*Banished Immortal*

# Banished Immortal

## *Searching for Shuangqing, China's Peasant Woman Poet*

Paul S. Ropp

*Ann Arbor*

The University of Michigan Press

First paperback edition 2002

Published in the United States of America by
The University of Michigan Press
Manufactured in the United States of America
⊗ Printed on acid-free paper

2005 2004 2003 2002 5 4 3 2



*A CIP catalog record for this book is available from the British Library.*

Library of Congress Cataloging-in-Publication Data

Ropp, Paul S., 1944–
Banished immortal : searching for Shuangqing, China's peasant woman poet / Paul S. Ropp.
p. cm.
Includes bibliographical references and index.
ISBN 0-472-11195-7 (alk.)
1. Ho, Shuang-ch'ing—Criticism and interpretation. I. Title: Searching for Shuangqing, China's peasant woman poet. II. Ho, Shuang-ch'ing. Poems. English. III. Title.
PL2710.0125 Z85 2001
895.1'148—dc21 00-10834

ISBN 0-472-08892-0 (pbk : alk. paper)

TO MARJORIE
*for hearing*
*and reading*
*everything*
*ten times over*
*and still smiling*

# Contents

# Preface

> He Shuangqing (1712–?) was a native of Jiangsu Province, and came from a family of farmers. She learned to read and write from her uncle, a teacher in a country school. She exchanged her embroidery for books of poetry. At eighteen she married a farmer of the Zhou family in a nearby town. Her husband was illiterate, had a bad temper and treated her cruelly, and her mother-in-law often tortured her.
>
> —Kenneth Rexroth and Chung Ling,
> *The Orchid Boat: Women Poets of China* (1972)

This short biography is the first thing I ever read about He Shuangqing. In the mid-1980s, I was just starting to study writings by women in the Qing period (1644–1911), and this anthology of English translations was the easiest place to begin. Intrigued by the idea of a peasant woman poet, I soon found a few more of her poems in Liang Yizhen's Chinese book, *A History of Women's Literature in the Qing Dynasty,* originally published in 1925 and reprinted in Taiwan in 1958. In China, Su Zhecong published a valuable anthology of Chinese women's writings in 1987. She offered a still more detailed picture of Shuangqing's life:

> He Shuangqing, style name Qiubi, was from Danyang (in the southeastern part of what is today Jiangsu Province) and lived in the vicinity of Xiaoshan [in Jintan County]. Her family had been farmers for generations. She was very beautiful, multitalented, and physically frail, and she had a gentle disposition. In 1732, when she was seventeen years old, she was married into a poor family of woodcutters, surnamed Zhou, who lived at Xiaoshan. Her husband was over ten years older than she was. Her mother-in-law was wicked; her husband had a violent temper, and she suffered from

> chronic malaria. From the time she was very young, she loved to study, and whenever she heard books being read aloud, she would break into a smile. Her uncle was a village tutor who used to teach next door to her house. When she heard him reciting from books, she would diligently and secretly write everything down. She had no writing materials, so to write her poetry and song lyrics, she would use powder to write on leaves. She eventually died from overwork and illness. Later someone collected her writings under the title *Lyrics from the Snow-Crushed Studio.* (Su Zhecong 1987, 408. All translations are my own, unless noted otherwise.)

Professor Su Zhecong included in her anthology seven song lyrics and one nine-verse poem by Shuangqing, and she listed two sources for her poems, an anthology of song lyrics and a book called simply *Random Notes from Xiqing.*

Having previously ignored the voluminous historical record of Chinese women's writings, I was anxious to believe that a peasant woman in eighteenth-century China might have the talent, the educational opportunity, and the personal experience to write great poetry. A more personal reason for my curiosity about He Shuangqing was that I grew up on a farm myself, raising corn and dairy cattle in central Illinois. I had long noticed—but never shared—the common assumption of city folk that rural people are by definition provincial, ignorant, and unsophisticated. My own grandfather, who died twelve years before I was born, was a poor farmer in two ways: he was not very good at farming *and* not very wealthy, in large part because he spent much of the family's money on books, and the rest to publish at his own expense two small volumes of his own poetry. So, the existence of a peasant poet in China seemed quite possible to me. I took all these poetry anthologies at face value and included several poems by Shuangqing in a paper for presentation in 1987 at the American Historical Association and a bit later at a seminar at Harvard University.

I quoted two poems by Shuangqing, citing her work as further evidence of the spread of female literacy in the Qing period and as a typical example of the expression of female unhappiness in women's writings. I argued that literacy in fact raised women's horizons and expectations in ways that Qing society was not prepared to accommodate. Therefore, we should not be surprised to find women expressing their sadness or unhappiness in poetry.

Having come of age in America in the 1960s, I have always been drawn to the dissatisfied and the dissenters in studying Chinese history.

I just assume that the eccentrics, the outsiders, and the misfits are more interesting as subjects of research, and more likely to be insightful social critics, than the wealthy, successful, and prominent scholar-officials who are at the center of most studies of Chinese history. It makes sense to me that powerless people, of necessity, understand the powerful better than the powerful understand the powerless.

My interest in gender relations also grew naturally out of the 1960s. My wife, Marjorie, and I had read and admired Betty Friedan in the early sixties, just before we got married, went off to graduate school, and started having children. The role of societies in shaping gender relations and expectations became something of an obsession for both of us, as it did for many in our generation. So He Shuangqing, whose life and poetry raises so many issues of class, power, gender relations, and literary creation, seemed a natural topic to explore in detail.

My general thesis on the rising but frustrated expectations of women was politely accepted at the AHA convention and at Harvard, though clearly some of my colleagues seemed unimpressed and puzzled by my decision to focus my research on writings by women. After all, so these (male) scholars seemed to think, men ran Chinese society and made the "big decisions," both in politics and in culture. Why study the writings of women? Didn't they just write about birds and flowers, boudoir daydreams, and domestic concerns? I also took some heat as a historian dabbling in literature. Historians tend to be suspicious of literary sources, and literary specialists often suspect that historians lack the specialized training to understand and interpret literature.

I was pleased, but also nervous, when invited to give a seminar presentation at Harvard on my research on women's writings. In a hot and crowded seminar room, I talked for about an hour and felt relieved on finishing my presentation. Ten minutes into the discussion period, Michael Fuller, a young assistant professor of Chinese literature, raised his hand at the other end of the long table. He asked with a hint of mischief in his voice, "What makes you believe your sources on the poet He Shuangqing? It seems highly unlikely that a peasant woman would ever have the time, energy, or opportunity to become literate, let alone write such highly stylized forms as regulated verse and song lyrics in classical Chinese." Touché! The question fairly knocked the wind out of me. I stammered something to the effect, "Well . . . I've seen poetry by He Shuangqing quoted in three separate sources. Given the nature of Chinese sources available in this country, we are heavily dependent on anthologies of women's writings. I just assume that these anthologies of Chinese poetry are based in historical fact." Michael kindly dropped the subject, but the half smile on his face let me know that he was not in the slightest convinced by my feeble answer to his question.

A few months after my Harvard experience, at the annual meeting of the Association of Asian Studies, *the* important scholarly meeting in our field, I met Dorothy Ko, a young rising star in Chinese women's history. I told Dorothy I was particularly intrigued by He Shuangqing, the peasant woman poet, partly because I found her poetry very interesting and partly because I had already run into serious skepticism about her very existence. I still believed my anthologies but knew that I would have to find more original sources if I was to convince others of her historical reality. I would need to know much more about this peasant woman if I was to have any hope of winning over those who doubted the value of women's literature in the first place.

A few months later, Dorothy sent me several notes on sources on He Shuangqing, and she mentioned that all the sources seemed to be based on a book called *Random Notes from Xiqing* by an obscure scholar, poet, and painter named Shi Zhenlin (1693–1779). Not long after that, in December 1990, while on sabbatical in Taiwan, I received a package from Dorothy, who was then living in Tokyo. Much to my surprise and delight, she had found a newly reprinted version of Shi's *Random Notes* in Tokyo; she immediately bought two copies, one for me and one for Grace Fong, another scholar with an interest in He Shuangqing. She enclosed a letter outlining her initial impressions of the book, giving me a preview of what I would find there:

> Much of the encounter between Shi Zhenlin/his friends and the peasant woman seemed platonic—the male literati were truly impressed by her talent, but much of it seemed sensuous if not erotic—men visiting her in her farm house, alone, and talking for hours; they kept going back for visits and maintained close communications via exchange of poetry. The peasant women were either immune from the norms of behavior that governed gentry women, or we are reading a scandalous tale. Interestingly enough, the authenticity of the Shuangqing story was, similar to the Xiaoqing story [another popular tale of a talented woman doomed to suffering], contested. I tend to believe that Shi Zhenlin did not make up the story. Real or imagined, we have here a rare glimpse into an interaction between the male, literati world and the female, peasant existence—a classic example of the interaction between class and gender. (Letter of Dec. 2, 1990)

What a godsend! Dorothy had sent me the key source I had been unable to find, and concisely outlined a research agenda for me. Her letter sent me rifling through the book to see what she might have found scandalous in the story. Much to my chagrin, I discovered Shi's memoir to be written in an extremely difficult classical Chinese prose style, full of obscure characters and arcane references. Many modern editions of classical Chinese texts include modern punctuation and annotations explaining allusions and particularly difficult passages. This work had none of that: no commas, no quotation or question marks, and no annotations or explanations of any kind. It had been reprinted in Beijing in 1987, from a 1907 version, with no crutches provided for the novice reader of obscure classical texts.

Back home in the states, the linguistic obstacles alone should have sent me looking for another topic, but as luck would have it, I just happened to be spending my sabbatical at the Inter-University Program for Chinese Language Studies in Taipei, popularly known as the Stanford Center. I had originally studied Chinese as a graduate student at the Stanford Center, and I now had a fellowship to spend the year in residence there, both to revive my spoken Chinese and to have expert help with my own Chinese research materials. I was doubly blessed that year with two talented teachers who functioned in effect as my personal tutors for the entire year.

As soon as Shi Zhenlin's *Random Notes* arrived in my mailbox, I read it with my senior teacher, Liu Chunhua, whom I called "Liu Laoshi" (Teacher Liu). My task each day was to read one or two pages, look up the characters I did not already know, and come to class prepared to explain in vernacular Chinese the meaning of the classical prose and poetry I had read. Many days I came to class with more questions than answers concerning the meaning of what I had read. We might get through a page in an hour, but some days we would only manage a few sentences, or perhaps one poem. After class, I would rush back to my office and type out in English my understanding of what we had just discussed in Chinese. Taking my fresh English translation back to class the next day, I would raise any lingering questions from the previous day's work, and because poems are so tricky, I usually explained one more time, in Chinese, how my English translation of the poem now read. Only after clarifying unresolved questions from the previous day's discussion would we proceed to new material.

Liu Laoshi was born into a wealthy family in China before the Communist revolution. Having received a classical education, including a master's degree in Chinese poetry, she astonished me with her knowledge of classical Chinese. She was an enthusiastic and demanding teacher. The words I most dreaded to hear from her were a sarcastic "Luo Jiaoshou!" (Pro*fess*or Ropp!) in response to my mistaken explanation of a term, or my confession of complete ignorance over something she thought I should know. Her chiding was all in my own interest, she and I both knew, and together we proceeded to be delighted by what we found in Shi Zhenlin's memoir. Her main field was the classical poetry of the Tang dynasty (A.D. 618–907), and she had never heard of He Shuangqing. I was consequently pleased to discover that I could serve as her informant on Chinese culture in the eighteenth century. She was in a sense an amateur reader of Shi Zhenlin, but a native wholly at home with the text at hand. By her own reactions to Shuangqing's poetry and her story, Liu Laoshi taught me more about Chinese culture than I ever could have learned from books alone. Thus, she became an important participant in my own search for Shuangqing.

In Shi Zhenlin's account, Shuangqing is so beautiful and talented that he and his friends regard her as a "banished immortal." Chinese people in the eighteenth century believed that extraordinarily talented people could achieve the supernatural status of an immortal, divine beings that live on forever in Heaven, a perpetually happy realm unlimited by the finiteness and suffering of human life. Shi and his circle, including Shuangqing, also believed in Buddhist concepts of karma and reincarnation. Sometimes an immortal might offend the higher powers of Heaven and be banished to live an incarnation in the "red dust" of the mundane material world. Since Shuangqing seemed too beautiful and too talented to be a mortal human being, it was assumed that she must have been an immortal banished to the human realm for one incarnation.

When I started reading Shi Zhenlin's memoir, I never dreamed what it would lead to: my dabbling in this topic for nearly a decade before getting my thoughts in publishable form; my raising doubts about Shuangqing's historical existence at a conference at Harvard in 1992; Du Fangqin and Elsie Choy writing books on Shuangqing soon thereafter, arguing that she was indeed a real historical figure; and my eventual teaming up with Professor Du herself and with Professor Zhang Hongsheng to travel to the rural county of Jintan in Jiangsu Province, where Shi Zhenlin once lived, to look for traces of the world he described as Shuangqing's. After an exhilarating trip to Jintan in October and November 1997, I turned to the task of writing a short book for a general audience. The adventure of this trip crystallized in my mind something I had not understood before: that the most interesting part of this project has been the process of discovery along the way. I want to try to recapture for the general reader the pleasures and pitfalls of an American scholar trying to understand and interpret a tiny piece of Chinese culture. The result is a memoir of my own, describing my quest to make sense of—and find truths in—the story of Shuangqing.

In *The Great Cat Massacre,* Robert Darnton suggests the value of historians' studying the past as anthropologists study alien cultures. Such an approach seems doubly appropriate when one is studying the past of an alien culture. Darnton illustrates with wit and wisdom what wonderful surprises one can find in dusty archives on eighteenth-century France. "When we cannot get a proverb, or a joke, or a ritual, or a poem, we know we are on to something. By picking at the document where it is at its most opaque, we may be able to unravel an alien system of meaning. The thread might even lead into a strange and wonderful world view" (5). I read these lines just as I was starting to read Shi Zhenlin's *Random Notes* with Liu Laoshi. They seemed a written prescription for what I should set about doing. On almost every page I found comments or actions that seemed strange, odd, puzzling. If I could understand these and make them familiar, I could perhaps illuminate aspects of life in eighteenth-century China that have been overlooked in studies of the famous and successful movers and shakers of that time.

The main threads running through this book are (1) my reading of Shuangqing's story in Shi Zhenlin's *Random Notes;* (2) the poetry and song lyrics of Shuangqing and their place in Chinese culture; (3) the evolution of opinion on Shuangqing and her poetry from the mid–eighteenth century to the present, including debates over whether she really lived or was just the fictional creation of Shi Zhenlin; and (4) my trip to Jintan and Danyang with Professors Du Fangqin and Zhang Hongsheng, in search of information about the vanished worlds of Shi Zhenlin and Shuangqing. I begin with my departure, accompanied by Professor Du Fangqin, from Beijing on the trip to Shi Zhenlin's home county in October 1997. Following Shi Zhenlin's own penchant for random wandering and travel writing, I intersperse chapters on the trip here and there throughout the book.

I have come to see Shi Zhenlin's memoir as a window on one part of eighteenth-century Chinese literati culture. It is not always a clear window, to be sure. As Robert Darnton would say, there are many "opaque points" in the text. That is what makes it so interesting. In each chapter on the memoir I take one particular topic or approach and try to clean that bit of the window from that particular angle, for a clearer look.

After getting each piece of the window as clear as I can, in chapter 14, "Reincarnations," I trace the evolution of Shuangqing's image in Chinese culture, from the first publication of *Random Notes* in 1737 down to the present day. That too is a fascinating story, because much of Shi Zhenlin's original narrative was left out of the accounts of Shuangqing that got passed on to later generations. And some details that have no basis in Shi's memoir got added to her later biographies.

Shi Zhenlin related Shuangqing's story in a very fragmentary and circuitous memoir of a decade of his life. After he passed from the scene, Shuangqing's story made its own way into Chinese culture in equally fragmentary and circuitous ways. She gradually became a cultural icon herself while Shi Zhenlin and much of his original story was ignored or forgotten. My own investigation into the Shuangqing story occurred in fits and starts, in bits and pieces, amid many other distractions, over more than a decade. This book is thus the story of three exploratory journeys through Chinese culture: Shi Zhenlin's, Shuangqing's, and my own.

### *Note on Pronunciation*

Chinese names present a challenge to the English speaker for three reasons: (1) Chinese is a tonal language, so inflection is far more important in Chinese than in English; (2) Chinese includes some sounds for which we have no ready equivalent in English; and (3) the pinyin romanization system used in China and in most newspapers and scholarly publications has some peculiarities that are not very user-friendly. Leaving the subtleties of Chinese pronunciation (tones and tongue position, etc.) to qualified language teachers, I list here a few of the idiosyncrasies of the pinyin romanization system. Many words in pinyin are not misleading to the English speaker: Beijing, Ming dynasty, and Zhou Enlai, to name a few. For the others, a few rules will help.

c = ts
cao = tsao

q = ch
qing = ching
qi = chee

x = sh
xi = she (with a hint of *see* thrown in)
xiao = sheeow (in one quick syllable)

u = ü (with the German umlaut)
yu = ü
xue = shüeh

shi = shr (or *sure* with a hard midwestern *r*)

Important examples (surname first, usually one syllable; given name follows, usually two syllables):

| | |
|---|---|
| He Shuangqing | Huh Shwang *(a* as in *father)* ching |
| Shi Zhenlin | Shr Zhen (rhymes with *fun*) lin |
| Liu Laoshi | Lēō (in one compact syllable) Lao (rhymes with *cow*) shr |
| Du Fangqin | Dū Fang *(a* as in *father)* chin |
| Zhang Hongsheng | Zhang Hong *(o* as in *hoof)* sheng (rhymes with *flung*) |
| Xiaowan | Sheeow (in one quick syllable) wan *(a* as in *father)* |

# *Acknowledgments*

I am profoundly grateful to the many people who have helped make this book possible:
to Dorothy Ko for starting the whole thing and reading it all near the end;
to Liu Chunhua for making me feel so lucky to be reading Shuangqing's poetry;
to Kang-i Sun Chang for her ardent support and encouragement all along the way;
to Du Fangqin for her warm friendship, infectious exuberance, and boundless energy;
to Zhang Hongsheng for arranging our trip and for cheerfully answering all my questions;
to Kang Zhengguo for his enthusiasm and erudition in checking every translation;
to Grace Fong for sharing ideas and sources, and for crucial help with cuts in the final stages;
to Wan Lijun and our many friends in Jintan and Danyang for being such gracious hosts;
to Brian Ibsen and Tom Levine for critical inspiration in the early writing stages;
to Hao Zhihang, Liu Long Ping, and Lisa Sun for research and translation assistance;
to an editor and two readers from another press, whose tough criticisms were needed;
to Max Hess and Tom Massey for aiding and abetting this project with their wise counsel;
to Wilt Idema, Ellen Widmer, and Judith Zeitlin for sharing their work and sources;
to the following friends who read all or part of the manuscript and offered helpful advice:
Michiko Aoki, Jack Costantino, Nichole Dupont, SunHee Kim Gertz,
Robin LeBlanc, Jonathan Spence, Ron Suleski, Stefan Tanaka,
Laura Val, Wang Ping and Suzanne Zhang-Gottschang;
to Anne Gibson of Clark University's Cartography Lab for the fine maps;
to my Clark History Department colleagues for collegial and financial support;
to Al LaPrade for efficient help with proofreading and indexing;
to Marcia LaBrenz for expertly coordinating the copyediting;
to Ingrid Erickson for believing in an offbeat book;
to my wife, Marjorie, for just about everything else.

RUSSIA
Lake Baikal
KAZAKHSTAN
Lake Balkhash
MONGOLIA
Karamay
Kulja
Urumqi
KYRGYZSTAN
Kashgar
XINJIANG
Hailar
HEILONGJIANG
Qiqihar
Harbin
JILIN
Changchun
Shenyang
LIAONING
NEI MONGOL
NORTH KOREA
SOUTH KOREA
HEBEI
Hohhot
Beijing
Tianjin
Dalian
Yantai
Qingdao
Yumen
GANSU
Yinchuan
Shijiazhuang
Taiyuan
HEBEI
Jinan
SHANDONG
NINGXIA
SHANXI
Golmud
Xining
QINGHAI
Lanzhou
Xi'an
SHAANXI
Zhengzhou
HENAN
JIANGSU
Nanjing
DANYANG and JINTAN COUNTIES
Shiqunhe
XIZANG
Shanghai
Hefei
ANHUI
HUBEI
Hangzhou
Wuhan
SICHUAN
Chengdu
Lhasa
Chongqing
Nanchang
ZHEJIANG
East China Sea
NEPAL
BHUTAN
Changsha
HUNAN
JIANGXI
Fuzhou
INDIA
Guiyang
GUIZHOU
FUJIAN
BANGLADESH
Kunming
YUNNAN
GUANGXI
Xiamen
TAIWAN
GUANGDONG
Guangzhou
Nanning
Hong Kong (U.K.)
MYANMAR
VIETNAM
LAOS
Haikou
Bay of Bengal
HAINAN
South China Sea
THAILAND
500 kilometers
0
500 miles

JIANGSU PROVINCE
Nanjing
Huning Expressway
DANYANG & JINTAN COUNTIES
Shanghai
Danyang City
DANYANG
Jiangshu
Mao Shan
JINTAN
XUEBU TOWNSHIP
Jintan City
Xuebu Town
Fang Shan & Shi Family Mountainside
Fang Shan Village
Guazhu
Yao Hu
LEGEND
mountain
county boundary
township boundary
water body/river/canal
road

*one* ·

# *Departure: "Soft-Sleeper to Nanjing"*

BEIJING, MONDAY, OCTOBER 27, 1997

"My daughter picked up the train tickets for us; we leave from Beijing Station tomorrow evening at 6:30! Ruan-wo!" Professor Du Fangqin, China's leading authority on He Shuangqing, reports over the phone in her bright and cheerful voice.

"Ruan-wo!" I repeat, buying time while trying to dredge up just what "Ruan-wo" means. Having been away from China now for six years, I silently curse my awkwardness with the language. Almost quick enough for her not to notice, I remember: "soft sleeper!" Of course! "Wonderful!" I reply in Chinese, "How convenient! We waste no time and save a night's hotel bill. So when and where shall we meet?"

We agree to meet at my hotel at 4:00 P.M. the next day. I still do not quite believe this trip is about to happen. I have studied Chinese history for thirty years, but mostly in archives and in published books. In the past ten years I have become increasingly intrigued with the case of He Shuangqing, China's great peasant woman poet. In 1737, the obscure poet and painter Shi Zhenlin described and quoted the poems and song lyrics of a beautiful and talented peasant woman named Shuangqing who he discovered living in rural Jintan County, east and south of Nanjing. A century later, local histories described Shuangqing as having been born in Danyang County, just to the north of Jintan. Until recently, it never even occurred to me to try to explore the world of Shi Zhenlin and Shuangqing by actually "going there."

### *The Mystery of Xiaoshan*

In the next week, we will do just that: visit the rural counties of Jintan and Danyang where Shi Zhenlin once roamed, and where he claimed to have found the beautiful and talented Shuangqing living in a remote village called Xiaoshan. No village with this name appears on any maps or in any local histories from any period of Chinese history. A decade earlier, a friend of mine, Kang Zhengguo, who teaches Chinese at Yale University, went to Jintan County to look for modern traces of the Shuangqing story, but he found no one who knew of Shuangqing, nor any place he could identify as Xiaoshan. He has given me a hand-drawn map of the area and some ideas about where to go and what to ask. Do people in this area know anything about Shuangqing? Have they ever heard of Shi Zhenlin? Can we identify any landmarks from the area that might help us locate this mysterious Xiaoshan?

### *Professor Du Fangqin*

This will be our assignment, and, most auspiciously, my traveling companions are two excellent Chinese scholars: Professor Du Fangqin, from Tianjin Normal University and the prominent feminist author of *Collected Materials on He Shuangqing,* and Professor Zhang Hongsheng, a leading authority on Chinese poetry and chair of the Classical Chinese Literature Program at Nanjing University. Professor Du has come to Beijing for a conference. Tomorrow night she and I will take the overnight train to Nanjing, where Professor Zhang will meet us and let us know what has been arranged for our visit. I have little idea what to expect on this trip, but I am thrilled to be able to make it with such superb scholars.

I will clarify below why some people suspect that He Shuangqing was nothing more than the fictional creation of Shi Zhenlin. Here it is enough to note that I wrote a conference paper on Shuangqing in 1992 raising doubts about her existence, and arguing that since we will never know with certainty whether she lived or not, we should emphasize the fact that she has been a plausible figure to most Chinese critics in the last two centuries. One year later, Du Fangqin published her *Collected Materials,* in which she argued forcefully that Shuangqing was a historical figure with a very distinctive poetic voice that could not have been created out of whole cloth by Shi Zhenlin.

As one of the founders of women's studies in China, Professor Du was a special guest at the 1992 Harvard conference where she had heard my paper on Shuangqing, but I did not meet her formally until February 1997, in unusual circumstances. She was visiting the East Coast and giving lectures at Amherst College and at Harvard. Unfortunately, I could not attend any of her lectures, but thanks to friends who knew of our mutual interests in He Shuangqing, I managed to insinuate myself into her schedule by serving as her chauffeur. She was speaking in Amherst one afternoon and needed a ride back to Harvard.

"If you can take a bus to Worcester," I told her graduate student escort, "I'll happily drive you back to Harvard." This worked, and we first got acquainted while speeding toward Boston on Interstate 90. She speaks little English, and my Chinese was rusty, but we managed to have a delightful conversation as I struggled to maneuver the turnpike traffic and speak Mandarin at the same time. We went to a Chinese restaurant in Cambridge and had fun eating, drinking, and joking about our continuing fascination with the peasant woman poet. A bit apprehensive about how we would handle our contrasting views, I happily discovered that Professor Du loves to laugh, and she easily joked about our differences. She spoke Chinese at about twice the speed my ears could comprehend, but with endless patience, she cheerfully repeated herself at half speed when asked, until I could catch what she was saying.

Because of the Cultural Revolution in China, Professor Du was of necessity a "late bloomer" in the field of scholarship. She was a college student in the turbulent 1960s and spent ten years as a middle school teacher during the 1970s. Only after the reforms of Deng Xiaoping did she have the chance to go to graduate school in classical Chinese literature. When I once asked her how she had liked teaching middle school, she replied with a frown and a terse declaration: "I hated it!" One reason for her distaste, no doubt, was the enforced political conformity and intellectual sterility of the last years of Mao Zedong's rule. The Deng reforms restored higher education and offered intellectuals a new lease on life. In the rebirth of Chinese universities in the 1980s, amid the seductive appeals of wealth and Western influences, only a few people in China received training in classical Chinese literature. And it was even rarer for people to pursue women's studies. In 1985, at the urging of Professor Li Xiaojiang, one of her graduate school classmates, Professor Du began to examine women's status and gender relations as seen in classical Chinese sources. She first made her mark with a truly pioneering book in 1988 called *The Evolution of Concepts of Women (Nüxing guannian de yanbian),* in which she traced the development of gender ideology in China from very early times down to the twentieth century. This was a courageous work that outlined women's subordination to men in almost every area of life, including philosophy, politics, society, economics, the family, and especially in the sexual arena.

Despite winning an award in Tianjin for *The Evolution of Concepts of Women,* Professor Du was not promoted in academic rank until her 1993 book on Shuangqing was published. Women scholars pursuing women's studies were regarded with some suspicion, as academic authorities assumed their topic was either too self-interested or too trivial to be considered worthy of true scholarship. In those years she was working with her colleagues against an ever-sluggish academic bureaucracy to establish an officially recognized Center for Women's Studies at Tianjin Normal University, a goal they finally achieved in 1992. A few months after her Shuangqing book came out, she also oversaw the publication of a contemporary study, *Chinese Women and Development: Status, Health, Employment (Zhongguo funü yu fazhan—diwei, jiankang, jiuye).* This work makes explicit the commitment that underlies all her work: to understand the subordinate status of women throughout Chinese history, with a view to ending that subordination.

Given Professor Du's status as a pioneering Chinese feminist, and her argument that Shuangqing was a historical person who wrote all the poetry attributed to her, I was a bit apprehensive about how to engage her in a discussion of this issue. As we waited for our order to arrive in a Cambridge restaurant, she put me at ease with her casual and good-humored manner. "I know you have doubts about He Shuangqing," she said, "but her poetry is better than Shi Zhenlin's. I don't think he could have made it up."

"I agree that her poetry is very good, but there are too many things in Shi Zhenlin's memoir that seem to me implausible." Then, trying to backpedal a bit, I added, "My real point in that Harvard paper was that we'll never prove one way or another whether she ever existed or not. We can only hope to establish some range of probabilities. The important thing is that she's a real figure in Chinese culture. She became much more famous than Shi Zhenlin."

"Professor Ropp," she now poured it on, "you are the American Shi Zhenlin, still looking for that beautiful peasant poet and trying to make her name famous!"

I laughed and replied, "She's quite famous on her own, without any help from me."

"But you carry her fame to the West! At that Harvard conference, I still remember you reading Shuangqing's poem in Chinese, 'Look at tiny tiny Shuangqing.' It was so touching I thought, 'I'm going to have to look into her story.' "

"But you put me to shame!" I said with mock indignation. "Here I am five years later still unpublished on Shuangqing, and you wrote a whole book in one year."

"Oh that book was mostly just citations from Shi Zhenlin and others. I just copied down what others have already said," she protested with undue modesty.

"I was so excited when Kang Zhengguo sent me your book," I told her quite truthfully. "Before it arrived in the mail, I didn't even know about it. And it's not just 'copied' from other sources. There is a lot of very important information in there that I didn't know before. I admit I was also excited to find myself quoted in your book. I don't often get to see myself quoted in a Chinese book!"

"I was too embarrassed to send you the book myself, but Kang Zhengguo said he knew you and would send you a copy."

### *Professor Kang Zhengguo*

"You know," I reported, "I was very lucky to be able to room with Kang Zhengguo at the Yale conference in 1993. He was scheduled to room with someone else, and he had no idea who I was. Fortunately, I got his attention with the provocative title of my conference paper on images of courtesan culture in late imperial China: 'Love, Talent, Glamour, Nostalgia, Sex, Bondage, and Shame.' It paid off in bringing me to Kang Zhengguo's attention. I think he was particularly intrigued by the 'sex, bondage, and shame!' So we roomed together. I had earlier been amazed by the depth of knowledge he displayed in his 1988 book on classical Chinese poetry by and about women. He had written insightfully in that book on Shuangqing, so I gave him my earlier paper on Shuangqing, and he would sit on his bed in our room, pondering the English, and discussing it with me in Chinese as he went along. We talked incessantly every night at that conference, and most of it was about Shuangqing. We joked about being latter-day literati ourselves, still poking around in the eighteenth century and imitating Shi Zhenlin and his literati friends in their obsession with the beautiful peasant woman poet!"

"See, you *are* the American Shi Zhenlin!" she laughed.

"Or maybe Kang Zhengguo is Shi Zhenlin and I'm Flower Lover Duan Yuhan [a close friend of Shi's and fellow admirer of Shuangqing]. After all Kang Zhengguo even went to Jintan to look for Xiaoshan [where Shuangqing supposedly lived]. Another reason for my skepticism about Shi Zhenlin's account," I couldn't resist adding, "is that Kang Zhengguo found no trace of a place he could identify as Xiaoshan, and most people there had never heard of Shuangqing."

### *Proposal: A Search for Xiaoshan*

"Oh, he only spent a few days looking for Xiaoshan!" Professor Du shot back. "You can't hope to succeed in this quest in a few days time. We should go there together and look for it ourselves, but we would need a few weeks at least! We would need to go to Danyang as well as Jintan."

Before she said this, I had never thought of such a trip. If Kang Zhengguo could not find anything significant, what chance would I have? But to go with a knowledgeable Shuangqing scholar like Du Fangqin, what could be better? "That would be great fun!" I replied.

"That's precisely what we *should* do," she quickly followed up. "When could you go?"

"Well, I have a sabbatical coming up next year. That would be a great time for me. Could you go sometime next fall?"

"Yes I could!" she replied with a quickness that amazed me.

### *Professor Zhang Hongsheng*

As attractive as the idea of a trip to Jintan sounded, I had no idea how to go about organizing such a thing. Fortunately, I had the good sense to mention our discussion to another friend, Kang-i Sun Chang, of Yale University. Along with Ellen Widmer of Wesleyan University, Kang-i had organized the Yale conference of 1993, and she had since invited Kang Zhengguo to Yale to teach Chinese. Within a month of my meeting Du Fangqin, Kang-i called me one day and said, "Paul, I know a Chinese professor from Nanjing who could be very helpful to you in organizing a trip to Jintan. He is Zhang Hongsheng, chairman of the Department of Classical Chinese at Nanjing University. He just happens to be spending the year as a visiting scholar at Harvard this year, and he's coming to give a talk at Yale. He's extremely knowledgeable about Chinese poetry, and Nanjing is not far from Jintan and Danyang. He could help you to make local arrangements. Kang Zhengguo and I could bring him up to Worcester to meet you."

"Kang-i!" I replied, "You're a saint to think of all this! I didn't even know anyone from Nanjing was at Harvard this year. By all means, let's do it."

We set the date, and within three weeks, Kang-i and Kang Zhengguo arrived in Worcester with Professor Zhang on a chilly March weekend. We had a party with our dozen Worcester China friends (scholars and spouses), and for breakfast, in honor of Shuangqing, I took our guests to the Miss Worcester Diner, the most famous diner in a city known for its high-cholesterol blue-collar diners (see figure 1). I was delighted to discover that Zhang Hongsheng was, as Kang-i said, extremely knowledgeable about Chinese history and culture, especially for one so young. By young, I mean in his early forties, which is young to those of us in our fifties. "This peasant woman poet, He Shuangqing, is certainly a fascinating case, whether she existed or not," he said to me early on in our visit. "I think we should be able to shed some light on the issue if we plan our trip carefully. We can arrange meetings with local scholars and officials in Jintan, look for some of the landmarks described by Shi Zhenlin, and see if any popular stories survive there today. Just give me a couple months advance warning before the trip."

Though he had written his doctoral dissertation on late Song dynasty poetry (twelfth–thirteenth centuries), Prof. Zhang was just then turning his attention to Qing-dynasty song lyrics (the genre for which Shuangqing is famous). Even with his new interest in Qing song lyrics, he seemed extraordinarily generous to offer his help to Du Fangqin and me in this way. "He'll make an ideal traveling companion," I correctly predicted to myself. Before he left for China at the end of August (1997), we had set the date for our trip, and his arrangements surpassed anything I could have imagined. Happily, he is a scholar of uncommon curiosity, and he seemed intrigued, if also bemused, by my interest in this peasant woman poet. He would be an invaluable asset on this trip, a disinterested but not uninterested third party, and a good honest broker between my skepticism and Du's belief. Professors Zhang and Du had never met, and I was gratified to serve as a go-between for two well-established Chinese scholars.

BEIJING, TUESDAY, OCTOBER 28, 1997

***Preparing for Departure***

It's a cool and cloudy day in Beijing. At 4:00 P.M. I return to the hotel from an afternoon of book shopping, get out of my cab, and discover Professor Du just walking up to the front door. We laugh and agree it's an auspicious beginning that we've arrived at the exact same time. I fetch my bags and together we board a cab. Du tells the driver our destination and immediately starts quizzing me: "Did you bring some good materials along?" She knows that the Harvard library, where I do my research, has one of the best Chinese collections in the world, and she rightly suspects that I have access to some materials there that are not even available in China.

"Yes, I brought a bundle of things." I pull a thick folder out of the side pocket of my suitcase to show her. I'm rather amazed to find ourselves discussing Shuangqing materials before we get three blocks from the hotel. She is so energetic, and so focused on our business, I realize, that this trip is guaranteed to be productive. Even if we find nothing of use to us, I will have a week or ten days of conversation with the world's most knowledgeable Shuangqing scholar.

At the bustling Beijing train station, we wheel our suitcases—Why did I bring so much stuff?—over to the office for long-distance phone calls, to call Professor Zhang and let him know our time of arrival. Train stations are invariably crowded and noisy places in China, and I was wondering what we would do for the nearly two hours before our departure. Luckily, the soft-sleeper class has its own waiting room, which is spacious, uncrowded, and surprisingly quiet. So we wheel our suitcases in, find a bench to ourselves, and proceed to pore over the materials I have brought along and to talk about the upcoming trip. Such is the abundance of Harvard-Yenching Library that I have photocopies of materials Du has never seen before. She is naturally excited by the things I've brought along: maps, bits of information from Jintan and Danyang local histories, two pages from a geographical dictionary, and several articles on Shi Zhenlin and He Shuangqing. The time passes quickly as I show her what I have, and we discuss the material, one piece at a time.

### *Soft-Sleeper to Nanjing*

At 6:00 P.M., we board the train, locate our bunks, and discover we are in adjacent compartments; I am with three other men, and Du is in a mixed compartment with two men and another woman. When she asks naively, "How can there be men and women in the same compartment?" a weary traveler with a bemused look on his face replies, "Bufen," meaning "no distinction" [by gender in these compartments]. Professor Du takes this news matter-of-factly, and we sensibly head for the dining car as soon as we've deposited our suitcases in our compartments.

Soft-sleeper is the most comfortable train ride in China, four people in a closed compartment, two beds on top and two on the bottom. The bottom beds double as soft seats for everybody in the daytime. It's clean, comfortable, uncramped, and quiet. "Hard-sleeper" is cheaper, but includes three levels of bunks and no private compartments. The trip to Nanjing takes thirteen hours. We should be there by seven-thirty tomorrow morning.

The trip is uneventful except for two dramatic stops in the first ten minutes. We are sitting in the dining car waiting for service, just as we begin to pick up speed, when there is a loud *Screech!* of wheels sliding on rails and we slam to a sudden stop. I feel my chest thrown against the table. A bowl of soup goes flying through the air, bounces off the unfortunate man who had ordered it, and lands with a loud crash on the floor. Two or three wontons scoot across the floor following in the wake of the bowl. I am surprised that the heavy bowl doesn't break, but that is no consolation to the poor customer, whose dark blue jacket is drenched with chicken broth. Visibly distressed by being soaked, he stares unbelievingly at his jacket, but doesn't appear to have suffered any burns.

Everyone in the car watches the accident victim as a waiter and waitress quickly bring towels and try to help him by wiping his jacket and cleaning up the table and floor around him. I am suddenly relieved not to have been served yet, and to be sitting toward the back of the car facing the direction in which we still have hopes of traveling. Had we already been served, Professor Du, sitting opposite me, would have been splattered with our dinner. There is a general shared sense of consternation in the car, as we all wonder what could have necessitated such a sudden stop, and whether or not we have hit something. I privately retract my impatience about the slow service on this car.

In a few minutes we start up again, only to come to an even more violently sudden and screeching halt five minutes later. This time I am more alarmed. We *must* have hit someone or something, I think. Otherwise, I don't see how we could have stopped so fast. Rationally I know that trains go from Beijing to Nanjing every day without anyone getting killed, or even scalded by their soup, but all the same, I can't help feeling apprehensive. Perhaps we should have taken a plane to Nanjing, but of course it's too late for alternatives. Within five minutes we are on our way again. Despite my heightened anxieties, we proceed to eat our meal without incident: two large dishes—beef and broccoli, beancurd and vegetables—with a big bowl of wonton soup and two large bowls of rice. The food is passable, and I am stuffed by the time we return to Du's compartment, where we sit together for a couple more hours and continue our discussions of my material and our upcoming explorations.

By 10:00 P.M. my mind is exhausted from the nonstop effort of speaking and hearing Chinese for the last six hours. We retire to our bunks. It is comfortable enough, and my compartment mates are all asleep. I am dead tired, and expect that the steady clackety-clack rumble of the train will soon put me to sleep. But the excitement of the trip, the relatively hot air in our compartment, and the snoring of my roommates all conspire to rob me of sleep.

NANJING, WEDNESDAY, OCTOBER 29, 1997

Just as I seem to have arrived in a state of peaceful slumber, at 6:00 A.M., a loudspeaker in our compartment blares out with music, the morning news, and information on arrival times. "Damn Communist country!" I think to myself, feeling somehow that my right to sleep, or at least my convenience, has been violated by being awakened so early with news and weather reports I can barely understand.

I get up around six-thirty to discover Professor Du already up and in line for the sink in the washroom. By seven, after dousing my face in cold water and brushing my teeth, I feel awake and ready for our arrival in Nanjing. We help two elderly women off the train with their bags, walk them to the depot waiting room, and immediately see a smiling Professor Zhang, who hails a cab and takes us to Nanjing University. We can't go to Jintan until tomorrow, he explains, so we agree to spend the morning in the university library, after first having a delicious Chinese breakfast in the faculty dining room. I've seldom eaten purely Chinese-style breakfasts in the past, but in the next few days I will quickly grow accustomed to the local breakfast fare: meat dumplings, steamed buns, pickled vegetables, occasionally corn bread or a sweet bun filled with bean paste, and always with a bowl of thin rice gruel and a glass of hot sweetened milk. I miss my coffee and orange juice and could probably ask for coffee, but I'm determined to "go Chinese" on this trip. The breakfast is tasty, filling, nutritious, and very cheap, about $1.20.

### *Professor Zhang Hongsheng: Connections in Jintan and Danyang*

Zhang Hongsheng is from Shandong Province, the home of Confucius, near the cradle of early Chinese civilization. He is tallish and handsome, with the high cheekbones I somehow associate with Shandong. He always seems easygoing and cheerful, but I can't help worrying that this trip is a bit of an imposition on him. His major research is on an earlier period, and it is only because of me and my Yale friends that he has gotten interested in Shuangqing. He is also clearly busy as a department chair in the middle of the fall semester. Over breakfast he explains that we are very fortunate because one particular student at Nanjing University is from a prominent family in Jintan and has made arrangements with the city government of Jintan for our visit. Tomorrow, in fact, this student is sending a car and driver to pick us up and take us to Jintan. We will spend three or four days in Jintan and then go to Danyang, where an old classmate of Hongsheng's works in the city government.

So we appear to be blessed with good *guanxi,* connections, in reference to the all-important network of personal relationships in Chinese society. Nothing is accomplished in China without good connections.

Whole books have been written about the importance of face-to-face social networks in Chinese society. This trip is itself a tribute to the power of *guanxi:* Through my Yale professor friend, Kang-i Sun Chang, I was able to room with Kang Zhengguo at the Yale conference in 1993. Through Kang Zhengguo I received Du Fangqin's book. Through Kang-i and another mutual friend, I was alerted to Du's visit to New England in early 1997 during which we first discussed a trip to Jintan in search of the village of Xiaoshan. And once again, through Kang-i, I was able to meet Zhang Hongsheng, who has now used his connections with a Nanjing University student and with a former classmate to set up our visit to Jintan and Danyang. Subtract any one of these people from the network and the trip might not have happened.

The three of us spend the morning in the Nanjing University Library, where we find a few local histories with references to Shuangqing, but nothing I hadn't seen before. In the afternoon, Hongsheng has meetings to attend to, so Du and I wander through the tree-lined streets of Nanjing and browse in bookstores. After sharing a large meal at a popular family restaurant, we return to the campus and retire early to be fresh for tomorrow's adventure.

JINTAN, THURSDAY, OCTOBER 30, 1997

By 9:00 A.M., we meet our chauffeur at the main gate of Nanjing University and are off to Jintan in a relatively new Dodge Caravan. Once we are ready to go, our escort, Mr. Huang, calls Jintan on his cellular phone to let our host there know we are on our way. Does anyone in China *not* have a cellular phone? Mr. Huang and his companion, our driver, are friendly and curious to hear what we three professors are up to. They are also curious to hear what professors get paid in America. I give them a range of salaries but hasten to add the average costs of a car, house mortgage, weekly food bills, utilities, et cetera, all to try to demystify "the good life" in the USA. In addition to their curiosity about America, they find our trio very quaint in our quixotic quest for information about an eighteenth-century poet they've never heard of.

### *Wan Lijun: Our Local Contact in Jintan City*

The brand-new Huning Expressway, which runs from Nanjing through Danyang to Shanghai, is very impressive, and the traffic is so light it hardly seems like we're in China. We exit the expressway at Danyang, to take a local two-lane highway to Jintan, and I am impressed by the large characters for Danyang atop the four-lane toll booth at our exit. This is definitely not how I envisioned my first glimpse of Danyang on a trip back to the eighteenth century. Within an hour and a half, we are in the attractive small city of Jintan, looking for the company where our local contact, the Nanjing University student, works. We stop, make a phone call, and in five minutes, to my surprise, an attractive young woman walks up to our party, extends her hand to Zhang and says, "Zhang Laoshi?" They have never met before, and she identifies him only because he is the Chinese male in our party of three. Since Professor Zhang had not mentioned the gender of our local contact, we had just assumed the student to be a man. Are we both sexists to have assumed this? We shake hands all around, and she introduces herself as Wan Lijun. She is attractive and thin, with a square face and bright flashing eyes. In her blue jeans, sneakers, and bright red windbreaker, she looks like she would be at home on any campus in North America.

### *Names: Xiaowan, Du Laoshi, Hongsheng, and Paul*

Names are interesting windows on cultural interaction. We quickly learn to call Ms. Wan "Xiaowan," meaning Little Wan, *little* being a friendly rubric that often gets applied to the younger people in any group in China. With Du and Zhang I develop two different systems. Zhang has spent a year in the states, and he well understands our American informality with names. So he calls me Paul and I call him Hongsheng, though I sense that it would be strange for his Chinese colleagues to call him that. With Du it is more complicated. She starts calling me Paul soon enough, in part because Hongsheng comments on the American habit of informality with names, but I can't really call a Chinese female professor by her given name. So following Hongsheng's lead, I settle on Du Laoshi. *Laoshi* is more informal and affectionate than *Jiaoshou* (Professor), and it feels nothing like the terribly stiff sounding "Venerable Old Teacher" of its literal translation. Just as younger people in China are often identified by a *xiao* (little) before their name, so are older ones identified with a *lao* (old) before their name. A year after this trip, Kang Zhengguo explained to me that Du Fangqin enjoys being called simply Lao Du (Old Du) because that was how China's greatest poet, Du Fu (712–770) of the Tang dynasty, is often identified. To be addressed as Lao Du is a nice reminder that she shares the same surname as this great cultural hero.

### *First Taste of Jintan Hospitality*

Xiaowan takes us to the Jinsha (Jinsha is another name for Jintan) Guest House, the number one hostel of the Jintan Municipal Government, which will be our base for the next five days. We have comfortable rooms with private showers and Panda TVs on which we see President Jiang Zemin's arrival at the White House in Washington. We go to lunch in a private dining room at the city government hostel and are joined by two young men from the city government and a young woman, Miss Cao, who is a personal friend of Xiaowan's. (We seem to run into personal friends of Xiaowan's everywhere we go in Jintan.) One of our hosts works in the Jintan County History Editorial Office, one works for the mayor, and Miss Cao works in the secret document section of the government, a department that sounds sinister in English but seems to carry no stigma in Chinese.

We have such an embarrassingly large lunch that I am inspired to write down the dishes. Early in the meal someone asks if I've ever eaten dog meat, and I confess that I haven't. "Would you if it were offered?"

Assuming the question to be purely hypothetical, I answer without much thought, "Yes, I suppose so. I will try anything once." A dangerous boast to make in China, I realize, but I continue, as if daring my hosts to shock me. "I grew up on a farm where we raised a variety of animals and regularly butchered our own pigs, cows, and chickens. So unlike city-bred folks, I know exactly where meat comes from and I'm not sentimental about it. I know it doesn't just grow in cellophane-wrapped cartons." Within ten minutes a large bowl of reddish stew arrives, *xiang rou,* "fragrant meat," the euphemism for dog meat. The host quickly fills the small bowl in front of me, and I dig in immediately lest I seem a complete hypocrite. The meat is tender, and frankly, quite tasty, seasoned with just enough red pepper to give it a little bite (pardon the expression). I can see why it's a popular winter dish. I finish my bowl but am careful to stave off having it refilled, which requires some considerable effort, with an assertive tone of voice and vigorous hand gestures. I don't want to overdo it.

Just as intimidating as the dog stew is the duck's blood soup—though it too is tasty—and the *bie,* or soft-shelled turtle. Not knowing that *bie* means *soft-shelled* turtle, but seeing quite clearly a turtle, perhaps eight inches in diameter, in a large bowl of broth, I am startled when our host stabs the back of the turtle with his chopsticks, breaks the shell into several hefty pieces, and plops one down on my plate. I know the Chinese consider turtle to be a delicacy, but I didn't know they eat the shell.

Around the edges, the shell is so soft it practically melts in my mouth, and I'm relieved to see others leave the hard parts of the shell on the table uneaten. The legs and feet are also a bit intimidating (no head sighted, I'm relieved to discover), but attached to the claws, bones and joints are tender bits of fatty meat. I watch others and follow along, put a claw in my mouth, separate the tender flesh and spit out the claw onto my plate. It's efficient and, given the tenderness of the turtle meat, easy.

With more than a dozen dishes, with beer and *baijiu* (a strong-tasting high-octane distilled clear liquor made from any of several grains), and with mandatory toasts with each of our hosts, we are ready for a nap before the afternoon's explorations begin. And today, after a short postlunch nap, I am amazed to suffer no ill effects whatsoever from going without coffee. Adrenaline, I decide, is a great substitute for caffeine.

### *Jintan County History Office*

With the entirely enjoyable preliminaries out of the way and refreshed by our short nap, we proceed to the Jintan County History Editorial Office to meet with Mr. Zhu Fulin, the deputy director of the office and of the Jintan Cultural Center. Mr. Zhu knows about Shi Zhenlin's memoir, *Random Notes from Xiqing,* but he says they have no copy in Jintan and had to go to Shanghai to borrow one. He had not heard of scholar Shi's other surviving work, *Scattered Drafts from Huayang,* so we promise to send him a copy. He notes that they include a biography of Shi Zhenlin in the Jintan County Gazetteer, but not He Shuangqing, because they "could not clarify her situation." An admirably responsible and scholarly approach, I think to myself. Mr. Zhu is quite surprised when we tell him that scholars in Canada, Hong Kong, Holland, Taiwan, and the United States are all interested in the life and poetry of Shuangqing and are now debating the significance of her poetry and arguing about whether she is a fictional or a historical figure.

### *Looking for Xiaoshan*

Much of our discussion focuses on the possible location of the village Shi Zhenlin described as Shuangqing's: Xiaoshan li, or Xiao Mountain Village. Mr. Zhu has never heard of this village nor seen any reference to it apart from Shi Zhenlin. But from other descriptions in Shi's memoir, Xiaoshan has to be near Mao Shan (a famous range of mountains just to the northwest of Jintan County) and Fang Shan (Square Mountain) on the western edge of the county. Apart from Taiwanese scholar Dr. Zhou Wanyao's assertion that Xiaoshan is in the vicinity of Fang Shan, there is another reason to think that Fang Shan is where we should be looking. A second name for Fang Shan is Siping Shan, and Shi Zhenlin says that Xiaoshan Village is at the foot of a Siping Shan. The only trouble is that the *ping* in Fang Shan's secondary name is the character meaning "flat or level," while the *ping* Shi Zhenlin uses means "guard or shield." Both *pings* have the same (second, or rising) tone, so if Shi was simply changing a few names "to protect the innocent" or to add a fictional touch to a real story, he could have deliberately chosen a same-sound-different-meaning character for Siping Shan.

### *Xiaowan's Belief in Shuangqing*

The most interesting part of the day comes after we return to our rooms in the late afternoon. Today is the first time Xiaowan has heard any details about the peasant woman poet Shuangqing and our quest for information about her. She had glanced through Du Laoshi's book this afternoon, read through some of her poems, and quickly skimmed Du's argument for the historical existence of Shuangqing. She now tells us that she has a very strong intuitive sense that Shuangqing was an actual historical figure. She is particularly impressed that Shuangqing was married to, and remained faithful to, an illiterate peasant who treated her very badly. Citing the contemporary Chinese equivalent of what we in America call "the battered wife syndrome," she argues that Shi Zhenlin's account described something very similar. She concludes with surprising confidence, "As a privileged male scholar, Shi Zhenlin could not have invented such a realistic account of female psychology without a real model as his basis!"

I am quite taken aback, but also very touched, by Xiaowan's fire and passion (as well as the breakneck speed of her speech) in discussing an issue that has always been for me primarily an intellectual exercise. She is so quick to jump to conclusions, I can't help thinking, but she is also throwing herself into our investigation with a sense of commitment that I find breathtaking. At the end of our discussions, Xiaowan gives each of us a copy of her own book of poetry, *Meili de liulang* (Beautiful wandering), published in 1996 when she was twenty-four years old (see figure 25). She has worked in her family's business throughout her youth and has not yet graduated from college, but she is already a published poet! Du Laoshi boasts: "In Xiaowan we have a modern-day Shuangqing, and in Professor Ropp we have a modern day Shi Zhenlin!"

I am flattered by the comparison, but confident that Xiaowan is a closer match for Shuangqing's talent than I am for Shi Zhenlin's. Yet, I can't let the analogy pass without comment. "Well, Xiaowan, if you find me sometime outside your window tearfully chanting your poetry, don't pay me any attention! I'm just a crazy old man like Shi Zhenlin!" (Shi Zhenlin and his friends used to loiter around Shuangqing's house and chant her poetry to express their profound sympathy for her.) We all have a good laugh and disband for the night. This is going to be an interesting week!

*two* ·

# *First Encounters*

*Shuangqing, a girl from Xiaoshan, was born of peasant stock. Shuangqing was brilliant from birth; upon hearing anyone read she would break into a smile. By ten-plus years of age she was adept at needlework. Her maternal uncle was a village tutor who used to teach next door to her house. When hearing her uncle teach, she would memorize everything. She would sell her needlework in exchange for books of poems and song lyrics, which she would chant from memory. She studied the xiaokai style of calligraphy and learned to make all the strokes extremely gracefully. She was able to write out the entire Heart Sutra [Xinjing] on a cassia leaf.*

—Shi Zhenlin, *Random Notes from Xiqing* (1907; reprint, Beijing: Zhongguo shudian, 1987), chap. 2, pp. 33–34 (hereafter abbreviated as *RN,* 2.33–34)

### *Shuangqing's Abrupt Introduction*

This is Shuangqing's introduction in Shi Zhenlin's memoir. When I began reading Shi's *Random Notes* with my teacher, Liu Laoshi, we were surprised to find nothing about Shuangqing in the first third of the book. In his first chapter he tells of his wanderings in scenic places, his friends, and the séances they hold in which they communicate with female immortals through a practice called "spirit writing" (described here in chapter 4, "Biographer"). Prefaces by Shi's friends highlight his profound sympathy for "young maidens" *(jiaren)* of extraordinary talent and beauty, but they make no mention of Shuangqing. Knowing that this is the only original source on Shuangqing and that Shuangqing is more famous than Shi Zhenlin, we had expected her to be the main feature of Shi's memoir. Instead, she seems almost hidden away in the middle of the book.

This first paragraph on Shuangqing is one of the few parts of Shi's *Random Notes* that has made it into many anthologies. It provides the essential information explaining how a peasant woman could become literate and identifies the village where she lived, Xiaoshan. Though a peasant, Shi reports, Shuangqing has acquired the skills one would expect only among the wealthy households of the elite: she does embroidery, memorizes and learns to write classical poetry with the help of her uncle, and writes in an elegant calligraphy.

### *Heart Sutra on a Cassia Leaf*

The paragraph concludes with a claim I found surprising: that Shuangqing could write out the entire Heart Sutra on a cassia leaf. The Heart Sutra, one of the most popular sutras in the Mahayana Buddhist tradition, was and is often memorized by lay followers of Buddhism. A meditation on the illusory quality of human form, feeling, perception, impulse, and consciousness, it is believed to disperse evil spirits when chanted regularly. This is the first of many references to Shuangqing's devotion to Buddhist teachings.

Du Fangqin had told me on our visit to Jintan that the Heart Sutra was around 200 characters. "That could fit on a cassia leaf," she said with at least a hint of jest in her voice. Yes, I agreed, if she wrote in small characters. Years later, in order to check this out for myself, I found and photocopied the Heart Sutra in the Harvard-Yenching Library. It is a short work, about 260 characters. When the Chinese woman working at the circulation desk saw what I had just copied, she became so excited that a Western Caucasian man would be interested in her favorite sutra, "the heart of Buddhism wisdom," that she forgot to give me my change. When I reminded her, she turned red, reached for the change drawer, and said, "I'm so embarrassed."

"That's okay," I replied, "I'm as delighted by your reaction as you are by my interest in the sutra." We parted feeling a kinship of quiet conspirators of contentment, fellow admirers of the Heart Sutra. I felt only slightly fraudulent, since I had never before seen the work in my life. In any case, I accomplished my mission, finding the sutra and seeing that perhaps it could fit, in small characters on a large cassia leaf, say, one foot square. Possible, I suppose, but I still wondered after reading this first paragraph, "Are we to take this narrative literally?"

### *Peasant Woman without a Surname*

A second surprise about Shi Zhenlin's introduction of Shuangqing is that he gives no surname for her. I had told Liu Laoshi that we would be reading the poetry of He Shuangqing, which is what she is called in every anthology. But here she is introduced simply as Shuangqing. Perhaps her surname would be made clear later in the memoir, but I had expected it here in the introduction of this peasant woman poet.

> *There was a neighbor girl married to a scholar who used to laugh at Shuangqing's humble rural background and her having no chance for contact with gentlemen scholars. In the tenth year of the Yongzheng reign (1732), Shuangqing was eighteen. The mountain folk had no way of recognizing her talent, but they all remarked on her beauty and so married her to the son of a farm family surnamed Zhou. Her husband's mother was a wet nurse, and they rented a place to live from* [Shi's friend, Zhang] *Mengzhan, and rented and tilled his land. When they saw their landlord, they called him Mr. Official. Her husband was over ten years older than Shuangqing. He only knew enough to refer to an almanac and note down the moon's phases.* (*RN,* 2.34)

Here we have a few more details about Shuangqing's husband and in-laws, poor tenant farmers who rent their land from Shi Zhenlin's close friend, Zhang Mengzhan. In the very first sentence, Shi Zhenlin highlights the social distance between Shuangqing's peasant family and the scholar-landlord class by quoting a neighbor woman who laughs at Shuangqing derisively because she "has no chance to meet scholars," a strange comment from someone who lives far away from scholars herself. Shi further emphasizes the social distance between landlord and peasant by reporting that the Zhou family doesn't really know how to address landlord Zhang properly, so they just call him *guanren,* "Mr. Official," the most formal and authoritative title they can imagine.

Against this rather vague rural background, having established the humble circumstances in which she lives, Shi gives us our first glimpse of Shuangqing and her poetic talent.

### *Shuangqing's Beauty and Talent: Song Lyrics on Leaves*

> *In the summer* [of 1732], *the fourth month, I went to Xiaoshan to escape the summer heat, staying at "Plowing-in-Pairs Hall"; Flower Lover* [Huaifangzi, literally "The one who yearns for fragrance (of flowers)," the style name of Shi's friend Duan Yuhan], *went along also. In the dusk we were looking toward the mountain. Shuangqing was just holding a trash basket outside the house, having just returned with a bamboo basket from planting gourd and melon seeds on the bank west of the*

*bridge. Her face was fine featured and attractive, but at the same time she looked lonely and forlorn.*

*The next day I received a song lyric of hers written in powder on a peony leaf, to the tune of "Huanxisha." It goes:*

*The warm rain falls unfeeling*
*Like scattered threads of silk.*
*The herd boy tucks a flower behind his ear*
*While peasants take new grains from the*
*Small field to the threshing floor.*
*Draw the water, plant the melons,*
*But he gets mad—too early;*
*Bear the smoke, cook the millet,*
*He's mad again—too late.*
*The day is long and my body is*
*racked with aches and weariness.*

*Also, on a tuberose leaf, I received a song lyric written in powder, to the tune of "Wang Jiangnan":*

*No sight of spring;*
*I've searched through west of the deserted bridge.*
*The pink that tints the dream*
*Cheats the butterfly;*
*The dark green that locks in my grief*
*Fools the oriole.*
*Deep regrets, best not stir them up again.*

*No sight of him;*
*Should I see him or should I not,*
*I wonder.*
*I salute the moon,*
*fragrance* [of incense] *only troubles my sleeves.*
*You pity the flower,*
*But no tears are left to wet your shirt.*
*The mountains are far away and the sun is low.*

(*RN*, 2.34)

In this passage we have the first two of Shuangqing's famous song lyrics, one written in powder on a peony leaf, and one in powder on a tuberose leaf. This powder could refer to the pollen of flowers, or the powder that women use for makeup. I discuss this issue in further detail in a later chapter, but here it is enough to note that Shi's description adds poignancy to his efforts to rescue this peasant woman poet from oblivion. Her writing is fragile and ephemeral until he gives it permanence in a printed memoir.

More consequential than the media in which they are written are Shuangqing's song lyrics, the poetic genre for which she is most famous. Interestingly, Shi Zhenlin and his friends interpret these first song lyrics of Shuangqing's as flirtatious, even though they always emphasize how loyal and obedient she is to her husband. Certainly, song lyrics often dealt in love themes, for the genre began with flirtatious songs exchanged by courtesans and their literati clients. Although the music of these tunes has been lost since the genre's origins in the eighth century, tune patterns still survive for about 825 tunes. The song-lyric writer literally "fills in" the lyric, as each tune title carries its own pattern including the rhyme scheme and length of each line.

Given its origins in popular song and the entertainment quarters, song lyrics were particularly associated with women, though often enough they were written by men in the voice of women. In Chinese poetic traditions, the lonely woman abandoned by her lover was frequently used as a metaphor for the official or aspiring official who was ignored or fired, unappreciated or persecuted, by the emperor. This popular device afforded the male writer a mask behind which he could criticize a boorish, ignorant, or immoral emperor indirectly and thereby avoid the punishment that a more direct assault would have risked. The song-lyric tradition in China was seen as a secondary poetic genre, less prestigious than the regulated verse (*shi,* the earliest form of Chinese poetry in which lines are all of uniform length) in part because of its associations with the pleasure quarters, and in part because it typically dealt with private emotions and was therefore seen as somehow "less serious" than regulated verse. Precisely because it was "less serious," it also allowed authors more freedom for the exploration and expression of personal feelings.

There developed two major and quite different modes of song lyric, and the two modes imply a gender division (despite the fact that both men and women wrote in both modes). "Heroic abandon" *(haofang)* represents an aggressive "masculine" style, often associated with themes of patriotism and heroic willingness to sacrifice oneself for the sake of one's country, region, or family. "Delicate restraint" *(wanyue),* by contrast, implies a quiet, gentle "feminine" style with an emphasis on private feelings, often of love. By the seventeenth century, song lyrics came to be written increasingly by women of elite status, far beyond the courtesan quarters. Although historians have long seen the song-lyric genre as reaching the peak of its development in the twelfth century, it also flourished in the Qing period and has continued to be written down to the present day. Given their emphasis on aesthetics and personal feelings, Shi Zhenlin and his friends were particularly drawn to song lyrics.

Shuangqing's first song lyric, to the tune of "Huanxisha," is a simple recounting of rural scenes, but with undertones of longing. The "unfeeling" rain is beautiful, "like scattered threads of silk," but it suggests an unspoken contrast with humans full of feelings. In keeping with the beauty of the rain, the farm boy with the flower suggests an idyllic rural scene of contentment, and the peasants taking grain to the threshing floor suggest an abundant harvest this year. The final half of the lyric provides a stark contrast as it certifies Shuangqing's hard work and unappreciated suffering. She diligently plants melons, draws water, and cooks millet, but her husband, or possibly her mother-in-law, is never satisfied with her hard work. She is left with only aches and pains and no one to offer thanks for her trouble.

The next lyric, to the tune of "Wang Jiangnan," is considerably more flirtatious. The nonarrival of spring (and springtime love) gives rise to an imagined spring (and an imagined love), but the beauty of the imagined spring and the imagined love only serves as a reminder of their absence. The female poet "looks for spring," read "longs for love," but cannot find either. The butterfly (male lover of flowers) dreams of pink but is deceived to think that spring (love) has arrived. The oriole sees dark green, another sign of spring, but this dark green is more dark than green; it only locks in the poet's grief and is not the green of springtime rebirth (or love). In the second stanza Shuangqing discusses a would-be lover whom she wants to see but is not certain she should. She implies the impossibility of their love-from-a-distance ever being fulfilled and is left alone with the moon as her only companion. In the next to last line, she certainly seems to highlight the ineffectuality of a would-be suitor: "You pity the flower / But have no tears left to wet your shirt." Given the implications of this line, it is not at all surprising that Shi and his friends read this poem as aimed flirtatiously at Duan Yuhan, known to his friends as Flower Lover. But Shuangqing denies any flirtatious intent and instead explains her devotion to her husband.

### *Shuangqing and the Literati: Flirtatious Poet or Chaste Wife?*

*Thereupon she turned away and sighed, "The farmer [my husband] may be coarse, but I can still find indirect ways to be tender toward him; how could I*

> *bear to cause him trouble? In this life I have no desire to know scholars face to face. Here is a song lyric to the tune of 'Shiluoyi':*
>
> *The hardest things in the world to declare are one's innermost feelings;*
> *Swallow all the tear drops, they just keep welling up.*
> *I twist the wilted flowers in my hands,*
> *Leaning speechless on the screen;*
>
> *Looking at myself in the mirror,*
> *I shock myself: so thin, erect, and alone.*
> *It is not the face of spring;*
> *It is not the face of autumn;*
> *Is it really Shuangqing?"*
>
> *Flower Lover felt very remorseful and wrote over a dozen song lyrics, hoping she would reply with matching rhymes, but she didn't answer. Then one day we saw Shuangqing again at her doorway looking very forlorn and sad; her countenance was completely changed from before. Flower Lover bowed to Heaven's emptiness* [as a way of saluting her]. *Another time, Flower Lover asked Mengzhan to hire a skilled painter to paint her likeness, and he sent her a parting song lyric, hoping for her to reply. This time she responded with a small letter all rolled up and tightly sealed, and she told him to break the seal and read it only out on the road where no one else would be around. Thrilled, Flower Lover slipped it in his sleeve and left. Mengzhan and I didn't know what she said, so the next day I sent a maid over to ask. Shuangqing smiled and quoted* [the female immortal] *Boluo's couplet: "The one with the most feeling is the crazy immortal / Now other scholars get involved, guessing all day long."* (*RN*, 2.34–35)

Immediately after declaring that she has no desire to meet scholars face to face, Shuangqing recites (or at least presents) another song lyric that seems to contradict her statement. It is a lyric steeped in a woman's disappointment through lost or unrequited love. Unlike many of Shuangqing's song lyrics that describe realities of farm and family life, this lyric is very typical of the female voice (or female mask) in the song-lyric genre proclaiming the disappointment of an abandoned lover. "Twisting wilted flowers while leaning on a screen" sounds suspiciously aristocratic. Do peasant families have screens for idle abandoned lovers to lean on? And the poem concludes in a highly self-conscious way, with the poet picturing for us the thin and solitary face she sees in the mirror and declaring it, not the happy face of spring nor the sad and weathered face of autumn. Rather, as if startled by her own appearance she asks, can it really be her own self, the face of Shuangqing?

Despite the clear flirtatiousness of the second song lyric and the clear overtones of disappointed love in the third, Duan Yuhan the Flower Lover immediately accepts Shuangqing's declaration of innocence at face value. He feels so remorseful over her "ill fate," and his having unfairly suspected her of flirtatiousness, that he writes her more than a dozen song lyrics, hoping for her to respond with matching rhymes. For all the pity he expresses for her "poor fate," and for all the admiration he has for her talent and her virtue, it certainly appears that he also still harbors the strong hope that she *will* eventually respond with poems that *are* flirtatious. The next time the literati catch a glimpse of Shuangqing, they are struck by how miserable she looks, her countenance "completely changed." This is certainly a realistic touch, for if her illiterate husband and cranky mother-in-law are as strict as Shi Zhenlin suggests, they can hardly look kindly on her exchanging poems with strangers. Thus it is not at all surprising that the arrival of these literati admirers in Xiaoshan might only serve to complicate Shuangqing's life.

Shuangqing's poor fate and poetic talent are not the only things on Flower Lover's mind, for he also suggests that his friends hire a painter to paint her portrait. There is an ironic and paradoxical cycle that occurs again and again in Shi's *Random Notes:* Shuangqing's virtue only serves to make her seem more desirable to the literati who cry for her poor fate, worship her talent and her beauty, and long for glimpses of her poetry and her person. She refuses to answer Flower Lover's poems but responds with a letter that sends him into fits of ecstasy. Zhenlin and Mengzhan, puzzled by the contents of her letter, send a maid to ask. Here again, Shuangqing appears as a precocious insider in Shi's memoir by quoting one of his own literary creations, a female immortal named Boluo. And by smiling and quoting the female immortal in a line about "the one with the most feelings" and scholars getting involved and guessing, she quite clearly seems to encourage the very kind of flirtatious poetic games that would get any married woman in eighteenth-century China into serious trouble. Shi Zhenlin, however, is quick to assure his readers of Shuangqing's virtuous reputation.

### *Shuangqing's Modesty, Virtue, and Beauty*

> *The old folks of Xiaoshan tell me that Shuangqing is by nature casual and direct, and warm and easy with other people; she has an air about her that floats as lightly as the clouds. She has none of the nervousness, narrowness, pettiness, or vulnerability of the "young lady" in her bearing. She in fact*

*hides her talent, so the people who have dealings with her family have never seen her writings. The villager she's married to is very poor and crude, and his mother (her mother-in-law) also forces her to work very hard without giving her any sympathy. Shuangqing handles all this bad treatment extremely well. Although unhappy, she never lets it show; although often hungry, tired, and ill, in her speech and in her laughter she seems completely contented.*

*The small courtyard at Xiaoshan is below Mount Siping, where bamboo and trees are thickly grown with a few scattered flowers. There is a bird there with glowing colored feathers whose voice is more beautiful than the yellow oriole. The mountain folks do not even know its name. Around the small courtyard are some earthen huts with thatched roofs, for renting out to peasants. Shuangqing lives in one on the west side of the small courtyard, opposite an old stream where the willows droop, entirely covering the eaves. Washing clothes and drawing water, so lovely sitting there on the rocks; those who see her are so amazed they suppose she's a goddess. Flower Lover would come here, and each time he came he would sit on the rock beside the stream where she always sat washing clothes. Mengzhan, returning from cutting wheat on the mountain, wrote the following* jueju:

*Mountain bees everywhere swarm on empty branches;*
*Waves of wheat, like yellow clouds; the day gets ever later.*
*Across the stream, I hear the soft call of an oriole.*
*When the day's tea is all boiled, I wake from my nap.*

*It was dusk already when we came out of the small village. Looking toward the western mountain in the rain, we saw a broken boat across the stream where Shuangqing used to sit washing clothes. Mengzhan got in the boat and chanted this poem:*

*A firefly, like a star, crosses the stream through the mist;*
*Clouds open a few inches, letting a patch of blue sky leak through.*
*Tonight the moon is waning. Will you still salute it or not?*
*Facing the flower, we crane our necks* [to see]; *out of her sight we sleep.*
(*RN*, 2.35–36)

At his leisurely pace, Shi Zhenlin gradually gives us more details on Shuangqing and her village at Xiaoshan. She is "casual and direct, warm and easy," with none of the nervousness or shyness associated with the cloistered young maidens in the elite class. Despite being mistreated by her illiterate husband and cruel mother-in-law, she never lets her anger show but always seems supremely contented. Although no one in the village knows of Shuangqing's literary talent, she is so beautiful that people who see her washing clothes in the stream by her house suppose she is a goddess *(shennü)*. As surprising as Shuangqing's ethereal beauty is the presence in this village of a mysterious beautiful bird with "glowing colored feathers" and a captivating voice. The peasants do not even know its name, and apparently neither does Shi Zhenlin. Though the village is poor, with peasants living in mud huts with thatched roofs, the surrounding landscape is almost magical it its beauty.

### *Landlord Zhang Mengzhan's Poetic Approach to Life*

In an interjection very typical of his writing style, Shi Zhenlin quotes two poems (*jueju,* short vignettes in four lines of seven characters each) by Shuangqing's landlord Zhang Mengzhan. Any scene or incident can inspire a poem from Zhenlin or any of his friends. They write poetry constantly. This is how they make sense of the world and how they communicate their innermost feelings to each other. In the immediate context of the discussion of Shuangqing, one might wonder what landlord Zhang Mengzhan's poems have to do with her. The first of the two poems simply recounts rural scenes of work followed by the idyllic soft call of an oriole, marking the end of the day. Mengzhan chants the second poem from the broken boat where Shuangqing sometimes washes clothes. In the last line, Shuangqing is clearly the flower these literati crane their necks to see, as Shi Zhenlin has just reported that these gentlemen scholars frequently loiter or lurk around Shuangqing's house and the stream where she washes clothes, just to watch her.

### *Shared Poems on a Buddhist Act of Mercy*

There follows an incident illustrating that Shi Zhenlin and Shuangqing share in common a devotion to the values of Buddhism. Though Buddhism was often criticized by orthodox Confucian scholars, it was quite popular in many regions, and Shi Zhenlin saw no contradiction between his Confucian duties and his belief in Buddhism. Along with Mengzhan and his brothers, Renzhi and Ling, Shi buys a bright green spotted frog from an old fisherman in order to free it from its cage, a typical Buddhist act of compassion that was quite popular in the eighteenth century as a way of building up one's own merit toward a future favorable reincarnation. Mengzhan wrote a poem commemorating this act of kindness; and Shi matched Mengzhan's rhymes with his own poem.

*On this night, the young boy Ling heard a voice chanting Buddha's name. I told him it was our frog. There was once a fisherman who had caught his boat full of fish. Halfway through the night the fish all chanted Amitabha. He was so amazed he let them all go; and from this good deed the clams of the sea became bodhisattvas, and the oysters were transformed into Lohans. That was the time when their merit became complete, giving rise to good fortune. Word [of my frog] spread to others; and Shuangqing matched our rhymes with the following:*

*Lotus leaves open as your many-tiered pavilion on the water's surface.*
*Their slight fragrance brings a joy that soon turns to sorrow.*
*The gentleman immortal sets you free from the heartless net;*
*In the nighttime rain you say your thanks from spring to fall.*

*Reflected in the water, you sit on the green ledge in solitary leisure;*
*Fed coarse greens, whether hot or bitter, dare you complain of hunger?*
*How then to affect your transformation into the Silver Moon Palace Toad?*
*Only wish your body to grow thin not plump [the easier to fly to the moon].*
(*RN*, 2.38)

Shuangqing fully shares Shi Zhenlin's Buddhist outlook. All sentient creatures are deserving of compassion. The Silver Moon Palace Toad is a divine being that lives with the moon goddess, Chang E, in her palace. To join the beautiful goddess Chang E on the moon is perhaps the highest aspiration a frog or toad could have. Just as these humans aspire to become immortals, so may the humble toad. And even the humble toad, freed from its cage by an act of Buddhist compassion, becomes associated in the minds of these poets with Chang E (as Mengzhan, in his poem, had also urged the liberated toad to "cultivate his virtue to become the Moon Palace Toad").

While translating Shi Zhenlin's memoir in Taiwan in 1991, I was very lucky to have as a tutor Liu Laoshi, a woman in her sixties, whose depth of understanding of Chinese culture and Chinese poetry always amazed me. When we began, she was mildly curious to see what Shi Zhenlin's memoir would be like. Very quickly she became a passionate fan of Shuangqing and an indispensable guide for me in my own search for Shuangqing. To illustrate how much I learned from her, I include some of our interchanges in these chapters of analysis. Horizontal lines precede and follow our conversations to set them off from my own analysis and from italicized translations of Shi's memoir.

•⁀ CONVERSATIONS WITH LIU LAOSHI The heater rattled against the January chill in our tiny cubicle of a classroom in Taipei. Liu Laoshi sat opposite me at the small table we shared, engrossed in this odd beginning of an odd tale. I jotted down notes toward a translation of Shuangqing's poem on the liberated frog and asked her what she thought of these first encounters between Shuangqing and Shi Zhenlin and his literati friends. "Well, her writing is good; there *is* something about her poetry that seems distinctive and powerful."

"What about Shi Zhenlin and his friends?" I continued. "Don't they seem curiously indifferent to or immune from the constraints of eighteenth-century society?"

"Yes, they seem completely infatuated with her, and quite reckless in the way they approach her and try to get her to respond. But Shuangqing *is* completely captivating in these first few pages. I don't ever recall any Chinese peasant woman being described with such loving care before. Her ambivalence is not too surprising. She can't help liking the attention from educated men who can appreciate her talent. At the same time, she has to be very careful in her dealings with them."

After years of seeing Shuangqing's poems only in anthologies, it was especially exciting to be able to read them now in their original context. The memoir itself was like nothing I had ever read before: so fragmentary, episodic, and seemingly accidental in its style, yet full of carefully crafted flights of rhetoric; dripping with erudition and at the same time very playful; so concrete and vivid in some of its descriptions and yet so frustratingly vague on other matters. After the first few pages, I had more questions than answers: What is Shuangqing's surname? How can these male strangers approach a peasant woman without getting her into serious trouble? Why does she respond with flirtatious poems? What did she mean about meeting gentlemen of talent in these *Random Notes*? If the memoir raised these questions, I was convinced, it would also surely provide answers to some of them.

Liu Laoshi was intrigued, above all else, by Shuangqing's poetry. She tended to see Shi Zhenlin's prose narrative as a distraction from the main event. It soon became evident, however, that Shi and his friends were attracted by more than Shuangqing's poetry alone. They were so taken with her beauty that they decided to capture it in several portraits. •⁀

*three* ·

# *Portraits*

### *Shuangqing and the Literati*

*Shilin, Zhang Fucang, came to Xiaoshan and painted two portraits of Shuangqing planting melons. He asked her to inscribe a poem on one to send to Flower Lover, and on the other one for himself to keep. Previously, when Flower Lover left, Shuangqing gave him a sealed envelope and directed him to read it only on the road. He went to a deserted temple, washed his hands in a stream there, licked the seal to moisten it, and pulled it open ever so carefully to avoid the slightest tear. He read it and let out an angry shout, and then he had to laugh. She had cut out a leaf in the shape of a butterfly, and on its two wings she had written two poems to the tune of "Huanxisha," making fun of Flower Lover. Flower Lover had earlier visited Danyuan (Tranquil Garden) to ask Wang Yueqiu to invite Shilin to come and paint her likeness.*

*. . . They arrived at Xiaoshan hoping to see Shuangqing but were not able to at first. Then in the evening she came out to wash clothes under the willows; they spied on her from one side and then crossed in front of her to look at her straight on, but she tried to turn away. Shilin said, "I can do it!* [I.e., I've seen enough to paint her.] *As for her bearing, her grace and beauty, that can be captured in paint; but that air about her, somewhere between shy and sad and not shy and sad, is especially difficult to capture." After completing the painting he presented it to Shuangqing. Shuangqing inscribed it with a song lyric to the tune of "Yujingqiu"; but then she felt remorseful and refused to give it back. She said, "You are just doing this to make fun of me."*

*Mengzhan wrote her a letter saying:*

> *This time when I had your pure likeness painted and implored you to inscribe it, I would not have dared such a thing to make fun of you. In fact, I will attach it to jade-studded scrolls, mount it on an antique bro-*

*cade, saturate it with rare perfume, bind it with a multicolored cord, and sheath it in an embroidered purse. I will not allow the vulgar masses so much as a glimpse to desecrate your elegance and purity, nor to breathe a single breath to despoil your sweet fragrance. I will invite talented gentlemen and young beauties to bow to you and empathize with you so that those in the human realm will know that a Shuangqing exists. I will invite the female immortals Boluo and Biye to chant poems in praise of you, so that all in Heaven will know that a Shuangqing exists. To correct for the creator who has allowed such unfairness to exist, I will raise your solemn beauty from the depths of its long obscurity and rekindle your burned ashes into a roaring inferno, so that all in Heaven and on earth will treasure what should be treasured [xi kexi] and cherish what should be cherished [lian kelian]. For you are certainly one who should be treasured and cherished: the single most beautiful woman in the world, born into this desolate and crude mountain area with no people* [i.e., no gentlemen].

*If you had the misfortune to be married to a man of scant learning and meager artistic sensibility, but who still tenderly cherished you and deeply treasured you, who could never wrong you, that would indeed bring you a happiness exceeding all your expectations. And if you had the good fortune to be married to a scholar, but* [a vulgar] *one who related to your cherishable and treasurable qualities by, contrary to all reason, drenching you with the sourness of pickled vegetables and smothering you with the stench of rotting garbage* [i.e., burying you in his wealthy household], *you would be like the eclipsed sun or the new moon. So meek and mild, with tousled hair and tattered clothes, if you were married to a common scholar [sushi], it would be hard for others to pity you. In fact Heaven has ordained you to be a peasant wife so the masses will not recklessly cherish and treasure you, so you hide all hints of your cherishable and treasurable nature and keep it repressed. But if you let it be revealed, it would certainly penetrate to the heights of Heaven and the depths of the earth. For Heaven must certainly know that there are those who cherish and treasure you, especially the one who basks in the sun and the moon! He takes as his task to rouse the whole universe to compete to cherish and treasure you.*

*Since there is a Shuangqing like no other, a portrait in painting is not like a portrait in words. In words one can capture her spirit, whereas a painting can capture her appearance. Thus the spirit that gets passed on in a painting is not her actual spirit, and the appearance that gets passed on in writing is not her actual appearance. The paintings that exist of the Luo goddess and Chang E are not based on people actually seeing them in the flesh. They are imitations of pure imagination. So on*

> *fans and screens, if their portraits border on the humorous, the goddesses do not get angry. For the phoenix or the magical* lingzhi *fungus, to be painted at all is regarded as auspicious, and to have their portrait hung is regarded as good a good omen, so that the blessings of genius and beauty* [i.e., of Heaven and earth] *will arrive. Heaven and earth do not play favorites, but in the end Heaven and earth do not prevent people from coveting true genius and beauty with their eyes, bragging on it with their mouths, and pursuing it with their hearts, to the point that they will steal it with their hands. Now the point of wanting to have your pure likeness in a painting is to have Heaven and earth treasure what should be treasured and cherish what should be cherished; to show people on earth and the gods in Heaven, whether vulgar or elegant, whether gods or mortals, so that they all will know there is a Shuangqing, and so that all might bow to her, cry for her, chant poems for her, and praise her. They must know that you exist, and that is why I have had your portrait done.*

*Shuangqing was thus gratified and returned the painting.*

[Shuangqing's] *song lyric to the tune of "Yujingqiu":*

*Eyebrows half in a frown,*
*Healthy color is already faded,*
*And the old remorse is not yet gone.*
*A thin figure in the painting,*
*Ashamed to be seen but hard to avoid it.*
*New illness still hangs on,*
*The painter applies light rouge but in vain.*
*In the cool of the night*
*The moon shines brightly,*
*Chang E shows no blemish.*
*Green sleeves still bear the telltale stains of tears;*
*The spot by the Haitang flower has been*
*Drenched with a thousand drops.*
*I wonder why recently everyday chores,*
*Combing hair and getting dressed,*
*Fixing dishes salty or sour,*
*All seem too much trouble.*
*Sweat makes her powder run and dry in streaks;*
*She dips the light cloth in blue water,*
*And repeatedly wipes the cold woven bamboo mat.*
*Who is there to realize*
*That this is a banished flower goddess?*

*Shilin sighed a deep sigh and said, "Steaming away in this cruel heat, my heart and eyes are all dizzy. It would be better to wait for the* [autumn] *cassia to bloom, and come again to paint an autumn face." Thereupon he left.*

*Mengzhan sent him this poem:*

*Now that you've departed, Xiaoshan's small eastern courtyard,*
*The Haitang flower bears the heat and blossoms forth.*
*Ethereal nighttime dream startles the flower and keeps her from sleep;*
*In the portrait her thin sleeves seem stirred by the autumn breeze.*
*In one scroll the springtime sorrow is still keenly felt.*
*The light rouge and black ink both give off a slight fragrance.*
*Deep in the night who will induce the elegant flower to sleep*
*In her now cool western hall until the moon becomes full?*

(*RN*, 2.38–41)

The structure of this segment is typical of Shi Zhenlin's rambling style. He circles back and forth in time, before and after the central events he describes: the literati spying on Shuangqing and Zhang Shilin painting two portraits of her. Although he has "seen enough" to paint her likeness, Zhang Shilin notes the difficulty of truly capturing an ambivalent "air" about her, shy and not shy, sad and not sad. The painter's lament echoes a recurrent theme in Shi's tale: the difficulty of capturing Shuangqing's infinitely good qualities with the finite power of words. She seems profoundly ambivalent toward the literati. Although she sends flirtatious song lyrics to Flower Lover Duan Yuhan, she tries to avoid the gaze of the scholars who find her washing clothes in her usual place, the stream beside her house. Once the paintings are done, she even inscribes them, but then she worries that the literati are making fun of her, and thus she inspires a nearly comic plea from her landlord Zhang Mengzhan.

### *Landlord Zhang's Letter to Shuangqing*

This has to be the most elaborate and flattering epistle ever sent from a landlord to a tenant. In the ornate parallel prose typical of the classical examination eight-legged essay, Mengzhan declares the purity of his motives and unbound strength of his worshipful admiration for Shuangqing. He promises to make her name known not only on earth but in Heaven as well, by having the female immortals Boluo and Biye chant her poems in the divine realm. Because she is the most beautiful woman on earth, born into a desolate place bereft of people who can appreciate her, he wants to assure that she will be treasured *(xi)* and cherished *(lian)* by all in Heaven and on earth. The term *lian*, which I translate here as "cherish," also carries a strong connotation of pity, but without the condescending tone we sometimes associate with pity. In treasuring/pitying unrecognized talent, the literati are also treasuring/pitying themselves. Mengzhan calls the place where Shuangqing lives *wuren zhi di*, literally "a place without people," as if the only people who qualify as human are the educated literati who come for a glimpse of her and her poems.

The references to the Goddess of Luo River and to Chang E, "imitations of pure imagination," suggest a parallel with Shuangqing. The point is not that the painting captures a true likeness of these goddesses, since who is to say what an imaginary creature really looks like? The mere painting of such a portrait is auspicious whether it is a true likeness or not. This is to assure Shuangqing she is not being made fun of, but the next sequence seems almost ominous in its implicit praise of her, as he notes that people cannot be stopped by Heaven from coveting genius and beauty and even from trying to "steal it with their hands." It is beginning to sound like Shuangqing is a bit too beautiful for her own good! Is this landlord threatening to steal the object of his desire with his own hands? As if to reassure her that is not the case, he ends with another flourish, assuring her that his only purpose is to make sure that all in Heaven and earth will know of her existence and praise her as she should be praised. He addresses her directly in the last sentence with the same term, *qing*, as in Shuangqing, the intimate term for "you" or "dear" that lovers use to address each other affectionately.

> Questions for Liu Laoshi  When a poet with romantic intentions writes to a woman, we ought not be surprised if he indulges in hyperbole. Isn't that what we mean by "poetic license"? Yet I couldn't help thinking that this letter was hilarious as we made our way through it. "In my own picture of rural Chinese society," I confessed to Liu Laoshi, "I imagine that if an ordinary peasant woman ever received such a letter from her landlord, she would either report the man to the authorities to have his sanity examined, or she would immediately propose exchanging her inscriptions on the paintings for a few months rent! The letter is so ornate, so elaborate, so overblown in its sentimentality and high-flown rhetoric, that it would seem to prove Shuangqing's original suspicions that these literati are simply making fun of a poor country woman."
>
> Liu Laoshi saw it differently. "Well, landlord Zhang is just show-

ing off his literary prowess here. He's writing for his friends as much as for Shuangqing, and Shi Zhenlin is quoting him for the same reason, to show his readers what a talented writer Mengzhan is." To her, this high-flown rhetoric was just setting up the more important revelation of Shuangqing's inscription on her portrait. She was not upset by the overblown literariness and sentimentality of his letter, but one element disturbed her: his use of the intimate term *qing* in addressing Shuangqing. She remarked with a frown, "I don't think a proper scholar would use such a term with anyone other than his own wife, and especially not in addressing the peasant wife of his own tenant."

### *Shuangqing's Self-Image: A Banished Flower Goddess*

To be sure, Shuangqing is no ordinary peasant woman. Rather, she seems to take landlord Zhang's overheated rhetoric right in stride. Without so much as a raised eyebrow, she promptly turns over one painting with her inscription, a commentary on her own appearance: a frail shy figure with tear stains on her sleeves, more tears drenching the spot by the nearby Haitang flower, and so sickly she has trouble with the routine chores of everyday life. The last images in the lyric are those of an upper-class woman, not a peasant. When she sweats, her powder runs and dries in streaks. Of course, peasant women would not normally be powdering their faces before taking to the hot and dusty fields. She dips a light cloth in blue water and wipes a finely woven bamboo mat of the kind found in wealthy households. This is a beautiful image, but it hardly sounds like a poverty-stricken peasant woman. And Shuangqing's last line puts her entirely at home with Shi Zhenlin's circle of female immortals: "Who is there to realize that this is a banished flower goddess?"

On the fifteenth of the second lunar month, there was a festival to the Goddess of a Hundred Flowers who presides in Heaven over the hundred female flower spirits or flower goddesses. There were many folktales of beautiful women portrayed as flower spirits reborn on earth. In the early nineteenth century, a talented literati novelist, Li Ruzhen, wrote a famous novel, *Flowers in the Mirror (Jinghua yuan),* centered on the earthly reincarnation of a hundred female flower spirits during the ninth-century reign of China's only ruling woman empress, Wu Zetian. The idea of a beautiful woman as a reincarnated flower goddess was common enough in Chinese culture, but it was a rare woman who saw and described herself in this way. Shuangqing here suggests that she too belongs in the divine realm but has been banished to the human world of the "red dust," the Buddhist term for the mutable impermanence, ego cravings, passion, pain, and suffering of material human existence.

> •⁀ LIU LAOSHI ON SHUANGQING'S SONG LYRICS Liu Laoshi was more impressed by Shuangqing's song-lyric inscription than by anything else in this section. "This lyric is good!" she exclaimed the second time we read it through, "and it very naturally describes in words what is shown on the portrait itself."
>
> "It seems to me," I started out tentatively, unsure of myself, "that Shi Zhenlin is playing games here, testing out various literary forms as ways to capture both Shuangqing's beauty and the impassioned literati response such beauty calls forth."
>
> "I think you have a good point," Liu Laoshi reassured me. "But what most impresses me is that Shuangqing's poetry is the best thing in this memoir. It's so natural, graceful, with vivid imagery, and it's never dull or ordinary."
>
> Perhaps, I began to think, it is not coincidental that Shi Zhenlin's narrative has been largely ignored while Shuangqing's poetry has become famous. •⁀

### *Growing Literati Obsession with Shuangqing*

When the painter Zhang Shilin leaves Xiaoshan to escape the summer heat, landlord Zhang Mengzhan sends him a poem that is a tribute to his portrait of Shuangqing and to Shuangqing's beauty. In Mengzhan's poem, Shuangqing, the Haitang flower, still bears the heat and blossoms forth, giving off her radiant beauty. Disturbing dreams startle the flower (woman), and the painting has captured her springtime sorrow even as it gives off the slight fragrance of "light rouge and black ink." The poem ends with a rhetorical question: who will comfort the flower and induce her to sleep? Who will help Shuangqing?

Following this poetic tribute to Shuangqing, Shi Zhenlin reports more wandering and poetry writing with his friends. He too has left Xiaoshan. He visits friends, goes on mountain hikes, and describes the scenery, and he and his friends all write poetry to commemorate these activities. In the eighth month, with autumn approaching, he returns to Xiaoshan with his friends Zhao Anshu, Zhang Mengzhan, and Duan Yuhan, and they resume their poetic interchanges with Shuangqing. In the ninth month, as promised, painter Zhang Shilin arrives back in

Xiaoshan to fulfill his earlier promise to "paint an autumn face" for Shuangqing. Shi Zhenlin tries at the same time to paint her portrait with words, describing her as ill but nevertheless hard at work in the busy autumn harvest season of 1733.

### *Malaria in Harvest Season*

*At the beginning of the ninth month, Shuangqing's malaria was still not better. But it was rice harvest time and she insisted on going to the threshing floor. She worked at laying out the wet grain, pulling off the grain and throwing it in the air* [to separate out the grains from the chaff], *drying it and then piling it up. She was so weak she became dizzy and had to put down some straw to sit on. As soon as she regained her balance she got up again, though the neighbor women tried to stop her. She cried and said, "My husband left early with his sickle hitched to his belt, walking barefoot in the frost, cracked heels and split toes, to go labor in the fields. How can I bear to sit and watch? My mother-in-law is also elderly, and she still comes to the threshing floor. How could an ill-fated person like me dare to imitate those wealthy ladies who fear the wind and sun and avoid the dust and dirt?" The neighbor women all felt sorry for her.*

*Shuangqing wore a green dress with her plain white sleeves rolled up, as fresh and clean as snow. When she was sweeping the threshing floor an old piece of paper fell out onto the ground. Young Ling picked it up and saw the line "In the shadows of the lamp are you still slightly ill or not?"* [This is a line from a poem Zhao Anshu had sent her.] *Shuangqing now seemed dull and listless. Each time she went out she would bow her head and keep her eyes lowered, not looking around anywhere. Once she carried vegetable baskets to the west side of the bridge and laid the baskets under a willow tree. There she wove together two willow branches, laughed, and said, "This is the tree of mercy."*

*On the ninth of the ninth month Shilin came. Shilin's family was poor and they made their living by painting. He also loved poetry and used to chant it endlessly.* [There follows a poem by Shilin, skipped here.] *Shilin painted three portraits of Shuangqing: one of her watching the moon, a second of her taking a lunch to the field, and a third of her washing clothes. After the paintings were finished Mengzhan sent Shuangqing a hairpin inlaid with silver, and two decorated azure blue shawls, and asked her to inscribe the paintings. Just then, because of the fall harvest, Shuangqing was terribly overworked. Her delicate hands were getting calloused, and her fingers were starting to crack; she suffered continuous pain, and her hands often showed traces of blood. She showed her wrists to Mengzhan's maid and said, "How could I hold the speckled bamboo brush and write fine calligraphy [zanhuatie]?*

*I went out with Shilin to pick wild chrysanthemums. We wandered around Nanpu and headed east. We saw Shuangqing wearing a white unlined garment. She leaned against the drying rack and pulled the grains of rice off the straw while the chaff flew all over her hair and shoulders. On the twenty-fourth Shilin left. I saw him off up to the elevated path. Mengzhan chanted Anshu's poem:*

*I watch you walk away and gradually disappear,*
*A human shadow in the twilight of the hillside.*
*Clouds descend over a thousand village trees;*
*The wind dries ten thousand bundles of grain.*
*In sad desolation, I stand utterly alone,*
*Feeling all forlorn. The evening fog is dense.*

*We watched him go until he was out of sight; then we returned. Shuangqing was wearing several layers this time, drying grain west of the wall. It was still very warm but she looked cold; we knew this was because of her malaria.*

*At the end of the ninth month, the sky cleared and it got quite comfortable. The farmers were all very busy harvesting the rice, repairing irrigation dikes, and preparing the soil. The harvest of all the crops (whether planted early or late) was so abundant that the women left their houses and went out to the fields, working all hours. Shuangqing's malaria was even worse than before. She was hot one minute and cold the next until her head swirled. Her complexion was pale and sallow. Her mother-in-law kept a close watch on her and admonished her more than ever; if Shuangqing was the slightest bit late in carrying out orders, she would get angrily scolded. In the afternoon she was first so cold that she trembled all over; yet she forced herself to get up and work. Though she wore several layers of coarse clothing, her hands still shook when she picked up the rice stalks to pull off the grain. Then she became so hot that she shed her clothes except for one layer, and still her face was all flushed, and she gasped for air. She got terribly thirsty but had no drinking water at hand, so she left the field and with her hands scooped up some water to drink from a stream. Her mother-in-law looked at her out of the corner of her eye and yelled at her harshly. Shuangqing just smiled and dared not say a word. She quickly complied with her orders and started working most strenuously, not daring to evade any of her mother-in-law's demands.*

*When they put down their bundles of grain that day, her mother-in-law had threshed several dozen bundles while Shuangqing had completed several hundred. All this Shuangqing bore with grace and dignity; her charming eyebrows*

> *looked like a painting; her earrings reflected the sunlight like stars; and when she lifted her shirt to wipe away her perspiration, she looked even more beautiful. But her mother-in-law was extremely suspicious and forbade any man from coming near Shuangqing or speaking to her. Shuangqing was always very cautious not to answer back if any man spoke to her. (RN, 2.77–79)*

These are the most realistic scenes of rural work that we see in *Random Notes*. Despite her weakness from malaria, Shuangqing works incessantly and threshes ten times the amount of rice that her mother-in-law manages. She sympathizes with her husband, who also works hard, and in these scenes generally ignores the nearby literati who are watching her and painting her portrait. When urged by the neighbor women to rest, she refuses even though she is near collapse, saying she would not dare to imitate those upper-class ladies who fear exposure to the elements. Yet, despite the dusty and dirty harvest she is engaged in, Shi Zhenlin describes her dress as "fresh and clean as snow." She is increasingly dull and listless, and careful to avoid any eye contact with the spying literati. One line of poetry falls out of her sleeve, and the servant boy Ling discovers it to be a line by Zhao Anshu.

> SHUANGQING AND THE GODDESS OF MERCY Neither I nor Liu Laoshi were certain how to interpret Shuangqing's act of sitting under the willow tree and weaving two willow branches together. Kang Zhengguo later explained to me that Guanyin, the goddess of mercy, Buddhist bodhisattva, and patron saint of all unfortunate women, is often portrayed holding a vase with willow branches in it. The willow was a symbol of salvation and of Buddhist mercy and compassion. Thus, Shuangqing's laughter would seem to be prompted by the contrast between these Buddhist ideals and the complete absence of mercy and compassion in her own family life.
>
> QUESTIONS ON SHI ZHENLIN'S PORTRAYAL OF RURAL LIFE Although I was sometimes slow to pick up on Shi Zhenlin's Buddhist imagery, I felt quite secure in taking exception to his descriptions of farmwork. Having experienced firsthand the dust and dirt of farmwork every summer of my youth, I found these portraits of Shuangqing's white sleeves and clean beauty in the midst of a rice harvest quite ridiculous. How can a malarial peasant woman in the middle of rice harvest season continue to look so dazzling? "Do peasant woman normally wear earrings?" I asked Liu Laoshi, somewhat mischievously.

"Probably not while harvesting rice," she replied, "but such adornments were not out of the question entirely, even for peasant women."

"I wonder what her husband thought about the silver-inlaid hairpin and blue shawls that Mengzhan sends Shuangqing," I said with a grin. "I would think he might not appreciate these expensive adornments."

"Yes, these gifts seem odd," she countered, "but perhaps he was just offering what he saw as a fair payment for her inscriptions on the paintings."

Liu Laoshi endured these prose passages, my suspicions, and my slow progress through them, as the penance to be paid for the fun of reading Shuangqing's poetry and lyrics. One day, out of the blue, she declared, "This material is too good not to recycle in a more modern art form. Professor Ropp, you should write a book about Shuangqing to bring her to the attention of China scholars in America."

"And what about you?" I asked. "Wouldn't you like to write a play or novel about her?"

"Indeed I would! But I may have to wait for retirement before I can find the time."

That day, Liu Laoshi asked me to photocopy the whole of *Random Notes* for her instead of just giving her a few pages each week. She was clearly impatient to forge ahead at a faster pace than I could manage!

### *The Meaning of Beauty for Shi Zhenlin*

Although Shi Zhenlin is adamant in declaring Shuangqing's beauty, he never describes her with precision. What did the term *beautiful* mean for Shi and his friends? In this connection it is worth noting the conventions of beauty in Shi Zhenlin's time and place. Shi clearly identified Shuangqing as a *jiaren,* a young maiden of the type celebrated in scholar-beauty romances.

In the Qing dynasty, the connotation of beauty conjured up by the *jiaren* was a very aristocratic ideal. Young beauties were invariably described as thin, frail, and delicate, with a light complexion. Of course they had tiny feet, which produced a lilting gait and a sense of vulnerability that men found captivating. Highly emotional and frequently ill, such heroines could easily die from a broken heart. They were usually described in elegant surroundings, in their boudoir, with many maids attending them. They were perfumed and powdered, with their hair worn in an elaborate "cloud-shaped pattern," and held in place with bejeweled pins and hair ornaments.

The seventeenth-century writer and connoisseur of women Li Yu once wrote an article on charm in women in which he listed his criteria for feminine beauty. He specified a light complexion, a full round face, small eyes with long curved eyebrows (presumably plucked and painted, since natural eyebrows do not grow in long graceful curves), a small mouth, pretty teeth, and small bound feet that produce a light yet natural gait (Chen Dongyuan 1967, 223–31; Eberhard 1967, 285–90).

Li Yu also described the importance of personality or charm in feminine beauty. He argued that women should be shy and modest, but not painfully so. This is best conveyed in his own description of his inspecting a lineup of potential concubines for a "distinguished gentleman" friend of his.

> There were great differences between the women who had appeared, dressed up and adorned before me. At first they all stood there with their heads lowered, and when they were told to lift their heads, one of them was not ashamed and lifted her head at once. Another one was much ashamed and embarrassed and lifted her head only after several requests. And then there was one who also did not immediately respond but, with some encouragement, she lifted her head, glanced at me briefly but without really meeting my eye, and quickly she detached her eyes from mine again. Only then did she lift her head fully. After everyone had looked at her, she glanced at me once more, and then lowered her head again. This was charm. (Eberhard 1967, 276; also in Lin Yutang 1963, 234)

Shi Zhenlin's description of Shuangqing seems to match very well Li Yu's definition of feminine charm. She is shy and modest, and yet not so shy and modest that she entirely spurns the attention she receives from the literati. Painter Zhang Shilin's characterization of Shuangqing as "between shy and not shy" seems to echo Li Yu's description of the charming young prospective concubine who made only the briefest sort of eye contact. In her demeanor, Shuangqing mirrors the sentiments most often identified with courtesans or maidens of the upper class.

It is admittedly frustrating to be told in a book without illustrations that Shuangqing's "charming eyebrows looked like a painting." Fortunately, we have many paintings of Qing-dynasty beauties to help us make sense of this comment. High and gracefully arching eyebrows were achieved by plucking them and then painting the desired design on one's forehead. Earrings that reflect light like stars would seem to suggest some kind of jewels, or at the least a shiny metal like gold or silver. Despite Liu Laoshi's assurances that peasant women did sometimes wear earrings, I see Shi Zhenlin's description here as appealing once again to an aristocratic ideal of beauty. The best exception to the aristocratic ideal is his concluding line about Shuangqing's being even more lovely when she lifts her shirt to wipe away her perspiration. Young maidens in scholar-beauty romances were not normally described as sweating.

Clearly Shi Zhenlin wants to have it both ways. Shuangqing is a hard-working, ill, and persecuted peasant woman, yet at the same time, in her dazzling appearance, she surpasses all the common aristocratic standards of beauty (except bound feet). He includes no illustrations in his *Random Notes,* but his prose descriptions and his assumptions about feminine beauty give us some idea of Shuangqing's appearance. At one point he describes her as sweeping leaves and looking "especially elegant, lovely, and dignified," even in her weakened malarial state (*RN,* 3.48). His description calls to mind a Qing-dynasty portrait by Fei Danxu (1801–1850) entitled *Sweeping Fallen Leaves in Autumn* (see figure 3). The beauty in the picture is thin and wispy, with a round face and high arched eyebrows. Though dressed a bit too elegantly for a peasant, she could pass for the Shuangqing described by Shi Zhenlin. In the nineteenth century the Zhejiang painter Ren Xun (1835–1893) depicted a female immortal in Heaven (see figure 4). She floats among the clouds with a beatific look on her face while scattering petals of heavenly flowers. Both these paintings convey the kinds of images Shi Zhenlin described in prose: Shuangqing gracefully sweeping fallen leaves, and Shuangqing the ethereal flower goddess banished to earth.

### *Class Constructions of Beauty*

While Shi conveys her talent, her personality, her demeanor, and her feelings in considerable detail, he tells us little about her physical features other than to say she is elegant, lovely, graceful, dignified, sensitive, modest, weak, and vulnerable. Her weakness and vulnerability result from her malaria, and from an emotional sensitivity that no one but her literati friends can appreciate. Despite a few signs of peasant influence—she does not have the nervousness or pettiness of spoiled aristocrats, her hands are rough, and on occasion she perspires—most of Shi's descriptions of Shuangqing sound very much like those of the upper-class women described in scholar-beauty romances. Francesca Bray has written insightfully about the role of class in the construction of a feminine ideal in the late imperial period.

> The ideal of elite womanhood stands in contrast to the elite image of the lower-class woman, constitutionally fertile and unconscious of any need to control her emotions. One of the signs of elite women's inferiority to men was their relative lack of emotional control. . . . Lack of self-control was a mark of inferior class as well as gender, but in the lower classes it was allied not to the elegant neurasthenia of gentlewomen, but to a robust physique and solid nerves. Peasant children grew up strong and healthy; direct exposure to sun, wind, and the *qi* of the soil strengthened their muscles and protected them from the nervous ailments to which well-born children were prey. (Bray 1997, 365)

Bray is speaking here of literati constructions of class distinctions and stereotypes. Needless to say, peasant women were not immune from illness, and there is no reason to believe they could not have been born with qualities of beauty as defined in elite terms. What is interesting is that Shi Zhenlin wrote entirely "against the grain" of the common literati stereotypes of peasant women. He saw in Shuangqing not the robust child-bearing peasant field worker but the beautiful maiden, the light-as-air goddess of the flowers, and the delicate melancholy *jiaren* idealized in art and literature by the Chinese elite.

Even after the first few pages of Shi Zhenlin's narrative of Shuangqing, it quickly became clear that I would never understand his odd tale without understanding more about its narrator. Who was Shi Zhenlin?

# *four*

# *Biographer*

*When I was very small, I was frightened by the sudden changing of daylight and darkness. People explained to me that this was simply the changing of day and night. I was perplexed by the appearance and disappearance of people. It was explained to me that this was simply the alteration of life and death. I was taught to distinguish the stars, to know the Sieve and the Dipper; to distinguish the birds, to know the blackbird from the magpie. That was how I first gained knowledge. As I grew up, sudden changes from daylight to darkness and from appearance to disappearance no longer seemed strange. However, at times, in the great confusion and muddle of things, my spirit would soar up into the vast universe to look down on it all, and I came to understand that in these alterations of light and darkness and of existence and nonexistence, there is a tinge of sadness.*

*As a tiny child I was enjoying a meal of chicken when the family members told me that the hen's baby chicks were still there. I crawled over to look and discovered a pair of chicks huddling over their mother's feathers. Out of sympathy, I could not eat any more; and that was how I first knew sadness. Once, when crawling beside a wall, I got hold of something I thought was candy, so I put it in my mouth to suck on it. My family pointed out my foolishness and told me it was only a piece of stone. On it were written two characters,* xi *and* qing. *They urged me to read these characters, and that was the beginning of my reading. The stone is hollowed out as a mortar, and I sit facing it still today as I write these* Random Notes. *On the twelfth day of the twelfth month of the second year of Qianlong (1737), composed in a dream.*

—Shi Zhenlin, preface to *Random Notes from Xiqing*

As every author knows, prefaces to books are read first but written last. There are several prefaces to *Random Notes,* this one by Shi himself, and two by his friends Wu Zhensheng and Cao Zhenting. Shi's preface is the shortest of the three. He uses the preface to recall his childhood and to explain his title. He speaks of his gradually gaining knowledge of the world, of coming to terms with darkness and death (mysteries to every child), of the experience of sadness upon realizing where his meat came from (with hints that he might have become a vegetarian very early). While he came to recognize darkness and death as natural, he suggests that he still finds something sad about life and its incessant changes. There is a hint here of a tragic outlook on life. Finally, he describes the first two characters he ever learned, *xi* and *qing*, "west" and "green," words he sees yet now, carved on a stone he found in his early childhood. These characters he takes for his title: *Random Notes from Xiqing.*

The most intriguing words in Shi's preface are the last three: *meng zhong zuo,* "composed in a dream." They could refer to the preface or to the entire work. As noted elsewhere (in chapter 13, "Clues"), Shi Zhenlin is very interested in the relationship between dreams and waking reality, and in several ways he implies that he does not recognize any distinction between the two.

### *Shi Zhenlin and the Civil Service Examinations*

Shi Zhenlin was born in 1693 in Guazhu on the banks of Yaohu (Lake Yao) in southern Jintan County, in Jiangsu Province. Jintan lies in the heart of south central China's prosperous rice, tea, and silk belt, and like many sons of prominent families in this area, Shi spent his youth in intense study for the civil service examinations that were seen as the key to wealth, rank, and fame in this society. He studied in many different places with a variety of friends, as if he needed to sample a variety of styles until he found one that would prove successful. He came to Xuebu District in the early 1730s in part to study for the examinations with Zhang Mengzhan, Shuangqing's landlord. We would never guess from Shi's preface, or from the contents of *Random Notes,* that it was written during the very time he was successfully completing his extended examination career. The work begins in 1723 and contains the most detail on the early 1730s. He first learns about Shuangqing in 1732 and last mentions her in 1734. In 1735 Shi passed the district examination in Xuebu District and the provincial examination in Nanjing. Then, a few months before publishing *Random Notes* in 1737, at age forty-four, he had won the coveted *jinshi* degree in Beijing that qualified him to hold office.

Although Shi mentions none of his examination experience, it is significant that his two preface writers included Cao Xueshi, his only close friend to have achieved the *jinshi* degree, and Wu Zhensheng, a lifelong examination failure who used his preface to show off his ability in the ancient parallel-prose style required in the examination system. Cao offered the stamp of approval of an "elder" who had attained his degree ahead of Shi, and Wu offered an eloquent and elaborate example of examination-style prose writing. Together their prefaces added luster to the work and signaled to the reader that this was no run-of-the-mill book, but rather the work of a talented, skilled, and above all, sensitive, writer.

The eighteenth century was not an easy time to compete in the civil service examination system. With the era's peace and prosperity came increasing literacy and, consequently, increasingly intense competition in the examinations. In Nanjing, the provincial capital of Jiangsu, the all-important provincial-level examination was held once every three years. The pressures on young men to succeed against great odds in this examination could be so intense that some of them literally went mad. On three occasions during the exam week, the candidates would carry food, drink, chamber pot, brush, ink and paper, into their tiny cubicles, spending up to three days and two nights in a single session, writing essays and poetry on assigned topics. In a large and prosperous province like Jiangsu, ten to twenty thousand men might qualify for the provincial examination in any given three-year period. Of this group, no more than ninety, less than 1 percent, would pass and thereby qualify for a low-level government post and, more importantly, for the even more prestigious metropolitan examination given every three years in the capital of Beijing.

The civil service examination system permeated and shaped elite Chinese society like no other institution. Benjamin Elman has called the system and the schooling that went with it an "educational gyroscope" that kept Chinese state and society on a steady and stable course (1991, 1999). The system guaranteed the state an unlimited supply of society's "best and brightest" minds and ensured that those minds would be thoroughly steeped in Confucian ideals. Given its near monopoly on prestige in society, the system also gave the state the de facto power to determine the size, shape, and character of the Chinese elite. No matter how well established an aristocratic Chinese family, or how long its distinguished pedigree, it could not hope to maintain its high status beyond a generation without continuing success in the civil service examinations.

There was a thriving publishing industry built around cram books of model essays whose only purpose was to prepare candidates for the examinations. Given the high stakes involved and the pressures on candidates to succeed, it is not surprising that some found ingenious ways to cheat. Candidates were carefully searched before entering the examination compound, but that did not deter all attempts to smuggle aids into the compound. In his history of the Qing examination system, Professor Miyazaki Ichisada includes a picture of what must be the world's most elaborate crib sheet: the lining of a scholar's gown, filled on the inside with seven hundred thousand characters, model essays, and quotations from the *Four Books* and *Five Classics* (Miyazaki 1963). As if the examination pressures were not bad enough, what made them worse, especially for a bright, creative, and dreamy boy like the young Shi Zhenlin, was that examinations depended on mountains of memorization rather than critical thought and had to be written in a rigid and formalized essay form called the eight-legged essay. Everyone complained about the eight-legged essay, but as examiners had their own pressures to deal with, sifting through thousands of essays to pick out and rank the few dozen best ones, they came to rely increasingly on formal criteria of the prose style because that was easier and more objectively measured than the more difficult and subjective areas of political and philosophical thought.

We do not know the detailed examination history of Shi Zhenlin, but we know that he failed several times, and that examination preparation dominated the early years of his life. Miyazaki Ichisada has estimated that Chinese boys were required to memorize passages totaling over four hundred thousand characters in classical Chinese texts (two hundred characters a day for six years) just to prepare for the first level of competition in the examination system (Miyazaki 1976, 16). Thus, we can be sure that Shi Zhenlin had a powerful memory and had thoroughly mastered the Confucian classics and the eight-legged essay form that dominated the examination system. In addition to the regular three-year cycle of provincial and metropolitan examinations, additional examinations were also given on special occasions such as the coronation of an emperor, or an imperial wedding. These were called *enke,* meaning special examinations granted by the grace of a magnanimous emperor. It was precisely at one of these special examinations at the capital that Shi attained his *jinshi* degree, an achievement often seen as the defining moment in the life of a Chinese scholar.

Yet Shi Zhenlin seemed curiously indifferent to his examination success. Offered an appointment as a district magistrate in Guangdong Province, far to the south, he declined it on the grounds that he could not leave his aging mother behind. Ten years later, in 1747 when he was fifty-four, he finally assumed his only official position, as an instructor in a prefectural school run by the government in Huai'an, on the Grand Canal about a hundred miles north of Jintan. What did he do in those ten years between appointments? From his fragmentary writings it appears that he traveled a great deal: to visit friends, scenic places, Daoist temples, and Buddhist monasteries and convents. More than anything else, he recorded the poetry that he and his friends wrote on their mutual visits and their wanderings.

Shi appears to have been a conscientious educational official at Huai'an. Early in his tenure there, a flood decimated the area, and he buried some of the poorest victims at his own expense. He also once furnished a New Year's feast at the school and invited the poor to attend. Apart from these small acts of compassion toward the poor, little is recorded of his time at Huai'an. In 1755, at age sixty-three, he resigned his post, with the excuse that he needed to return home to care for his aging mother. Nothing in the Chinese value system, whether political obligations or career ambitions, could trump filial piety, so no one could fault him for his decision. He was, no doubt, a loyal and filial son, but it is abundantly clear from his writings that he was not a conventional orthodox Confucian, and he was not very interested in an official career. Rather, he was drawn to Daoist and Buddhist philosophy, and to the world of the upright recluse who turns his back on politics and an official career as too dirty and too messy a business for a true scholar to spend his time on.

So why did he devote the first four decades of his life preparing for and competing in the examination system? For one thing, it was a matter of self-esteem. Examination success was society's definition of success par excellence. For another thing, attainment of the highest degree, the *jinshi,* bestowed high status on the degree holder and his family, whether he served in government or not. A high- degree holder could call upon officials personally and meet them face to face, which mere commoners could never do. Social contacts with high local officials helped protect a family from lawsuits and from charges of tax evasion. Shi Zhenlin undoubtedly benefited in all these ways from his civil service degree and his contacts in officialdom, but he clearly preferred to spend his time in pursuits far removed from politics and officialdom.

Retiring in 1755, Shi lived another twenty-five years until 1779. These years were spent much like his earlier years, traveling, sightseeing, visiting friends, drinking, writing, and painting. He had two sons, born in 1723 and in 1732, and a grandson in 1757. In all of his surviving writings, he respectfully mentions his wife a few times, but is mostly silent about her and about their relationship. He makes no references to personal experience with concubines or courtesans anywhere in his writings. About his economic situation, we know almost nothing. His family no doubt owned enough land to support his literati lifestyle, and he occasionally was asked to write epitaphs for friends and acquaintances and prefaces to their books and collections. Although he was known as a skilled painter and calligrapher, we have little or no information about whether he made any money from these endeavors. Some people probably paid him for the commemorative essays and epitaphs they implored him to write. He once spent a busy day inscribing 120 paper fans for a monk at a Buddhist temple, but we are not told whether his payment was in cash or in merit toward his next reincarnation (Yuan Hua 1988, 103). Whatever the extent of payment he received for his works, and it was probably not much, he liked to give the impression that he was living out the amateur ideal of the refined literatus who painted and wrote poetry as forms of self-cultivation and self-fulfillment, untainted by the demands and corruptions of the marketplace.

### *Self-Chosen Names*

For all that Shi Zhenlin wrote, he left us frustratingly little documentation about the concrete realities of his life. We can get a clear sense of his values just from looking at some of the names he chose for himself and for his writings. Beyond their given names, chosen by their parents at birth, Chinese scholars often chose a courtesy name when they reached the age of twenty, and additional style names or poetic names as they grew older. These additional names often reflected something of a person's values or his personality. Shi's original courtesy names were Gongdu (with no particular meaning), and Hugang (meaning simply wooded ridge). In 1725 a friend chose for Shi Zhenlin the style name Wugang, meaning the "ridge of the Wutong tree." Since the Wutong tree has a very straight trunk, it is a symbol of moral uprightness and thus an appropriately flattering style name. Some time later, signaling his strong interest in Buddhism, Shi changed the *wu* (meaning Wutong tree) in Wugang to the *wu* meaning "enlightenment," as in "Buddhist enlightenment." At various times in his life, he signed his name as the White Cloud Professor (Baiyun jiaoshou), Moon Admirer (Nongyue xianlang), the Gourd Ridge Hermit (Hugang jushi), the Wild Old Man of Gourd Ridge (Hugang yelao), the Retired Official of Gourd Ridge (Hugang tuishi), the Old Man of Huagang (Huagang weng), and the Unofficial Historian of Huayang (Huayang waishi), in reference to the famous Huayang grottos of Mao Shan (Yuan Hua 1988, 98). Taken as a whole, these names suggest a very self-conscious literatus and Buddhist-Daoist recluse who shuns the machinations of politics and power, who lives in quiet harmony with nature, and who treasures beauty and aesthetic pleasure over wealth and splendor.

The *Chinese Biographical Dictionary* says of Shi that "he loved to paint trees, rocks, orchids, and bamboo," and that "he loved to copy the calligraphy of old inscriptions from stone tablets." The 1935 edition of *Random Notes* contains a sample of Shi Zhenlin's calligraphy, written in his eighty-seventh year (see figure 6). The standard semicursive style of the piece is rather plain, but it suggests a steady and confident hand, especially for a man well on in his ninth decade. Unfortunately, as far as we know, none of Shi Zhenlin's paintings survive.

Shi spent much time in the Mao Shan area (just to the north of Jintan County), a mountain range famous as a center of Daoist religious belief and practice, including belief in immortals. His only surviving work besides *Random Notes* is called *Scattered Drafts from Huayang*, Huayang being the name of a famous cave on Mao Shan, the site of Daoist religious activity from the fourth century A.D. onward. What I have translated as random and as scattered in these two titles is the same character, *san*. It is a word close to Shi Zhenlin's heart, and it implies a certain freedom and the absence of order. These are just sketches and drafts, disorderly and desultory notes, nothing systematic or formal here, so the word suggests.

### *The Wandering Immortal*

Another word close to Shi Zhenlin's heart is *you*, wandering or roaming. His *Random Notes* records a peripatetic, wandering lifestyle. The Xuebu district that includes Fang Shan was once called Youxian District, the District of the Roaming Immortals. There is listed in Shi Zhenlin's biography another book that he wrote that no longer survives (so far as we know). It is called *Youxian shicao*, literally, *The Scribbled Poetry of a Wandering Immortal*. The title is thus connected to the Xuebu District, and Shi mentions spending time visiting friends, studying for the examinations, and holding poetry gatherings at several places in Xuebu, including Ji Shan and Fang Shan. In addition to its identification with Xuebu Township, *Wandering Immortal* also conjures a frame of mind implying a palpable sense of freedom. The term *immortal* already suggests one unburdened by the cares, ambitions, ego desires, and anxieties of ordinary life. Thus, the wandering immortal is doubly free; he wanders wherever his momentary desire takes him, and he scribbles his poetry without calculation, revision, or so much as a second thought.

Shi Zhenlin was by no means the first Chinese poet to project this carefree image, and he may have done so, however contradictorily, like some of his predecessors, with a self-conscious sense of calculation. The most famous of all Chinese poets, Li Bo in the Tang period, quite self-consciously crafted just such an image with his own poetry, of a carefree-undisciplined-Daoist-drinker-singer-poet-genius. The very term *banished immortal* is most often associated with Li Bo for his superhuman genius and carefree style. Given the rich range of cultural models available in eighteenth-century China, it is not surprising that Shi Zhenlin's life style had plenty of precedents. What is more worthy of note is that his interests and his self-image were so strikingly at odds with his own times.

### *Eighteenth Century: Powerful Emperors and Literati Conformity*

This was an age we associate with powerful emperors reigning over a peaceful and prosperous empire. The population of China doubled in the eighteenth century, a feat unparalleled in any previous age. Etienne Balazs, a brilliant French historian of China, once called the eighteenth century, with a tad of cynicism, "one of the least unhappy periods" in the country's long history (1965, 73). It was an age of conformity, as emperors tolerated little dissent. The only mention of anything about an emperor in Shi's *Random Notes* is in the way he identifies the years in which he is writing, with Yongzheng years, starting with year one, 1723.

The Yongzheng emperor came to power in suspicious circumstances; many believed he poisoned his father, usurped the throne, and killed the rightful heir. He was brilliant, suspicious, energetic, and determined to prove his critics wrong. He could be forgiving, as when he pardoned a man who confessed to writing accusations against him, but who then, most importantly, recanted. But he could be demanding, suspicious, and paranoid. In 1726 an unlucky examination official in Jiangxi Province assigned an exam topic with a phrase from the *Book of Songs*, *weimin so zhi* 維民所止, an unexceptional phrase meaning "where the people rest." When the phrase was brought to the emperor's attention, he was alarmed that the first and last characters of the phrase, *wei* and *zhi*, are similar to the characters for Yongzheng 雍正, only with the top of each character missing. Accused of purposely implying that the emperor was headless, the official was imprisoned in Beijing, where he starved to death. Several members of his family were executed and others exiled (Hummel 1967, 22). Given the strength of family ties and the obligation of sons to be above all filial and loyal to their fathers, emperors who killed officials had to kill their families too, lest they invite attempts at revenge. So political careers promised great rewards, but also great risks. It is not surprising that Shi Zhenlin, having spent the first half of his life trying to qualify for government service, declined his first appointment and served in his second for only a few years before taking early retirement.

Shi Zhenlin was not much inspired by Confucian orthodoxy and ideals of public service. Rather, he drew his inspiration from cultural trends and models that had become especially popular a century before he was born. The late Ming period (sixteenth and early seventeenth centuries) was one of rich cultural ferment along with political disintegration. There was in the late Ming a movement to promote combining China's "three teachings"—Confucianism, Daoism, and Buddhism—into one. One idealistic school of Confucianism in the late Ming promoted egalitarian ideas such as mass education, and some advocated a Confucian mass movement to unite people from all social classes. The late Ming was also known for its thriving urban entertainment areas where a number of elegant, brilliant, and beautiful courtesans achieved an unprecedented degree of celebrity, in part through their liaisons with some of the most prominent literati in the empire. Urban entertainment districts also encouraged a growing interest in vernacular literature of all kinds; romantic ideas flourished in fiction and poetry. By the eighteenth century, however, rather than being praised for these developments, the culture of the late Ming period was blamed for the collapse of a native Chinese political order and castigated for the breakdown of social hierarchies, social order, and discipline.

### *Eighteenth Century: Social Change and Status Anxieties*

In addition to their unsettling memories of late Ming excess and collapse, many eighteenth-century Chinese literati perceived new threats to their own social status. They saw the rapidly growing and changing economy, the rapid urbanization of society, and the growth of a money economy as serious threats to fundamental Confucian values and, not coincidentally, as threats to their own position in society. In response to all these pressures, there was a major movement in the eighteenth century to rethink and to revive classical Confucian traditions. The Manchu rulers promoted the most conservative schools of Confucian thought, emphasizing hierarchical relationships and the importance of unflinching obedience to familial and imperial authority. And for their part, many Han Chinese scholars, traumatized by memories of late Ming chaos, were content to cooperate fully with the Manchus in promoting social, political, and cultural conservatism.

Like many others, Shi Zhenlin was dismayed by the social trends of his time, especially the competitive quest for wealth in the economy and for rank and fame in the examination system. Yet his response to these trends was very different from that of most orthodox Confucian scholars, even though he accepted many Confucian values such as the importance of family and filial piety, and the responsibility of the ruler to provide for the welfare of the people. He serves to remind anyone who reads him today that not everyone in the eighteenth century participated in the classical Confucian revival that we associate with that age. The most fundamental impulse behind Shi Zhenlin's *Random Notes* is the impulse to escape the "real world" of his time and to create in its place an ideal world of his own making. For this purpose, he took much inspiration from the culture of the late Ming period.

### *Popular Religion, Female Immortals, and Spirit Writing*

Shi Zhenlin was fascinated by the folk world of immortals *(xian)*, celestial beings of the spiritual (and ideal) world, by which he may have meant the world of the imagination. He was particularly fascinated by the idea of female immortals, who, he felt strongly, were more talented, sensitive, beautiful, and virtuous than earthly mortals. There was a strong fascination with female immortals in China, especially from the sixteenth century onward. Shi and his friends regularly held séances in which they communicated with talented female immortals through a process called *fuji* (literally, planchette), a form of spirit writing, in which two participants held a stick from which a stylus was suspended over a tray of sand. The participants concentrated and reverently invited the spirit into their presence. They knew the spirit had joined them when the stylus moved by its own power and wrote characters, one at a time, in the sand.

As Judith Zeitlin has noted, the popularity of spirit writing in late imperial China owed much to the common poetic practices of the day, in which men were trained to write poems in imitation of various styles, on demand, spontaneously and in public. Moreover, men sometimes wrote poetry in a female voice, and they saw poetry as a powerful way to transcend "the borders between life and death, past and present, reality and imagination" (Zeitlin 1998, 107). Writing about You Tong

(1618–1704), a famous scholar and calligrapher who practiced spirit writing, Zeitlin is particularly insightful on the reasons why many literati in the seventeenth and eighteenth centuries were fascinated with the writings of women. "Women's poetry," she suggests,

> usually devalued and unpublished, represented writing most at risk of being lost, and consequently, most in need of pity, protection, and preservation. The fragility and vulnerability projected onto women's writings reveals the common tendency to conflate female body and text in this period, but it also betrays the anxiety that the male subject's own writing will not last, his own self disappear without a trace. Spirit-written poetry by women, which ought to signify permanence—the continuation of writing beyond the grave—could paradoxically be seen as nothing but "writing in the sand" (*shayu;* a term for planchette)—that is, the most fragile and ephemeral of all writing. By empowering the male subject as protector and savior, the reclamation of women's poetry from death—often through the imagination—may have served a quasi-apotropaic function. (1998, 116)

Although inspired by You Tong, who lived a generation before Shi Zhenlin, Zeitlin's comments are particularly apt in explaining the connection between male anxiety in this period and male efforts to pity, protect, publicize, and, on occasion, imagine and invent "the writings of talented women."

Early in *Random Notes from Xiqing,* Shi Zhenlin describes divination sessions and records the poetry, dictated by planchette, of several female immortals, including one named Boluo. He and his friends regarded these female immortals, summoned spirits, as real members of their circle. On the first page of his *Random Notes,* he notes that he was given the name Moon Admirer (Nongyue Xianlang) by one of these summoned spirits, a female immortal, in the first year of the Yongzheng reign (1723). Several things about this name are worthy of note. Literally, *xianlang* might be read as "young immortal." In Chinese folklore, immortals (the *xian* in *xianlang*) were people of superhuman talent and skill who become elevated to the status of immortals or divine beings after death. A living person with any extraordinary talent (whether for poetry, martial arts, drinking, or even lovemaking) might be called an immortal, and worshiped as such after death. (Mao Zedong is a most recent example.) It was a common conceit for courtesans to use the term in their stage names, suggesting a superhuman level of beauty or artistic ability.

In this case, however, the term *xianlang* has nothing do to with immortals. It was used in the late Tang period (tenth century A.D.) by female singers and entertainers to refer to their male lovers. At that time, a reasonable translation would have been "my dear," or "honey." But by the eighteenth century it was simply a very antiquated personal pronoun that had lost its earlier sexual connotations.

### *Moon Admirer: Fascination with Ill-Fated Young Beauties*

*Nongyue,* admiring the moon, or playing with the moon, implies a romantic who appreciates the beauty of moonlight. There is at least a hint here of an interest also in women. Wolfram Eberhard writes that such phrases as "to enjoy flowers and play with the moon" describe "a man who consorts with prostitutes" (1986, 111). Courtesans or prostitutes are never mentioned by Shi Zhenlin, and my good friend Kang Zhengguo assures me that Shi was anything but a rake. Yet at the very least, his whimsical name, Moon Admirer, given him by a female immortal through divination, clearly signals to the reader that this man has a deep interest in the aesthetic appreciation of beauty, especially feminine beauty.

### *Wu Zhensheng: Literati Admiration/Emulation of the Feminine*

In his preface to Shi's memoir, Wu Zhensheng presents himself as a romantic poet unconcerned with politics or career, but we know that he sat for the civil service examinations on many occasions and never passed. He also served very briefly as a secretary in the Ministry of Justice. His examination failures undoubtedly sharpened his sensitivity to the beautiful maiden *(jiaren)* whose literary talent, he took for granted, was doomed to go unappreciated. Wu's examination preparation shows through in another way in his preface, for it is written in the most ornate and elaborate parallel prose.

Above all else, Wu Zhensheng's preface highlights his and Shi Zhenlin's obsession with "young beauties," but not as "dirty old men" looking for sexual thrills. Rather, Wu writes about young beauties as moral and aesthetic models, and the "proper" response that truly talented and sensitive men should have toward them. His preface is a connoisseur's guide to the qualities of young, beautiful, and talented maidens, and the proper way for male scholars to appreciate them. He begins his preface by proclaiming Shi Zhenlin's obsession with talented and doomed young beauties:

> *Moon Admirer heaves a deep sigh, "Alas!" for the poor fate of the young beauty [jiaren]. He grieves for her and aches for her.* (Wu Zhensheng Preface, part 1, p. 1).

### *Wu Zhensheng's Companionate Marriage to a Young Beauty*

Shi Zhenlin refers to Wu Zhensheng as the Jade Hook Master of the Song Lyric (Yugou Cike), and occasionally in *Random Notes* we find references to Wu's loving relationship with his wife, Zhuanhua Furen. Near the end of Shi's memoir, after recounting many tales of Shuangqing's talent, beauty, virtue, and suffering, Shi laments that Wu's beautiful and talented wife had never met his beloved Shuang-qing.

> *The Jade Hook Master of the Song Lyric especially respected Shuangqing's virtue. He deeply regretted that Zhuanhua Furen had died* [without meeting Shuangqing]. *Otherwise, he knew she would have gone to Xiaoshan to honor her and commiserate with her. She would have welcomed Shuangqing to their Choose Your Dream Pavilion, and their Moon without Regret Garden. Zhuanhua Furen once wrote a poem praising a beautiful woman, which contained the lines: "Not yet awakened from the embroidered-curtained and jade-carved bed; / In the next life I would search out only you* [to marry]." *This was in reference to a woman of great beauty but no special talent.*
>
> *In their ability to sympathize with each other, women far surpass men. If Shuangqing were a man, although many gentlemen would sigh for her and cry for her, in the end they would do not a single thing to save her from her situation. Some couples appear united but are not in love; some appear in love but are not in spirit; and if they are not together in spirit, how can they not drift apart? If Zhuanhua Furen had ever seen Shuangqing, she would have undoubtedly wiped Shuangqing's tears, summoned her spirit back, and been a model for men to follow in truly cherishing talent. But alas, Heaven did not allow this to happen.* (*RN*, 4.66–67)

Here we have a glimpse of a devoted couple truly in love with each other, and at the same time so freely romantic that the wife can write a love poem to another woman and freely share the poem with her husband and his friends. If Shi Zhenlin's portrait is accurate, Wu Zhensheng had lived through his own scholar-beauty *(caizi jiaren)* romance, complete with a tragic ending of the heroine's premature death. Wu's signature to his preface includes the appellation "an old widower," a reminder that he wrote of the beauty's (*jiaren*'s) tragedies from personal experience, for he was married to one in his optimistic youth.

In paying tribute to Wu Zhensheng's wife, Zhuanhua Furen, Shi Zhenlin makes one of his most interesting arguments about gender differences, that "in their ability to sympathize with one another, women far surpass men." His comment that men might sympathize with a male Shuangqing, but would do nothing to help him is an uncannily accurate representation of most of his friends' reactions to Shuangqing. Shi is saying, in effect, that true empathy and sympathy are feminine qualities that he and his friends admire, and attempt, not always successfully, to emulate. After all, his entire treatment of Shuangqing is a declaration of the depth and profundity of the identification and sympathy he and his friends feel for the beautiful, talented, and abused peasant woman poet.

If we see feminine-masculine qualities on a yin-yang continuum, *Random Notes* belongs much more to yin-feminine side of the ledger than to the yang-masculine side. Both Shi Zhenlin and Wu Zhensheng appear to be obsessed with such qualities as empathy, sentiment, deep feeling, artistic refinement, and delicate beauty, all of which reflect what we might call the feminization of literati culture in late imperial China. Neither of these men expressed in their writings an ounce of concern for the traditional "male sphere" issues of public policy, political career, Confucianization of society, or even the practicalities of making a living. Instead, in emulation of a feminine ideal, they wrote about private feelings and emotions, artistic and scenic beauty, cultural refinement, sensitivity, and emotional bonds between friends.

### *Ill-Fated Women of Beauty and Talent*

From the sixteenth century onward there was a deep fascination in Chinese culture with the notion that a beautiful and talented woman is doomed to suffer an ill fate. Whether this kind of deep concern for the ill fate of young beauties indicates sympathy for women, the lusting fantasies of polygamous males, or male anxiety over women's literacy or women's sexuality is a matter of debate. Quite possibly it reflected all those things. In any case, the issue resonated powerfully with the social forces at work in China from the sixteenth century onward.

For one thing, there were movingly documented cases of beautiful and talented women who lived tragic lives. Two famous examples were sisters, Ye Xiaoluan (1616–1632) and Ye Wanwan (1610–1633). These were the talented daughters of Ye Shaoyuan (1589–1648), a poet and scholar-official, and Shen Yixiu (1590–1635), his highly accomplished wife. Xiaoluan was especially beautiful and talented, and her father was crushed when she died suddenly at age sixteen, five days before her marriage was to take place. Her older sister, Wanwan, who was also very talented, died seventy days later, at age twenty-three, having suffered from a particularly unhappy marriage. Ye Shaoyuan and his wife communicated with their daughters' spirits after death through séances, and they were convinced that the girls had become Daoist immortals who then, in the spirit world, converted to Chan Buddhism. (Daoism or Buddhism, it didn't make much difference which to a man like Ye Shaoyuan, who believed in both.) Two years later, Ye's dear wife, Shen Yixiu, also died, and he believed that she too joined the happy world of immortals. He published eulogies to these women, along with their own writings.

### *Romance and the Power of Imagination*

From the literary world, Shi Zhenlin was undoubtedly inspired by one of the most famous plays in the southern drama tradition, *The Peony Pavilion,* a romantic comedy written by Tang Xianzu (1550–1617) in 1598. Tang's heroine in the play, Du Liniang, is aroused by thoughts of love after reading romantic poems in the Confucian classic *The Book of Songs.* (Confucian scholars managed to interpret these poems as political allegories, but young readers naturally read them as love poems.) In an erotic dream, she makes love with a young scholar in a pavilion beside blooming peonies. Deeply moved by this dream, she longs for love so intensely that she dies before her parents can find a proper mate for her. She is buried beside her self-portrait, which is then seen by the very young man she had dreamed about. He falls in love with the portrait, and she is given permission to return for a visit to the world of the living. In spirit form (i.e., in a dream), she seduces the love-struck scholar and then has the delicate task of convincing him to dig up her corpse so that body and spirit can be reunited. Romantic that he is, he undertakes this task, after which the couple is left with the challenge of trying to persuade her parents that there is nothing salacious or immoral about this unusual resurrection and self-arranged marriage. Once the wedding is properly performed, her virginity is revealed to have survived intact, since making love in spirit form leaves no impact on the body. And to complete the happy ending, the newly married young scholar comes in first place in the palace examination.

Filled with earthy dialogue and bawdy double entendre, *The Peony Pavilion* was extremely popular from the time of its writing on through the eighteenth century. It was frowned upon by conservative Confucians as frivolous and risqué. Women were especially moved by it, and many wrote commentaries on it. Tang Xianzu's preface to his witty play contains a paragraph on love that I think applies equally to the views of Shi Zhenlin.

> Love is of source unknown, yet it grows ever deeper. The living may die for it, by its power the dead live again. Love is not love at its fullest if one who lives is unwilling to die for it, or if it cannot restore to life the one who has died. And must the love that comes in dream necessarily be unreal? For there is no lack of dream lovers in this world. Only for those whose love must be fulfilled on the pillow and for whom affection deepens only after retirement from office is it entirely a corporeal matter. (Tang Xianzu 1989, ix)

For Shi Zhenlin, as for Tang Xianzu, the power of love and the power of imagination are two sides of the same coin. For both writers, literature's power is precisely the power to create an ideal world as a believable alternative to the "real world," where good does not necessarily prevail over evil, and where love does not always triumph.

### *Cult of* Qing: *Passion*

What Cyril Birch translates as "love" is the concept of *qing*, which might also be called passion. This is a concept very important to Shi Zhenlin. My friend Wang Ping, a talented poet, novelist, and scholar, recently mentioned to me that Shi's very title for *Xiqing sanji* 西青散記 (Random notes from Xiqing), is an appropriate homonym for *xiqing sanji* 惜情散記, "random notes on treasuring passion." It is this passion—strong feelings of love, pity, admiration, attachment, and excitement—that Shi Zhenlin and his poetic and artistic friends all share in their fascination with Shuangqing. One of the great fiction writers in the late Ming period was Feng Menglong, who compiled a virtual encyclopedia called *A History of Qing*, in which he included more than 850 short classical tales and anecdotes, on twenty-four different types of manifestations of *qing* or passion. Although the cult of *qing* is associated in particular with the late Ming period, it clearly retained its hold on many artists and writers in the seventeenth and eighteenth centuries.

### *Xiaoqing: Ill Fate of the Talented Beauty*

Under the influence of the cult of *qing,* Tang Xianzu's heroine, Miss Du Liniang, inspired romantic idealism in countless young men and women in China from the sixteenth century onward. Not surprisingly, few of them had as happy an ending as Miss Du's resurrection in *The Peony Pavilion.* One particularly famous example of a tragic figure inspired by Tang's play was the (quite possibly apocryphal) story of a young concubine from Yangzhou who is known only by her given name, Xiaoqing (1595–1612). Some have claimed that her name, Xiaoqing 小青, was purposely chosen from the two components of the homophone character for *qing* meaning passion 情. From a poor family in Yangzhou, she was, according to many popular accounts, sold to become the concubine of a Hangzhou gentleman, Mr. Feng. A concubine "belonged" to her master as a mistress, but she was not a wife and did not have a proper wedding. She remained subordinate to her master's wife, and even the offspring she bore were considered as children of the wife to whom they owed their primary filial respect and obedience. Mr. Feng's wife was a cruel and jealous woman who forbade her husband to see his new concubine. She kept Xiaoqing in seclusion in a house on beautiful West Lake in Hangzhou and tried to force her to leave the Feng household altogether. Inspired by the romantic ideals of *The Peony Pavilion,* Xiaoqing refused to leave, remained steadfast in her love for Mr. Feng, and pined so intensely that she soon died. She left behind a few romantic poems, though most of her poetic output was burned by Mr. Feng's jealous and vengeful wife.

To this day, we do not know if Xiaoqing existed or not, but she became one of the most famous literary heroines in the Qing period. Publishing houses brought out editions of her biography, her poems, and plays and short stories based on her tale. Painters sold portraits of her, and entrepreneurs erected her tombstone as a tourist site at West Lake. Ellen Widmer attributes the amazing popularity of Xiaoqing as a literary heroine to three trends: (1) the alienation of intellectuals who saw Xiaoqing as a metaphor for their own marginalization; (2) the boom in publishing women's writings; and (3) the popularity of *The Peony Pavilion.* Widmer also notes the wealth of different and even contradictory messages people could take from the story. Satirists could use the story to criticize jealous wives who persecute concubines. Conservatives might see it as a cautionary tale about the dangers of young girls reading romantic plays. Women might interpret the story very differently, to show how even a persecuted concubine could achieve fame through her literary talent and her romantic ideals (Widmer 1992; see also Ko 1994, 91–112).

There are many parallels between the story of Xiaoqing the persecuted concubine and Shuangqing the peasant woman poet. Both heroines were beautiful, talented, frail, sensitive, and miserable. Both seemed doomed to short lives of misery but were also blessed with the possibility of posthumous literary fame. Both were made famous by male biographers, and their lives were open to many interpretations from many angles. Conservative males could use both stories as cautionary tales warning against the dangers of literacy for women. Promoters of female literacy could marvel at these examples of extraordinary female talent. In pitying these heroines, marginalized male intellectuals also pitied themselves.

Shi Zhenlin wrote his memoir a century after Xiaoqing became famous, yet in many ways, he seemed more attuned to the romanticism, idealism, and religious ferment associated with the late Ming period rather than the Confucian orthodoxy we tend to identify with his own time, the eighteenth century. He was drawn to Buddhism and Daoism as much as to Confucianism. He celebrated women of talent and virtue, arguing against conservatives that there was no contradiction between talent and virtue in a woman. His ideal of marriage was a love union of superbly talented, attractive, and sensitive intellectuals. He was fascinated with dreams and imagination and with the power of writing, not only to buy one fame and fortune in the examination system, but to create alternatives to the "real worlds" of money, politics, and power.

### *Literary Ambition and Alternative Worlds*

Shi feigned indifference to the quest for fame that filled the climate of his time, but he was not very convincing. He took a highly circuitous route in cultivating what he cared most about: his literary reputation. Even examination success, he seemed to say, could be disappointing in a success-crazed world. He turned instead to the ideal world of aesthetics: literature, poetry, random essays, belles lettres.

In Shi Zhenlin's ideal world, there is freedom to roam at random through an idyllic natural landscape of breathtaking beauty. The sensitive scholar is a painter-poet-writer-calligrapher-musician who associates with like-minded men and women and nurtures, recognizes, admires, and cherishes genius wherever he or she finds it. There is no competition between friends, except in the playful form of matching rhymes and the mutual teasing that naturally occurs on those enjoyable occasions of hiking, admiring beautiful scenery together, eating, drinking, and writing poetry.

Shi Zhenlin creates a utopia, but one not wholly independent of the real world of eighteenth-century China. Rather, his utopia exists on the margins of the real world. He and his circle of friends cherish these ideals, but they are quite clearly and self-consciously in the minority. Most of his contemporaries, Shi implies, are small-minded, conventional folks who see his literati circle as ne'er-do-wells and impractical aesthetes of little accomplishment. To the majority, "getting ahead" is the most important thing in life, and that means prosperity through landowning or other sound investments; examination success; official career; a "good marriage," meaning a marriage between families of prominent scholar-officials; and the strict training of the next generation to carry on the family's success. Although the conflict is muted, more often assumed than stated, Shi Zhenlin's memoir makes most sense when seen to represent the tension between these two worlds.

For all his self-declared modesty and his projected air of carefree romanticism, Shi Zhenlin was ambitious to make a literary name for himself, and Shuangqing's poetic talent was one of the vehicles of his own ambition. By his self-proclaimed discovery of the brilliant and beautiful peasant woman poet, he demonstrated his profound understanding of literary talent, his deep sensitivity to the suffering of the downtrodden, his superior ability to recognize great beauty in surprising surroundings, and his keen aesthetic sensibilities. The product of an anxious age for male literati, he found in Shuangqing a sublime heroine of beauty and talent whose tragic life story and moving poetry left his friends and acquaintances filled with admiration, pity, and awe. For Shi Zhenlin, this was far more satisfying than any level of success in the civil service examinations.

### *Random Notes: Unstructured Genre for a Wandering Immortal*

Shi Zhenlin's fragmentary writings reflect his penchant for aimless wandering. In his *Random Notes,* he draws on several traditions of writing, including the *biji* tradition that we might call simply "jottings," made up of a scholar's personal observations, possibly arranged by topic or chronology or by nothing at all. These autobiographical jottings drew from both historiographical and fictional traditions and were always briefly episodic and informal. Poems in various styles by Shi and his friends and acquaintances appear on almost every page. Like notebooks or journals that scholars or fiction writers might keep, these jottings were only loosely organized if organized at all. Grace Fong has succinctly summarized the form of *Random Notes* as

> an assortment of seemingly disparate materials haphazardly arranged that fall into several generic categories: the informal essay, personal journal, autobiographical memoir, diary, and records of dreams, travel, and other miscellaneous jottings. . . . Although the chapters follow a vague chronology of the years 1723 to 1736, the sense of narrative temporal sequence is disrupted by sudden shifts, insertions, overlaps, and flashbacks in passages dispersed throughout all four chapters. The overall effect is narrative fragmentation. (1997, 267)

Travel writing, which began at least by the fifth century, was a popular genre for intellectuals in China from the eleventh century onward. As Richard Strassberg has noted, there were two major inspirations for travel writing: a Confucian view of "travel as a purposeful activity whose ultimate goal was the restoration of moral and political order," and a Daoist vision of "travel as liberation from the unnatural constraints of society" (1994, 21). Obviously, Shi Zhenlin was drawn more to the Daoist than the Confucian purpose in his travel accounts.

### Dream of the Red Chamber *and* Six Records of a Floating Life

Two other authors should be noted here who shared Shi Zhenlin's literary ambition, his distaste for officialdom, and his fascination with *qing,* passion or love, and its frustration. These are Cao Xueqin (c. 1715–c. 1763), the author of China's greatest novel, *Dream of the Red Chamber,* also known as *Story of the Stone,* first published in 1796, and Shen Fu (1762–after 1809), a failed scholar-painter-dreamer who completed a memoir, *Six Records of a Floating Life,* in the early nineteenth century. *Dream of the Red Chamber* is framed as a Buddhist allegory illustrating the transience and illusory quality of "real life" in the "red dust," and the inability of most humans to see through the illusions of earthly life with all its attachments and ambitions. Yet inside this "otherworldly" framework, Cao Xueqin spins the most elaborate, realistic, and detailed re-creation of the daily life and material reality of a Chinese family that has ever been done. Cao vividly captures the passions, hopes, and disappointments of all the members of the large and wealthy Jia family (masters and servants alike) over a brief period of joy and prosperity followed quickly by the family's inevitable and painful decline. As a novelist, Cao Xueqin seems obsessed with women and their hopes, aspirations, and frustrations. All of Cao's heroines are meticulously portrayed as vivacious and talented individuals, each with her own unique personality. Yet their talent and beauty only serves to make their disappointments, frustrations, bad marriages, widowhoods, and early deaths seem more poignant. Even more than Shi Zhenlin, Cao Xueqin is an author obsessed with the complementary relationship between illusion and reality, permanence and impermanence, art and life. While paying lip service to the Buddhist quest for transcendence of human attachments and material life, Cao portrays these attachments and the pleasures of material life so lovingly, carefully, and realistically, as to give them a permanence in art that they conspicuously lack in the life of any individual.

Writing a generation later than Shi Zhenlin, Shen Fu paid more direct tribute to the ideals of the scholar-beauty romance in his autobiographical memoir of his twenty-three-year love affair with his beloved wife, Yun. Shen himself failed in the examinations and worked in a succession of unsuccessful jobs, as a yamen clerk and secretary, as a painter, and as a tradesman. He loved poetry, painting, calligraphy, and gardening too much to be worried about the practicalities of making a living. His beloved Yun was a romantic, beautiful, talented, and self-educated poet. Though she tried to serve her in-laws faithfully, she was constantly misunderstood and criticized, in part because she shared her husband's romantic view of life, and together they consistently put their own conjugal relationship before the needs of Shen Fu's parents. They were both much too free-spirited to meet the expectations of the Confucian family system. The last straw came when Yun fell in love with a courtesan whom she tried to bring into the family as her husband's concubine (to his bemusement, and to his parents' chagrin). Shi Zhenlin was not nearly as unconventional as Shen Fu, but he shared with Shen Fu, and with Cao Xueqin, a fascination with male-female love and passion, a fatalistic conviction that too much passion would doom a person to a short and unhappy life, and a dedication to portraying the joys and frustrations of personal passion in highly artistic forms of prose and poetry.

All of these works suggest that the aesthetic ideals we normally associate with the sixteenth century lived on in artistic writings of the eighteenth. Shi Zhenlin shared many of these ideals with the above authors. With the writer-compiler Feng Menglong and the dramatist Tang

Xianzu, he shared a deep fascination with *qing*, passion. Like many others in his time, he was obsessed with ill-fated women of talent and beauty. He shared with the novelist Cao Xueqin an obsession with art and beauty and a philosophical fascination with the transience of all things and the relationship between illusion and reality and literature and life. And with Shen Fu, he shared a commitment to aesthetic ideals over material success and a determination to pay tribute to these ideals in the artful prose form of a rambling memoir.

*five* ·⁀

# *Searching for Xiaoshan, Part 1*

Jintan, Friday, October 31, 1997

After breakfast at the Jintan City government hostel dining room, Hongsheng and I are waiting in our room for Xiaowan to arrive. Today we hope to go to Fang Shan, the most plausible location of the elusive village of Xiaoshan. Fang Shan is on the west edge of a township called Xuebu Zhen, about fifteen miles due west of Jintan City. Although Xuebu Zhen is only a half hour's drive away from us, we are official guests of the local government and will have to wait until a government car is available to take us to Xuebu Zhen. While we wait, Hongsheng and I decide to look at Shi Zhenlin's *Random Notes* for clues about the location of Xiaoshan. As I browse through Elsie Choy's partial translation of *Random Notes,* Hongsheng leafs through Du Laoshi's Chinese copy. I soon come across this description of the scenery around Xiaoshan:

> *North of Xiaoshan there was a huge rock that stands erect like a screen forty to fifty feet tall and half again as wide. There were old cypress, cedar, and pine trees growing in distorted forms, hugging the ground or hunch-backed, all bound by ancient vines. Under the precipice it was sunless. There was a thatched pavilion facing north with the name plaque of "Xiang xia" (Resounding Sunset's Glow). Danyuan once wrote a poem about it. A meandering brook came through the rambling rocks, keeping the stones awash. In the front the water converged and gathered into a pond about four feet deep. At the shallow portion where there were pebbles, you could wade across. In the middle of the pond a stone jutted out like the spine of an ox, complete with shoulders and a head. Hollow underneath, it harbored some fish that were very delicious. About a hundred paces from the west of the pavilion, a studio had been built, wrapping around the precipice. It faced east and was named Ougeng (Farming in Pairs). Bamboo, well trimmed, surrounded it. Toward*

*the north was Chonggang Peak; ten li further north was Mao Shan. From the upper story of this studio you could actually see the steps leading to the mountain top.*

*Mengzhan's studio, Gudian shanfang, was located at the southwestern edge of Xiaoshan. The route from the western foot of the hill to Xiang xia Pavilion was about 500 paces, running through a bamboo forest with huge rocks on both sides. There were eight turns and five ups and downs.* (Choy 1993, 59–60)

I ask to see the Chinese copy of *Random Notes,* find the original basis for Choy's translation, and show it to Hongsheng, who reads with interest. We don't know if anyone here has ever heard of Chonggang Peak, Xiang xia Pavilion, or Ougeng Hall. But Shi Zhenlin provides a concrete description of a mountainside covered with rocks, bamboo, and steep winding pathways. Most importantly, for our purposes now, Shi locates Xiaoshan precisely ten *li* (three and a third miles) south of Mao Shan, which is a famous landmark. We check my Xeroxed map of Jintan County, taken from the Jintan County Gazetteer I had checked out of Harvard's library, and are pleased to see that Fang Shan (Square Mountain) looks indeed to be about ten *li* due south of Mao Shan! I am, on the one hand, pleased with this discovery, and on the other hand, privately chagrined that I didn't notice this Mao Shan connection years ago. Oh well, today is the first day I've ever been in a position to put this knowledge to concrete use in any case, and Hongsheng and I are both feeling optimistic now that we should be able to follow up on Shi Zhenlin's description, and see if there is indeed any *there* there.

### *"We've Discovered Xiaoshan!"*

Suddenly there is a loud knock on the door, and before we can even get to the door, Xiaowan and Du Laoshi burst into the room full of excitement. They are talking simultaneously and so fast that it takes me about ten seconds to decipher what has them so excited. The words come out in torrents!

"We've discovered Xiaoshan!" they exclaim almost in unison.

Xiaowan blurts out, "There *was* a Xiaoshan Academy! A man named Yu Zhao visited the site in 1984, and he wrote a poem about it in 1988! I have it right here!"

"How did you get the poem?" I ask with amazement as she shows me her notebook with a scribbled verse I can't begin to decipher, except for the date, April 1988.

"He dictated it to me over the telephone!" she says with a giggle.

Du Laoshi chimes in: "He says Xiaoshan was a real place, and Shuangqing was a real peasant woman!"

Hongsheng asks, "Can we meet this Mr. Yu sometime?"

Xiaowan laughs and replies, "I was so excited I didn't think to ask about a meeting, but I'll call again to see if we can arrange a time to meet with him."

Mr. Yu Zhao is head of the Economic Commission of the Jintan Municipal Government, not the office in which I would have thought to look for information about Shuangqing! And of all the evidence I expected to find in Jintan about Shuangqing, I didn't anticipate it would come in the form of poetry. But for this investigation, what could possibly be more appropriate? The literati are still writing poems about Shuangqing! Unable to read Xiaowan's "grass writing," I ask her to copy it more clearly in my notebook. She does, and I work out a translation over the next few days:

> Amid flowers and trees in the mist are several cottages;
> Sounds of dripping spring water mix with the calls of perched crows.
> It was said a peasant woman leaned on her door chanting songs;
> And she composed song lyrics full of sorrow to express her innocence.
> From morning to night, exhausting work, she still managed to write;
> Through all her years of hardship, she still maintained her elegance.
> Up to the present day, this beauty's story lives on and on,
> All one sees are blue-green mountains in the sunset's glow.

### *Xiaoshan Academy*

Mr. Yu says that Xiaoshan is indeed at Fang Shan. Hongsheng, who comprehends this story more quickly than I do as it pours forth from Xiaowan and Du Laoshi, gives me a slower and clearer explanation: "He went to Xuebu Zhen in 1984 and was told that there was once a Xiaoshan Academy *(Xiaoshan shuyuan)* near Fang Shan. [In the eighteenth century, there were many private academies in China where scholars pursued common interests in poetry or classical scholarship.] According to Yu Zhao, a number of scholars, including Shi Zhenlin, gathered at this Xiaoshan Academy to study, and He Shuangqing used to help the scholars there with various menial tasks. Although a poor peasant woman, she clearly had literary interests and talents, and the scholars would teach her to write regulated verse and song lyrics, and help her revise and polish her own writings." This is a story we have never heard before!

"The amazing thing to me," I remark to Hongsheng, "is that this story is in many ways more plausible than the one told in Shi Zhenlin's memoir. Here we have a woman of humble background who has a functional connection to a group of scholars, running errands at the academy where they study. Not only that, the scholars tutor her in the arts of poetry and help her revise and perfect her poems. Here we have a popular story that attempts to make sense of the brilliant poems of He Shuangqing by describing (and creating!) a believable context which would help explain how such poems could be written by a poor peasant woman."

### *Waiting for Chauffeur*

As Xiaowan makes more calls on her cellular phone to find us a car, Hongsheng reports to Du Laoshi on our own conclusion, reached just before they burst in with their exciting news, that Fang Shan must indeed be the original site of Shi Zhenlin's village of Xiaoshan. We show her the section of Shi's *Random Notes* that led us to this conclusion, and she is even more excited at the thought that we are really on the verge of finding a real place to identify as Xiaoshan. Our elation over these developments begins to cool as Xiaowan makes call after call on her cellular phone, only to discover that all the government cars in Jintan seem to be tied up this morning. Du Laoshi remarks that Fridays are meeting days for local governments all over China, so our chances of getting to Fang Shan today may not be very good. It begins to dawn on me also that we are fast approaching a weekend, which may mean cooling our heels another two days in Jintan before we can have the apparently necessary government escort to Fang Shan.

We twiddle our thumbs in our room and talk with Xiaowan about contemporary Chinese society and its ills. She tells of a particularly unscrupulous young woman in her writers' class who is extraordinarily selfish. This woman picks up and discards boyfriends right and left. She broke off one affair to take up with a married man twenty years her senior. She wrecked his family, bore a son by him, and then divorced him. She takes no responsibility for raising her son, but farms him out to others. Against the background of our discussions of Shuangqing, Xiaowan seems worried that there is no moral anchor for young people in China today, yet the fact that she is deeply troubled by this suggests that some young people have not lost their moral bearings.

### *Detour: Jintan's Most Famous Son, Duan Yucai*

Our conversation drifts back to Shuangqing, and we begin to realize that we are not likely to get to Xuebu Zhen this morning. There is a memorial hall in Jintan City in honor of the county's most famous intellectual, Duan Yucai (1735–1815), a scholar-official and expert in the evolution of classical Chinese. While waiting for a car, we decide to visit the Memorial Hall of Duan Yucai, which was established by the city in 1985, on the 250th anniversary of his birth.

We start out walking and almost immediately run into a young woman with a cute four-year-old boy in her arms. As seems true of everyone in Jintan, she is a good friend of Xiaowan's. Within thirty seconds of our meeting, we invite her and her son to join us on our visit, and she agrees to come along. We hail a cab and very quickly arrive at the museum, an attractive compound in the style of a traditional elite family's home, set on the edge of a small lake. The architecture is Ming style, which seems odd for a memorial for a Qing-dynasty figure. I speculate to myself that Chinese patriotism might be at work here, as the Ming (1368–1644) was the last native Chinese dynasty, and the Qing by contrast represents the conquest of China by the Manchus.

It is a beautifully clear, bright, sunny, and crisp autumn morning. The lake is deep blue, and the Duan Yucai Memorial Hall has several rooms and a small scenery-viewing pavilion, with a number of colorful chrysanthemums scattered around in full bloom. Impressed by the glorious chrysanthemums in the bright sunlight, Du Laoshi and I cheerfully inform our friends of Shuangqing's special love for chrysanthemums, and we then take turns snapping pictures of each other in various combinations with and without the flowers in front of the museum (see figure 7).

Duan Yucai was thirty-seven years younger than Shi Zhenlin, and we have no evidence that they ever met. Although Duan never passed the metropolitan examination in Beijing, he passed the provincial examination in Nanjing in 1760, and he served in a variety of official posts before retiring in 1780. He became a disciple of one of the leading philosophers of the Qing dynasty, Dai Zhen (1724–1777), and he published an extremely influential study of China's oldest dictionary of classical Chinese. The official and scholarly careers of Duan Yucai are spelled out on large posters around the main hall of the memorial compound. On the strength of his etymological and phonetic studies of classical Chinese, and because of the pioneering rigor of his textual research, he is today regarded as one of the first "modernizers" of China's classical heritage and easily the most famous scholar ever produced by Jintan.

The unequaled prominence of Duan Yucai today suggests something about the strength of China's scholarly culture and the official concern to promote "progressive" intellectuals from China's past. Many others from Jintan rose much higher than Duan through the examination system and in official circles, but there are no memorial halls to them. In the provincial examination compound at Nanjing, which is a museum today, there is a chart showing that two scholars from Jintan County actually attained the highest rank in the metropolitan examination, in 1723 and in 1737 (this latter, the very same year that Shi Zhenlin himself passed the metropolitan examination). This number one scholar rank, called the *zhuangyuan,* was the most coveted award that could be bestowed in Qing society. To be the highest-ranking scholar in the triennial metropolitan examination was to achieve instant immortality. By today's terms in the United States, it was the prestige equivalent of winning an Academy Award, a Grammy Award, a MacArthur ("genius") Fellowship, and the Heisman Trophy all in one act. Nothing was as prestigious as winning the rank of a *zhuangyuan.* That this modest-sized county of Jintan, one of over 1800 in China, produced two such winners in Shi Zhenlin's own youth, would have been a matter of great pride for the entire region. It also suggests the intensely competitive examination-taking atmosphere in which Shi Zhenlin and Duan Yucai were raised.

Interestingly, we are told in the posters of the main hall that Duan Yucai liked poetry, but his father forbid him from immersing himself in the study of poetry and song lyrics, feeling that these were frivolous and potentially corrupting subjects for young men to study. Duan's father's strictness must have had the desired effect, for his own scholarly career as an etymologist and phonetician could not have been more different from the wandering poet Shi Zhenlin. One of Shi's best friends, as described in *Random Notes,* is one Duan Yuhan, or Flower Lover. The *Duan* and *Yu* in *Duan Yuhan* are the same characters as the *Duan* and *Yu* in *Duan Yucai,* suggesting the possibility of a blood relationship, as families often named brothers with one common given name. Duan Yucai had a younger brother named Duan Yucheng, but we have found no reference to a Duan Yuhan in any writings about the family of Duan Yucai. So whether Flower Lover Duan Yuhan existed or not, or was a relative of the famous Duan Yucai, remains a mystery.

We cannot help wondering, as we tour Duan Yucai's memorial, whether his prominence will ever be approached or eclipsed by that of Shi Zhenlin. Duan was clearly more in touch with his own age, as no scholarly calling in those days was seen as more important than probing the intricacies of the classical language of China's long past. Shi Zhenlin, by contrast, remained relatively obscure despite his own greater examination success. Yet we cannot help speculating that Shi Zhenlin's writings may speak to future generations with more immediacy than the dry etymological analyses of Duan. His romanticism, his Buddhist-Daoist philosophy, his love of nature and poetry, his playful fragmentary writing style, and especially his blurring of the boundaries between experience and imagination all seem made to order for the kinds of skeptical, text-based, self-reflexive literary analyses that are so popular in the West today. If Duan Yucai represents a modernist hero for China, holding up the past to rigorous empirical testing and analysis, perhaps, I mischievously speculate to myself, Shi Zhenlin will one day be held up as a hero in a postmodern tradition that questions the modernist faith in empiricism and delights in the ambiguous interplay of experience and imagination in the human definition of reality.

### *Mr. Chen's Rainbow Elegance Restaurant*

Finished with the Duan Yucai memorial, we go next to lunch at the restaurant where we had dined the previous evening. We say farewell to Xiaowan's friend and her son and proceed to the Hongya Meishi Cheng, Rainbow Elegance Restaurant. Its proprietor is a delightfully gregarious and engaging host named Chen Xiqing. He loves playing the *laoban,* "the boss," and is determined to make his guests feel at home. He joins us in our private dining room every fifteen minutes or so, to make sure we have plenty to eat, and to question us about our investigations. He laughs easily and is quick to tell the waitresses to refill our tea glasses, bring more beer, or order another dish or two if our table is less than covered with food. Chen is such an engaging host that I don't even mind the cloud of smoke he creates wherever he goes. Only on our third visit to the Hongya does he give up pushing us to share a cigarette with him. He is amused by our quixotic quest for information about the peasant woman poet Shuangqing and proudly regales us with stories of his own multifaceted careers. He worked in several occupations, as a farmer, then a factory worker, and then a policeman, before becoming an entrepreneurial restaurateur. From humble beginnings selling only dumplings, he has built his Rainbow Elegance complex, which includes the sit-down restaurant where we have our private dining room, and a variety of recreation rooms upstairs, where people can play cards or mahjong or sing at the Karaoke bar. Chen Xiqing is obviously thriving in "market-socialist China."

Last night our foursome (Xiaowan, Hongsheng, Du Laoshi, and I) had dinner here in our own private room, and we were showered with the most lavish hospitality. We started with four cold appetizers and a unique and delicious tea called tributary chrysanthemum iced tea. Despite its name, it is served piping hot in tall clear glasses. None of us had ever had this tea before, but it immediately got our attention as the most visually stunning tea we had ever seen. Each glass of tea seemed to come alive, with chrysanthemum flowers, seeds of various shapes and colors, and most curiously, a steadily expanding brown translucent spongy matter that reminded me of a fungus or mushroom seen growing by the miracle of time lapse photography. We joked that some of our glasses looked too ominously dangerous to drink, but the tea tasted sweet and mild, and with regular infusions of boiling water, we knew it couldn't carry anything very dangerous. We expressed our wonderment at this tea to Mr. Chen, and he showed us a package with a description of the contents: chrysanthemum flowers, nolfberry, sugar crystals, a hawthorn lotus seed core, and a variety of medicinal herbs. Each time we drank as much as half or a forth of the glass, new hot water was added, and the tea never lost its flavor through the hour and a half we took to eat the lavish meal. On seeing our obvious pleasure from this unique tea, Mr. Chen insisted on sending each of us home with a complementary package of fifteen tea bags. It is one of my most prized souvenirs of Jintan.

After enjoying Mr. Chen's warm hospitality and a spectacular meal last night, we are delighted to be able to return today. We suggest that we don't need as much food for lunch, but our suggestion falls on deaf ears. This time we don't even order anything; the food simply appears. We have five cold appetizers (including thin-sliced pig ears!) followed by two soups and seven other delicious dishes. As Xiaowan's guests at Mr. Chen's restaurant, we never pay a penny here, no matter how lavish the meal. It is never quite clear to me who is paying, Xiaowan or the Jintan municipal government. In any case, we are certainly made to feel like honored guests. Having again eaten more than we needed, we walk back to our hotel where fortunately a car is now ready to take us to Xuebu Zhen.

### *To Xuebu Township*

Thanks to our connections through Xiaowan, we arrive at the government offices of Xuebu Zhen with a letter of introduction from the office of the mayor of Jintan. Letters of introduction are essential to get the cooperation of any work unit in China. A week later I would be turned away from the Rare Book Room of the Beijing Public Library because I did not have a letter of introduction from any recognized authority. But here in Jintan County, well armed with the mayor's letter, we are warmly received by Mr. Secretary Sun, and are introduced to several other Xuebu Zhen officials, including the congenial township head, Mr. Zhang Jinsheng.

We explain our purpose and give these officials some background on Shuangqing and Shi Zhenlin's story. It helps a great deal that we have Du Laoshi's book, which we give them and which immediately establishes our credibility as serious scholars with a serious purpose. To bolster our case, we also show them all the materials I have brought along, including my conference paper on Shuangqing, Elsie Choy's book on Shuangqing, a recent article on Shuangqing from Taiwan, and several scholarly Chinese articles from earlier in the twentieth century. We also tell our hosts that other scholars in Canada, Holland, and Hong Kong are interested in Shuangqing and her place in Chinese culture. We suggest to Secretary Sun that he is welcome to photocopy any and all of these materials, and he carries them off to another room. I am impressed that these local government officials actually seem interested in our topic, as they pass Du's book around and eagerly leaf through it.

As we sit in the Xuebu Township office, I begin to doubt that we will ever get to Fang Shan. Mr. Sun seems a bit puzzled by our mission, and he is not sure that he can help us out. As soon as we got out of our car, our driver immediately returned to Jintan, leaving us again without transportation. Mr. Sun says he doesn't know if anyone is available to show us around the Fang Shan area. He makes several calls and tells us that no one he talks with has ever heard of Xiaoshan, a Xiaoshan Academy, or He Shuangqing. Contemplating the approaching weekend (and thinking in American terms), I begin to worry that we could be politely turned away this afternoon and told to try again next week. After several more minutes of waiting, Mr. Sun comes in and says he has found an escort for us, an older gentleman, Mr. Duanlin, who is the head of Fang

Shan Village. (Fang Shan Village is within sight of Fang Shan the mountain, but not actually at the mountain.) Because we no longer have our own car, we are given the personal car of Xuebu Zhen's town head.

### *Jianguo Village: No Memory of Shuangqing or Xiaoshan*

Xiaowan manages to call Mr. Yu Zhao on her cellular phone, and he reports that, to the best of his recollection, Xiaoshan Academy was originally located at the site of a temple called Eight-Li Temple (Bali Miao, the *li* here being the distance marker of one-third of a mile), in a village called Jianguo. *Jianguo* literally means "construct the country," a sign that the name dates either from the Nationalist era, the 1930s, or the early Communist period, the 1950s. We drive to Jianguo Village and meet there the village head, Mr. Duan Mingde. Mr. Duan looks to be in his sixties, though he may be younger. He has the deeply tanned and weathered face of someone who makes his living out in the elements. He seems happy to meet with us and is interested to hear of our investigations, but he has never heard of Shi Zhenlin, Shi's *Random Notes,* He Shuangqing, Xiaoshan, the Xiaoshan Academy, or any other name we mention in connection with our inquiry.

Mr. Duan senses our disappointment with his answers to our enquiries about Shi Zhenlin and the peasant woman poet Shuangqing. He tells us that it isn't too surprising that no one today seems to know of Shuangqing, because this entire region was decimated in the mid–nineteenth century by the Taiping Rebellion that swept through all of south China and eventually made its headquarters in Nanjing for twelve years before being repressed by the forces of the Qing dynasty. All the original inhabitants of this area were killed or fled the wars associated with the Taiping movement. So although this area has been densely populated for at least two millennia, no one living here today has roots farther back than the late nineteenth century.

Noting our interest in history, Mr. Duan volunteers to show us a bronze mirror that was found in a nearby field a few years ago. He brings us the mirror, which we estimate could date as early as the Ming dynasty (1368–1644). It is a round bronze mirror, about ten inches in diameter, flat on one side with swirling designs on the other. The flat side was polished to give off a reflection, and the decorative side made the object something to be treasured and often used in ceremonial burials for the wealthy. I recall Shuangqing's line about pawning her hairpins to buy medicine, using a twig to fasten her hair, and using water for a mirror. Although peasants would not likely have a bronze mirror, it is a nice thought. Since peasants found this one in a field, perhaps Shuangqing found it first. The thought is so far-fetched that I keep it to myself. Even so, I am impressed with Mr. Duan's mirror and thank him for showing it to us. It is the first time I have ever held such a rare artifact in my hands.

### *First View of Square Mountain*

We return to our car a bit downcast. Our main purpose has not been achieved, and Xiaowan and Du Laoshi are especially disappointed that we have not yet found anyone who can tell us anything about popular lore on Shuangqing or give us any bit of evidence connecting this place with Shi Zhenlin's *Random Notes.* Our one consolation is that from Jianguo Village we get our first clear view of Fang Shan the mountain and get out of our car to soak in the view. As befits its name, Square Mountain, it really looks square and flat on top, not terribly high, perhaps three thousand feet, but nevertheless a very clear landmark standing in sharp contrast to the surrounding level plains (see figure 8). As we walk a few hundred feet away from the road, we come upon a beautiful little pond beside a bamboo grove, with a few rocks at one end. Du Laoshi and I immediately recall Shi Zhenlin's description of Shuangqing's village:

> *Shuangqing lives in* [an earthen hut with a thatched roof] *on the west side of the small courtyard, opposite an old stream where the willows droop, entirely covering the eaves. Washing clothes and drawing water, so lively sitting there on the rocks; those who see her are so amazed they suppose she's a goddess.* (*RN,* 2.36)

We could easily picture Shuangqing on the rocks on the other side of this little pool, washing clothes in the shadows by the bamboo grove (see figure 9).

To the south we see the twin peaks of Yaji Shan, which Dr. Zhou Wanyao, a Taiwan scholar, recently mentioned as an additional possible location for Xiaoshan. The *Ya* of *Yaji* is a character shaped very much like a capital letter *Y,* and it stands for anything that has two branches forking upward, as the letter *Y* does. Yaji refers to the erect pigtails of a child, and Yaji Shan has two peaks that bear just enough resemblance to that hairstyle to see how it got its name. We calculate that Yaji Shan is a bit too far to the south of Mao Shan to fit Shi Zhenlin's description of the location of Xiaoshan, so we make no attempt to visit Yaji Shan, though our driver takes as close as we can get from the regular highway so we can take pictures. It is exciting for us to be between these two mountains and close enough for clear pictures.

### *Surprise Guests in Xuebu Town*

We return to the Xuebu Zhen government headquarters and gather in the reception and meeting room where we had earlier met Secretary Sun. I sense that we have arrived at a critical turning point in our investigations. It is late on a Friday afternoon; we three outsiders have just arrived on a rather esoteric and quixotic quest; and we have been politely hosted for several hours. But we have much more we would like to do. We still want to get closer to Fang Shan, and we would like very much to interview some of the older folks in Xuebu Zhen, preferably people with a fairly high cultural background and level of education. We are still hopeful that we might find someone with some knowledge of Shuangqing or Shi Zhenlin. We want to share with them Shi Zhenlin's descriptions of Xiaoshan and see if his descriptions sound familiar to any of them. After we talk for a while longer and make clear our larger goals, we are told, somewhat to my surprise: "This can be arranged tomorrow." But now, Xiaowan alarms our hosts by saying that since we have more investigations to carry out here tomorrow, and it is not convenient for us to return to Jintan City this evening, we need a place to stay in Xuebu Zhen tonight, and perhaps the following night as well! This comes as a surprise to Du Laoshi, Hongsheng, and me! We had not talked about staying in Xuebu Zhen and had brought nothing but our notebooks, cameras, and materials on Shi Zhenlin. If her suggestion catches us by surprise, it floors our hosts at Xuebu Zhen. There is a general sense of consternation for a time, with several people talking at once. Mr. Sun and other Xuebu Zhen officials say they have no government guest house or hostel in the town.

Xiaowan is a persistent negotiator, and before long, to my astonishment, we are invited to dinner with half a dozen Xuebu Zhen officials and are told that we can spend the night at a *private* guest house in Xuebu Zhen. As Hongsheng later explains to me, our letter from the mayor's office makes it very difficult for any local officials in Jintan County not to help us with our investigations. He also politely adds that it doesn't hurt to have a visiting foreign scholar in our group. I am pleased to have this small but crucial ceremonial role in our joint quest.

Our dinner is a lavish affair, with ten or twelve dishes, including a variety of cold appetizers, two soups (including, of course, duck's blood soup), a whole fish, lamb, beef, chicken, pork, all washed down with liberal quantities of beer and *baijiu* (the high-octane firewater). For the nonalcoholic drinkers, there is a sweet creamy coconut drink. Amid all the toasting, we sense a warm feeling of camaraderie. I am simply amazed at this treatment, and at how far we have come since our arrival a few hours earlier, when I thought Secretary Sun was quite puzzled as to how to handle our unusual and somewhat esoteric scholarly concerns. The toasting is led by a Mr. Pan, a Xuebu Zhen official who makes it a point to toast everyone at the table at least once, and to challenge anyone with a small *baijiu* class to *ganbei,* literally "dry the glass," the equivalent of "bottoms up." Not liking the taste nor the alcoholic potency of *baijiu,* I stay with beer for the evening, but undaunted by this, Mr. Pan challenges me to empty my beer glass. In mock panic, I point out that my beer class is much larger than his shot glass of *baijiu.* He counters by noting the comparatively low alcohol content of beer compared to *baijiu* and assures me that I can "take my time" in draining the beer glass and take a breath or two as needed. I cheerfully comply without much trouble. At one point, Mr. Pan challenges Mr. Zhang, the genial town head, to drain his glass of *baijiu* even though he is drinking the strong stuff not from a shot tiny glass but from a half-full beer glass. Without hesitating, in one grand gesture Mr. Zhang tosses the *baijiu* down, proudly sticks his empty glass in Mr. Pan's face (the polite way to show that one has indeed emptied the glass), and slams the glass down on the table with a force that makes me wonder whether he is having fun or not. It is an impressive performance, though I can't help noticing that Town Head Zhang is pretty quiet after this and just sits hunched over his plate looking very weary, perhaps not feeling entirely well after so much firewater.

### *Lake of the Wandering Immortals*

After dinner, we are taken to the Kangle Lüguan, the Health and Happiness Hotel, a rather misleading name for a very small family-run guest house, much like a bed-and-breakfast, minus the breakfast. More impressive than the Kangle Hotel is the small lake next to it: Youxian Hu, Lake of the Wandering Immortals, with the very same name, Wandering Immortal, that Shi Zhenlin used to call himself! This whole district was once called Wandering Immortal District, thus it seems indeed the appropriate place to look for clues into Shi Zhenlin's now-vanished world.

Our hosts don't quite know how to register me, though it helps when

I pull out my passport with a number they can record, and they are especially relieved to see that I not only have a Chinese name, but can write it, Luo Puluo. Since nothing in Chinese is very close to Ropp, my early Chinese teachers had given me the surname Luo, and the given name, Puluo, seemed clever enough to me, since the Pu can play the double function of the *pp* in *Ropp* and the *P* in *Paul.* On this very trip, someone in Shanghai told me my name was very poorly chosen, but I could only tell him he was twenty-five years too late with that information. What particularly troubled him was that my name is not immediately identifiable as the name of a foreigner! That's precisely why I like it. But all this is irrelevant to my hosts at the Health and Happiness Hotel. Just the fact that I have a Chinese name is comfort enough for them. I am the first *waiguoren,* foreigner, to stay in this guest house, and that alone makes me feel very privileged to be here.

Our quarters are quite Spartan, but compared with the hospitality of everyone we have met in Xuebu Zhen, the quality of the Health and Happiness Hotel pales into relative insignificance. After all, we have pretty much brought this onto ourselves, or at least Xiaowan has brought it on for us. Having negotiated our stay here, rather to our surprise, she somehow found a ride for herself back to Jintan for the night. I can't help wondering if perhaps Xiaowan just needs to be rid of us for the evening. The next afternoon we would learn what she was up to when she arrived back in Xuebu Zhen with a camera crew from Jintan Television!

It becomes quite clear in the course of the night that Hongsheng is no more pleased than I am to be camping out in Xuebu Zhen rather than back in the relative luxury of the government hostel in Jintan City. The screen door to our room doesn't close; let's hope mosquito season is past. There is a television set in the room that doesn't work, but we've no time for TV anyway. Our hosts furnish us each with a hand towel, a new tube of toothpaste and a toothbrush. They put a clean sheet on each of our hard beds and a towel over each of our pillows, which are very large, hard, and filled with beans. I am reminded that Chinese nobles were often buried with their heads resting on large cubic porcelain pillows, not my idea of resting in peace! It is a cold evening, probably under fifty degrees Fahrenheit; we have no heat, and precisely one large quilt apiece. My quilt is quite warm enough, but Hongsheng's has a hole in it where there is no quilting, so he endures a long night of shivering.

Before we retire, Du Laoshi and Hongsheng and I confer on tomorrow's schedule and prepare a list of questions to ask: Any large protruding rocks on the mountainside? Any flower goddess temple? Any Yanzhi Dong? (This refers to a Rouge Cave near Xiaoshan, where Shi Zhenlin said that women ground down the colored rock found there to use as a kind of makeup for the removal or covering of freckles.) Any Xiaoshan Academy? Any Ougeng Hall? Any Chonggang Peak? We will read (or translate into vernacular Chinese) Shi Zhenlin's descriptions of Xiaoshan and its surroundings and see if anything sounds familiar to our informants.

Despite our differing perspectives, we make a pretty good investigative team, and we have a comfortable division of labor. Du Laoshi is the expert on the details of Shi Zhenlin's *Random Notes* and on the life and poetry of Shuangqing as described there. Hongsheng understands the local accents better than Du and I, and he can make the initial introductions and summarize for me, in his clear precise Mandarin, all the answers we receive, so I have some hope of understanding what's going on. My role is to demonstrate, just by being here, the international significance of our quest for information about Shuangqing. Occasionally I am called on to tell our hosts about the international scholarship on Shuangqing, but mostly I am happy (and relieved) just to listen and try to follow the conversations.

I'm a little uneasy with the way that Hongsheng, and especially Du Laoshi, introduce the story of Shuangqing as entirely factual with no ambiguity at all. On the other hand, I agree, we would look rather silly to introduce ourselves by saying we believe Shi Zhenlin's account is entirely fictional. ("You have a local heroine, a cultural icon really, who you've never heard of, and who we don't believe ever existed. But she's a great fictional character! Can you shed any light on how this might have happened?") Du Laoshi's view is that Shi Zhenlin's *Random Notes* is a straightforward factual account of his experiences and observations. Given her guiding assumption about this, she is very excited about the story of a Xiaoshan Academy, which she sees as important evidence that Shi Zhenlin did indeed discover a talented and beautiful peasant woman poet named Shuangqing. Because I am more skeptical about Shi's memoir, I think it is just as likely that the Xiaoshan Academy, if it existed, was so named *following,* and *in imitation of,* Shi's memoir. Certainly, all the local histories that talk about Shuangqing's village of Xiaoshan are simply based on Shi's memoir and nothing more. Liu Laoshi also takes great comfort from the fact that the Taiping cataclysm of the nineteenth century transformed this region into a population of newcomers. This fact alone easily explains why no popular stories of Shuangqing seem to have survived in Jintan. For me, I must admit, if I did find popular stories here about Shuangqing, I would tend to see them as oral traditions passed on from readings, misreadings, retellings, and mishearings of the Shuangqing story as first told by Shi Zhenlin.

Despite our different perspectives, however, we share a common goal to find out as much as possible about this area in our short time here. After we agree on this list of issues to raise tomorrow, we retire for the evening. I climb under my thick quilt and take out my notebook to summarize the day's events. Before long, I drift off to sleep, not quite feeling the serene guarantee of health and happiness suggested by the name of our domicile, but nevertheless very pleased to be staying beside a place as close to Shi Zhenlin's heart as the Lake of the Wandering Immortals.

*six* ·

# *Poems*

*Shuangqing is frail and compliant by nature, but she is also able to bear much hardship; even when she feels depressed, she still maintains a calm and pleasant demeanor. Once she found a neighbor lady quarreling at her home, and Shuangqing, despite her weakened condition, tried to calm the old lady down. The old woman scowled and said, "What are you, a dead toad? How come you seem so timid?"*

*One day Shuangqing was pounding rice with the mortar and pestle. Out of breath, she stood still for a moment, holding onto the pestle. Her husband saw her standing there and suspected she was just loafing. He gave her a hard shove, and as she fell down beside the mortar, the pestle fell on top of her midsection with a loud crack. She bore this pain in silence and just got up and resumed pounding the grain. Her husband glared at her, and she smiled apologetically and said, "I'll soon be finished with this pounding."*

*She was then heating their gruel for lunch when she suffered a malarial attack. The fire flared and the gruel started to boil over. Shuangqing panicked and hurried to pour cold water into the boiling gruel. Her mother-in-law grabbed her by an earring and tore it off, yelling "Get out!" Her earlobe was torn and blood ran down on her shoulder. She tried to cover her ear, and started to cry. Her mother-in-law waved the ladle at her and yelled, "How dare you cry!" She just wiped the blood up in silence, but because she had let the gruel boil over, her husband forbade her from joining in the noon meal. Shuangqing just smiled and kept on grinding grain with the mortar. The neighbor lady asked if she was hungry. When Shuangqing answered, "No," the woman sneeringly laughed and said, "So, the toad has some fire in her belly after all! Perhaps that has filled you up!"*

*At this point Shuangqing leaned on the mortar, stared at the floor, sighed, and said to herself, "Heavens! I hope that this life of Shuangqing's can atone for all the world's most beautiful young maidens, and that after I absorb all the endless sufferings and tribulations of this world in their stead, young beauties will never again have to bear what I, Shuangqing, have had to bear." She then asked the young Ling* [landlord Zhang Mengzhan's brother] *to copy* Random Notes *for her, and to have it buried with her when she dies. Then, matching Boluo's poem, she wrote a regulated verse [shi] in nine stanzas, writing with rouge on a head kerchief. Mengzhan asked to see it, but she refused. He then swore an oath saying, "Whoever fails to return this kerchief will be reborn in the next life as an ill-fated beauty the equal of Shuangqing!" Thus, he got the kerchief from her, copied the poems, and quickly returned it. On the kerchief now there were spots that looked like tear stains.* (*RN,* 3.6–7)

### *Preface to a Poem*

This is Shi Zhenlin's introduction to a long poem of Shuangqing's, a regulated verse of seven characters per line. In introducing these verses, Shi Zhenlin gives more background than usual, detailing her life of persecution at the hands of her husband and mother-in-law. Despite the physical abuse that she suffers, Shuangqing maintains her dignity and never seems to lose her temper or her calm demeanor. A rather cold and cantankerous neighbor lady tauntingly scolds Shuangqing for being so timid, so lacking in *qi,* a word that means breath as well as courage, anger, and physical vigor. Of course, Shuangqing is often short of breath, but the neighbor lady also implies that she is simply timid rather than virtuous. After Shuangqing takes considerable physical abuse at the hands of her husband and her mother-in-law, she is not even allowed to eat the gruel she has cooked for the family. When Shuangqing bears all this in silence and denies to the neighbor lady that she is hungry, the old woman jokes that perhaps this toad has some *qi* after all, some breath, or some fire in her belly that has left her no room for food. A toad puffs its cheeks with air when it croaks, and its *qi* is thus quite visible. By crudely likening Shuangqing to a lifeless or barely croaking toad, the old neighbor lady makes fun of her even when the young victim of malaria and wife abuse is most in need of comforting. But no provocation will rouse the virtuous peasant wife and daughter-in-law to an expression of anger or self-defense. Instead, talking curiously of herself in the third person, she takes solace from the hope that "this life of Shuangqing's can atone for the world's most beautiful young maidens *(jiaren),*" so that they will never again have to bear what she has had to bear. She asks Mengzhan's younger brother, Ling, to copy Shi Zhenlin's *Random Notes* for her and to have it buried with her when she dies. She is so ill that she does not expect to live long. She writes her poem matching a rhyme scheme that the female immortal Boluo had used in one of the poems Shi and his friends had received through their divination practice of spirit writing.

Shuangqing's landlord, Zhang Mengzhan, asks to see her poems that she has written in rouge on a head kerchief. She refuses, but relents when he swears an oath that he will return it or suffer rebirth as a beauty with an ill fate to equal hers. When Mengzhan returns the kerchief with its nine-verse poem, it is stained with tears, presumably his. This poem is distinctive in its descriptions of ordinary scenes of rural life, and perhaps for that reason, it is also one of the most frequently anthologized of Shuangqing's regulated verses.

### *Conventions of Regulated Verse*

Popular from the Tang dynasty (618–906) onward, seven-character regulated verse was probably the most common type of classical Chinese verse. All educated people were expected to be able to write and to appreciate this kind of poetry, and they wrote it daily, on social occasions, in journals, as letters, and for men, in the all-important civil service examinations. Chinese literati saw poetry as the highest form of communication, "an activity appropriate to all human beings on certain occasions and in certain states of mind" (Owen 1990, 295).

For Shi Zhenlin and his circle, poetry was the greatest expression of one's humanity. And they spent as much energy reading and listening to each other's poems as they did writing their own. *Random Notes* is as much about being a good reader as a good writer of poetry. Shi Zhenlin in many ways staked his own claim to fame on his ability to read, understand, and appreciate Shuangqing's poetry.

One final point, before looking at Shuangqing's nine-verse poem. Chinese readers tended to assume that poetry, especially regulated verse, was autobiographical, not fictional.

> The traditional Chinese reader had faith that poems were authentic presentations of historical experience. Poets wrote, as readers read, under those assumptions. No one felt uncomfortable in constructing biographical chronologies from poems or in using poems as direct sources for cultural history. (Owen 1985, 57)

Of course it is possible that Shi Zhenlin was exploiting precisely these kinds of assumptions in his reconstruction of the life and poetry of Shuangqing. I say this here, however, not to question these assumptions or raise doubts about this nine-verse poem attributed to Shuangqing. My point, on the contrary, is how well this poem fits with the assumptions of Shi Zhenlin's Chinese readers. Of all the poems by Shuangqing, this one seems the most fitting for a peasant woman to have written.

***Nine Verses Matching a Rhyme of the Female Immortal Boluo***

*1.*

*Not ready for vows and incense in a cloistered convent,*
*My heart is cold and unrippled as a clear still pool.*
*Don't blame a starving swallow for bringing nest mud too late;*
*Who pities an ailing silkworm for spinning a flimsy cocoon?*

*2.*

*This year torrents break forth from the autumn clouds.*
*To fill out new rent, I have again pawned my skirt,*
*Saving a quilt to protect you from the cold.*
*My heart like honey, how could I fault you?*

*3.*

*Coiling and stitching hemp, I make [you] a pair of shoes,*
*To ascend the western peak for grass at dawn tomorrow.*
*The sudden cold brings a night of gusty winds;*
*I implore them to blow my way instead of yours.*

*4.*

*In the chilly kitchen, smoke hangs heavy and damp over the room.*
*With the Wutong trees all burned, the phoenix has no perch.*
*Alone I pick wild vegetables and wash them in the cold.*
*The chrysanthemum though ill still has to bear the frost.*

*5.*

*My fate, like a cicada's wing, is thin and insubstantial.*
*I used to be as fragile and pampered as the girl next door.*
*Would mother still recognize me now with*
*My bitter jaundiced face, all its cheerful color gone?*

*6.*

*My heart is soaked through with a springtime bitterness.*
*In my illness, sparse dreams easily fall into oblivion.*
*Having sold my few cheap hairpins for a dose of medicine,*
*I cut a poplar twig to fasten in my hair, with water as a mirror.*

*7.*

*Mount Siping looms like a platform in the distance,*
*From where you, carrying cold kindling, descend many times.*
*On your return I urge you to get up a little later,*
*Though the sun is high, I privately bar outsiders from rousing you.*

8.

*The chickens sleep in pairs, mock the luan bird perched alone,*
*They fly in pairs as well, their purple crowns aligned.*
*The dim lamp wick now flares with green [a good omen];*
*[If true] my humble stove is better to lean on than a balcony rail.*

9.

*I live in a simple house, beside a wealthy establishment.*
*Incense smoke drifts down at night, rousing my sense of loss.*
*Opening my sleeves, I pour out these sad lines of autumn.*
*Withering grass, setting sun, I dream of roaming afar.*

(*RN*, 3.7–8)

Taken as a whole, these nine verses are less intensely emotional than Shuangqing's more famous song lyrics, but like the lyrics, they create a self-portrait in which images of the natural world both reflect and alternate with images of a wounded self. In verse 1, Shuangqing shows her Buddhist outlook, cultivating a motionless heart, Buddhist detachment, even though she is "not ready" to become a nun in a convent. She alludes to all the blame she suffers in the family, likening herself to a starving swallow and an ailing silkworm. Verses 2, 3, and 7 are rather striking departures from most of her work in that they express tender affection for her husband and address him directly with the intimate pronoun, *lang*. Her affection seems puzzling in light of the immediate context Shi Zhenlin has outlined. In verses 4, 5, and 6 she describes her hard life, her loneliness, and her deteriorating condition, alternating direct images of her frail self with such self-reflective images as the lone phoenix, the mythological *luan* bird, and the ailing chrysanthemum. Verses 5 and 6 both hint at a lost youth and lost hopes, contrasting her former beauty with her current sickness, poverty, and disappointment. Autumn is the season associated with the sadness of parting and mortality, and such associations permeate all nine verses. The "springtime bitterness" in verse 6 suggests that the memory of springtime, symbolizing the hopes of youth and love, now seems bitter because those hopes have been so totally disappointed.

In contrast to the earlier passages referring to affection for her husband, the final two stanzas emphasize Shuangqing's loneliness and lack of an understanding companion. Chickens in pairs suggest the naturalness of conjugal love in contrast with the beautiful *luan* bird perched alone. In other words, the lonely Shuangqing has no understanding mate to appreciate her beauty and talent. She wants to interpret the flaring of an untrimmed oil lamp wick as a positive omen of luck changing for the better. With this image following that of the lonely *luan*, she implies that if her luck changed only slightly, if her husband were more sensitive and understanding, she would be quite content with her life of poverty and illness. The final stanza suggests, however, that poverty is difficult for such a proud poet to bear. The incense from a wealthy neighboring house drifts by her poor hut to remind her of her unhappiness and disappointment.

"THIS REALLY DOES SOUND LIKE SHUANGQING!" When I read this poem with Liu Laoshi, she found it very moving and very convincing as a self-portrait of a proud but ill and poverty-stricken woman. The focus of the poem is unusual because upper-class women who defined the genre of "women's poetry" seldom wrote about housework drudgery. They wrote of embroidery, to be sure, the defining work of the elite woman, and of the strains of supervising a large household. But Shuangqing gives us a view of peasant life from the kitchen floor.

"This really does sound like Shuangqing!" Liu Laoshi exclaimed with pleasure. "It is simple, straightforward, with touching imagery and vividly sketched scenes."

She didn't say what I detected as implicit in her praise: there is not a hint of flirtatiousness about this poem. Shuangqing describes her own hard work, her loneliness, and her sorrows in six verses and expresses her tender concern for her husband in three verses. She clearly refers only to her husband here and throws nary a glance at the literati. This is not true of all of Shuangqing's poems, but it is a striking characteristic of this one, and I think it is the main reason Liu Laoshi found it so appealing.

"Given the background Shi Zhenlin gives for this poem," I asked, "do you find it odd that Shuangqing is so solicitous of her husband here? He is always described as such a brute. How can Shuangqing feel so tenderly toward him?"

"This is her duty!" Liu Laoshi said emphatically, as if I had forgotten the basic rudiments of Chinese family life. "She is a wife, after all! And her husband works hard to eke out a living for all of them. So she is grateful for what little she has."

To Liu Laoshi, this poem defined the authentic Shuangqing. It became the measure by which other poems were judged and sometimes found lacking. In fact, she was not at all hesitant in judging some of Shuangqing's poems as authentic and some as fabricated by Shi Zhenlin. At times she would simply say, "This doesn't sound like Shuangqing. You need not spend precious time translating it." (I interpreted her to mean: "I don't want to spend my precious time going through the painstaking process of helping you translate it!") Consequently, in my year with Liu Laoshi, I did not translate all of the poems attributed to Shuangqing in *Random Notes*. I only recently got around to translating the following poem, alas, without her expert help. ·⌣

### *Literati Assign Poetic Topics to Shuangqing*

At one point in *Random Notes,* the literati get discouraged when they give Shuangqing rhyme schemes to match, because her rhymes are so much better then theirs, so they decide instead to give her topics to write on. Three of them choose three topics for her: "Plantain" (the banana-like plant first mentioned in the Confucian classic of early poetry, *The Book of Songs*), "Tianzhu Seed" (the seed of an evergreen plant called nandina) and "Clearing after a Snowfall on West Mountain," West Mountain being what the villagers of Xiaoshan call Mount Siping, situated west of the village. Shuangqing responds to this request with three poems, a total of eighty-four characters, written in light ink, almost illegible, on a one-inch square leaf of a rush!

PLANTAIN

*Fragments of clouds want to align, but are blown all the more apart.*
*Through their fissures come bits of light to mark my sad and lonely heart.*
*From Mount Jingshan Bian He's tears cascade down in double streams*
*For the hundred flowers with their hidden beauty and their lost dreams.*

TIANZHU SEED

*Damp kindling only smolders, winter vegetables rot with mildew,*
*Fallen leaves now dry, get swept to the fence of woven bamboo.*
*Under the stove are kept—thread by thread, strand by strand—*
*A whole array of tight bundles, kindling grass, bound by hand.*

CLEARING AFTER A SNOWFALL ON WEST MOUNTAIN

*The fragrant bits of clouds, once here, now disband;*
*The beautiful maiden seamstress adds another strand.*
*Plantain is hard to locate; Tianzhu seed I find not any place;*
*But snow is past, sky now clears, I'm cheered to see West Mountain's face.*

(*RN*, 3.32)

• LIU LAOSHI: "DON'T BOTHER WITH THIS POEM!" This is a clever poem, and I have tried to capture the cleverness with a rhyming translation. But Liu Laoshi was so suspicious of the authorship of the poem that we only discussed it in general terms. She found it too clever by half. To begin with, she found the reference to Bian He a bit too esoteric for Shuangqing. Bian He lived in the kingdom of Chu in the eighth century B.C. He found a piece of pure jade on a mountain called Jingshan. When he presented it to the prince of Chu, the prince accused him of presenting a fake piece of jade, and he sentenced Bian He to have his left foot amputated. When the prince died and his successor took the throne, Bian He again brought the stone as a gift, only to be accused of deceit once more. This time his right foot was amputated. When this prince died, Bian He again presented his jade piece and wept tears of blood. When asked why he wept, he replied that he cried not for the loss of his feet, but over the fact that a genuine piece of jade was regarded as an imitation, and a loyal subject was regarded as disloyal. The stone was examined once more and discovered to be genuine. The jade was named after him in his honor, and he was offered a noble title, which he declined (Choy 1993, 143–44; Giles 1868, 627–28).

Bian He's tears in Shuangqing's poem are for "the hundred flowers with their hidden beauty and their lost dreams," that is, for people like Shuangqing whose talent goes unrecognized and unappreciated in this remote village. The story of Bian He is quite appropriate to the theme of unappreciated beauty, and I was not so sure that peasants would not know his story. For once, I was less skeptical than Liu Laoshi.

The next verse, on Tianzhu seed, was less objectionable with its nice image of those tight bundles of hand-bound grass that Shuangqing's husband spends his winter days on the mountain cutting and carrying back to the village. But the last couplet was particularly objectionable to Liu Laoshi. "Look at this!" she exclaimed, her voice dripping with disapproval. "She cleverly combines all three of her assigned topics in the last couplet. This smacks of literati cleverness to me. Shi Zhenlin might go in for this sort of cleverness, but not Shuangqing!"

It amused me to see how Liu Laoshi could scold Shi Zhenlin! •

### *Shuangqing as the Autumn Lotus*

*On the twenty-eighth* [of the seventh month, 1734], [Zheng] *Chi'an invited* [Bi] *Keshan to a farewell dinner. I was sick and unable to go.*

> [Jing] *Zhenxiang returned from Xiaoshan, having gotten Shuangqing's Autumn Lotus poems, written on the leaves of a rose (Yuejihua, rosa indica). Each stem has five leaves, and she had written one verse on each leaf. The leaves were extremely small, and the characters were so tiny they looked like shadows.* (*RN,* 4.41)

Thus Shi Zhenlin introduces Shuangqing's "Autumn Lotus poem," ten interlocked verses in which the last line of each verse is echoed in the first line of the next verse. To highlight this aspect of the poem, the repeated terms are printed in bold type. Because the structure of English is so different from that of classical Chinese, these repetitions are not quite as striking in translation as in the original. There is a lot to unpack in this poem, apart from the clever interlocking couplets. The lotus flower in autumn is the mirror image of Shuangqing and her sadness. As a summer flower, the lotus cannot long survive the autumn cold. The poem speaks in the voice of the lotus, which is the same as Shuangqing's own voice. Filled with literary allusions and a veiled eroticism, the poem's sheer "literariness" made Liu Laoshi suspicious. But this time I prevailed on her to work with me anyway, citing my need to learn how to translate interlocking couplets effectively. In the end, she didn't mind taking as much time as I needed to get it right.

*1.*

*Wait for a letter, it doesn't come, I cry like the autumn locust.*
*My heart is like the plantain leaf tightly folded up.*
*I gloomily await the frost, but the frost can't bear to come;*
*The* ***plum*** *has barely blossomed; the* ***mum's*** *in sturdy full bloom.*

*2.*

*The* ***mum's*** *heart and the* ***plum's*** *soul understand each other;*
*At the setting sun when people retire, then the egret returns.*
*Does the gentleman want to worship the flower spirit?*
*You can use me to sacrifice at the shrine of the world's wronged* ***women****.*

*3.*

*The* ***woman's*** [i.e., the lotus's] *pure grievance, at dawn the cold wind blows,*
*Drops of dew hit the water, the resting fish coldly stares.*
*The heart of the lotus seed in autumn is bitterest of all;*
*If I cannot love the* ***moonlight,*** *whoever can I love?*

*4.*

*The* ***moonlight*** *looks like water, no butterflies in sight;*
*My remaining color almost gone, standing upright, alone.*
*Night rains come again, breaking my red petals in pieces;*
*When the mermaid sees me, she cries her* ***tear*** *ducts dry.*

5.
*Her* ***tears*** *exhausted, she will give up no more pearls;*
*The sins of a former life create this life's suspicion.*
*One stalk consigned, ten thousand threads are broken;*
*In Jiangnan's seventh month the* ***wild goose*** *comes early.*

6.
*By the clouds a new* ***wild goose****; by the moon a lonely person;*
*The caltrop competes to show up the water lily's weakness.*
*The yellow oriole knows how to pity the white egret;*
*The wild pond's poor flowers cannot compete with* ***spring****.*

7.
*Pale reflection, ashamed to face* ***spring*** *feelings in the mirror.*
*Like water the heart stirs, hard to find nighttime peace.*
*My leaves impede the fierce rain, and flowers collect the dew;*
*Sweet protection of the* ***mandarin duck*** **[lover's]** ***dream****, is it cold or not?*

8.
*The* ***love-crazed duck*** *without a* ***dream*** *grasps hold of spring;*
*One feels sadness before the cassia buds of the autumn moon.*
*Repair all the five colors of West Lake's flowers;*
*But I am as heartbroken as Nügua in her* ***Heaven****.*

9.
***Heaven's*** *five colors fill the horizon at lonely dusk,*
*Under the moon, apply autumn's powder mixed with tears.*
*Carefully gather flower petals, lightly lightly roll them*
*Into* ***fragrant tablets*** *for burning by the bed curtain.*

10.
***Fragrant tablets*** *all burned, azure smoke abounds,*
*Marriages are allocated, how can there be mistakes?*
*From now on loving couples should not be parted,*
*With my broken reds and tattered greens, I'll mend your fisherman's cape.*

(*RN*, 4.41–42)

In the opening line, the poet waits for a letter that doesn't come. This is a conventional image of the lonely abandoned lover. Here she can't be referring to her husband since he is illiterate. She must be waiting for a letter from one of the literati. The lotus awaits the frost, and even though the frost "can't bear to come," we know that it inevitably will come, with predictable consequences for the lotus. The plum and chrysanthemum are both cold-weather flowers, and because of that, we see in verse 2, they "understand each other." The unspoken implication is that although they understand each other, they do not understand the lonely lotus (Shuangqing).

Since Shi Zhenlin's friend Jing Zhenxiang retrieved these verses, the reference to the gentleman *(xianlang)* in verse 2 suggests the poem is directed to one of the literati, perhaps Jing or Shi Zhenlin himself. Shuangqing tells this gentleman that if he wants to worship the flower spirit (and she sees herself as a flower spirit banished to live on earth), he may invoke her as a sacrifice to the shrine of the world's wronged women.

In verse 3, the woman and her lotus mirror are aggrieved by the cold autumn wind, and, immersed in water, the lotus is doubly cold, its heart "bitterest of all" at this season. The moonlight could suggest a love interest, and given Shi Zhenlin's style name, Moon Admirer, it may suggest an interest in Zhenlin. "If I cannot love the moonlight, whoever can I love?" If she cannot feel love for the one who has made her name known to the world, how can she feel any love at all? But the beauty and the lotus remain alone with the moonlight to remind them of love, and there are "no butterflies in sight," no admirers or lovers to keep them company. The lotus and Shuangqing are both ailing, color faded, petals broken by the rain.

The mermaid in verses 4 and 5 refers to the mermaid of the southern seas who lives and spins under water and cries tears of pearls. She has cried so much she has no more tears to shed for the poor dying lotus. This suffering must result from sins of a previous life. The lotus stalk, though fragile, contains many tiny threads, and threads are what bind people together in ties of mutual affection. The poet is frail, but she still harbors many passions, deep desires for human connection. In looking for connections, she turns to nature. The wild goose returns early this year, in the seventh month, on its way south. Verse 5 shows, however, that connections are rare and difficult, even in nature. When the goose returns, it sees only a solitary person in the moonlight (wishing in vain for moonlight romance). The caltrop, like a woman jealous of another's beauty, competes with the water lily rather than offering sympathy. The yellow oriole, by contrast, can feel empathy for the white egret, but the wild flowers on an autumn pond cannot compare with the radiance of spring.

The poet returns to the lotus's, and her own, sad state in verse 7. Both pale, they are "ashamed to face spring feelings in the mirror." Their aspirations (for love and survival) are so far out of the question that they are ashamed even to admit them. Because of their unfulfilled passions (and in the poet's case, her sickness), it is "hard to find nighttime peace." The lotus shields the pond from wind and rain, bearing the brunt of the storm with its own leaves. And it protects, or keeps alive, the dreams of mandarin ducks. A pair of mandarin ducks symbolizes love, and their dreams are dreams of love. Although both poet and lotus are battered and chilled by the autumn wind and rain, they still harbor hopes and dreams of love. The "love-crazed duck," even without the hope of a dream, still "grasps hold of spring," still holds the love ideal in its heart.

In verse 8, the "sadness before the cassia buds of the autumn moon" refers to the moon goddess, Chang E. The line literally reads, "One feels sadness before the cassia buds of the silver toad." The silver toad is the toad that lives on the moon with Chang E, and the autumn-blooming cassia tree grows in the courtyard of Chang E's moon palace. The meaning of the line is to emphasize the sadness of the lotus (and the author) under the full autumn moon. The second part of the verse concerns the heavenly goddess Nügua. In ancient times, according to Chinese folklore, the gods of Heaven were fighting with each other, and they accidentally broke one of the pillars holding up the firmament. Nügua mended the pillar by smelting stones. She managed to keep Heaven from collapsing, but her repair work was not perfect. Consequently, the firmament sags in the northwest corner, and the crashing pillar caused the earth to slant toward the southeast, thus explaining why China's rivers all run toward the southeast. West Lake is one of China's most famous scenic spots. As Nügua repaired Heaven, so the five colors of West Lake will be restored when spring arrives, but the lotus (poet) is as sad as Nügua because the autumn lotus has no hope of complete restoration. That others will enjoy the spring radiance of West Lake only makes her sadder.

Verses 9 and 10 concern the practice of grinding flower petals with pollen and water, to be used as a kind of women's makeup. Flower petals were also sometimes ground or wrapped tightly into "fragrant tablets" to be burned in autumn or winter as a kind of incense or room freshener. The poet mixes her flower petals and pollen with her own tears and later burns the dried tablets by her bed. Bedside fragrance suggests the sweetness of lovemaking, but the lotus and poet have no hope for such sweetness in this twilight hour of their lives. The phrase "Marriages are allocated" suggests that marriages are controlled by fate, and fate cannot be changed. If the lotus (poet) is doomed to a lonely death, at least she can hope that others not suffer her same plight. "From now on loving couples should not be parted / With my broken reds and tattered greens, I'll mend your fisherman's cape." Marital bliss may be impossible, but it can still be imagined. As the autumn lotus disintegrates into broken reds and tattered greens, she promises to use those sad remnants of her self to mend the fisherman's cape, the woven-straw rain cape, of her lover.

PEASANT GENIUS OR LITERATI CONCEIT? I was impressed with the interlocking verses of this poem, and with that Shuangqing hallmark the intense identification with another living object, in this case the autumn lotus facing the coming winter. By contrast, Liu Laoshi was not very happy with the poem. "This is too intricate, too literary, too flirtatious for Shuangqing. It's a good poem, but it just isn't the kind of poem she would write."

I envied her cultural self-confidence. She read the poetry like a true *zhiyin,* "one who knows the tone." She seemed to know all the tones and many of the allusions without having to check a single dictionary! Of course, she also "prepared for class" by looking up the obscure characters and allusions that Shi Zhenlin delights in sprinkling through his text. In the course of our readings, she had taken on Shuangqing as her own best friend, and she had a very clear sense that the "Autumn Lotus" poem, good as it was, wasn't the authentic Shuangqing voice. For the real Shuangqing, the true voice of the beautiful sensitive peasant genius, Liu Laoshi was quite certain, we had to look to her song lyrics.

*seven*

# *Lyrics*

### *The Autumn Chrysanthemum*

*Shuangqing loved chrysanthemums, and she kept a wild one in a flower pot so that she could face it whenever she was cooking or pounding grain. For this chrysanthemum she wrote the following song lyric to the tune of "Er lang shen":*

*The fine fine fragile willow leaves*
*Quiver and vanish, leaving the mist as before.*
*Facing the setting sun in an autumn mountain shadow,*
*I am cheered by your still hearty stem.*
*You've endured the heavy autumn rains past Double Ninth*
*And fortunately survived to a brief spell of Indian summer.*
*I know tonight you'll be dipped in light frost;*
*As the butterfly departs you'll bow your head.*

*So many hardships, early autumn cold chills to the bone*
*And my sickness returns again.*
*Is it just my own Shuangqing heartlessness*
*To abandon you in the quiet dusk out back?*
*In the cold moonlight by the balcony rail, sleep impossible,*
*For several nights on end I never unbutton my jacket.*
*Useless to apologize for letting you down;*
*You've blossomed in a destitute home, a place of gloom;*
*Sorrows need washing away, but there's no more wine.*

(*RN*, 2.80)

Flowers are symbols for beautiful women in Chinese poetry, and above all other flowers, Shuangqing identifies with the autumn chrysanthemum. As the last flower to bloom in the season, the chrysanthemum symbolizes the upright, righteous, and unappreciated beauty, facing the coming frost alone. The chrysanthemum is Shuangqing's companion in hardship and a mirror reflection of her own self. Together they both persevere through hard times (autumn) to face the inevitable chilling frost of the coming winter. The approaching cold stirs Shuangqing's illness and threatens the chrysanthemum with death.

Double Ninth was an autumn festival celebrating longevity on the ninth day of the ninth month of the lunar calendar. On that day people would take a picnic to the mountains, where they would enjoy the autumn scenery and drink a tonic promoting long life: wine in which chrysanthemum petals had been steeped. The final line, "Sorrows need washing away, but there's no more wine," alludes to one of China's greatest poets of reclusion, Tao Qian (365–427), who also wrote a poem about being too poor to afford wine at the celebration of the Double Ninth festival. Tao extolled the virtues of simple country life in contrast to the machinations of those seeking wealth, power, and fame. Thus, though describing nothing beyond her own humble circumstances, Shuangqing displays through this allusion an affinity with an important cultural symbol of Daoist withdrawal from a corrupt society.

Both flower and poet have survived hardship. The chrysanthemum has lived past the first cold nights of autumn and has just enjoyed a brief spell of Indian summer. But a killing frost is on its way, and Shuangqing apologizes to her flower friend for abandoning it to the cold. The poet, having her own difficulties with sickness, poverty, sleeplessness, and the coming of winter, cannot save the flower from its inevitable sad fate of death.

Shuangqing became particularly famous for her song lyrics, and some have regarded her as one of the best lyric writers in the entire Qing dynasty. Her lyrics are mostly in the typical feminine style called "delicate restraint" *(wanyue).* They are gentle, soft, and quiet in tone. Several of the lyrics discussed in this chapter focus on objects outside the poet herself, and in each case she deeply identifies with the object in question. This too was a convention of the lyric, called *yongwu* (singing of objects), in which the poet expresses his or her own feelings through the object being described. Shuangqing is particularly adept in giving a sense of her own very profound identification with these objects.

The lyric on the autumn chrysanthemum made a deep impression on Liu Laoshi. "This is really good!" she exclaimed as we read it through the first time. Following our normal practice, I read it through once for the pronunciation, and then we discussed its meaning line by line. Whenever the bell rang announcing the end of class (and the ten-minute break between classes), we often continued on for few more minutes. This time, she ignored the bell entirely and said, with no attempt to hide her enthusiasm, "Shall I read it through once?" In other words, "Do you want to hear how it really sounds?" Of course I did. She then read it once very slowly, with feeling, while I listened and tried to make mental notes on her inflection, tones, and pacing. Some lines she read fast, some slowly, and the last line she took especially slowly, as if mulling over and savoring each character. She emphasized the tones much more than in normal speech, so that her reading sounded almost like singing. As she began, I realized that I had very rarely if ever heard Chinese poetry expertly read aloud by a native Chinese speaker. From this day onward, if Liu Laoshi didn't volunteer to read each lyric aloud, I asked her to, and she happily obliged. Before I left Taiwan she recorded all of Shuangqing's lyrics for me to take back home

The next two days, following this class on the autumn chrysanthemum lyric, we discovered two equally moving and famous lyrics in rapid succession, with just enough explanation to give each a context. This was the one piece of *Random Notes* that I had already seen quoted verbatim in many anthologies. But I had not previously translated these lyrics, and Liu Laoshi was reading them for the first time. It felt as if we had come upon some buried treasure.

### *Lonesome Phoenix; Lonesome Farm Wife*

*One day she was late in taking a meal out to the field. Her husband angrily brandished his hoe as if to hit her. Shuangqing returned and wrote this one-verse song lyric to the tune of "Gu luan" (Lonesome phoenix):*

*Noontime cold arrives, alas, on schedule,*
*So early my fevers begin;*
*Under my plain green shirt I add a layer.*
*Too tired to comb my slept-on hair,*
*I wrap it up untidily in a kerchief.*
*So busy my plain skirt goes unwashed,*
*Along the edges of the folds threads are*
*broken and worn—a double loss.*

*Looking closely at my hands and wrists, all filled with calluses,*
*Yet these cheeks retain a hint of youth.*

*Though one whole life may be sorrowful and wasted,*
*Yet [one has to] bear it;*
*Though everything only comes to dust and ashes,*
*Still, take more thought before you marry.*
*Profound thoughts and elegant feelings*
*All get consumed in kitchen heat, grease, and smoke.*
*Rush a meal to the eastern field, scolded for being late;*
*Cold spell returns, then warm spell, who cares?*
*Get back fast, I have yet to gather the drying cotton;*
*What's more, it will soon be time to cook supper.*

(*RN*, 2.80–81)

This lyric is one of the plainest that Shuangqing wrote. It is simply a description of her busy life despite illness during an autumn harvest season. As the days grow colder, her chronic malaria flares up, and she adds a layer under her shirt to stave off the chills. Ever conscious of her appearance, she wraps her slept-on hair in a kerchief, laments her unwashed tattered skirt, complains of her rough calloused hands, and yet proudly notes that her cheeks still retain a hint of youth. Is this what literary critics call "the male gaze" at work here? If this seems unusual for a peasant woman to be writing so elegantly about her appearance, it is also a far cry from the courtesan self-portrait song lyrics that paint seductive pictures of boudoir beauties.

The beginning of the second stanza may be addressed to the lone phoenix of the tune, but it could also serve as a kind of self-admonition to the poet anticipating eventual rebirth in a Buddhist world. The implication is that although this world of pain and suffering may indeed be illusory, as the Buddhists teach, it still hurts to have to endure pain and to be unappreciated. The Buddhist poet also reveals her romantic and artistic side. "Profound thoughts and elegant feelings" represent aesthetic ideals that are quite real to this women. Yet in her humble circumstances, these ideals "all get consumed in kitchen heat, grease, and smoke." How can the busy farm wife—running meals to the fields at noon, drying raw cotton in the sun, and rushing back to cook supper—ever hope to develop her artistic yearnings and talents? This is the most striking example I can think of in the Chinese tradition where we find a woman artist outside the traditional elite class pleading for something like "a room of one's own."

In the context of verse 1 with its mention of "taking more thought before you marry," Shuangqing implies that a more appropriate husband-lover could comprehend and share in her profound thoughts and elegant feelings and thereby relieve her psychologically, if not physically, from the numbing drudgery of farm life. In recounting her hardships, Shuangqing shows her unhappiness in her marriage more directly here than in any other of her writings.

***The Lone Wild Goose***

*One day near dusk, with a basket in one hand and a broom in the other, Shuangqing was returning from the fields when she saw a lone goose and heard its mournful cry. It was actually resting on a path between fields. Shuangqing just stopped and stared at it toward the east. Her mother-in-law yelled at her suddenly from behind, and she dropped her basket in fright. Shuangqing was always somewhat weak and easily frightened, and now she became worse and was easily agitated by the slightest sound. Her mother-in-law took advantage of this condition to oppress her even more. She wrote a song lyric on the lone goose, to the tune of "Xi huang hua man":*

*Blue fills the distant sky,*
*But sunset clouds scatter in patterns*
*Like flecks of tiny red buds.*
*When I hear you call, I fear you're too near.*
*When I look your way, I fret, you're too far.*
*A lone goose, just one,*
*How can you know where to fly?*
*Heavy frost already chills the sandbar cattails,*
*Worse still, you've no other birds to ask for solace.*
*Find a hidden spot to rest;*
*Though the phoenix pair exemplifies love,*
*How can we share such ties of affection?*

*Anxiously, I implore you, keep still,*
*Find a narrow bank or stream,*
*To let the fleeting years pass.*
*With the grains all gathered,*
*The nets are cruelly fixed,*
*Entranced, you're easily frightened.*
*On all sides, cold and mist.*
*Does your broken heart match the beauty's feelings?*

*How much love can your small heart hold?*
*The night is not yet old,*
*But flight-weary, you rest by mistake*
*in an open field.*

(*RN*, 2.81)

As with her lyric on the chrysanthemum, Shuangqing here identifies herself profoundly with the subject of this lyric, the lone goose she sees resting on a path between two fields. The bird is lost, disoriented, cut off from its flock, and thus vulnerable to loneliness and ultimately to capture by hostile hunters. The suffering poet, also lonely, frightened, and forsaken, offers the solace of close friendship and understanding. She fears for the bird's safety and notes that she and the goose, in contrast to the happily paired phoenixes, both suffer the absence of an understanding mate. She implores the goose to seek shelter and notes that the hunters' nets are "cruelly fixed," just to catch such a bird for a meal. She compares herself directly to the goose, and asks, "Does your broken heart match the beauty's feelings?" in reference to herself. The second question, "How much love can your small heart hold?" implies that it can hold a lot, but as with the beauty, such love only results in a "broken heart" because they are both alone without companionship or comfort in an ever colder and more hostile environment. Finally, though the night is still young, the bird is so tired that it ominously rests "by mistake in an open field." As in her lyric on the chrysanthemum, the poet sympathizes so deeply with her subject that the two are one and the same, yet she is not able to save the flower from the killing frost or the goose from the hunters' nets. Both the poet and her friends are lonely, unappreciated, and left to suffer in their hostile and desolate surroundings.

LIU LAOSHI: THE AUTHENTIC LYRIC VOICE OF SHUANGQING

The three lyrics quoted here from Shi's *Random Notes* had a profound impact on Liu Laoshi. I had read them in anthologies early on in my study of Shuangqing but had not attempted to translate them into English. I was still learning the rudiments of the song lyric as a genre at this point, but to Liu Laoshi, reading these lyrics was like eating candy. As a specialist in earlier Chinese poetry, and like many other Chinese literary scholars, she had never bothered to read much poetry from the Ming and Qing dynasties, assuming it to be derivative and uninspired. But she quickly fell in love with these three lyrics. She was amazed at their power, the beauty of their imagery, and the simple yet subtle and profound way the author identifies so completely with the living objects she describes. In her excitement over Shuangqing's song-lyric voice, Liu Laoshi found herself growing impatient with Shi's rambling narrative, his endless description of his friends and their second- and thirdhand reactions to Shuangqing's poetry. It was steadily becoming clearer to me why Shuangqing became a famous poet on the strength of her song lyrics. They are distinctive in their focus on simple observations of everyday rural life, in the intense way Shuangqing identifies with her subjects, and in her simple yet self-conscious way of describing herself as an overworked, sick, and lonely farm wife and poet. These three lyrics in particular came to define for Liu Laoshi "the authentic voice" of Shuangqing.

After these three distinctive lyrics, Shi Zhenlin switches to other topics related to Shuangqing and her interactions with her literati admirers. Finally, after about two dozen pages of miscellaneous anecdotes, we have another famous song lyric. As with the others, Shi introduces it very briefly.

***Ode to the Fading Lamp***

*Shuangqing once admonished her husband about his gambling. He got angry and locked her in the kitchen; she sat there on a pile of firewood facing the dim lamp and crying. For the fading lamp she wrote this song lyric:*

*You are already dim and I forget to blow;*
*You want to brighten, but who will trim you?*
*You face me like an unlit firefly.*
*On the earthen steps I hear cold rain*
*Dripping past the third watch.*
*Alone, weak, weary, and sleepless,*
*Hard to extinguish,*
*You harbor too much passion.*
*Your scented oil is all gone,*
*But your fragrant wick is not yet cold.*
*Keep Shuangqing company for a little bit longer.*

*Your tiny tiny flame*
*Slowly fades into a motionless speck.*
*I still hope you can linger*
*and blossom with a flare.*

*Better here than on a wild windswept pond*
*as a wavering flickering fisherman's lamp.*
*Once the toiling autumn moths have scattered,*
*I am already ill,*
*And when has my illness ever improved?*
*We stare at each other for a good long while.*
*I hazily drift off to sleep;*
*but sleep only leads to frightening dreams.*

(*RN*, 3.12)

Here Shuangqing identifies herself not with a living object but with a fading oil lamp beside her sickbed. The scented oil in the lamp is about gone, and the wick has just enough oil to flicker dimly. She implies that both the lamp's light and the poet's life are weak, nearly extinguished, but still desiring to survive. As with the chrysanthemum, Shuangqing sympathizes deeply with the dim lamp in its struggle to keep burning, but she is too weak to sustain or protect it. She forgets to stimulate its flame by blowing on it, and she has not the strength (or perhaps resources) to add oil or trim the wick. Yet the lamp, like the poet, though weak and sick, is "hard to extinguish" because it "harbors too much passion." This passion, *qing*, is the same passion, often defined as love, that some of Shuangqing's literati admirers are crazed by. Who harbors too much passion? The absence of personal pronouns makes the reference ambiguous, but the implication is clear: both the lamp and the poet. Yet passion is after all what keeps them "hard to extinguish" and still alive. As with the chrysanthemum, Shuangqing finds solace and companionship in the lamp's presence, and she implores it to keep her company and not to abandon her to the cold darkness of a rainy night in late autumn. Despite the absence of oil in the lamp, she still has hope that it might not only survive but actually flare up with an auspicious flash of illumination to give her cause for hope, even if against all reason.

Shuangqing offers encouragement to the fading lamp, even as it is reduced to a tiny motionless speck of light. Things could be worse, she reminds the lamp. It could be struggling for survival, tossed hither and yon on a wild windswept pond as a fisherman's lamp. Better to be in Shuangqing's poor hut, out of the wind and rain, even if its companion is ill and trying to get to sleep. The poet and the lamp do keep each other company for a long while, and then the poet drifts off to sleep. The term that modifies the verb *to sleep* is *menglong*, which means both "hazily" and the time when the moon sets just before dawn. So the night is almost over by the time Shuangqing drifts off to sleep. The final line ends the lyric ominously, as "sleep only leads to frightening dreams."

Shuangqing's identification with the fading oil lamp is much like her earlier identification with the chrysanthemum and the lone goose. She excels in this *yongwu* (singing of objects) tradition, identifying so completely with the object described that it mirrors her deepest self. What is impressive about Shuangqing's lyrics is precisely that her metaphor images seem so natural and unforced. She paints a very convincing self-portrait through these objects.

### *Shuangqing's Lyrics for Hanxi*

Near the end of chapter 3, Shi introduces Shuangqing's only close female friend, a neighbor girl named Hanxi. Although she is illiterate, Hanxi appreciates Shuangqing's art and shares her Buddhist outlook. Unfortunately for Shuangqing, Hanxi is married and moves away from Xiaoshan. When she returns to visit her parents, Shuangqing is too ill to attend a feast in her honor, but she responds with two song lyrics that were to become two of her most famous works.

> *A neighbor girl, Hanxi, was newly wed and had just returned to visit her parents. She was quite intelligent. When she saw Shuangqing pounding rice or carrying water by herself, she would always help her. When Shuangqing was ill, she would sit on her bed crying for Shuangqing. She was not literate, but she loved Shuangqing's calligraphy. She asked her to write out the Heart Sutra and to teach her to recite it. This time she was about to return to her new husband's home, so her parents had a feast for her and invited Shuangqing. But because of her illness, Shuangqing could not attend. Hanxi refused to eat and instead took her portion and had it sent to Shuangqing. Shuangqing cried and wrote a song lyric for her to the tune of "Mo yu'er":*
>
> *Cheered by the end of the rains,*
> *The evening clouds in the west appear;*
> *Beyond the lonely mountain haze, sky light blue.*
> *Where strips of moss are dry, fragrant shoes can tread,*
> *Sharp prints left on the dark mud still soft.*
> *Clamor of people's voices:*
> *Want to go but have to lean on the brushwood door*
> *Vainly harboring deep deep desire.*
> *My thoughts of you are all one strand,*

*Spun under the moonlight,*
*Threaded with grief, strung with remorse,*
*Pearls of tears enough for one whole string.*

*After dusk, this fever persists,*
*Who will comfort my struggle to breathe?*
*Through the small window the wind*
*Shoots in like an arrow;*
*Springtime red, autumn white, no awareness.*
*Small bud like me, difficult to pick.*
*Our next meeting is so far off*
*I hear the heart-broken one*
*Has already been sent her lavish feast.*
*The sunset hurts the eyes;*
*Don't look to the horizon,*
*The horizon only shows a few cold clouds drifting apart.*
(*RN*, 3.51–52)

This is an unusual lyric for Shuangqing in that it is written for another woman, her closest female friend, Hanxi, who lived next door before she married and moved away. Against the background of a sunset following heavy rains, this lyric pours out Shuangqing's regret at missing Hanxi's feast and makes clear her own suffering in sickness and pain, her gratitude for Hanxi's gesture of close friendship, and her great affection for Hanxi and sorrow on their having to part.

She paints beautiful imagery of a clearing sky after a rain and closely observes the footprints in the mud left by the one who has brought her Hanxi's portion of a feast given in her honor. Many of the terms of endearment that Shuangqing uses suggest parting lovers: "Vainly harboring deed deep desire"; "My thoughts of you are all one strand"; "the heart-broken one." But such terms were also common expressions of friendship that men often used with other men, and women with other women. She concludes verse one with a whole series of spinning and sewing images to express her sense of longing for her friend.

This is the kind of skill with imagery that one comes to expect in Shuangqing's lyrics. She describes her discomfort in sickness and her disappointment at not being able to participate in Hanxi's feast. Other hallmarks of the Shuangqing style: she observes nature's seeming indifference to human suffering, "Springtime red, autumn white, no awareness," and she portrays herself as a flower, "small bud like me, difficult to pick," suggesting that she remains an isolated beauty out of reach of any would-be lovers. After lamenting that "our next meeting is so far off," she concludes the lyric by observing that even the beautiful sunset is too painful to watch (though watch it she does): "The sunset hurts the eyes; / Don't look to the horizon, / The horizon only shows a few cold clouds drifting apart."

Immediately following this lyric is a second one for Hanxi, even more romantic in tone. It is full of doublets, repeated characters, in the style of Li Qingzhao (1084–c. 1151), China's most famous woman poet.

*And with light ink finely written on a reed, she wrote the following song lyric to the tune "Fenghuang taishang yichuixiao":*

*Tiny tiny flecks of cloud,*
*Fine fine threads of light;*
*here and gone, bright and dim, hard to quench.*
*Just now despairing, despondent*
*Flicker, flicker, waver, waver,*
*Stare and stare at hill upon hill, stream after stream.*
*The person moves away*
*Dimmer dimmer, farther farther.*
*From now on,*
*sickness upon sickness, suffering upon suffering,*
*Just like tonight.*
*A deep blue sky,*
*I ask Heaven, no reply;*
*Look at tiny tiny Shuangqing,*
*Wavering, weary, and bored.*
*What's worse: Whom do I see? Who sees me?*
*Who will mourn the delicate fragile flower?*
*Who will see her joy and delight, secretly using plain powder*
*to write and transcribe, depict and describe.*
*Who still cares, life upon life, age after age, night after night, day after day?*

(*RN*, 3.52)

LIU LAOSHI: "LOOK AT ALL THESE DOUBLETS!" While Liu Laoshi admired Shuangqing's first lyric for Hanxi, she was utterly amazed by this one. "Look at this!" she exclaimed, even before I read it through the first time. "It's full of doublets *(diezi)!*"

I was still such a novice at reading song lyrics that I had to ask, "Why are you so excited about doublets?"

"See all these double or repeated characters?" she patiently asked. "Li Qingzhao was famous for this kind of repetition."

I did a quick count. Twenty-one times Shuangqing repeats the same character twice. Another four times, she repeats a pair of characters but reverses their order. There are only ninety-five characters in the entire lyric, so this kind of repetition fills over half of the piece.

To me this appeared to be a fairly simple technique of endless repetition. "Why is this so noteworthy?" I asked naively.

"In fact it's very difficult to do this well," she explained. "The trick is not just repetition but to use doublets (also called reduplicatives) in a way that still seems natural in the speech pattern and rhyme scheme of the lyric form. The beauty of this lyric is that Shuangqing executes these repetitions so naturally."

During my year in Taiwan, Grace Fong kindly sent me a conference paper she had written in 1990 (and later published in 1994) in which she translated and analyzed this lyric. I shared Fong's analysis with Liu Laoshi and was pleased for a change to be able to use my English expertise to explain something my teacher would otherwise not understand. Fong commented on the particular use of "feminine discourse" in this lyric, "that intense preoccupation with the relationship between being and being seen. The subject, in order to constitute its identity, needs an external perceiver. Though the perceiver would function as a reflector, thereby affirming the being of the woman perceived, it is not just the mirror, the male gaze, but that longed-for, absent *zhiyin,* the understanding and caring friend who can break through the boundaries of loneliness and alienation to touch the heartstrings of the self. *Qing,* emotion, desires its fulfillment in the other."

Fong concluded her discussion with an unanswered question: "Who is the feminine subject of the song?" (1994, 133). Obviously, the subject was Shuangqing herself, but Fong also pointed out the many ambiguities in Shi Zhenlin's account of Shuangqing. How could we ever be sure just who Shuangqing was?

Liu Laoshi was very interested in my Chinese account of Fong's incisive analysis, and I was pleased to be able to share it with her. Yet Liu Laoshi was also troubled by the uncertainty of our poet's identity. On the one hand she was utterly thrilled by this lyric, and on the other hand she was suspicious. It didn't quite fit her intuitive Shuangqing authenticity test. It seemed too self-consciously manipulative, too contrived with doublets, and too "romantic" to be consistent with Shi Zhenlin's characterization of Shuangqing.

"You know, " she said reluctantly, "I'm a bit bothered by the very tune of this lyric. It seems more suited to a high-class courtesan than Shuangqing. I'm just doubtful that a modest woman like Shuangqing would even write a lyric on this tune."

"How to write such a poem on a reed is another problem!" I thought to myself, but not wanting to raise more doubts at this point, I asked her instead to read it aloud so we could both hear an expert's rendition of it.

For a change, I found myself ready to argue against Liu Laoshi's doubt. "Concerning the issue of flirtation," I started out cautiously, "Don't you think it's significant that this romantic sounding lyric is directed to another woman? Here, finally, Shuangqing has found a female *zhiyin,* the intimate and understanding friend."

"Yes," Liu Laoshi agreed. "You're right about that."

With this vote of confidence, I continued. "In contrast to most village women, Hanxi (despite her own illiteracy) appreciates Shuangqing's abilities and offers her the sympathetic love and understanding needed to inspire her best poems. And in contrast to Shuangqing's literati admirers, Hanxi offers love and understanding that is more unconditional, and unburdened by flirtatious overtures; she doesn't send or demand matching rhymes of passion. In addressing a female *zhiyin* Shuangqing can express romantic longings without risking scandal."

As the bell rang, Liu Laoshi concluded our class by taking some solace in my argument, even if she still had doubts. In any case, she admitted, "Whoever wrote this, it is the most amazing of all the lyrics attributed to Shuangqing." At my urging, she read it through, very slowly and deliberately, one last time.

All the lyrics I have discussed thus far were supposedly written in 1733. As the narrative of Shuangqing in *Random Records* nears an end, Shi Zhenlin talks more about Shuangqing's admirers and less about her. The last two of her lyrics in *Random Notes* Shi reports that he received in the second lunar month of 1735.

***Persecution and Springtime Disappointment***

*I left Xiaoshan in 1733. In the summer of 1734, I traveled around Menghe. In the spring of 1735, I stayed at Lanling. I heard that Shuangqing was ever more careful in serving her mother-in-law so that the neighbors all referred to her as especially filial. Her husband was becoming more and more cruel, but Shuangqing catered to his every whim, never daring to cross him in the slightest. She worked hard all year long, leaving her tattered writings and drafts all locked up, never even stealing a glance at them. One evening she happened to pick up the Surangama Sutra and began reading it by the kitchen lamp. When her mother-in-law came back from her evening out, she grabbed the book from Shuangqing and scolded her saying, "This broken book is just waste paper for* xiucais [lower-level examination degree-holders] *to stare at. Do you think a dirt-poor silly slave girl like you can hope to take an exam to become a female government student?" Once Shuangqing began to wash her inkstone when her husband saw her and angrily said, "So you want to steal some loafing time playing with that piece of mud. You'd be better off scraping the charcoal off the pots and pans to fertilize the fields." Shuangqing's calligraphy was both dignified and graceful. She wrote only on coarse fire-starting paper, to keep a daily record of the fermented wine for her husband. Her husband couldn't read, but he stared warily from one side and rebuked her saying, "That character is upside down." She just laughed and said, "No it isn't!"*

*Her Plum Blossom lyric goes:*

*I laugh at my sickly state.*
*I've been busy with spring for quite some time,*
*Going out to inspect the high blossoms.*
*My face is now worn and haggard,*
*Who knows on whose behalf?*
*Since my sickness, I share misfortune with the flowers.*
*Just now winter clothes must be quickly washed.*
*Springtime waters are so cold,*
*My wrists fear the drenching.*
*The harsh east wind*
*Blows the* [plum's] *cold fragrance;*
*A fine sliver of new moon returns.*
*Spring passions fill the sky, blossoms falling everywhere,*
*Enough to tire Shuangqing;*
*In my dream I pick them up in vain.*
*I summon the spirit of the butterfly,*
*Wipe the tears of the oriole,*
*And deep in the night read the Surangama Sutra.*
*There are many moving lines on the sadness of spring's passing,*
*On the sour, the bitter, life, and death,*
*All so movingly written.*
*I pray to the springtime years,*

*And kowtow to Guanyin,*
*So often the divination slips are all used.*

(*RN*, 4.46–47)

As the chrysanthemum symbolizes autumn, so the plum blossom signifies spring. And of course, spring to the poet conjures images of rebirth, youth, life, and love. This is a song of spring, the happiest time of year, but because of her sickness and her lost hope for love, Shuangqing can find little pleasure even in spring. She wants to partake of the hope and love associated with spring and so goes out to inspect the season's first plum blossoms, but her illness makes her too tired to enjoy the experience. She records her worn and haggard appearance (to satisfy the male gaze?) and hints that the cause might be pining for a lost and secret love: "Who knows on whose behalf?" In her sickness, she shares misfortune with the early-blooming flowers, as the weather still chills to the bone, threatening poet and flowers alike. Yet the work of springtime washing must be done. Though able to recognize the beauties of spring—the plum's fragrance, the new moon, and blossoms filling the sky—such recognition alone drains Shuangqing of strength. She manages to pick up the blossoms only in her dream, a glimmer of hope for love, but that too is in vain. Her only solace in the end lies in religion, the Surangama Sutra, and the worship of Guanyin, the goddess of mercy. Spring ultimately offers no hope and no solace; the only guarantee of spring seems to be that it will soon pass.

The final song lyric by Shuangqing in *Random Notes* is a bittersweet song of springtime.

*Here is her song lyric on taking lunch to the plowing field:*

*Purple paths in springtime brightness.*
*Slowly tie on my head a spring scarf,*
*And take a meal out to spring plowing.*
*The tiny plum is thin in spring,*
*The fine grass shines with spring,*
*Step after step the springtime field is alive with spring.*
*Recall that year when spring was fine,*
*To a springtime swallow*
*I poured out spring's desire.*
*But now this year,*
*I think spring notes and spring tears*
*Have been frozen into springtime ice.*

*I have cherished spring, ached for spring, for how many springs?*
*A layer of spring mist*
*locks in a spring oriole.*
*I give spring to you,*
*You give spring to me;*
*Which of us is the spirit of spring?*
*I can distinguish spring's head from spring's tail;*
*But it's hard to tell a spring dream from a spring awakening.*
*What demon of spring*
*Makes a springtime illness last one whole spring?*
*Spring has wronged Shuangqing.*

(*RN*, 4.47)

Something of a stylistic tour de force, this lyric uses the character *chun* (spring) at least once in every line, some twenty-one times in all. Given the happy connotations of spring—love, youth, optimism, rebirth—it is quite a feat to paint a picture of such despondency with such a shower of springtime imagery. Shuangqing begins with a rural scene in spring, notes the special qualities of spring, life and rebirth, that suggest hope. She recalls the spring when she "poured out spring's desire," that is the *qing*, passion or love, that Shuangqing shares in common with her literati admirers. She contrasts the hope and excitement of that year with the despair of the present, when her notes or letters and her tears are frozen in "springtime ice." As in other lyrics, she expresses her own profound identification with a personified object, only in this case the object is springtime, or the spirit of spring, itself.

She has cherished spring and ached for spring year after year. She is solicitous of spring, addresses spring directly, and takes on the role of spring herself. "I give spring to you, / You give spring to me; / Which of us is the spirit of spring?" The problem Shuangqing now has with spring is that it brings her only illness, and none of the other things spring is supposed to bring. She is the spring oriole locked in a layer of spring mist. She is so ill that she has trouble distinguishing dreams from waking consciousness. She may also be expressing her own echo of Shi Zhenlin's argument that dreams and waking reality are on the same plane of existence, equally real and illusory, and in any case indistinguishable.

In the conclusion of this lyric, Shuangqing's normal sense of compassion gives way to anger. She moves from cherishing spring and aching for spring to blaming spring for having wronged or deceived her. The wrong and the deceit is the illness that spring brings. Such is the poet's romantic worldview that the poetic associations of spring come to be seen as a personal betrayal of the poet by springtime itself when those associations fail to materialize in her life.

There was a palpable sense of disappointment in our tiny classroom when Liu Laoshi and I finished reading these lyrics and approached the end of Shi Zhenlin's Shuangqing narrative. We wanted more Shuangqing lyrics to compare with these, and we kept hoping we would stumble on some key to the various puzzles Shi Zhenlin left unsolved. But Shi simply let Shuangqing fade gradually out of the picture. We were left on our own to try to decipher his message. Because of the many implausibilities, inconsistencies, and contradictions in Shi Zhenlin's narrative, I came to suspect that Shuangqing might be a fictional character. Liu Laoshi was equally inclined to believe in Shuangqing's historical reality, precisely because of the power and distinctiveness of these lyrics. She dealt with the implausibilities and inconsistencies in Shi Zhenlin's narrative by sifting them out and keeping the best lyrics—on the chrysanthemum, the lone goose, the fading lamp—as works too good and too distinctive to have been fabricated by Shi Zhenlin.

I had to agree with Liu Laoshi that the following qualities make Shuangqing's song lyrics very distinctive:

Her simple depiction of rural life and its everyday chores

Her profound personal identification with other lonely objects, animate and inanimate alike

Her self-conscious self-portrait of a persecuted but proud and principled peasant woman poet

Her powerful manipulation of the feminine style of song lyrics, and her ingenious employment of doublets

In contemporary debates over the historical reality of Shuangqing, these distinctive qualities of her poetry become very important. But whatever contemporary scholars may think, the vast majority of Chinese literary critics and historians, from the eighteenth century to the present, have seen these lyrics as authentic works by an authentic peasant woman poet.

*eight* ·

# *Searching for Xiaoshan, Part 2*

Xuebu Town, Saturday, November 1, 1997

I wake up at 7:30 A.M., pleased to have the night at the Peace and Happiness Hotel behind us, and cheered to see bright sunshine and clear blue skies. Today we interview our local informants, explore Fang Shan, and just possibly discover the original site of Shi Zhenlin's (or Shuangqing's) village of Xiaoshan. This should be the climax of our trip!

After paying our bill for the night (eighty yuan, or about ten dollars for our party of three) and sharing an ample breakfast of meat-filled steamed buns *(baozi)* and a giant bowl of beancurd soup at a crowded open-air restaurant, we walk a couple of blocks to the township government headquarters for our morning discussions. We are joined in a conference room by three elderly gentlemen from Xuebu Township, Wang Rongsheng, a retired newspaper reporter, Bao Jiujing, from the Xuebu Township Historical Records Office, and Ye Furong, a seventy-eight-year-old retired worker, and by our local hosts, Mr. Zhang, the town head, and his assistants Mr. Pan and Mr. Sun. After introductions all around, as boiling water is poured over local tea leaves in tall clear classes, we begin our discussions. I marvel at this hospitality from local government officials on a sunny autumn Saturday morning.

### *"Can You Help us Find Xiaoshan?"*

Hongsheng explains our purpose in coming here. We are studying Shi Zhenlin's eighteenth-century memoir and have come to Xuebu Township to learn anything we can about this area that Shi Zhenlin described as the home of the peasant woman poet Shuangqing. Noting that Shi Zhenlin described a village called Xiaoshan at the foot of Mount Siping, Hongsheng reports that we have reason to believe that Shi Zhenlin's Mount Siping might be today's Fang Shan, also called Mount Siping, only with a different character for *ping*. We pass Du Laoshi's book around and note that we have heard there was once a center of learning here called the Xiaoshan Academy.

Mr. Bao explains some historical background about Fang Shan and notes that many changes have occurred in this area in modern times: modern highways were constructed through here in the 1930s, and in 1993 an expressway was built to Nanjing. Two large reservoirs were built in 1955 and 1958 (the latter during Chairman Mao's disastrous economic experiment called the Great Leap Forward). In the 1970s a collective tea farm was established, and many trees have been planted throughout the area in the past two decades.

### *Shuangqing Connection Number 1: Cutting Kindling on Mount Siping*

Hongsheng notes that Shuangqing's husband made his living cutting firewood on the mountain, and this gets a lively response from everyone. At times, with three people talking at once in local accents, I think they might as well be speaking Korean for all I can understand. Fortunately, Du Laoshi has a tape recorder, and she would later send me her complete account of our discussions. I try to focus on one person at a time and frantically jot down what I manage to catch. Mr. Pan notes that cutting kindling was a major occupation in this area, as Fang Shan was covered with a coarse wild grass that was cut, tied in large bundles, and carried down to Xuebu Town to be sold for kindling. Mr. Ye ventures that in Qing times, people went to Fang Shan just for cutting kindling. There was even a knife associated with Fang Shan that was cleverly designed solely for the purpose of cutting twigs and grass for kindling. It had a double-sided detachable and reversible blade, so when one side got dull, one just turned the blade around and continued cutting. I recall that Shuangqing once described her husband leaving for the mountain with his grass-cutting knife.

Mr. Wang adds, "People spoke of Fang Shan as a 'storehouse' of wealth. There were popular sayings about this: 'If you want Xuebu Town to get rich, you have to open up the "storehouse" of Fang Shan.' And another, 'When the store house of Fang Shan is open, every household is rich and content.' "

### *Connection Number 2: Rock-Strewn Mountain*

But I know people don't get rich cutting wild grass for kindling. And these sayings are from the twentieth century. What they are talking about is the rich stone and mineral deposits of Fang Shan. Mr. Wang continues, "The Xuebu area is rich in stone, mineral ores, and iron ore. Everybody in Fang Shan today lives in a two-story house [i.e., is wealthy]. The way to get rich is mainly in running a factory. Quarries are at the base of all the local industries, which include building materials, cement, lime, and stone. This too, I think to myself, would be consistent with Shi Zhenlin's description of Mount Siping as covered with stones of every shape, color, and size.

### *Connection Number 3: Peasant's Straw and Hemp Sandals*

We are not so interested in the current economy of Xuebu Town and try to bring the discussion back to the eighteenth century. Hongsheng notes that Shuangqing made her husband straw sandals for his trips up the mountain. This triggers another outburst of opinion. As Du Laoshi's notes attest, "Everyone chimed in at once: 'In those days a pair of sandals lasted only a day. Every household made its own sandals. They didn't have shoes back then.' "

Hongsheng remarks, "Shuangqing's family was poor. Was it a luxury to have sandals made of hemp?"

Again, several responses, all to the effect that hemp and straw sandals were made by everyone. Hemp grew wild on the mountain, so it was not a luxury item. Hemp sandals were more durable than straw sandals, and when wet they would stretch, whereas straw sandals would get tighter. All agree that hemp and ramie sandals were better than straw ones. Mr. Wang explains the evolution of footwear in the area as follows: Originally people wore straw sandals; then they developed "mountain stockings," or stockings worn over their sandals and pulled nearly up to the knee. In the 1950s, people wore shoes or sandals with cloth sewn to soles made of used rubber tires. Finally, in the 1970s, leather shoes came into general use.

I think to myself that this is all very interesting, but we're not learning much directly about Shi Zhenlin or Shuangqing.

### *Connection Number 4: "Where Is Eight-Li Temple?"*

Hongsheng must be thinking the same thing, because he tries now to bring us back to Shi Zhenlin by asking about the possible location of the Xiaoshan Academy, which Mr. Yu Zhao has told us was located at a temple called Bali Miao (Eight-Li Temple). Mr. Ye responds, "There are two places with that name: a South Bali Miao at Jianguo Village (where we visited the day before), and a West Bali Miao at Wuli Peng (meaning five-*li* shacks). No one seems ever to have heard of a Xiaoshan Academy or an Ougeng Hall (the Plowing in Pairs Hall where Shi Zhenlin claimed to have stayed and studied with Shuangqing's landlord, Zhang Mengzhan).

### *Connection Number 5:*<br>*Prominent Landlord Family Named Zhang*

Although they draw a blank on these references, our Xuebu friends proceed to tell us all they know about every temple in the area, from the Tang dynasty onward. They also note that another academy, a center of Confucian studies, was built here in the Song period (960–1279), for the education of a family surnamed Zhang. The genealogy of this Zhang family is one of the few family genealogies from this area to survive the Cultural Revolution. In the frenzy of the attack on all traditions in the Cultural Revolution years of the mid-1960s, young Red Guards ransacked private homes and destroyed every private library they could find. Many families destroyed their own old books to forestall such humiliating and destructive attacks. Somehow, the Zhang family genealogy, spanning many centuries, escaped destruction in those terrible years. It is housed, in over fifty volumes, in Jintan City. Lightbulb! Perhaps this is the same family as Shuangqing's landlord, Zhang Mengzhan. Du Laoshi whispers to me that we must ask about seeing this genealogy later in Jintan.

### *Connection Number 6:*<br>*"Xiaoshan Sounds Like the Shi Family Mountainside!"*

Hongsheng tries to keep us on track by reading, or rather, paraphrasing in vernacular Chinese, the passage from Shi's *Random Notes* where he describes Xiaoshan's location and scenery. This is the passage I showed Hongsheng the day before, which locates Xiaoshan ten *li* south of the famous Mao Shan. Once Hongsheng completes this passage, there is, most amazingly, unanimous agreement from all six Xuebu people in the room: "This sounds like Shi Jia Shan Linchang (the Shi Family Mountainside), located in the West Bali Miao district." We are surprised and delighted to have such immediate unanimity on the location of Xiaoshan. This might also corroborate the information we got the day before from Mr. Yu Zhao, locating the Xiaoshan Academy with a temple (or district) called Eight-Li Temple.

### *Connection Number 7: Local Caves and Temples*

Other landmarks in Shi Zhenlin's account of Xiaoshan include a "Yanzhi Dong," Rouge Cave, where he says women ground colored rock into powder for makeup, and Huashen Miao, the Temple of the Goddess of Flowers. These references mean nothing to our informants, but Mr. Wang says, on the way to Fang Shan, there is a Nainai Dong (Grandma's Cave), where women would enter and sit for a time in order to improve their health and insure a safe childbirth. Du Laoshi is quick to assume this might be the same place as Shi Zhenlin's Rouge Cave, and she points out that the rich mineral deposits in this area would naturally produce the kind of colored rocks that Shi Zhenlin describes in his account of Rouge Cave.

There was also a very old Buddhist temple, Shifuo An, Temple of the Stone Buddha, in this area, dating from the tenth century. It was destroyed in the Cultural Revolution. Women also went there to pray for good health. Du Laoshi asks whether the goddess of flowers was worshiped in this area, and Mr. Ye says indeed she was. For the prevention of smallpox, acting troupes would perform plays in praise of the goddess of flowers on the twelfth day of the first lunar month, at the end of the New Year celebrations. Du Laoshi sees this as confirming Shi Zhenlin's description of a Temple of the Goddess of Flowers.

### *Connection Number 8: Importance of Education*

Du Laoshi asks whether or not this area ever had a tradition of talented women writers. Her question draws a complete blank from our friends, but they are quick to point out that Jintan County in general, and Xuebu Town in particular, have always had a relatively high cultural level. The oldest member of our group, Mr. Ye, recalls his youth, when private tutors recruited students from local families to study with them, for a fee, at a Buddhist temple. He himself went to this kind of school and learned to recite the *Four Books* and *Five Classics* (even though he was born eight years after the fall of the Qing dynasty and fifteen years after the old examination system was abolished). Du Laoshi is quite pleased with all this and sees the high cultural level of Jintan County as further circumstantial evidence supporting the literal truth of Shi's memoir.

### *Connection Number 9: Transportation in the Eighteenth Century*

Hongsheng then asks about what kind of transportation Shi Zhenlin might have used to travel from his home on Lake Yao to this area. All agree that he could have made the trip very conveniently on the Xuebu Dahe, the Big Xuebu River, which extends from Fang Shan to Lake Yao. He might have had to walk only three or four *li* (just over a mile) at the end of his voyage to get to Xiaoshan Village (i.e., Shi Family Mountainside).

### *Connection Number 10: Xuebu Zhen Equals Township of the Wandering Immortals*

My brain, tired of following the rapid-fire Chinese from five or six people at once, literally checks out of the conversation. And my stomach suggests it is time for lunch. Just as I am drifting off in a daydream, Mr. Wang gets my full attention with the remark that in Qing times, Xuebu Zhen was also called Youxian Township, that is, the Township of the Wandering Immortals! However tenuous some of these "connections" are between contemporary Xuebu Zhen and the question of Shuangqing's existence, this is clearly the right place to search for the vanished world of Shi Zhenlin's memoir.

### *Connection Number 11: Zhang Ting (Xiaomei), Another Contemporary Shuangqing!*

After a round of photographs in front of the town government headquarters (see figure 10), we all go to lunch together. We dine again in a private dining room of the Xuebu Township government headquarters. We are joined at lunch by a seven-year old girl, Zhang Ting, the granddaughter of Township Head Zhang Jinsheng. Yesterday she sat in on some of our meetings, sometimes drawing pictures, sometimes listening to our discussions, and sometimes entertaining herself quietly in a corner of the room, oblivious of the adults around her. Zhang explains that her parents are both out of town on business right now, so she is staying with him and his wife. I call her Xiaomei, Little Sister, and marvel at her unself-conscious independence. Her front baby teeth are missing, and when she walks her jet black pair of pony tails bounce against her bright red jacket. She is utterly charming! At lunch, she astonishes me when she explains to one adult how to write the character for Xiao in

Xiaoshan. She must have heard this yesterday in our initial discussions of our purpose in Xuebu Town. She seems to take this adult world right in stride, even while remaining firmly in her own preferred childhood world. I joke with Du Laoshi that we have found yet another modern-day Shuangqing!

### *Explorations of Fang Shan*

After lunch we prepare to board a large pickup truck that will be our vehicle for the day. Although the cab has double seats, enough room for six people, there are ten or twelve of us, and I quickly make a move to sit in the back of the truck. It is a bright sunny day, and the open air views should be spectacular. Everyone objects, presumably on the grounds that the foreign guest, middle-aged professor, should sit in the cab. I boast that I grew up on a farm, used to drive a pickup truck to high school, and would be more than comfortable in the open air. To prove my point, I jump in the back of the truck and sit on the floor. Du Laoshi, as insistent on her farm background as I am on mine, promptly joins me. This is too much for our hosts to take, and they quickly produce two wooden folding chairs that they place at the front of the truck bed, insisting that Du and I use them. As we graciously accept the chairs, several of our group, including Xiaomei and Mr. Wang, the retired newspaper reporter, sit on the floor of the truck bed. Hongsheng sits in front with our driver and with the township head, Mr. Zhang.

As we pull out of the government headquarters I think to myself, "What a silly way to die! Riding on a folding chair in the back of a pickup truck! All it would take is a quick sharp turn, or hitting a rut at forty miles per hour, and we go sailing into the ditch, or worse, onto the pavement. No helmets, skull fracture. Local headline reads: 'American and Chinese professors die while exploring Jintan's past.'" But we are not driving at high speeds on superhighways, after all, and fortunately our driver seems to take the corners slowly. So very quickly my attention turns back to the search for Xiaoshan.

Crossing the Big Xuebu, we notice some small wooden boats on the river, and Du Laoshi remarks that Shi might have come here on a boat just like one of these. All afternoon, Du Laoshi and I delight in imagining Shi Zhenlin on these rivers, canals, and dusty roads. In our shared excitement at being here, our differing viewpoints seem completely irrelevant. Our first stop is Wuli Peng (Five-Li Shacks). Mr. Wang explains that this was the place Shi Zhenlin called Wuli Ting (Five-Li Pavilion) in *Random Notes.* It was called Five-Li because it's about five *li* from Xuebu Town. Originally a pavilion was here, but later there were only some humble straw shacks left, so its name changed to Five-Li Shacks. We proceed another few kilometers down the Changli Highway and stop beside some tall brush, where Mr. Wang explains there once sat West Bali Miao, or West Eight-Li Temple, the site where Mr. Yu Zhao had located the Xiaoshan Academy.

### *Tile Shards at West Eight-Li Temple*

At this point, much to my surprise, the town head, Mr. Zhang, gets out of the truck carrying a shovel, climbs the roadside fence, and walks into the thick brush to see if he can dig up any remnants from the Eight-Li Temple. I quickly join him and am amazed that within ten minutes we have a dozen or more pieces of bricks and roof tiles (see figure 11). What a place to be an archaeologist, I can't help thinking to myself. Someone provides a sack to hold these relics, and I am pleased to realize that we might have souvenirs of a Qing-dynasty temple, or perhaps even the Xiaoshan Academy, a place we had never heard of before our trip here. Whether we find anything else of significance today, we have to call this a success!

### *Our Xiaoshan: The Shi Family Mountainside*

Next we drive to the Shi Jia Shan Linchang, the Shi Family Mountainside, that everyone this morning has identified with Shi Zhenlin's description of Xiaoshan. We drive up to Fang Shan from the east and pass through level fields surrounded by hills or mountains on three sides. To the north is the famous Mao Shan, embodying fifteen hundred years of Daoist religious history (see figure 12). Immediately in front of us is Fang Shan, now the site of a stone quarry. We face layer upon layer of multicolored rocks. It appears that half of Fang Shan has been blown away. Within ten minutes of our arrival, there are dynamite explosions in the distance, near the top of the mountain, and smoke and dust rises while large boulders fall. We are several hundred yards away from the action, which is okay with me. To the south of us is a small hill that Mr. Wang identifies for us as the site of Nainai Dong, where women came and sat for hours to improve their health. Du Laoshi thinks this must be Shi Zhenlin's model for Rouge Cave and asks if we might go see Nainai Dong. I am not so confident that Grandma's Cave and Rouge Cave are one and the same, but I have to admit that the multicolored rocks in this quarry make Shi Zhenlin's claim that rocks from here were ground up for women's makeup seem not entirely far-fetched. Mr. Wang says that Nainai Dong no longer exists, thanks to the blasting and quarrying of the past two decades.

We can only try to imagine what Fang Shan looked like in its natural state. Our hosts seem quite confident that this is the place Shi Zhenlin describes, with a stream, bamboo groves, and fields at the foot of a mountain covered with brush, strange protruding rock formations, and steep winding paths. I am much surprised once again as we discover ourselves standing beside a brand-new prison, recently built by Jiangsu Province on land just purchased from Xuebu Township (see figures 13 and 22). There are about a hundred inmates here, and we see prisoners hauling stone (see figure 14) and working in the fields with hoes while being watched by guards. Clearly our hosts are not trying to manipulate our location of Xiaoshan for their own convenience as a future tourist site. I think to myself, "Shuangqing felt herself imprisoned at Xiaoshan, and punished for some unknown sins of a former life. Here today we have people imprisoned at Fang Shan for known sins of this life. Somehow it all seems appropriate."

Du Laoshi marvels, "This does look like the description in *Random Notes:* Shuangqing talked of a stream west of her cottage, and fields to the south."

Hongsheng asks, "Was there a large pond in this vicinity?" He's thinking of Shi Zhenlin's reference to a pond near Xiaoshan.

"Yes," says Mr. Wang, pointing to the east, behind us. "There was a pond back that way called Yazhu Tang, Wild Boar Pond, and beside the pond was the Shifo An, the Stone Buddha Temple. It was a temple at first and later became a convent."

"So," I think to myself, "maybe Shuangqing actually considered life in a convent." I recall her nine-verse poem on her husband cutting kindling on the mountain. It begins with the line, "Not ready for vows and incense in a cloistered convent, / My heart is cold and unrippled as a clear still pool." Maybe I'm finally getting into the spirit of fitting all these pieces neatly together.

Mr. Wang continues, "There were many carved stone Buddhas at this temple, and a small path led from the temple through a bamboo grove, with a stream on the right, to the foot of the mountain. It then wound its way, with both steep dips and inclines, up the side of Fang Shan." This sounds very much indeed like what Shi Zhenlin described.

Hongsheng is carrying Du's copy of *Random Notes* with us, and he again reads, or paraphrases, Shi Zhenlin's description of Xiaoshan. The landscape matches pretty well (as much as we can tell in rubble left from twenty years of dynamiting), but Shi made no mention of a Stone Buddha Temple or convent. Hongsheng ponders the issue a minute and muses out loud that maybe this report of a temple is just a legend, or possibly it was built after Shi Zhenlin's time. My own view, which I keep to myself, is that at best Shi Zhenlin fictionalized his account of this peasant village and may have created the entire landscape out of his imagination. I can't help recalling having read that in the middle of rural Iowa one can now take a tour exploring the "Bridges of Madison County." Don't we all commingle history, myth, and legend in creating our own remembered past? Are we looking for a Chinese equivalent of the bridges of Madison County?

As we consider Shi's description of Xiaoshan in *Random Notes* and the location of Shuangqing's own humble house in the village, the group's conclusion is that it must have been right where the prison stands today! I take as many pictures as I can of the mountain, the quarry, our group, the nearby fields, and even the prison, feeling exhilarated to be in the shadow of Fang Shan, and out in the countryside of the District of Wandering Immortals where Shi Zhenlin once roamed. Meanwhile Du Laoshi and Hongsheng pepper our hosts with more questions about the possible correlations or noncorrelations between Shi's memoir and this site (see figure 16). Du Laoshi is particularly excited by all the parallels between this place and Shi's description of Xiaoshan, and she is quick to conclude that today's Grandma's Cave must have been Shi Zhenlin's Rouge Cave. When one of our hosts says there was also a nearby temple to the God of the Soil (ubiquitous temples in the Chinese countryside), she asks if possibly that was a later evolution from the Temple of the Goddess of Flowers described by Shi Zhenlin. Despite my private reservations about all these correlations, in the spirit of the afternoon's explorations, I'm happy to suspend disbelief.

### *Photographing a Young Shuangqing and Wild Mums at Xiaoshan*

At the beginning of our afternoon journey, Xiaomei will not let me take her picture. She is quite outgoing, friendly, and unself-conscious, until I pull out my camera and point it in her direction. Then she turns shy and waves me off with a curt "Buyao!" ("Don't want [my picture taken]!") From the moment she surprised me at lunch with her precocious explanation of how to write Xiaoshan, she has become the young Shuangqing in my mind. Months later, when writing this chapter, I would become conscious, for the first time, of the parallels between my desire to photograph Xiaomei and Shi Zhenlin's portrait-painting escapades in Xiaoshan. The problem with the "male gaze" is the power differential between the viewer and the person being viewed, a differential that is greatest when the viewer is bent on creating and controlling a permanent image of the viewee. Shi Zhenlin and his friends assumed that Shuangqing resisted their attempts to view her and paint her portrait because of her modesty, but she was also trying to preserve her dignity, to prevent her own self and her own image from being turned into objects for the use and pleasure of others. In any case, during our afternoon field trip, Xiaomei starts to warm up to me, and at some point in the afternoon, she sits on my lap on the folding chair in the back of the truck. ("So now I'm also endangering the life of a child," I fret briefly to myself!)

After we finish at the Shi Family Mountainside, our driver takes us to the banks of the Big Xuebu River and lets us off. He has to deliver Mr. Wang to his home, near Mao Shan, and he can drive faster without a human cargo in the back. I am more than happy to walk now because the sun is rapidly moving toward the horizon, and the breeze on the truck is getting chillier by the minute. Besides, it is a beautiful afternoon, and a pleasure to walk along the banks of a river Shi Zhenlin once traversed. Xiaomei asks to carry what she playfully calls my "bag of treasures," the roof tile and brick fragments. And finally, she lets me take her picture on our walk (see figure 17). I am pleased to have won her trust. We enjoy the scenery along the river with fields on both sides. Coming upon some lovely blooming wild yellow chrysanthemums outside a small one-story peasant home, I joke with Du Laoshi that "Shuangqing's autumn mums still grow in Xiaoshan!" And we take turns snapping pictures of each other with the flowers.

After walking over an hour, we begin to wonder if our driver has gotten lost on the way to Mao Shan. Xiaomei gets tired of walking, and her grandpa carries her for a while on his back, another good chance for a picture (see figure 18). I've grown very fond of Town Head Zhang. He strikes me as the kind of person whose natural charm puts others at ease. He has been so helpful to us, and so cheerful, feeding us lavish meals and spending his weekend showing us around. Would he rather be doing something else? Or are we a welcome diversion from other more boring tasks of local government?

We finally stop for a rest beside the road, and Town Head Zhang asks the people living there if they have any chairs so we can sit for a bit. Folding chairs appear immediately, followed by glasses of tea just as our truck arrives. We thank our momentary hosts, decline the just-poured tea, and board the truck. The sun his not quite set, and Hongsheng pushes our luck a little further, and asks if we might drive up to the top of Fang Shan. "Fine!" comes a quick reply. We let off a couple of people, including Xiaomei, back in town, which makes room for all of us to sit in the cab. We take a small winding road up the west side of the mountain. It is peaceful and beautiful on the mountainside, with tea fields aglow in the sunset. The mountain is aptly named Square Mountain. It not only looks square from ground level, it is also flat on top. We drive all the way to a lookout point from which we have a clear view of Mao Shan to the north, Yaji Shan to the south, and the stone quarry and the prison to the west, directly below us. Hongsheng remarks that the *fengshui* (geomancy) would have been ideal in this spot for the Xiaoshan Academy.

### *Dramatic Sunset at Xiaoshan*

As we proceed back down the west side of the mountain, we are treated to a dramatic sky streaked with clouds and a golden ball peeking through the clouds (see figure 19). Mr. Bao remarks that the "sunset at Fang Shan" is one of eight famous scenes for which Jintan is known. I think of Shuangqing's mention of sunsets in some of her song lyrics, especially her lyric written for her girlfriend and neighbor, Hanxi, which ends with the line: "The sunset hurts the eyes; / Don't look to the horizon, / The horizon only shows a few cold clouds drifting apart." One part of me says, "Every place has dramatic sunsets occasionally, so what?" Another part says, "This is too good to be just a coincidence. The spirit of Shuangqing still lives in the sunset at Xiaoshan."

### *Banquet at the Welcoming Immortal Pavilion in Xuebu Town*

We arrive back at the government compound and are surprised to see Xiaowan there with a carload of her friends including a TV crew and several others from Jintan. Included in her entourage are a lawyer friend, Mr. Xu Donggong, as well as the highest-ranking official we have met so far, a Mr. Zhu, the head of security for Jintan City and the vice secretary for the city's Committee on Politics and Law. They came two or more hours ago, hoping to film us on our explorations, but we were out in the countryside, and they had no way to reach us. Now it's too dark for filming. Undaunted, Xiaowan suggests that we'll just have to come back tomorrow. Mr. Zhang graciously invites all of us to have dinner at a nearby restaurant, the Yingxian Lou, the Welcoming Immortal Pavilion! As we all file into the private dining room with one large round table, it becomes clear that there is not room for everyone. I watch closely to see how this awkward situation will be handled. With a barely noticeable gesture, Town Head Zhang motions to Mr. Pan and another secretary that they'll just have to leave. As Mr. Pan is the one who seems to enjoy the toasting at banquets more than anything else in life, I feel uncomfortable at this apparent expulsion, especially since all these TV people have just arrived without any advance warning. But this is clearly not my problem to solve.

The plan to return tomorrow with the TV crew is fine with us, but I can't help wondering, as we sit down to eat, where we will spend the night tonight. One day without a shower and deodorant may not be so bad, but if we spend another night in the Health and Happiness Hotel, I think to myself, we not only won't look very good on TV, the cameraman and reporter won't want to get within ten feet of us. Just as we sit down at the table, Xiaowan says she's arranged a ride back to Jintan for us this evening. Hongsheng and I exchange relieved smiles that proclaim all is well with the world.

We settle into yet another lavish meal, with polite toasting all around, though the atmosphere is not quite as boisterous as the night before when we were a smaller, more intimate group. To my surprise and delight, half an hour into the meal, Mr. Pan comes walking back in with his glass and a bottle of *baijiu,* the strong stuff, and proclaims with a good laugh that he cannot let us get through this meal without a round of toasts. Starting with me and Mr. Zhu from Jintan, he works his way around the table, insisting on a *ganbei* ("bottom's up") with each of us. I stick with beer and manage, just barely, to keep my glass only half full for this toast. Having toasted each of us individually, he proposes one last toast to the whole group and cheerfully bids us all farewell. I am pleased that at least Mr. Pan has been able to have some fun after all.

After dinner we happily head back to Jintan in a car with Xiaowan. Ten minutes into the trip, the cellular phone rings, and Xiaowan asks me, out of the blue, if I like Chinese calligraphy. She has to repeat it twice because I don't understand the context of the question. When I finally understand and respond, "Of course I like it!" she follows up with a surprising announcement. Her friend, lawyer Xu (this is definitely a new China where a young man can make a living as a lawyer), is on the phone, suggesting that we might stop on our way home at a little art gallery in Jintan run by a local calligrapher and painter named Shi Han.

Several friends have gathered there and would be happy to do some calligraphy for us. Tired and dirty though we are, this sounds like too good an opportunity to pass up, so we readily accept.

### *Calligraphy Party in Honor of Shuangqing*

Much to our delight, there are half a dozen people awaiting us at the Xinjiade Gallery, including Xu, Mr. Meng Jiyuan, the author of *Random Notes on Mao Shan,* and Shi Han, the self-taught calligrapher-painter and gallery proprietor. All three of these demonstrate their calligraphy for us. First Xu, who insists he is strictly an amateur lover of calligraphy, takes a foot-long brush an inch in diameter, and on a large (two feet by four feet) piece of paper writes the characters *Xiaoshan shuyuan* (Xiaoshan Academy), followed by two large characters, *Shuangqing,* on another large sheet of paper. After these, he writes out the name of the studio of landlord Zhang Mengzhan, *Ougeng tang* (Plowing in Pairs Hall). Xu also writes out three short poems, one for me, one for Hongsheng, and one for Du Laoshi. Next, Meng Jiyuan, whose book we had earlier been given, proceeds to write a long poem describing a beautiful sunrise over mountains, in Li-shu script, old-official-style calligraphy, to present to me. And to cap off the celebration, Shi Han takes a brush and writes in his graceful and fluid calligraphy one verse of a Shuangqing lyric on a beautiful piece of special paper flecked through with gold (see figure 20).

Shi Han looks to me like any college student anywhere in the world. He has an attractive mane of shaggy black hair, black-rimmed glasses, and is wearing faded jeans, sneakers, and a baggy winter coat over his sweatshirt. He says he is largely self-taught in painting and calligraphy, having taken some classes at Henan University. I marvel at the smooth fluidity of his strokes, as the brush seems to fly over the paper, leaving characters running together in its wake. He also introduces us to another young woman, Xu Shuping, who writes song lyrics herself. We read several of her lyrics and all marvel at them (though I marvel, doubtless, with less understanding than my Chinese friends).

Looking around the gallery, with three walls covered with scrolls of paintings and calligraphy, I am particularly attracted to a painting that Shi Han has done of bamboo, flanked on both sides with the two small scrolls containing a five-character couplet in elegant calligraphy (see figure 21). The bamboo and calligraphy are both in the style of a famous eighteenth-century painter-calligrapher named Zheng Xie (more commonly known as Zheng Banqiao), another of my favorite eighteenth-century eccentrics. Xheng Xie was in many ways similar to Shi Zhenlin. He had no interest in officialdom and preferred a simple life uncorrupted by power and money. The three scrolls together are priced modestly at three hundred yuan, about forty dollars, and I tell Shi Han I would like to buy the set. He starts to take it down, saying, "In that case, I'll just give it to you, no need for you to pay."

I protest in the only way possible, by pulling three hundred yuan from my pocket immediately and putting the money on his countertop. Seeing my determination not to accept such a lavish gift, he eventually relents and takes my money, but insists on giving me a refund of fifty yuan. Thus is face saved all around. I am exhilarated by the enthusiasm of all these people for our venture in exploring the background of Shi Zhenlin's memoir, and by the thought of taking home these beautiful souvenirs of the Jintan intelligentsia.

We finally take leave of Shi Han and get back to our room at the Jintan Guest House, which looks more luxurious than ever after our two days away. Before falling asleep, I write as much about the day as I can, lest it escape unrecorded from my memory. It has been an eventful day, and tomorrow promises more of the same: breakfast with Mr. Yu Zhao, our discoverer of the Xiaoshan Academy, and a televised trip back to Fang Shan.

# nine ·

# *Flirtations and Admirers*

*Zhang Shilin . . . came to Xiaoshan and painted two portraits of Shuangqing planting melons. He asked her to inscribe a poem on one to send to Flower Lover [Duan Yuhan], and on the other one for him to keep for himself. Previously, when Flower Lover left, Shuangqing gave him a sealed envelope and directed him to read it only on the road. He went to a deserted temple, washed his hands in a stream there, licked the seal to moisten it, and pulled it open ever so carefully to avoid the slightest tear. He read it and let out an angry shout, and then he had to laugh. She had cut out a leaf in the shape of a butterfly, and on its two wings she had written two poems to the tune of "Huanxisha," making fun of Flower Lover.*

—Shi Zhenlin, *Random Notes from Xiqing,* 2.38–39

### *The Xiaoshan Quartet of Shuangqing Admirers*

Shi Zhenlin and his three friends, landlord Zhang Mengzhan, Flower Lover Duan Yuhan, and Zhao Anshu, spend a lot of time in Xiaoshan. We might call them the Xiaoshan quartet. At times, Duan and Zhao, in particular, get so carried away with their feelings for Shuangqing that they make a public spectacle of themselves. They say they are moved by feelings of admiration, empathy, and pity, but they act like obsessive aspiring lovers. They want so badly to see Shuangqing, to comfort her and soothe her, that one can't help asking, "Where does compassion end and lust begin?" Shuangqing, usually described by Shi Zhenlin as the picture of modesty and wifely loyalty to her husband, nevertheless responds to the poetic overtures of these gentlemen with poems and notes of her own. They are not blatantly erotic, but erotic overtones are unmistakably present. "Making fun" of a man in song lyrics is, after all, one way of flirting, and in the context of gender relations in eighteenth-century China, such behavior could have gotten a married woman into serious trouble. In this case, it only serves to make Shuangqing's literati admirers bolder than ever in seeking her out.

They steal glimpses of Shuangqing when they can, discuss her sad circumstances, and chant her poems to each other. They compete with one another in seeing who can most eloquently describe her in prose and poetry, and who can win the favor of her reply. Shuangqing seems ever careful to avoid direct contact with these men, though Zhao Anshu goes so far as to pace back and forth outside her house chanting her song lyrics. He writes her a poem fretting about her illness and implying that in their dreams they can be together, intimately, while in waking reality they must remain apart. Uniting in dreams was not an outlandish idea, as dreams represented experiences of the soul unshackled by the limitations of the body. But Anshu concludes that with the arrival of chilly autumn rains, even his dreams are cold, that is to say, even this avenue of communication with Shuangqing seems temporarily cut off.

Flower Lover Duan Yuhan writes a lyric for Shuangqing that is a song of love for a departed lover. He laments their physical separation and urges that they maintain contact with letters. He "secretly peaks" at her "new lyrics on old leaves" and fears that the breeze will scatter the fragrant powder. His felt need for secrecy hints that others would easily interpret their exchanges of poems as violating the bounds of propriety. Her tiny indistinct characters fill him with "uncontrollable sorrow." In his final line, he "endlessly calculates" how she is and vows never to forget her even in the next life.

### *Shuangqing's Response*

*Shuangqing rolled these poems up and put them in her sleeve without saying a word. Toward evening she went out to wash clothes with her hair wrapped in dark silk; she looked too weak to bear the weight of her clothes. Anshu climbed a willow tree and loudly chanted her poems. She finished her wash, held her head low, and quietly walked back to her house, shutting the door behind her without ever glancing his way.*

*Mengzhan received from a maid a bouquet of Golden Phoenix [Jinfeng] flowers with tiny characters written in powder on one of the petals. They were so fine they were difficult to see. This was the* jueju:

*Faint writing in light red, a plea to the Jade Emperor;*
*Dark clouds spit out a heart-breaking frost.*
*Tender sorrows finely printed on a cassia leaf;*
*The entire night the Flower Goddess is hard at work.*

*He also received this seven-character regulated verse written on an autumn Haitang leaf:*

> *Time to dry the autumn clothes in the afternoon sun;*
> *Beautiful mountains shine so bright they chase illness away.*
> *Parting feelings linger in the grass, turning into fireflies;*
> *This deep sorrow is clearer and harder than ice, like crystal.*
> *Springtime swallow then autumn goose, in constant alteration;*
> *Rain ends, new moon ascends: death gives rise to life.*
> *From the small window the light has always been dim;*
> *For the flare of the lamp I will wait till dawn.*
>
> (*RN*, 2.73–74)

Shuangqing describes herself very self-consciously in her poems as deeply unhappy, describing her own writing in powder, pleading to the Jade Emperor (for a better fate), and expressing tender sorrows on a cassia leaf. She refers to herself once again as the Flower Goddess, "hard at work the entire night," presumably writing her poetry in powder on leaves. In her longer seven-character regulated verse, she speaks directly and suggestively of "parting feelings" that "linger in the grass, turning into fireflies," and followed by "deep sorrow." There is nothing explicitly erotic here, but it is very easy to conjure from this image a spot in the grass where lovers made love before their reluctant parting. The ever dim light from the small window suggests the poet is kept in darkness, lonely and unappreciated. The flaring up of an oil lamp was seen as an auspicious sign, a flash of illumination against the lonely darkness, and in the context of the poet's deep sorrow in the dead of night, such a flare might suggest communication from or contact with a lover. In any case, the literati are encouraged by Shuangqing's verses to intensify their expressions of love and pity for her.

The next time Anshu returns to Xiaoshan, he "chanced to see Shuangqing three times," and once again "paced back and forth in front of her gate and chanted her song lyrics over and over." At one point during his performance, she returned from picking cotton and leaned on her door with her back to Anshu, who caught a glimpse of her "lifting her sleeve again and again as if to wipe away her tears." He is so moved that his heart trouble flares up and he has to take a good deal of bitter-tasting medicine before he recovers. Then Shuangqing adds fuel to the fire by sending him a *jueju* teasing him with a line about "the crazy autumn wind [that] still tries to blow the willow catkins" (*RN*, 2.74).

•⌣ LIU LAOSHI'S DOUBTS I asked Liu Laoshi about this line. "Isn't this a bit flirtatious for such a modest woman as Shuangqing is supposed to be?"

"Yes," she admitted, adding her standard qualifier, "it sounds more like Shi's fantasy than an actual quote from Shuangqing."

Still, by this time, Liu Laoshi was hooked on Shuangqing's poetry, and especially her lyrics, such as the odes to the chrysanthemum, to lone goose, and to the fading lamp, that minor discrepancies or oddities in Shi Zhenlin's narrative did not faze her. She took them right in stride and tended to assume that part of the story was quite real, however fictionalized other parts of it may have been. •⌣

### *"A Wandering Immortal"*

Despite the flirtatious hint in Shuangqing's kidding of Zhao Anshu, Shi Zhenlin asserts without any hint of irony that Shuangqing is completely loyal to her husband, and even scornful of educated folks who ridicule or look down on him for his lack of culture. Hearing this, Anshu exclaims, "She is indeed a wandering immortal," that is, *youxian,* the same term as in Shi Zhenlin's *Poetry Drafts from the Wandering Immortal,* and the same term as in the Wandering Immortal Lake in Xuebu Zhen. The implication is clear, in the context of their discussion, that this is a woman whose unbending loyalty to her brute of a husband shows superhuman moral fiber. In response to Shuangqing's beauty, talent, and virtue, the painter Zhang Shilin vows to worship Shuangqing as an immortal, to pray to Buddha for the forgiveness of her sins, and to paint three thousand portraits of her to present to people "of true feeling" (*RN,* 2.74–75). It is the assumption of everyone in *Random Notes,* including Shuangqing herself, that the only logical explanation of her sad fate (being a beautiful genius cursed to live in poverty and obscurity) can be the sins of a previous life, or some heavenly offense by an immortal now in exile.

### *Shuangqing Explains Her Ambivalence*

Shi Zhenlin occasionally reports conversations between Shuangqing and others, in which she has a chance to explain herself. In one such conversation, a rather strange neighbor lady asks Shuangqing why she doesn't just commit suicide since her life is so miserable. Shuangqing explains that suicide would be the easy way out, and it would not fully repay her bad karma, leaving her to be reborn in an equally ill-fated next life. Moreover, she continues, her husband is better than most, for "the men of this area all seem either to be deformed, stupid, or cruel; they neither look like human beings nor share human feelings." And in a very interesting piece of logic, she observes that since Heaven has already cursed her with talent and beauty, she would only be making this malevolent Heaven all the happier if she further harmed herself by taking her own life.

In response, the neighbor asks why Shuangqing doesn't just behave like some scholars' wives *(shiren fu)* and go right out and have an affair since her husband is so lowly in status anyway. This gives Shuangqing the chance to proclaim her loyalty to her husband, and even to deny that male scholars are any better than peasants. Here, in contrast to some of her actions in sending flirtatious notes and poems to her literati friends, she shows great sensitivity to the social mores of her place and time, noting that "the mistake of one instant" can bring a hundred years of shame. In response, the neighbor lady points out that she already risks censure by sharing her poems with outsiders. Shuangqing explains that she is only human, and she is stirred by powerful emotions "to write elegant thoughts and beautiful feelings." She intends herself to be an inspiration to other "ill-fated beauties" but admits, in the end, that she still "feels some remorse" over her relations with her literati admirers (*RN,* 3.8–9). This Shuangqing seems like a different person from the writer of teasing notes and tender song lyrics to Flower Lover Duan and Zhao Anshu.

### *Anshu and Shuangqing: A Chaste Scholar-Beauty Romance*

Gradually Shi Zhenlin spreads word of Shuangqing to a wider and wider circle of friends and acquaintances, but no one gets as close to Shuangqing as Zhao Anshu and Duan Yuhan. At one point, to console Shuangqing, Shi Zhenlin sends her a letter entirely devoted to reporting to her the suffering that Zhao Anshu has endured in his life. He was orphaned very early in life, once suffered an illness very much like Shuangqing's malaria (and was miraculously cured only after meeting Shi Zhenlin), and is so sensitive that he once went into a deep depression when his pet kitten died! Shi concludes his letter to Shuangqing by pairing Zhao Anshu's unparalleled talent with her unparalleled beauty, using the terms "talented scholar" *(caizi)* and "beautiful maiden" *(jiaren)* of the scholar-beauty romance tradition in which such couples are destined to fall in love and marry.

As Keith McMahon has noted, the "chaste scholar-beauty romance" was very popular in the seventeenth and eighteenth centuries in China. In these stories the man and woman who fall in love epitomize the best of civilization: they are supremely talented, attractive, sensitive, and moral. They usually meet by chance and fall in love through the exchange of brilliant and heartfelt love poetry. Because they are so well matched, it is obvious that they should be married, but there are always obstacles in their way, either uncooperative parents or various evil people who want to prevent their union (McMahon 1995, chap. 5). By referring to Anshu and Shuangqing as "talented scholar" and "beautiful maiden," Shi Zhenlin identifies them with this chaste scholar-beauty tradition. However, the scholar-beauty novels are mostly comic, and the boy invariably gets the girl. Shi Zhenlin's tale, by contrast, is more tragic than comic. There are several potential mates for Shuangqing, and they all share and understand the ideals of the scholar-beauty romance, but since Shuangqing is already married, there is no possibility that she will ever have the kind of talented, handsome, sensitive, and upright mate she deserves.

> *"Anshu is the most talented gentleman in the world, but Heaven has afflicted him; Shuangqing is the most beautiful maiden in the world, but Heaven has afflicted her. Are these not the same?"*
>
> *Shuangqing then wrote a song lyric on her illness. She prefaced her song with this: "[Zhao] Anshu suffers illness; [Duan] Yuhan suffers poverty; the one who suffers both is me, Shuangqing. Moreover, I was born into a woman's body; is that not even more tragic?" Her song lyric:*
>
> *Side by side with my lonely shadow,*
> *Muddled as in a dream,*
> *Who can I count on to wake me?*
> *I bear so many tantrums of the butterfly,*
> *and so much anger from the bee,*
> *even with medicine I get no better.*
> *At this busiest season,*
> *How can I find a spare moment?*
> *Sorrowfully I start the stove*
> *to brew my medicine.*
> *I have poured out all my sorrows*
> *and cried out all my tears.*
> *The abuse the beauty suffers no one knows.*

*Endure through the evening,*
*then comes the morning,*
*days drag on and nights seem endless.*
*The whole night tossing and turning,*
*Just as sleep nears it is time to rise.*
*The sharp cry of the wild swan*
*breaks apart the last remnants of cold sunlight.*
*The hillside in twilight is like a mirror,*
*The small brushwood gate*
*enveloped in the mist;*
*The maiden in blue-green sleeves is in a sickly sickly state.*
*I look forward to springtime's early return,*
*but I fear the east wind will not consent.*

*She wrote this to the tune of "Boxing," on the leaf of a reed, and added with a sigh, "I wish I could turn into a colorful cloud and fly away."* (*RN,* 3.14)

This lyric is a convincing description of illness, albeit by a very self-conscious beauty who likens herself to a flower harassed by butterflies and bees (would-be suitors). Her illness keeps her muddled, as if in a dream, and she would like to be awakened from the nightmare of her life. In actual fact, she would welcome some dreams, but she cannot get to sleep, tossing and turning all night until dawn. With scenic imagery, she turns the hillside into a mirror in which she herself appears in "blue-green sleeves . . . in a sickly sickly state." She wants to welcome spring, symbol of young love and hope for escape from her situation, but she fears "the east wind will not consent."

### *Shuangqing and Flower Lover Duan Yuhan: Shared Poverty and Desire*

There soon follows more exchanges of poetry between Shuangqing and Duan Yuhan, the Flower Lover. Duan is extremely poor, and Shuangqing notices that his coat is so thin that he suffers greatly from the cold in winter. She asks Zhang Mengzhan's younger brother, Ling, to bring her Yuhan's coat so she can add some cotton for a lining. Ling tells her that she needs inner and outer layers of a coat in order to add lining, but Duan's coat has only a single layer. So Shuangqing instead wrote a song lyric in Duan Yuhan's honor (*RN,* 3.42). Shortly after this, Yuhan sends her a song lyric that ends with the remark that he both likes Shuangqing and is tormented by her. She responds in kind with a lyric on the same tune addressed to him. He is so excited by this that he starts talking and crying in his sleep. One night soon thereafter, he manages to see Shuangqing sweeping willow leaves by her door.

> *She wore a thin cotton dress and an old scarf. Although she was ill with malaria, her appearance was especially elegant, lovely, and dignified. Her eyes were so bright and spirited that their beauty extended to people dozens of paces away, so gloriously bright and beautiful. Yuhan paced to and fro watching her; that was the night he cried out in his sleep and wrote this song lyric, crying out even more sadly.* (*RN*, 3.49).

The last line of the lyric by Yuhan refers to his

> *springtime dream of orioles and swallows [yingying yanyan] frolicking everywhere.*

Orioles and swallows represent young beauties in Chinese poetic imagery, and spring is the season of love. So orioles and swallows in a springtime frolic conjure in a Chinese reader's mind at least as many sexual overtones as any Western reference to "the birds and the bees."

When I read this section with Liu Laoshi, she was not terribly pleased, but at least it was Flower Lover Duan Yuhan, not Shuangqing, doing most of the flirting here. Immediately after this, however, we read the following letter by Shuangqing to Duan Yuhan, and this began to strain Liu Laoshi's credulity.

***Shuangqing's Letter to Duan Yuhan***

*Shuangqing sent a letter written in powder on a jixiang [good fortune] leaf, saying:*

> *Yesterday a neighbor lady heard that I wanted to give you a lining for your coat. She sneered at me, so I said to her, "Flower Lover is over fifty years old; I am twenty-one. I once fell into a dry well so I couldn't even see the sun or moon, and poisonous insects descended upon me. Flower Lover with great sympathy peered down into the well. Day and night he chanted Buddha's name and cried for me like a father or mother. Down in the well I kowtowed to him with such gratitude that I could have died without any regrets. Most people in this world are cold at heart, but the friends of Mr. Moon Admirer are all men of great warmth, humanity,*

> *filiality, bravery, and pure hearts. Wherever there is trouble in the world, they will rush to help, with hair flying and hats askew; they could not bare to hide behind closed doors. Flower Lover is full of passion [qing], but still very righteous* [i.e., he may love me, but does not harass me]*; he forgets male and female distinctions just like a mother or father. How could I imitate the vulgar village women who outwardly avoid contact even with male kinfolk while secretly seeking out the male servants? Who parade their chastity in broad daylight and pursue their fallen ways under cover of darkness? Who put on a brave front to hide their inner fright while they sneak around like thieves? Am I that vulgar and disgusting?*
>
> *But in this age of ours we have no jealous wives at home and no carousing men outside; everyone is happily established in loving couples. So I happily manage all the housework and help my husband with the field work too, never thinking of leaving him. And every evening I bow and wish the emperor a long, long life and burn incense to Heaven's benevolence, never once forgetting. Fortunately I have the chance to meet and exchange poems with true gentlemen of purity and talent. Although my poems are poor and simple, you still cannot say they belong to those of Zheng and Wei* [sensual poems in the *Book of Songs*]*."*
>
> *You have compassion for me, I know this myself. But if you pay me too much attention, we risk improper intimacy; if you say too much, we risk going overboard. I must preserve my body like a fine jade; you must treasure your writing like rare gold.* (*RN*, 3.49–50)

As we began reading, Liu Laoshi and I first discussed the unlikely medium of this letter. I took *jixiang* to mean good fortune, which it normally does, but Liu Laoshi explained that it also is a name for grass. Jixiang grass grows easily and is regarded by most farmers as a troublesome weed. One type of Jixiang grass is associated with Buddhism, and that is probably the association Shi Zhenlin is after. "A piece of grass," I said to Liu Laoshi in mock seriousness, "seems an awfully narrow medium for a two-page letter written in powder."

She found this only mildly amusing, but I got her laughing hard with my soulful rendition of Shuangqing's opening lines, where she explains to her suspicious neighbor lady how heroic her literati admirers really are. The image of a young Shuangqing trapped in a dry well, attacked by poisonous insects, only to be comforted by the crying and prayerful chanting of Flower Lover peering down at her, struck me as patently absurd. How about offering a rope or a ladder along with the sympathy? Mencius once declared that it might be okay for a man to touch his sister-in-law if he had to do so in the process of rescuing her from drowning. This would appear to be a comparable case, but just like her impassioned admirers, Shuangqing seems concerned only with sentiment, not with actions. She presents the most flattering portrait of Shi Zhenlin and all his literati friends who rush about "wherever there is trouble in the world . . . with hair flying and hats askew," presumably to have a front-row seat to the world's suffering and to offer their heartfelt sympathy.

Following this fanciful rhetorical opening, Shuangqing offers her most direct defense against the charge of reckless flirtation with men (or men's reckless flirtation with her). Here she explicitly puts the best face on Flower Lover's actions. He is passionate, full of *qing*, but still upright. He so admires talent and so empathizes with suffering that "he forgets male and female distinctions *just like a mother and father.*" (Never mind that his style name is Flower Lover!) As for herself, she defends her exchange of poems with these men, suggests her association with them is chaste, we might say Platonic, and contrasts her own honorable behavior with that of the village gossips who avoid men in public while seeking out lovers in private. "Doesn't this sound suspiciously like the literatus Shi Zhenlin, insulting the low morals and hypocrisy of peasant village life?" I asked Liu Laoshi.

"Yes," she agreed. "Almost all of the prose passages attributed to Shuangqing seem like they could as well have been written by Shi himself." •⌣

Despite what Shuangqing has just said about hypocrisy and immorality, she suddenly turns quite orthodox and offers praise for "this age of ours" where everyone is happily and loyally married, including she herself! And she pays her respects to the emperor and burns incense to Heaven's benevolence! So much for the poor fate Heaven has dealt her. Then she defends her own poetry as innocent and contrasts it against the sensual poetry in the *Book of Songs,* the Confucian classic whose sensual poems (like the Songs of Solomon in the *Bible*) had long been interpreted by moralistic commentators as allegories condemning the behavior described.

In concluding her letter, Shuangqing addresses Duan Yuhan directly, advising that he not pay her too much attention lest they risk "improper intimacy," and that he should not "say too much" lest they "risk going overboard." She is saying in effect, "If you don't tone down your passionate language, we both may not be able to control ourselves!" In her final line, she speaks of preserving her chastity, a highly orthodox goal, but the language she uses—"I must preserve my body like a fine jade; you must treasure your writing like rare gold"— nearly sends Flower Lover off the deep end.

> *That night he shouted, screamed, and cursed in his sleep. When he awoke, he sighed and said, "I am both poor and old. Shuangqing alone forgets both of these realities. If I cannot feel passion [qing] for her, for whom can I feel passion?* [Literally, if I cannot apply my passion here, where can I apply it?] *There have been no passion-crazed fools on earth for a long while. Apart from me, who else is there?* (*RN*, 3.50)

## Qing: *Flower Lover's Passion*

Flower Lover's passion, or *qing*, can be variously translated as feelings, passion, sentiment, or love, and the term is freighted with at least an implication of carnal or sexual desire. As noted in chapter 4, the cult of *qing* was especially popular with Chinese literati in the sixteenth and seventeenth centuries, but it received considerably less attention in the more conservative eighteenth century. Flower Lover Duan Yuhan calls himself a passion-crazed fool, reminiscent of the kinds of passion-crazed men and women once chronicled by Feng Menglong, and he notes that there have not been many such passion-crazed fools for a long while, alluding indirectly to his seventeenth-century predecessors. In any case, the *qing* or passion with which he is overcome carries clear erotic overtones and echoes the romanticism so popular in the late Ming dynasty.

> Up to this point in our reading of *Random Notes,* Liu Laoshi had been a bit suspicious of some of the flirtatious aspects of some of Shuangqing's poems, but she was generally tolerant of Shuangqing's mildly flirtatious poetry and kibitzing with her literati admirers. But now we came to a passage that made her indignant. It is a sentence buried in the most abstruse and difficult prose attributed to Shuangqing, in a letter she sends to her other chief admirer, Zhao Anshu. Shi Zhenlin, in his typical way, circles around the relationship of Shuangqing and Anshu for some time before getting to his punch line.

### *Anshu's Delirium*

Zhenlin meets Anshu one day and finds him feeling especially miserable. He wants to see Shuangqing but cannot bear to. Shi quotes Anshu's poem on springtime and his deep sympathy for Shuangqing and notes that Anshu still regrets the time he implicitly criticized Shuangqing and failed to understand her. Whenever he reads her song lyrics, he cries helplessly and says he no longer cares to go on living. Then one day he gets a letter from Shuangqing that contains the line, "One word from the gentleman is better than a precious pearl." Anshu clutches her letter and sobs, and then he disappears and goes to a deserted pavilion where his friends eventually find him and urge him to return home. This happens every day for three days, and each time his friends find him and counsel him to go home. The third time, he is so distraught, he bows to Heaven and declares that he no longer wants to live. Danyuan laughs at his love-crazed sickness. Anshu responds by saying that it is not only for Shuangqing that he feels so forlorn. He feels this way for all people in distress, whose suffering

> *Heaven gives us in writing through the person of Shuangqing.* (*RN*, 3.63)

Anshu's protestations to the contrary, his own profoundly stirred feelings seem tightly bound up with the person of Shuangqing.

Mengzhan's maid brings him a poem from Shuangqing written on two orchid petals. Anshu loves this poem and finds some relief in it, but the orchid petals dry up and the poem is lost, so he again becomes completely distraught. He just clutches Shuangqing's letter, keeps reciting her line about the gentleman's one word being "better than a precious pearl," and says he wants to die for Shuangqing. Mengzhan's maid tells Shuangqing about Anshu, and laughs at her, presumably for having driven Anshu crazy with passion. Shuangqing tells her,

> *He's mistaken* [about the reference to a "gentleman" in her letter]. *The gentleman refers to my husband. He is illiterate, so I teach him under the nighttime lamp. He already knows over ten characters. Other people may know ten thousand characters and think it nothing special, but if my husband knows one character, we regard that as a precious thing, so I call it a priceless pearl. Why should I envy Xu Ling* [507–583, known for his extravagantly elegant poetry with little meaningful content]? *Since my husband does not know how to write, I hold his hand to trace characters;*

> *he can only manage a dot and a simple stroke. How could I be thinking of an Yishao* [style name of Wang Xizhi, 321–379, one of China's greatest calligraphers]?" (*RN,* 3.63)

Shi Zhenlin then quotes Shuangqing's letter to Zhao Anshu in its entirety. It is written in the most elaborate parallel prose, quoting the *Book of History* and using very elegant and abstruse language in the style of the *Chuci* (Songs of the South). Elsie Choy declines to translate any of the letter, saying of it, "He Shuangqing demonstrated the depth of her scholarship by using the defunct, though exquisite, ancient style of writing in which sentences run in couplets and many literary allusions are used. It can only be appreciated in the original; any attempt to translate it would do it a disservice" (1993, 114–15).

> LIU LAOSHI'S INDIGNATION My normal procedure with Liu Laoshi was to read as much as we could in each class. I read a sentence in its classical form (to show that I knew the proper pronunciations) and then translated it into vernacular Chinese. When I got stuck, which I did with depressing consistency, I looked to Liu Laoshi for her explanation of the allusions I had missed, the characters I had misread, et cetera. And on this letter, I was more lost than usual. I had only tried reading the very beginning of the letter in my preparation for this class, and in class I got stalled very quickly. Liu Laoshi usually read ahead as we worked our way through the text, so she normally knew what was coming. But this day, much to my surprise, she was reading the letter for the first time along with me. She began by describing the letter in general terms and remarking that it did not sound very much like Shuangqing. She found it much too erudite and full of allusions. Then, as she was just scanning the letter, she suddenly turned red in the face, without my fully understanding why, and exclaimed in her most excited voice, "Shuangqing could *not* have written this sentence; this is pornographic!" For the first and only time during my year of studying with Liu Laoshi, she proclaimed, "I will not explain this sentence, and there is no point in our discussing it. It's too disgraceful!" There was an anger in her voice that made me glad I wasn't Shi Zhenlin sitting across the table from her. I was not familiar with several key characters and so remained in the dark until class was over and I went back to my office. We spent the rest of our session discussing not the sentence itself, but the possible meaning of this little bombshell. What kind of joke is Shi Zhenlin trying to play here? And why would

he attribute such a thing to Shuangqing, after all he has tried to say about her strict virtue? As our class ended, we were nowhere near any resolution of these issues. It was the shortest one-hour class I ever had with Liu Laoshi! Usually, if I was not sufficiently prepared for a class, I suffered through a torturously long hour, with Liu Laoshi saying things like, "Well just look at that sentence again, you should know that! Surely you know what *this* character means. We discussed this just last week!" One hour would seem like three. But this time, to my relief and amusement, Shi Zhenlin had taken all the heat.

I was on my own to figure out the precise meaning of the "smoking quote," and it did not take long after class for me to get to work with my dictionaries. I soon had the general meaning of the sentence. Something about his tongue on her cheek, and his hand (actually wrist, to my puzzlement) on her soft breast. Is there some erotic attachment to the wrist that I don't know about? Is Liu Laoshi the one to ask about this? Probably not. After the buildup, this passage was almost a letdown, a bit too tame, but I reminded myself, perhaps not in the context of Shi Zhenlin's time and place, eighteenth-century China.

LIU LAOSHI RELENTS AND DISCUSSES THE SMOKING QUOTE The next day, after a little time to adjust to the idea, Liu Laoshi was, after all, willing to discuss the offending passage in its general meaning, and the larger context of the letter. Yes it did say wrist, and no that didn't make any more sense to Liu Laoshi than it did to me. In the letter Shuangqing describes her intense longings, feelings she must keep hidden. The erotic sentence about her husband comes right before the statement Zhao Anshu kept quoting to his friends, about the one word from the gentleman immortal. By the end of the class I had a translation:

> *He licks up the tears on my fragrant cheeks; his tongue washes away my longing. He gently wipes the perspiration from the soft skin of my breasts, his hand* [literally, wrist] *soothes my aching heart. One word from the gentleman is better than a precious pearl.* (*RN*, 3.64)

Liu Laoshi's spontaneous reaction to the passage told me more about its significance than the literal words themselves. By contemporary American standards, the passage *is* pretty bland. What offended her was not that the words themselves are so prurient, but that they were attributed to the pen of Shuangqing, which directly contradicted Shi Zhenlin's claims about Shuangqing's wifely modesty and chastity. Even before we happened upon the offending passage, Liu Laoshi had remarked that this letter of Shuangqing's to Zhao Anshu "doesn't sound like Shuangqing," and this convinced her all the more that Shi Zhenlin was the letter's author. •⌣

For years, I saw this flash of erotic description in Shuangqing's letter to Zhao Anshu as a kind of writerly joke, an ironic wink to the reader, by Shi Zhenlin. To me, the wink signified a larger writerly joke at work throughout the whole of *Random Notes.* And above all, Liu Laoshi's angry response to this passage confirmed my sense of Shi Zhenlin's playful purpose. But several problems still troubled me. For one thing, other readers like Du Fangqin and Elsie Choy did not see this "erotic smoking gun" as a problem for Shuangqing's image as a virtuous wife. And for another, in light of the following passage that Shi wrote near the end of *Random Notes,* it was difficult to imagine how Shuangqing could endure making love to her husband, much less describe the experience as a tender one in a letter to a literati friend.

> *Shuangqing prided herself on cleanliness, so despite the poverty of her home with all its dust and smoke, her hair never seemed to get soiled. Her husband was so dirty his reeking body odor assaulted the nose. The dirt and grease was so thick on his face and neck that you could rub it off in balls. She urged him to bathe, but he would only get angry, so she dared not push the matter.* (*RN,* 4.47).

If this man really made love to Shuangqing as her letter describes, presumably she held her nose and closed her eyes.

•⌣ Kang Zhengguo: An Alternative Explanation After finishing my first draft of this manuscript in 1998, I asked my good friend Kang Zhengguo of Yale University to read it. He performed a heroic service by checking every one of my translations against Shi Zhenlin's original. He caught an embarrassingly large number of minor mistakes, and in this chapter, he found what he considered my most serious mistake. As I have noted earlier, classical Chinese is frustratingly ambiguous compared with the precision demanded by English grammar and syntax. On my translation of the "smoking gun" erotic passage, Kang's response was clear and harsh. "Why do you assume a third-person pronoun in this passage? Shuangqing is only talking about herself. A more accurate translation would be, "I lick away the lovesick tears on my cheek with my own tongue and wipe away the sweat on my chest with my own hand." In other words, she has only herself to turn to for comfort. Your Liu Laoshi is an oversensitive Victorian prude! There's really nothing overtly erotic here."

Looking at the original passage again with him, I had to admit that he was probably right, though I pointed out that Liu Laoshi's reaction was still important to my story. A day or two after our discussion, he bought up the matter again, "So, what do *you* think? Are you inclined to accept my interpretation or Liu Laoshi's?"

"I agree that the third-person pronoun is not really there in the Chinese version," I conceded, "but I still have some qualms about your interpretation because the very next sentence reads, 'One word from the gentleman is better than a precious pearl.'" Since Anshu thinks the *gentleman* refers to him even though Shuangqing says it refers to her husband, it still seems possible that Anshu pictured himself licking Shuangqing's tears and wiping the perspiration from her breast. By the way, is there any sexual connotation in that term for breast?"

"None at all," he replied confidently. "It could just as easily be translated as chest, and it's a term used for male and female alike."

Kang Zhengguo was probably right, I have concluded, though he had not remembered that Shuangqing refers in her very next sentence to "the gentleman" from whom "one word . . . is better than a precious pearl." I had won a minor concession and was at least gratified to be able to argue the point. In any case, even without an erotic "smoking gun," this letter was enough to send Zhao Anshu into alternating fits of agony and ecstasy. Despite Kang Zhengguo's criticism of my earlier translation, he did agree with Liu Laoshi that this letter seems much too erudite and ornate, in any case, to fit Shi Zhenlin's image of the peasant woman Shuangqing.

However frustrating she sometimes found Shi Zhenlin, Liu Laoshi was always much more inclined than either Kang or me to believe in the veracity of Shi's account. She tended to see parts of *Random Notes* as authentic history and parts as unreliable. Shuangqing could not have written such a letter to Zhao Anshu, but she must have written those compelling song lyrics. It has frequently occurred to me in the time since my sessions with Liu Laoshi that in many ways she replicated, in her own response to *Random Notes,* precisely the response the work has received in Chinese culture over the 250 years since it was written. And this is a response that Shi Zhenlin himself first reported in the latter parts of *Random Notes,* where he described Shuangqing's growing fame among an ever-expanding circle of admirers whose sole contact with her was through exposure to her poetry.

### *An Expanding Circle of Admirers*

> *The day after I arrived at* [Zheng] *Chi'an's,* [Zhao] *Nazhai arrived, and the day after that* [Yun] *Ningxi arrived. Ningxi read Shuangqing's song lyrics halfway through the night. He pulled open my bed curtain and yelled: "For this kind of young woman to exist in the world is truly a miracle of Heaven and earth! In talent and in beauty Shuangqing is incomparable, and in poverty and sickness she is also incomparable. On top of that she has an evil husband and a cruel mother-in-law who fiercely yell at her and compel her to work and suffer all day long. But whereas Shuangqing should be expected to die, she weakly continues to live; whereas she should be expected to be angry, she remains pleasantly unperturbed. Her strength is all spent, but she works hard anyway and is completely and sincerely filial and respectful. Now all the other ill-fated beauties in the world cannot match Shuangqing in talent, beauty, poverty, and sickness; they should all be thankful for Heaven's grace, turn their tears into laughter, and determine to keep on living." Then he presented an offering of chrysanthemums to Shuangqing.*
>
> *He took down the flute and started to play it but stopped short and began sobbing, with tears falling like rain. He took a chrysanthemum blossom to wipe his tears, laughed, and said, "In this world there is nothing that can assuage my tears." Ningxi's face was square and wide, with a long beard. He wore short sleeves, and under the lamp he danced wildly and let out a great laugh. He continually pulled open my bed curtains, held his hands up in respectful greeting, and squatted down in front of me, his eyes gleaming like the morning star and his words tumbling out nonstop.*
>
> *From Danyuan, Jing Zhenxiang also copied Shuangqing's song lyrics all night long. Zhenxiang was twenty years old, with talent, passion, and elegance, but without the flippancy and fickleness of most young people. His refined sensitivity was like that of Mengzhan.* (*RN,* 3.3–4)

In the later portions of *Random Notes,* Shi Zhenlin delights in reporting his travels and the frenzied reactions of his many friends to his account of Shuangqing's life and poetry. Wherever he goes, he carries his memoir and portraits of Shuangqing with him, and then he adds to the memoir a full report of his friends' reactions to both. He seems to be preparing the book for publication by adding long endorsement blurbs attributed to anyone and everyone he happens to meet. Some of these people sound suspiciously like Shi himself. If so, he probably wasn't the first aspiring author to make up his own book blurbs. In any case, once exposed to her song lyrics and her sad story, these admirers literally worship Shuangqing as a divine being, and they hold her discoverer in the highest esteem.

### *"This Is Truly a Banished Immortal!"*

*Zhang Laiyu, the younger brother of Zhang Xingjian (who passed the provincial examination in 1732), was a perceptive critic and a talented singer. On the ninth I went to visit* [Yun] *Ningxi, and the next day Laiyu arrived. He bade Ningxi to play the flute and he sang along. Looking at Shuangqing's likeness he said, "Her face is like the shape of the moon, only thinner; her complexion is like snow, only her countenance is downcast. She is a plum blossom spirit with the moral strength of the lotus; her talent is like a fine brocade and her virtue is like jade. This is truly a banished immortal!"*

*Ningxi had a paternal uncle, Du'an, who had been ill for a decade. He painted landscapes from his bed and invited poets to inscribe them. When he saw Shuangqing's portrait, he cautioned Ningxi, saying, "This is an immortal! Don't be casual with her. You should burn incense and worship her." As for his basic nature, Ningxi is somewhat forlorn, but pure, strong, and incorruptible. He is much like Cao Zhenting.* (*RN,* 3.4–5)

All of Shi Zhenlin's friends are described as handsome, talented, passionate, upright, and indifferent to wealth, fame, and power. They all proceed to regard Shuangqing as a supernatural being, a banished immortal or flower goddess, and often enough, as seen here, they set up a shrine to worship her. Interestingly, Yun Ningxi and his uncle both proclaim Shuangqing's divine status on the basis of her portrait, not from seeing her in the flesh. Many of Shi's friends appear only briefly in *Random Notes,* long enough to make clear their awe and admiration for his memoir and the poetry or portrait of its most famous heroine, Shuangqing. Some of these men beyond the Xiaoshan circle manage to send their own poems to Shuangqing and receive her replies, often matching their rhymes with hers. When Shi Zhenlin reports carrying the portrait of Shuangqing washing clothes to Menghe, the scholars of Menghe all write and chant poems before it. One of these is a seven-character ancient-style poem by Yun Ningxi. Shuangqing somehow learns of this and replies with a long poem in regulated verse. She refers to herself as a forlorn beauty and implies that she is indeed an immortal banished from Heaven. Key lines from this long poem include the following:

*The beauty's home is in Huayang's eighth Heaven,*
*But now she lives by streams and fields.*
*I twist the fragrant silk, soft as raindrops;*
*Want to bind lovers with it, is that not sad?*

*My face is haggard and his face is old;*
*The small room has too much dust to sweep away.*
*The peony is so poor that it cannot bloom;*
*It's glory cannot even match the fragrant grass.*

*I recall the mulberry shade, learning to plant melons;*
*To relieve his thirst I send him a pot of tea.*
*In the cool night I sit in sickness by the open window;*
*I blow out the lamp and spin hemp under the moon.*

*You literati all cherish talent in vain;*
*A simple farm woman, I cannot be moved.*
*After the rain the yellow oriole lets out a cry;*
*Spring sorrow thus roused with the green green leaves.*

*My pure heart wonders will there be calm or distress;*
*There is no space by my bed to pace to and fro.*
*Even if I could turn into a lonely flying phoenix,*
*I would not go the Jade Terrace of Qin.*

*With sundry bits and scraps of old cloth,*
*I'll patch my worn clothes with yards of thread.*
*The white fog covers all, I dream of plum blossoms;*
*Thick frost of night washes over the beauty's face.*

(*RN,* 3.11)

LIU LAOSHI: "THIS IS TOO FLIRTATIOUS!" Liu Laoshi had a very strong reaction against this poem. "This doesn't sound like Shuangqing!" she said dismissively. "It's too intricate, too self-conscious, and too flirtatious to be genuine. She talks of wanting to unite lovers with fragrant silk, refers to herself as a beauty, and implies that she herself is an immortal."

"I'm intrigued by her reference to 'Huayang's eighth Heaven,'" I remarked, wanting to see what she made of this. Huayang is the name of the cave palaces at Mao Shan, that famous center of Daoist religion just north of Shuangqing's village, Xiaoshan. Female immortals dwell in these Huayang caves, and Shi Zhenlin titled his second collection of miscellaneous notes *Scattered Drafts from Huayang.* "Is she implying here that she herself is one of the female immortals of Huayang?"

"Yes she is," Liu Laoshi replied. "But there is something stranger than that here. Look at this personal pronoun, *lang,* which she uses several times. This is the intimate term a woman uses in addressing her lover. Shuangqing wouldn't write a poem matching rhymes with a stranger like Yun Ningxi and address him as *lang!* She doesn't even know him!"

Liu Laoshi saw other problems as well. The reference to the Jade Terrace of Qin is an unusually oblique literary allusion for Shuangqing to use. In Chinese folklore, Nongyu was the daughter of the prince of Qin. She was so taken with the flute playing of an immortal named Xiaoshi that she ascended to Heaven with him on the back of a phoenix. Thus Shuangqing implies that she would not seek a love affair even with an immortal, much less with a wealthy literatus. Liu Laoshi quite liked the implication of this line, but she found the erudite reference and the flirtatious connotations of the poem highly inconsistent with the Shuangqing we had seen in earlier parts of *Random Notes.*

AN ALTERNATIVE READING: SHUANGQING AS CHASTE WIFE However, not everyone shares Liu Laoshi's doubts about this poem. Elsie Choy, for example, translates *lang* as "my husband," giving the poem a very different slant, and Kang Zhengguo agrees with Choy. Commenting on my translation, he noted, "When Shuangqing refers to herself as *qie* [the conventional term for humble wife], it is clear that *lang* refers to her husband and no one else. Liu Laoshi failed to see the term *lang* in the overall context of the poem. There is nothing very flirtatious here." So Elsie Choy was right! I accepted Liu Laoshi's reading of the poem at the time, but Kang Zhengguo has convinced me that I was wrong. He does agree, however, that there is a self-conscious ornateness in this poem that is not very consistent with Shi Zhenlin's image of Shuangqing the humble peasant wife.

### *Shuangqing Rebuffs a Farmhand*

Not all of Shuangqing's admirers fare as well as Yun Ningxi. Soon after quoting her poem matching rhymes with Yun, Shi Zhenlin describes a very different response to a young servant (whose approach is not nearly so subtle as Yun's).

> *There was a farmhand named Qian Qinglang. He sometimes worked alongside Shuangqing's husband. He saw his reflection in the pond and decided he was very handsome. He pounded rice for people for pay. He went out and bought a purple coat to wear, along with a black felt hat and a pair of dark shoes. He washed his face, brushed his teeth, cut his hair, and scrubbed his neck; and then started to sing popular love songs in a loud voice. All spruced up like this he went to Shuangqing's on the pretense of borrowing something from her. He extended his hands to receive it from her directly* [something clearly taboo], *but she blurted out, "Stop!" He was so chagrined and deflated that he tore his new clothes off and sold them straightaway. Whenever he saw Shuangqing thereafter, he did not even dare to look directly at her.* (*RN*, 3.12)

Of course a young farmhand has none of the status of a literatus who writes a clever poem. Following on the heels of her poetic exchange with Yun Ningxi, this incident serves to highlight the status hierarchy, even in Shuangqing's world. It also suggests how strictly she observes the village rules of etiquette whereby there should never be physical contact between unmarried men and women. With one forceful cry of "Stop!" she not only fends off the young man's advances, she shames him so completely that he sells his new clothes and can never look her in the eye again. If only he could have managed an elegant poem, he might have gotten a very different response.

In contrast to this simple peasant, the literati hold Shuangqing in awe but never approach her quite so boldly or directly. Yun Ningxi, for example, has exchanged poems with Shuangqing but never seen her.

> *Ningxi wanted to meet Shuangqing, so he asked Mengzhan to introduce him to her, but Mengzhan did not do so. Thus Ningxi went out walking through the lanes. He saw a number of young girls, but none of them looked like Shuangqing. Then he saw a very poorly dressed woman drawing water. Completely startled, he blurted out, "Shuangqing!" It had just been raining, but he stood there in the mud, spellbound, until his sandals were completely submerged.* (*RN*, 3.32)

Shi Zhenlin is typically vague in his description of Ningxi's sighting of Shuangqing. First, Mengzhan ignores Ningxi's request for a proper introduction to Shuangqing, so he goes off looking for her. In yelling out her given name, Ningxi seems about as provocative as the peasant boy who tried to touch her. But Shi has such fun describing the spell-bound Yun Ningxi that he ignores Shuangqing's reaction altogether. He never even confirms that this woman is Shuangqing. We can only assume that she continues drawing her water and ignores her gawking admirer. Yun Ningxi's reaction is really an aesthetic one. Awestruck by the sight of Shuangqing, he may be a voyeur, a connoisseur of beauty, but he is not a would-be suitor. He treats her quite literally as a banished immortal, not as a real woman, peasant or otherwise.

### *Shi Zhenlin: "I Want to Make Her Name Known throughout the World."*

In the final sections of Shi's *Random Notes,* he spends less time in Xiaoshan and more time traveling.

> *In the eleventh year of the Yongzheng reign (1733), on the eighth of the twelfth month I left Xiaoshan. Packing for the return trip, I planned to travel next year in the north. To encourage Shuangqing to cherish herself, not to be anxious or to overwork, and to take care of her illness lest she die, on this trip I want to make her name known throughout the world.* (*RN,* 3.51)

On his trip, he meets more friends who become instant admirers of Shuangqing. These include Shen Zhilun, who calls himself the Drunken-on-Books-Immortal. Shen proclaims at one point,

> *I only want to seek out those people in books who have true feelings.*

Not surprisingly, when he reads Shuangqing's lyrics, he exclaims,

> *The Drunken-on-Books Immortal will never again be sober.* (*RN,* 3.65)

Shen Zhilun is so moved that he writes forty-four poems matching Shuangqing's rhymes, and six prose essays to express his profound identification with her. Shi Zhenlin paraphrases three of these essays. One of them, entitled "Sweeping Away the Mist," is the most eloquent justification in *Random Notes* for the exchange of poetry between men and women.

***Literati Love of Female Talent and Beauty Is No Sin***

> *There was a Mr. Trunkful of Books who saw the Drunken-on-Books Immortal matching the rhymes and tunes of Shuangqing's regulated verses and song lyrics. He angrily stared* [at the latter] *and cried, "Stop! For men and women to match poems is not according to propriety [li]. You must quickly destroy those works, lest you desecrate the words invented by Cang Jie." The Drunken-on-Books Immortal leaned on his desk, laughed, and said, "The ancients only warned against licentiousness; they did not forbid the cherishing of talent. So when we meet talent, we must cherish it; why worry about male and female? As for this profound emotion, although you can call it romantic, it was originally quite in accord with Neo-Confucian principles [daoxue]. Moreover, does the gentleman truly understand the sorrows of Cang Jie? He went to great pains, with great vitality and inspiration, applied all his strength and suffered great hardship. And later generations use his invention in their poetry and essays, turning it into something dry and dull. Shuangqing uses this invention with the talent of an immortal. The Drunken-on-Books Immortal uses this invention to cherish her talent. Now you would put a stop to this and destroy a thing of beauty* [literally, *fengjing,* or scenery]. *If Cang Jie is still conscious, he must also be crying night after night. It is not only angry ghosts* [of the wronged who have reason to cry]." (*RN,* 3.67)

By paraphrasing, or claiming to paraphrase, Shen Zhilun's essays, Shi Zhenlin blurs the line between himself and this new friend and ardent admirer of Shuangqing. Whatever the ultimate authorship of these essays, the language and sentiments are Shi Zhenlin's. I have never seen Shen Zhilun's name anywhere outside of Shi's memoir. He might be a fictional character. In any case, his defense of gender-blind exchange and appreciation of poetry is written in the same sarcastic style as other parts of *Random Notes* where Shi Zhenlin criticizes hypocrisy and narrow-mindedness.

Mr. Trunkful of Books presents the conservative view that the exchange of poetry between men and women is immoral. His very name suggests a pedant who collects books as status symbols, but who is too limited in feeling and imagination to actually be moved by his reading of a book. By contrast, Shen Zhilun's own self-chosen style-name, Mr. Drunken-on-Books Immortal, suggests precisely the depth of passion and feeling so prized by Shi Zhenlin and his circle of friends. In response to the conservative pedant's charge that men and women who exchange poems in effect desecrate the sacred invention of Chinese characters by Cang Jie, Shen Zhilun hurls the charge right back at him: to write with genuine talent, passion, and feeling is to honor Cang Jie. By contrast, the conservative pedants who write their dry-as-dust examination essays and their imitative "moralistic" poetry are the ones who truly desecrate the sacred invention of Cang Jie.

Shen Zhilun (like Shi Zhenlin) holds an emotive aesthetic view of poetry. Poetry is to be judged by the authenticity of its sentiments, the beauty of its images, and the depth of its feeling. This is in direct contrast to the conservative Confucian view that the main purpose of poetry is moral, "to carry the Dao," to encourage virtuous thought and behavior. Shen defends poetic exchanges between men and women by saying these admirers of Shuangqing are simply cherishing talent wherever they find it, and they just happen to have found it in superabundance in the person of Shuangqing: "When we meet talent, we must cherish it; why worry about male and female?"

To conservatives, this kind of argument is only a veil behind which to hide licentiousness. They have a long list of reasons for "worrying about male and female," including the clear erotic overtones in many places in Shi's *Random Notes:* the flirtatiousness of some of the poetic exchanges, the literati flocking to catch a glimpse of a married woman, chanting her poetry and tapping their feet in rhythm to her cadences through long sleepless nights. In all of these examples, conservatives would see two major problems: first, there are clear overtones and undertones of intense passion; and second, this passion threatens the stability of the family and one of its chief organizing principles, gender-based hierarchies. None of this is moral, natural, or healthy in the conservative view.

### *Jing Zhenxiang: Ambivalent Admirer of Shuangqing*

Another of Shuangqing's distant admirers is Jing Zhenxiang, a romantic who once wrote a biography of a female immortal under the influence of a medium. Jing visits Xiaoshan with his nephew, meets Shi Zhenlin, and reads his *Random Notes.* He initially shares other people's doubts about the existence of Shuangqing, but once he sees her poetry, he is so moved that he cannot eat or sleep. He copies out *Random Notes,* chants Shuangqing's poems, and paces to and fro in his bamboo grove. He carves Shuangqing's poems and song lyrics on bamboo and proclaims that under the intoxicating power of her poems, he has lost all interest in life and death (*RN,* 4.30).

Jing Zhenxiang chants Shuangqing's song lyrics to the devout Buddhist farm family of Zhang Tianshen. The illiterate seventy-year-old mother is so moved by the story of Shuangqing that she wants to meet Shi Zhenlin and discuss the brilliant peasant woman poet. She and her daughter repeatedly cry for Shuangqing. Thus, even young and old illiterate women are profoundly moved by Shuangqing; it is not just flirtatious literati who concern themselves with her. Why, we might ask, does Zhang's mother wish to meet Shi Zhenlin rather than Shuangqing herself? Perhaps she understands the story of Shuangqing as just that, a story.

### *Bi Keshan: Admirer of Shi Zhenlin*

Some literati seem to admire Shi Zhenlin as a writer and Shuangqing as a character in his book. Bi Keshan, for example, describes Shi's memoir in extravagant terms, as more valuable than the Buddhist sutras (*RN,* 4.42). He tells Shi that he wants to take a trip north to solicit funds to subsidize the publication of *Random Notes* and to provide help for Shuangqing's family.

> *And when I return south, I'll present some money to her husband so that he can build Shuangqing a pavilion called Delivering Lunch Pavilion* [in commemoration of her lyric on taking lunch to the field; see chapter 7, "Lyrics"], *and he can buy some land where she can plant melons, and dig a pond where she can wash clothes.* (*RN,* 4:40)

This relief scheme for Shuangqing is another humorous example of how far removed her literati admirers can seem from any of the realities of peasant life. Bi Keshan is the only person in *Random Notes* who suggests concrete financial help for Shuangqing's family, but his goal is the construction of a memorial pavilion, and the reconstruction of other sites related to her and Shi Zhenlin's poetic descriptions of her washing clothes and planting melons! Without a shred of practicality, this is not the kind of financial help a poor peasant family is likely to welcome! How about a tax break, or some rice for seed? Why not send her some books, or high-quality paper, brushes, and a nice inkstone? But a memorial pavilion and a pond? The extra land for planting melons would at least represent a real capital improvement, but the purpose is aesthetic, not financial, to provide a scene for the poetic description and painted portrait of Shuangqing planting melons. And the pond for washing clothes is hardly necessary since Shuangqing already has a stream running by her house. As with all the literati expressions of sympathy with

Shuangqing, the purpose is symbolic and aesthetic, not practical or tangible.

### *Shuangqing's Spreading Fame*

Near the end of *Random Notes,* as Shuangqing's fame spreads, she herself gradually fades from view. Some of her later admirers become farther and farther removed, so they are reported in second- and third-hand accounts.

> *A girl from Biling told us that a dozen or more people there know of Shuangqing's song lyrics. They all try to get others to get her works for them, and quite a few of them try to send poems to her* (*RN,* 4.44).

### *Eighteenth-Century Debates on Female Talent and Virtue*

Shi Zhenlin's account of Shuangqing's many admirers may be seen as one side in a running debate among Chinese intellectuals in the eighteenth century on the relationship between talent and virtue among women. Some conservatives argued that talent, especially poetic talent, was ethically suspect in a woman. Most within the elite agreed on the value of educating daughters, and articulate elite women certainly made a strong case for the compatibility and complementarity of talent and virtue among women (see, for example, Mann 1997, chap. 4). Even conservatives saw the value of female literacy so that daughters could read Confucian morality books and mothers could educate their sons at an early age. As women began to become literate in larger numbers, they formed networks of mutual support and encouragement. Some elite families sponsored the publication of poetry by the women in their clan, and a few literati, like the famous poets Yuan Mei (1716–98) and Chen Wenshu (1775–1845), even took in female students from other families and encouraged the publication of their poetry.

Shi Zhenlin clearly advocated female literacy and the compatibility of talent and virtue in women, though as far as we know, he never took any practical steps, beyond praising talented women, to promote female literacy. He mentioned his wife a few times, always respectfully, but also in a matter-of-fact way, without any of the tension or excitement he put into his descriptions of Shuangqing, the female immortals, or other talented and beautiful maidens he saw during his wanderings. He was a romantic, but primarily a literary romantic. In his memoir, he was not bound by the normal constraints on elite society. He appeared to be free to wander for weeks and even years at a time, to find the most beautiful women, on earth or in Heaven, and to communicate freely with them through exquisite and heartfelt poetry.

### *Romanticism and the Realm of Imagination*

His unconventionality is played out mostly in his head: he does not teach female students, he does not frequent courtesans, he does not take concubines, and he does not have a real-life "love affair" (that he reports to his readers anyway). His romanticism is confined to the realm of imagination: he finds the world's most beautiful, talented, virtuous, and soulful woman in Shuangqing, and he befriends her, becomes her guardian, and to put it in contemporary terms, appoints himself to be her literary agent.

In describing the many admirers of Shuangqing and her poetry, Shi was also collecting advertisements for himself and his memoir. Many of the admirers he describes sound suspiciously alike. They are all handsome, passionate, sensitive, refined, and indifferent if not hostile to wealth and power. Many are so profoundly moved by Shuangqing's story and her poetry that they nearly lose their bearings. Lovers of literary talent above all else, they admire Shi Zhenlin as much as or more than Shuangqing. While they see Shuangqing as a banished immortal, an exiled flower goddess, or, perhaps, a literary figure, they know that Shi Zhenlin is a flesh-and-blood scholar-poet-painter.

Whether real or imagined, this is a highly literary crowd of admirers. For them the line between fiction and fact, between literature and life, is almost nonexistent. Shen Zhilun "only wants to seek out people *in books* who have true feelings." Bi Keshan wants to give money to Shuangqing's family to build scenic memorials commemorating aesthetic images of her taking meals to the field, washing clothes, and planting melons. Such memorials would make no sense for a real peasant woman in a real peasant family. But they would make sense for a real immortal, already passed from life back to the comforts of Heaven. And they would make sense for a woman poet understood to be a literary creation.

The worshipful attitudes of these admirers toward Shi Zhenlin also suggest that he may be the creator, not just the discoverer, of Shuangqing. If he only found her poems and circulated them, why would everyone be in such awe of him? Why did Zhang Tianshen's mother wish to meet Shi Zhenlin but not Shuangqing herself? Why did others not collect and circulate Shuangqing's poems on their own? In some cases, Shi tells us that others have retrieved her letters or poems or song lyrics from Xiaoshan, but his memoir is the only vehicle by which these works survive.

Shi was quite aware that his account of Shuangqing would be viewed with suspicion by some. He offers this growing list of her admirers as one kind of proof of her existence. Yet some of those who most admire Shuangqing's poetry also raise explicit questions about her existence. In a variety of ways, Shi sprinkles doubts about Shuangqing throughout his narrative.

*ten* ·

# *Doubts and Silences*

*Shuangqing, a girl from Xiaoshan, was born of peasant stock.* (*RN,* 2.33)

### *Peasant without a Surname*

This is Shuangqing's introduction, about a third of the way into *Random Notes.* For years I thought little about the curiosity of her name, except to be puzzled how she had later acquired the surname He in the nineteenth century. It is not surprising that someone eventually assigned Shuangqing a surname, because every Chinese is assumed to have a surname. What is odd, especially given Shuangqing's peasant status, is that Shi Zhenlin says nothing about a family name. Women, as men, in eighteenth-century China, were identified first and foremost by their surnames rooting them in a family. Peasant women at many times and places in the long history of China did not even have given names (Watson 1986). A peasant woman was identified simply as the daughter of so-and-so, or the woman surnamed such-and-such. She might be numbered to differentiate her from her siblings in birth order (as in Wang Sanmei, Wang sister number 3), and when she married she then became known as the wife of so-and-so. There are sections of local histories on virtuous widows in the Qing period that never mention a woman's given name. Yet here is Shuangqing, identified with *only* a given name and no surname, no family to root her within the fabric of society. In this regard, she is like the female immortals whom Shi Zhenlin and his friends contact through divination. They too have no family names; they are not bound by human limitations nor by any family ties of obligation.

### *What's in a Name?*

The name *Shuangqing* is itself a very unusual name for a peasant family to give a daughter. *Shuang* means double, or a pair. *Qing* is an intimate term of endearment between husband and wife that can be used by either spouse. It can be translated as the equivalent of *you,* but with a much greater sense of intimacy than *you* implies in English. A more accurate rendering would be "my dear." *Wo* [my] *qing* means "my wife" or "my husband"; *Ai* [love] *qing* means "my dear" or "my love," with the implication that my spouse is also my lover; and *qingqing* is a particularly affectionate way of addressing one's spouse. *Qingqing wowo* (rendered literally as "you you, me me," but with a degree of intimacy not conveyed by the English pronouns) is a shorthand term meaning "lovers' talk" or "whispers of love." *Shuangqing* ("double qing" or "a pair of qings") can be seen as another way of saying *Qingqing,* so the very name of Shuangqing carries clear connotations of conjugal intimacy and love. A final twist is that *Shuang,* meaning double, could hint that this is a love or a lover with a double identity, part real and part imagined, or part male and part female.

### *Absence of Children*

Another striking thing about Shuangqing's biography is that there is no mention of children or the expectation of children in her peasant family. Perhaps, in her malarial state, she was too weak to have children. And if that were the case, her inability to have children might account for some of the persecution she suffers. A woman's failure to produce children was recognized in Qing law as legitimate grounds for divorce. At the same time, the great emphasis on filial piety in this society insured a woman a secure place in her husband's family, *if* she could bear and raise children. The predominant rationale for women's literacy in the first place was to enable a mother to educate her sons. Yet in his *Random Notes,* Shi Zhenlin seems oblivious to the pressures any peasant woman like Shuangqing would have faced regarding her obligation to produce children. People mistake her for a flower goddess, and Shi's friends, in response to her talent and virtue, proclaim her to be a banished immortal. Would not the mundane bearing and nursing of a child reduce her to an ordinary human level and diminish her erotic aura for her literati admirers? Shi Zhenlin's silence on the issue of Shuangqing's bearing children bolsters her image as an ethereal genius but makes it more difficult to picture her as an earthbound peasant.

### *"Meeting Scholars in* Random Notes*"*

In response to the first of Shuangqing's song lyrics that Shi and his friends receive, they assume that she is teasing Flower Lover Duan Yuhan.

> *We took this* [Shuangqing's lyric] *to be making fun of Flower Lover, who got quite angry. When Shuangqing heard of this she said, "I've been born and raised among mountain folk. It is not my fate in this life to be blessed by meeting literati; though fortunately in these* Random Notes *I can make the acquaintance of gentlemen of talent. Every evening I burn a stick of incense and bow to the empty sky, like a caged bird longing to see a flying phoenix." Thereupon she turned away and sighed, "The farmer* [her husband] *may be coarse, but I can still find indirect ways to be tender toward him; how could I bear to cause him trouble? In this life I've no desire to know scholars face to face.* (*RN,* 2.34–35)

I was quite startled when Liu Laoshi and I came upon this passage on just the second page after Shuangqing is introduced in Shi's narrative. "Though fortunately in these *Random Notes* I can make the acquaintance of gentlemen of talent." "Is this any way for a peasant woman to talk?" I blurted out to Liu Laoshi, "as if she's a character in a book?"

"Yes, this seems a strange comment," she agreed, but she was clearly not as disturbed by it as I was. Her attitude seemed to be, "Look, we've just begun to read this story. Don't get so worked up over an odd sentence here and there. Let's just plunge ahead and see what the poetry is like. That's what we're here for after all." In effect, she was telling me, politely and by inference, "It's the poetry stupid! Don't be such a literal-minded twerp!"

Admittedly, much hinges here on the way one translates Shi's classical Chinese prose. My translation, with Liu Laoshi's blessing, is a fairly literal rendering of the sentence: The original Chinese is 妾生長山家。自分此生，無福見書生。幸於散記識才子。. A literal character-by-character version would be "wife [literally concubine, but a humble first-person pronoun for a wife] born and raised in mountain family. My fate in this life not blessed to know scholars. Fortunately in *Random Notes* I know men of talent." The *yu* 於 here can be translated as "in" or "through," and Elsie Choy makes the statement seem less strange by using *through* and by putting the sentence in present-perfect tense: "Fortunately through the *Sanji* [*Ran-*

*dom Notes*] I have made the acquaintance of a few men of talent" (1993, 51). When I discussed this passage with Zhang Hongsheng in Nanjing, he suggested a third interpretation that would solve the problem in another way: "Fortunately, I have the opportunity to meet the scholars described in *Random Notes*." Such is the ambiguity of classical Chinese that all these possibilities coexist.

I see every one of these alternatives as problematic. In my original version, she is saying she can meet scholars in the pages of this book. This still seems to me the most straightforward English rendering of the original Chinese, and it amounts to a declaration of her own fictionality. In Choy's rendering, Shuangqing says she has already met scholars through the influence of this book. This solves one problem but creates others. Shuangqing suddenly appears as an insider and member of Shi Zhenlin's circle even though Shi claims he has just seen two of her song lyrics for the first time and has never yet even met her. In Zhang Hongsheng's version, she observes that she can meet the scholars described in this book. Here again, since the book is just now being written and she has yet to meet its author, how can she know already that the book will bring her into contact with scholars, or that through the book, she will get to know Shi Zhenlin's entire circle of friends?

### *Writing in Powder on Leaves: Liu Laoshi's Experiment*

> *On the twenty-sixth of the tenth month Shuangqing cut a three-inch section of a madder leaf and wrote on it in powder a letter to her uncle, saying . . .* [The letter concludes:] *In writing poems I use leaves instead of paper and powder instead of ink, because leaves quickly wither and powder easily scatters. I do not want my writing to survive.* (*RN*, 3.9)

When Liu Laoshi and I began reading *Random Notes,* we were both taken aback by the idea of Shuangqing writing her song lyrics in powder on leaves. As we continued on with the text and discovered that most of her poems, and some letters, were so described, Liu Laoshi became more and more intrigued. She decided to try an experiment. Assembling a variety of leaves large and small, she took several kinds of facial powder and used a brush to see if she could make any lasting visible marks on the leaves. Dry powder yielded nothing beyond perhaps a vague outline of one crude character per leaf. She wet the powder and tried that; again, no luck. She tried every possible combination: wet leaves with dry brush and powder; dry leaves with wet brush and powder. No success. She experimented by coating the leaves with powder and then writing characters with a wet brush. That didn't work either. Liu Laoshi loved these song lyrics and she wanted to believe this tale from start to finish, but as for writing in powder on leaves, nothing worked! Her experiment brought her to the conclusion that Shuangqing's writing in powder on leaves was a figment of Shi Zhenlin's romantic imagination.

### *Elsie Choy's Solution*

Not all scholars are troubled by this writing on leaves with powder. Elsie Choy notes that court women in the Tang period (618–907) would float love poems written on red leaves through the sewer system, in hopes that they might eventually be freed of court service so they could marry the men who found their poems. But Choy sees Shuangqing's writing on leaves in a different light:

> He Shuangqing's dependence on leaves and pollen from flowers as her chief media transcended romanticism. Her use of these media suggests that she was an unconventional person, creative, resourceful, practical, aesthetic and philosophic at the same time. In her husband's home she was not free to read and write, nor could she find time to earn pin money as she had been able to do in her own family. Yet, as she told a neighbor, "With all the emotions constantly welling up in me, my poetry simply comes by itself." Therefore, it was a natural thing for her to use the leaves and flower pollen from the many flowering shrubs that she loved so well in the foothills around her farm house. These were nature's answer to her prayer, an answer that might seem odd to others, but one that well suited her outlook on life. After all, what better way was there for her to achieve an idealistic and transcendent union with the universe than to allow her work, which represented her heart and soul written on fragile leaves, to hasten an early return to the substratum of existence that is believed to be the void out of which all things ceaselessly arrive and into which they endlessly return? (1993, 20–21)

Choy's sweet seriousness is almost enough to make me retract my irreverence and repent! I quite agree with her that this is the philosophical rationale for the powder on leaves as expressed in *Random Notes*. I do not question the philosophy here, though the impudent sophomore in the class might ask: If you do not want your poetry to survive, why write any to start with? Moreover, Shi Zhenlin completely defeats the purpose of Shuangqing's use of ephemeral powder and leaves by copying everything down immediately with pen and ink, and circulating it far and wide. The main problem with powder on leaves is not the philosophy behind it; the problem is the physics! Perhaps, I am happy to grant, this powder on leaves is a literary conceit that should not trouble us. Perhaps, but in my own reading with Liu Laoshi, it was one of the first things that suggested to me that *Random Notes* is a fanciful work not always to be taken literally.

### *Shuangqing's Prose: "In a Different Voice"*

There are more substantive signs of fictionalization in the prose writings that Shi Zhenlin attributed to Shuangqing. In some of these writings we find a decidedly different tone and sensibility than we see in the simple and soft "feminine" poetry that made Shuangqing famous.

> *There was a Mr. Chen Xigu who was strikingly handsome from the time he was young, and who was very talented and arrogant. He came back from Zhejiang, saying he was a cousin of Shuangqing's on her mother's side. He wrote ten verses imitating the four- and five-line ancient style, using plain unembellished language and affecting a naive simplicity, and he sent these to Shuangqing along with a scarf, hairpins, earrings, and some fine silk. Shuangqing's husband came bowing to him and humbly offered him some food. Mr. Chen just squatted informally and disrespectfully and laughed at Shuangqing's husband.*
>
> *Shuangqing cried and refused to accept Chen's gifts. In inscribing his poems, she wrote,*
>
>> *This is worth a tongue comb for Master Qiwu or a toothpick for Mr. Danyuan! Yet you bring them to flatter me. Cheap cloth, beans, and grain: there is nothing special about these things at all, yet even little children understand their beauty, and we poor mountain folk must take care to save such things. Do they not exceed in value Suiren's discovery of fire and Shen Nong's discovery of herbal medicine? As for Qin-dynasty steles and Han-dynasty stone tablets, immortals' volumes and sacred classics, the world passes them on, but only a few can recite them. Yet the songs and sorrows of each generation cannot be contained in these things; how much less can you capture them with three bottles of vinegar stuck up your nose and your tongue sticking ten thousand* li *up into the sky!*

*Mr. Chen was totally shamed and chagrined, and he came over to tell me what had happened. He cursed her saying, "She's an ill-fated devil to harbor such anger toward people." Mengzhan tried to console him, and then he* [Chen] *left.* (*RN,* 2.81–82)

I had to laugh as we came to the end of Shuangqing's letter to Mr. Chen. I looked to Liu Laoshi for her reaction and remarked, "This doesn't exactly sound like the meek and mild young bride who endures constant abuse at the hands of her husband and mother-in-law. Compared to their rough treatment of her, Mr. Chen's sin doesn't seem to deserve such a scolding. What do you make of this?"

"You're right," she agreed, "This doesn't sound much like Shuangqing. Of course, in insulting her husband, Mr. Chen has also insulted her. But even so, I think Shuangqing would be much more likely to refuse the gifts without fanfare, not to launch into such an overheated verbal attack. The rhetoric here, with the references to Suiren, the mythological discoverer of fire, to Shen Nong, the founder of China's herbal medical tradition, and to Qin- and Han-dynasty steles, stone inscriptions, all sound like references of a scholar, not a peasant woman."

"What do you think of the note's conclusion?" I asked mischievously, suspecting I might get a strong reaction. "What about the line, 'with three bottles of vinegar stuck up your nose and your tongue sticking ten thousand *li* up into the sky'?" I had to laugh as I read the phrase.

"That's ridiculous!" she said dismissively, confirming my suspicions. "It's utterly out of character for Shuangqing. This sounds more like Shi Zhenlin writing fancy phrases to show his disdain for the arrogant and the rich. In contrast to her song lyrics, which are so compelling and distinctive, these prose passages are just too erudite, too temperamental, and too sarcastic to fit with Shuangqing's personality."

A dozen pages later, we came upon another piece of prose writing attributed to Shuangqing. In a letter to her uncle, she shows her sympathies with upper-class women who are supposedly better off than she is. While less sarcastic than her earlier letter to Mr. Chen, this one also seemed to us a bit odd for a peasant woman to write.

### *Shuangqing's Letter to Her Uncle*

*On the twenty-sixth of the tenth month Shuangqing cut a three-inch section of a madder leaf and wrote on it in powder a letter to her uncle, saying:*

*Everyone supposes that I am ill-fated, but my fate was not originally bad. The virtuous young women of red chambers and the young beauties of green windows* [i.e., young women of upper-class families] *are buried deep in their boudoirs, and there are many like this in the world. Recalling their long nights, they have no joy; looking at spring, they dare not cry* [i.e., show emotion]. *The peach blossom reds quickly fade, and the willow's rich greens soon decay. How could they not want others to sing their praises or cry for them? But instead they meet with countless taboos and very little praise. They are bright and shining pearls cast into the blackest waters. Even the echoes of the bird's mournful cry and the bit of life left in the tangled grass are still paid homage from the pretty mouths of poets and carved into the wondrous book covers of the literati* [i.e., noticed in the literary world]. *How much more disappointing is it for the refined and upper-class ladies to be looked upon as cheaply as so much fertilizer?*

*Those who chant my song lyrics on the chrysanthemum or the lone goose all suppose that I am expressing my resentment. I am not so virtuous that I don't honestly feel resentment, but I cannot bear to express resentment toward my husband. Thus Shuangqing maintains some self-respect. Formerly, Xiaoqing did not want to ascend to Heaven but only wanted to find a mate on earth. But in my life to come I would be born a man who cultivates Chan to eliminate the broken heart and propagates Buddhist tales for the discarding of enchantment.* [I.e., she has no wish for romance or marriage in the life to come.] *In writing poems I use leaves instead of paper and powder instead of ink because leaves quickly wither and powder easily scatters. I do not want my writing to survive.* (*RN*, 3.9)

LIU LAOSHI'S REACTION After we finished reading this letter, I began with an observation: "It is interesting to me that on the one hand she shows uncommon sympathy for the upper-class women who are far more pampered than she is, but who are also more secluded than peasant women. Would a peasant woman really suspect that women in elite families are 'looked upon as cheaply as so much fertilizer'? This sounds to me suspiciously like the Shi Zhenlin, who 'aches and weeps for the young beauty' [as Wu Zhensheng noted in his preface to *Random Notes*]."

"You have a point," Liu Laoshi somewhat reluctantly admitted. "This too is a bit out of character for Shuangqing. But look at her hope to be reborn as a man who 'cultivates Chan to eliminate the broken heart and propagates Buddhist tales for the discarding of enchantment.' This much at least rings true for Shuangqing. She is clearly a devout Buddhist."

"It also rings true for Shi Zhenlin," I pointed out. "He was a strong devotee of Chan Buddhism, so in this regard, Shuangqing might simply be his alter ego."

She was not particularly pleased to hear this. I was going too far with my doubts. "But still, I think her poetry *is* better than Shi Zhenlin's. I just can't believe he could have invented her song lyrics by himself."

"What about Shuangqing's final claim that she doesn't want her writing to survive?" I asked. "Isn't she contradictory on this point?"

"Well," she replied patiently but firmly, "she knows she opens herself to attack by exchanging poetry with scholars, but they are the only people who appreciate her talent. I think she may be profoundly ambivalent, but not necessarily contradictory."

None of my doubts about Shi Zhenlin's story did anything to dampen Liu Laoshi's enthusiasm for Shuangqing's poetry. She continued to talk about her desire, some day, to write a novel or play about Shuangqing. "This is too good a story to pass up!"

### *Parallels with Xiaoqing: Ill Fate of the Talented Beauty*

Shuangqing's mention of Xiaoqing in this letter is one of her few references to a famous literary woman. As mentioned in chapter 4, Xiaoqing was the tragic, talented, beautiful (and possibly fictitious) Yangzhou concubine who was made so famous in many late Ming plays and stories. There are many parallels between Shuangqing and Xiaoqing. They were both associated with Buddhism and particularly with the Heart Sutra. Xiaoqing was supposedly educated by a nun, and very early in her education she learned to recite the Heart Sutra from memory. As Shi Zhenlin reported in his first paragraph on Shuangqing, she could "write out the entire Heart Sutra on a cassia leaf." In her letter to her uncle, Shuangqing imitates the following well-known poem attributed to Xiaoqing: "I bow in front of a bodhisattva / I'll neither be reborn in the Western Paradise nor ascend to Heaven. I only want a drop of water from Guanyin's willow / So as to be reborn on earth with my loving husband" (conversation and correspondence with Kang Zhengguo, July 1998). Both women pine away under the persecution of a cruel higher-ranking woman, and both find solace in Buddhism and in poetry. For both women, literacy is a blessing and a curse. On the one hand, literacy gives them an expressive power that ultimately achieves their cultural immortality, although it comes primarily through the mediation of their male admirers. On the other hand, their literacy helps expose them to romantic literature and inspires in them the stirring of romantic longings that can have no fulfillment in their lives. Each writes captivating poetry, suffers alone, seeks solace in Buddhism, and dies young (Kang 1994).

The one point of contrast between these two literary women is that Shuangqing is less overtly romantic than the Yangzhou concubine. Whereas Xiaoqing asks to be reborn with her loving husband, Shuangqing has no loving husband and no way to acknowledge openly any desire for any other lover, for that would compromise her virtue. Instead she asks to be reborn as a man who cultivates Chan so as to extinguish desire and "to discard enchantment." In other words, Shuangqing takes the more orthodox Buddhist position that all attachments, including romantic attachments, are illusory and a source of human suffering.

A final parallel between the two women is even more pertinent to the theme of this chapter: to this day we do not know whether either woman ever existed in the flesh, while both, through their tragic stories and the elegant poetry attributed to them, have become undisputed cultural icons. Together with many unambiguously fictional women (for example, Du Liniang in the drama *The Peony Pavilion,* and most of the young women in the novel *Dream of the Red Chamber*), Xiaoqing and Shuangqing are part of the powerful literary trope in late imperial China of the ill-fated woman of beauty and talent. The captivating appeal of this trope (a metaphorical figure of speech) owed much to the parallels between these women and their male hagiographers, marginalized literati who felt their own talents and virtues were unappreciated by remote and capricious rulers, and unrecognized and thus wasted in a money-and-status-crazed society. By lionizing and sympathizing with such women, Shi Zhenlin and other like-minded literati were also celebrating, and mourning for, themselves and their own values, ambitions, and frustrations.

### *Doubts Unanswered*

One of the most intriguing aspects of Shi Zhenlin's *Random Notes* is that he occasionally quotes his own friends as raising doubts about Shuangqing's existence. As often as not, he simply leaves these questions hang in the air without any reply or explanation whatsoever.

> *On the twenty-first of the seventh month, Jing Zhenxiang came to Ganlu Mountain Retreat to bid me farewell. He left for Xiaoshan in order to chant his poems on the autumn lotus for Shuangqing, and to ask her to match*

> *them. He said to me, "Those who have doubts about Shuangqing all say she does not exist. Here is a farm woman who is literate, who also writes essays, and who moreover writes very skillfully. She makes Yuhan drunk, she startles Anshu, and she leaves Ningxi awestruck. These three, whether hungry or thirsty, happy or sad, all become completely crazed so that they can't even control themselves. How can this happen again and again?" He then left; I wasn't feeling well.* (*RN*, 4.39)

As seen in chapter 9, Jing Zhenxiang is an ambivalent believer in Shuangqing. While he is on his way to Xiaoshan to chant his poems to her and to try to get her to respond in kind, he reports to Shi Zhenlin the doubts that others have expressed about her. How could a farm woman write such poetry? And how could she drive her trio of admirers, Zhao Anshu, Flower Lover Duan Yuhan, and Yun Ningxi, so stark raving mad? The most interesting part about this passage is the ostentatious way Shi Zhenlin lets the issue hang in the air without one word of an answer. Where we are led to expect some response of the author to this challenge to his veracity, there is only silence. "He then left; I wasn't feeling well." This is followed by the kind of abrupt change of subject the reader learns to expect in *Random Notes:*

> *Chi'an wrote ten poems on autumn insects, of which I have chosen five* [to quote].

By such silences as these, Shi Zhenlin sprinkles additional doubts about Shuangqing at various places in *Random Notes.* Sometimes, as in the above passage, he lets the doubts stand and coyly avoids addressing them further. In other passages, he raises the doubts and addresses them in elliptical and ambiguous ways. In understanding the story of Shuangqing and her transformation into a cultural icon, these ambiguities and silences are as revealing as all of Shi Zhenlin's explicit statements about her person and her poetry.

Occasionally Shi Zhenlin will say he received a Shuangqing poem from a maid or from the young boy Ling, landlord Zhang Mengzhan's youngest brother. These two serve as go-betweens for Shuangqing and her admirers. But in many cases Shi never clarifies just how he receives her poems written in powder on leaves. He never describes a direct face-to-face conversation between himself and Shuangqing, and he never explains how he knows of the conversations he records between her and her family or her neighbors.

Beyond noting how much she suffers at the hands of her cruel mother-in-law and her hot-tempered husband, Shi Zhenlin shows no anxiety about the likelihood that he and his friends, by exchanging poems with her, by chanting her poems right outside her own house, by their frequent attempts to spy on her and paint her portrait, must surely make her persecution all the more intense and unavoidable. There is just silence where one might expect to hear, at the very least, arguments over whether the best favor the literati could grant Shuangqing would be to leave her alone.

### *Wang Danyuan's Scruples*

Shuangqing is cautioned occasionally by her literati admirers to be discrete in whom she shows her poetry to, a laughable piece of advice in light of the behavior of these men who go to great lengths to have contact with her. A close friend of Shi Zhenlin's, Wang Danyuan criticizes Shuangqing openly at one point, for having the temerity to have contact with men outside her own family.

> *On the twenty-third of the eighth month Anshu left the Five-Li Pavilion, walking back to Donghu. Yuhan and I stayed at the Southern Chan Temple. Under the lamp with Shushan we discussed Shuangqing. Shushan wrote three poems he wanted to send to her. Danyuan sat alone facing south, looked up from the prayer mat, and confidently discussed the Confucian Way and ritual propriety* [*daoxue* and *lifa*], *and he used them to disparage Shuangqing. Yuhan, very upset by these old-fashioned remarks, lay down and refused to listen.*
>
> *I said, "When Shuangqing received Danyuan's poems, she carefully washed her hands and held them respectfully, rinsed out her mouth and chanted them. She vowed to carve the gentleman's figure in sandalwood and to bow to it morning and evening. So I did not think you would denigrate her like this." Danyuan got up, smiled, and shrugged, holding out his hands and asking, "Is that really true?" I replied, "Yes indeed it is!" Then he apologized and said, "My poetry is difficult for most men to understand; now to have a* zhiyin [one who understands the tone, i.e., a true understanding friend] *in the powder quarters! I regret that I am thirty years older than she so that I am ashamed even to look at her." Thereafter he never again used Confucian theories to criticize Shuangqing!" Yuhan was very pleased at this.* (*RN*, 2.75)

Wang Danyuan is laughably susceptible to flattery here and quite ready to drop his Confucian scruples once he hears that Shuangqing not only understands but also admires his difficult poetry. But if he wondered about Shuangqing's morality in the first place, why did he not question the morality of the literati who are, after all, the initiators of this flirtatious violation of the Confucian proprieties? In all the discussions of Shuangqing, there is a curious lack of interest shown in the possible consequences of the actions of the literati toward Shuangqing. She is often discussed and treated as a fictional character in the sense that she seems well beyond the reach of any possible help from her admirers beyond receiving their heartfelt sympathy.

### *Yun Ningxi's Doubts: Proof in the Poetry*

Every time Shi Zhenlin is asked about proof of Shuangqing's existence, he responds in ambiguous ways. When three friends of Shi Zhenlin, Yun Ningxi, Zhao Nazhai, and Wang Danyuan visit Xiaoshan, they come upon Shi and Shuangqing's landlord family, Zhang Xiuyuan and his two sons, Mengzhan and Renchi. Yun Ningxi immediately proclaims his praise of the Zhang family "for protecting and not slighting what Heaven loves." Xiuyuan does not understand the meaning of this, so Yun Ningxi explains that Heaven has placed Shuangqing on their land precisely because they protect her from harm (presumably by the very depth of their sympathy for her). Ningxi then salutes Shi Zhenlin as another hero.

> *You are the jade ladder to Ironclad Mountain* [Tiewei Shan, a mountain in Buddhist lore]. *Although Shuangqing has talent and beauty, I think you have embellished* [literally, added color to] *her portrait. If I could see just one leaf with writing in powder, my doubts would disappear.*

Shi Zhenlin describes his response, or nonresponse, to this request:

> *I then brought out ten or more poems written to Shuangqing by Qian Lingxiao and Zheng Chi'an.*

And he then launches directly into a description of Qian Lingxiao, after which Yun Ningxi begins to write his own poems for Shuangqing (*RN*, 3.31).

I am not the only one who has trouble believing that all these poems can be written in powder on leaves! Yun Ningxi says he is impressed by all the stories about Shuangqing, and he credits Shi Zhenlin as the vehicle by which Shuangqing has become known to the world. But he uses a curious term to describe Shi Zhenlin's work. "You have embellished her portrait." This could be read in several ways: You have added color. You have brought her to life on the page. You have idealized her. Or perhaps, you have polished her poetry yourself. But by the request that follows, it is clear that Yun Ningxi has real doubts about the literal truth of Shi Zhenlin's account of Shuangqing. "Show me the powder on leaves, and I'll believe!"

Shi Zhenlin is nothing if not consistent in his response to these kinds of queries from his friends and acquaintances. He ignores the doubts that have been expressed. He never stoops to argue the case directly for Shuangqing's reality. He never says, "Let's go over to her cottage to see her." Or, "Speak of the devil, there she is now!" In each case, instead, he appeals to the images of her poetry or, in this case, the poetic images that others have created in her honor. He shows Ningxi the poems Shuangqing has inspired two of his other friends to write. And then the doubts are dropped. His nonarguments never meet with objections. In this case, which is typical in *Random Notes,* Yun Ningxi is so impressed with the testimony of others that he immediately joins in with poems of his own for Shuangqing. As we have already seen in the previous chapter, Yun Ningxi, who began with such serious doubts, was to become one of Shuangqing's most ardent admirers.

### *Li Yunchou's Doubts*

As noted in chapter 9, Shen Zhilun, the Drunken-on-Books Immortal, was a kindred spirit of Shi Zhenlin's. One of his essays is "Heaving a Long Sigh," which Shi summarizes this way:

> *The Drunken-on-Books Immortal said to Li Yunchou, "I have seen Shuangqing in person, not only seen her but wept for her as well." Yunchou said, "Nonsense!" I replied, "In the chrysanthemum and the lone goose I see the dark loneliness of her setting; in the 'soul of the moon' and the phrase 'dripping with beauty' I see her dazzling appearance; in the 'hungry swallow' and the 'ailing silkworm' I see her soft warm nature; in elegant words and profound feelings I see her unparalleled talent." Yunchou said to this, "Why do you cry for her?" I replied, "First, I cry for her misfortune. She is like a broken sword by a mountain spring, like a broken pine tree uprooted in a valley; I therefore cry for Shuangqing's fate. Second, she is like a famous flower ruined by the rain or the new moon hidden by the clouds; I therefore cry for*

> *Shuangqing's beauty. The pearl cannot rise from the depths, and polished jade cannot easily be extracted from a rough block of stone; I therefore cry for Shuangqing's talent. The plum blossom cheerfully bears the snow and the chrysanthemum happily endures the frost; I therefore cry for Shuangqing's virtue."* (*RN,* 3.67)

Li Yunchou is not a major character in *Random Notes,* but curiously enough, he is the person credited with bringing Shuangqing to the attention of the Drunken-on-Books Immortal. He gives Shen a copy of *Notes on Shuangqing,* apparently consisting of the portions of *Random Notes* dealing with her. Yet, notice Li Yunchou's role in the dialogue reported here. When Shen says he has seen Shuangqing, Li replies, "Nonsense!" Why is Li Yunchou so dismissive of this claim? Is he saying Shen has never been to Xiaoshan, so he couldn't have seen her? Or that he couldn't have seen her because she is only a character in a book? Whatever his views, "Nonsense!" is a pretty strong reply to a friend's claim. Shen makes no attempt to persuade Li by normal means: "No, I went to Xiaoshan and happened to see her," or even, "I saw her portrait by Zhang Shilin." Rather, he appeals to the imagery of Shuangqing's poetry, the chrysanthemum, the lone goose, the hungry swallow, and the ailing silkworm.

Li Yunchou's reply to this is equally curious. "Why do you cry for her?" After all of Shen Zhilun's outpouring of sympathy, and his cascade of vivid imagery to capture Shuangqing's desperately sad situation, how can Li remain so oblivious to her suffering? Is he just an insensitive clod? One way to make sense of Li Yunchou's question, it seems to me, is to recognize the implication that Shuangqing is in all likelihood a fictional character. If she is fictional, what is the use of crying for her? And Shen Zhilun replies with his own series of images and analogies that make clear her beauty, talent, suffering, and virtue, whether she is real or fictional. She is like a broken and abandoned sword, a broken pine tree, a ruined flower, a new moon hidden by clouds, a buried pearl, spring plum, and autumn chrysanthemum. We might add to Shen's list, she is very much like a failed examination candidate, brilliant but not recognized, beautiful but ignored, virtuous but persecuted. Shen's argument is typical of Shi Zhenlin's method at many points in *Random Notes.* The reality of Shuangqing is to be seen in her poetic imagery, in the emotional power of her words, and in the beauty of Shi Zhenlin's descriptions of her tragic story.

### *Story without an Ending*

The final silence, or omission, in the story of Shuangqing in *Random Notes* is the lack of any conclusion to the story. Shuangqing is introduced abruptly about one-third of the way into the memoir. Her story and her poetry come to dominate the middle part of the book. Shi gives a little information about her background, sprinkles his text with observations about her, quotes her poems, song lyrics, and prose letters, and then begins to circulate her poetry and his narrative to his friends and acquaintances. As he moves to the later portions of the memoir, Shi seems increasingly preoccupied with the reactions of others to Shuangqing's life story and her poetry (as conveyed by him) and less interested in her life itself.

The last four or five references to Shuangqing in *Random Notes* concern only other people's comments about her. She has ceased being an active participant in the story well before the memoir concludes. Shi Zhenlin laments the fact that some of his friends, particularly Cao Zhenting and Zhuanhua Furen, the wife of Shi's good friend Wu Zhensheng, have never had the chance to meet Shuangqing. Shi tells Cao Zhenting the story of a beautiful pair of sisters whose father has died, leaving them to an uncertain fate in marriage. After hearing this story from Shi Zhenlin, Cao Zhenting becomes very restless and worries that evil go-betweens might doom these girls, just as was the case with Shuangqing.

A few pages later (4.75), Shi Zhenlin notes that it is mostly the young who have a great capacity for love and virtue *(zhixing);* only Shuangqing, he says, carried this sensitivity through her whole life. Cao Zhenting then tells Zhenlin about a young woman who is extremely talented in swordsmanship. She meets a renowned teacher who sees her talent and talks with her at length about the martial arts. He wants to take her as his concubine but her mother won't agree because she is too young, and they leave. He sees her years later, and she performs magnificently. The implication is that this girl matched Shuangqing in maintaining lifelong virtue, sensitivity and accomplishment.

This is the last mention of Shuangqing in *Random Notes*. So despite the declared love of all his friends for this peasant woman poet, despite their deep pity for her and their undying admiration for her, in the end they do nothing to relieve her suffering, and she fades from view without any apparent resolution of or change in her situation. She is seen as more and more desperately ill and increasingly persecuted by her husband and mother-in-law. But there is no word of her death, no relief of her suffering, and no sense of any conclusion. Shi Zhenlin just stops talking about her. She drops silently out of view.

### *Shi Zhenlin's Silence after 1737*

In 1762, twenty-five years after finishing *Random Notes,* Shi Zhenlin published his notebook *Scattered Drafts from Huayang* (Huayang being the cave on the famous Mao Shan). In many ways, *Scattered Drafts* is a continuation of *Random Notes,* with occasional references to dates and recording miscellaneous observations and travels. But in other ways it is a more mundane and earthbound book. It includes descriptions of people, letters to friends, and prefaces to their poetry collections, but with fewer lyrical descriptions of immortals and fairies, and nothing approaching the long narrative passages of his earlier work. What is most striking for our purposes is that the name of Shuangqing appears not even once in *Scattered Drafts.* How could she feature so prominently in one of Shi's notebooks and drop from view so completely in the second?

Shi saw his *Random Notes* as his most significant work and as an important work of imagination, and at one point he makes the following curious boast about it:

> In the four chapters of *[Random Notes from] Xiqing,* the writing is without feeling and filled with regrets, but also without regrets and filled with feeling. In the passages concerning dreams of beautiful women, the writing is without fragrance and full of shadows, and without shadows and full of fragrance. (*Scattered Drafts* 1935, 71)

This is partly just playful rhetoric, with contradictions or paradoxes that sound perfectly logical in the parallel prose of classical Chinese. But the most interesting comment concerns the "dreams of beautiful women," literally *dai meng,* or dreams of black eyebrows [of beautiful women]. Shi ended his preface to *Random Notes* with the comment "written in a dream," which could imply that the preface was written in a dream, or that the whole work was written in a dream, in other words, that it is above all a work of imagination. Are all the women in *Random Notes* to be seen as imaginary? By making no mention of Shuangqing or any of the female immortals from his previous work, Shi Zhenlin gives the reader plenty of grounds for such speculation.

Fig. 1. *Left to right,* Zhang Hongsheng, Kang-i Sun Chang, and Kang Zhengguo, in front of the Miss Worcester Diner, Worcester, Massachusetts, March 1997

Fig. 2. Liu Chunhua (Liu Laoshi), poetry teacher and Shuangqing admirer who taught at the Stanford Center in Taipei, Taiwan, 1990–91

Fig. 3. *Sweeping Fallen Leaves in Autumn,* by Fei Danxu (1801–1850)

Fig. 4. *Heavenly Immortal Scattering Flowers,* by Ren Xun (1835–1893)

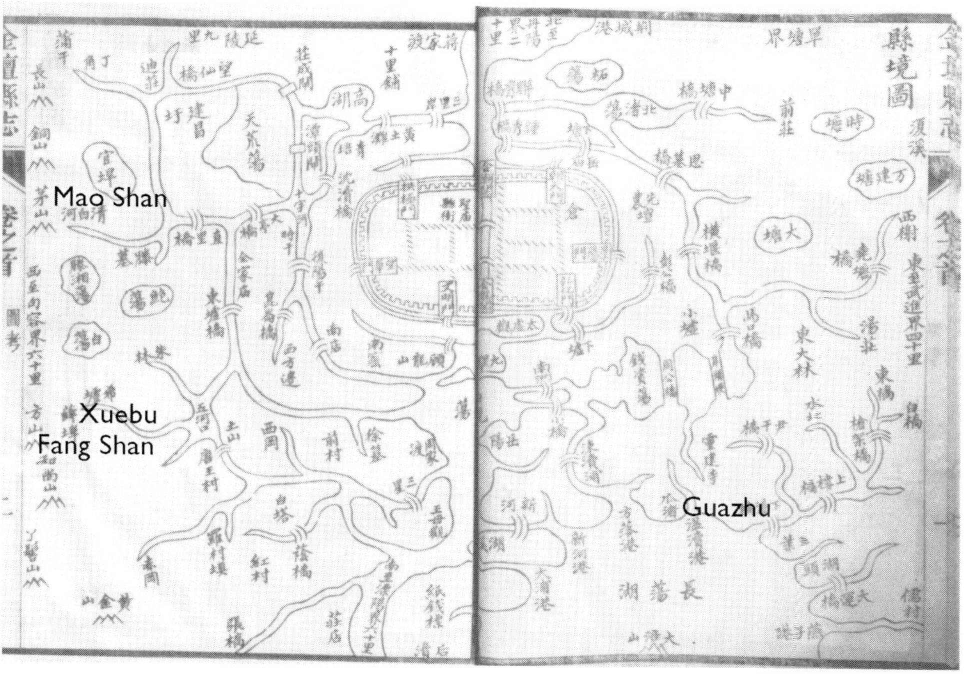


Fig. 5. Map of Jintan County from the *Jintan County History,* 1885

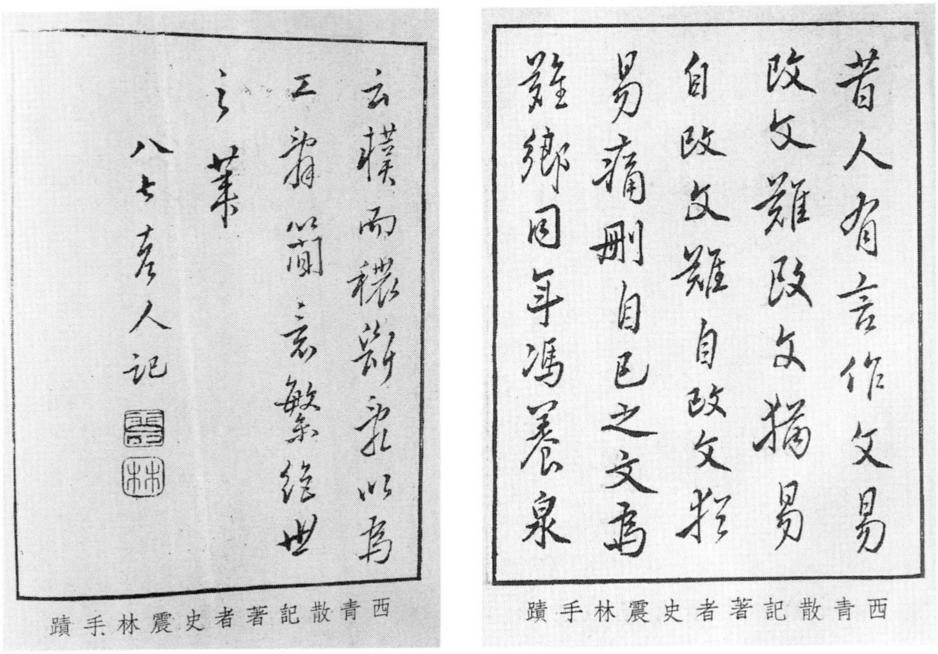


Fig. 6. Calligraphy in a plain semicursive style by Shi Zhenlin, written in his eighty-seventh year. From the 1935 edition of *Random Notes from Xiqing*.

Fig. 7. At the Duan Yucai Memorial Hall in Jintan, October 1997. *Right to left,* Wan Lijun (Xiaowan), Du Fangqin (Du Laoshi), Xiaowan's friend with her baby boy.

Fig. 8. Fang Shan (Square Mountain), also known as Siping Shan (Four[-sided] Flat Mountain), the probable location of Shuangqing's village, Xiaoshan

Fig. 9. Stream and bamboo grove at Jianguo Village near Fang Shan, reminiscent of Shi Zhenlin's description of a site near Shuangqing's house where she often washed clothes

Fig. 10. Discussion Group at Xuebu Zhen (Xuebu Town), November 1, 1997 (chap. 8). *Left to right,* Zhang Hongsheng, Mr. Pan (Xuebu township official), Zhang Jinsheng (Xuebu town head), Wang Rongsheng (retired newspaper reporter), Bao Jiujing (Xuebu Township Historical Records Office), Ye Furong (retired worker), Paul Ropp, Du Fangqin.

Fig. 11. Digging for roof tile shards at former site of the Eight-Li West Temple in Xuebu Township, possible location of the Xiaoshan Academy

Fig. 12. The sacred mountain in Chinese Daoism, Mao Shan, as seen looking north from Fang Shan

Fig. 13. Approaching the Shi Family Mountainside at Fang Shan in Xuebu Township, probable site of Xiaoshan village. (The provincial prison is just visible behind the pine trees.)

Fig. 14. Tractor and cart loaded with stones from the quarry at the Shi Family Mountainside

Fig. 15. Approaching the stone quarry at the Shi Family Mountainside. Blasting work at the quarry left us content to stay several hundred yards away.

Fig. 16. Field investigations at Fang Shan. *Left to right,* Zhang Hongsheng, Bao Jiujing, Xuebu town head Zhang Jinsheng, Du Fangqin. With back to camera, seven-year-old Zhang Ting, granddaughter of Xuebu Township head Zhang Jinsheng.

Fig. 17. Zhang Ting (whom we called Xiaomei, Little Sister). She relented and allowed this photograph after resisting several earlier attempts.

Fig. 18. Zhang Ting and her grandfather, Zhang Jinsheng, on our walk through the countryside in Xuebu Township

Fig. 19. Dramatic sunset at Fang Shan, recalling Shuangqing's lines: "The sunset hurts the eyes; / Don't look to the horizon, / The horizon only shows a few cold clouds drifting apart."

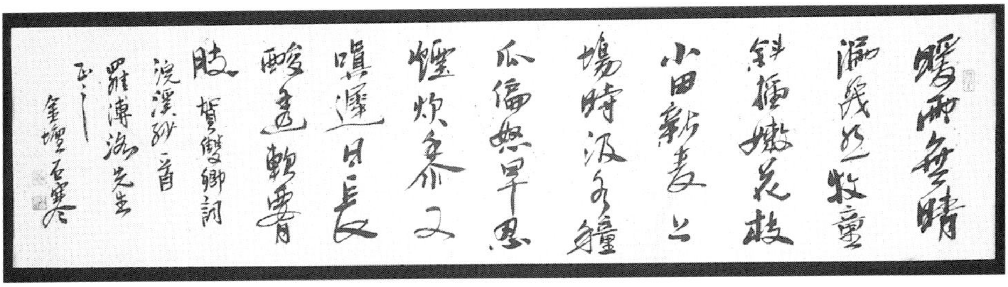

Fig. 20. Shuangqing's first song lyric, to the tune of "Huanxisha," as written by the Jintan painter and calligrapher Shi Han

Fig. 21. *Bamboo and Rock with Calligraphy in the Style of Zheng Xie* (eighteenth-century painter-poet-calligrapher), by Shi Han

Fig. 22. TV crew interviewing Zhang Hongsheng beside the provincial prison at Shi Family Mountainside. *Left to right:* Du Fangqin (taking picture), Secretary Sun, Xuebu town head Zhang Jinsheng, Jintan security chief Zhu, Wan Lijun (Xiaowan), Zhang Hongsheng, TV interviewer, TV technician (obscured), TV cameraman, Jiangsu novelist Chu Fujin, lawyer Xu Donggong (friend of Xiaowan), last two unidentified.

Fig. 23. Two sisters with a young boy, at the gallery of Shi Han, the Jintan artist and calligrapher. If I could chose an aesthetic standard for the beautiful peasant Shuangqing, this would be it.

Fig. 24. The waitstaff of the Rainbow Elegance Restaurant in Jintan, with the proprietor, Mr. Chen Xiqing, and Paul Ropp

Fig. 25. Portrait of Wan Lijun (Xiaowan), from her book of poems, *Beautiful Wandering*, published in 1996 when she was twenty-four years old

Fig. 26. Zhang Hongsheng and Du Fangqin in Danyang. Slogan on wall reads: "Help Danyang progress; manage well the Yellow Wine Festival."

Fig. 27. At the Jiangshu Township Government Headquarters in Danyang. *Left to right:* Our driver from Danyang City, newspaper reporter and our escort Mr. Shi Shenghua, our local host Miss He from the Jiangshu Township government, Du Fangqin, and Miss Yin from the Danyang County Records Office.

There are those who see references to Shuangqing in *Scattered Drafts,* but the most they can come up with are two phrases. One, in a letter to his friend Wu Zhensheng, where he writes very cryptically, "The family of immortals in the Wanyi Garden, long separated by the clouds in the sunset; washing clothes at Xiaoshan, illness without recovery. Lamenting people, lamenting things. Half in the women's quarters, half in a dream" (1935, 15). I've made this translation as literal as possible, to illustrate how open such a passage is to multiple interpretations. The reference to washing clothes in Xiaoshan is the closest Shi Zhenlin ever comes to mention of Shuangqing in *Scattered Drafts.* Some have argued that "washing clothes in Xiaoshan" refers to Shuangqing, and "illness without recovery" refers to her death. Elsie Choy dates Shuangqing's death to about 1737 based on this one cryptic reference (1993, 30).

But Professor Zhou Wanyao in Taiwan has recently pointed out that a different interpretation of this whole passage is equally plausible. The Wanyi Garden, as described by Shi Zhenlin near the end of *Random Notes,* was named after two beautiful young women in the family of Jin Boyan. Jin had four concubines and a beautiful and talented daughter named Wanjuan. When he acquired a fifth young concubine from West Lake in Hangzhou, everyone in his family was shocked to discover that the newly arrived young woman looked and talked exactly like his own daughter Wanjuan. The two girls immediately embraced and proclaimed that they were in fact long-lost sisters. Somewhat bemused by this turn of events, Jin Boyuan agreed that he had acquired a second daughter rather than a fifth concubine. They chose the name Yijuan for this new daughter and named their lovely garden Wanyi, combining the names of the two sisters. The sisters became so inseparable that they said they would never agree to marry different men. They would either remain unmarried or would become the wife/concubine of one husband to be shared in common. (As strange as this may sound, such a practice was not unheard of in China, and particularly in one area of south China, premarital sworn sisterhoods were quite common in which young women would even live together and pledge their loyalty to each other, while vowing to remain unmarried or to marry one and the same man.)

The most important point, for our purposes, is the reading that Professor Zhou points out as one possible interpretation of the sentence quoted above on Wanyi Garden and washing clothes in Xiaoshan. Why does Shi Zhenlin say "half in the women's quarters, half in a dream"? Dr. Zhou suggests that he might be implying that his story of the sisters Wanjuan and Yijuan actually came from the women's quarters, while the story of Shuangqing, the clothes washer of Xiaoshan, was the product of a dream.

The second possible reference to Shuangqing in *Scattered Drafts* comes at the end of a letter to Shi's friend Cao Zhenting and is equally cryptic: "Under the peaks of [Ya]ji Shan, there is Xiaoshan. The Washing Clothes Pavilion is still there in the sunset" (1935, 17). Like the passage quoted above, this one raises more questions than it answers. In the Xiaoshan that Shi Zhenlin describes, the peasants do not have any pavilion for washing clothes. As noted in the previous chapter, one of Shuangqing's admirers, Bi Keshan, once proposed building a pavilion to commemorate her taking lunch to the fields, and building a pond where she could wash clothes. His purpose, however, was not utilitarian aid to a poor peasant family but the construction of memorials to famous poetic images associated with Shuangqing. This "washing clothes pavilion" not so much suggests a real peasant village named Xiaoshan but conjures up that indelible poetic image: of the beautiful banished flower goddess washing clothes on the banks of a stream in a beautiful sunset.

### *Cao Zhenting's Silence*

Cao Zhenting is Shi Zhenlin's only close friend whose collected works survive. With a helpful tip from Du Laoshi, I was able to find Cao's collected writings, *Xiangxue wenchao* (Prose writings from the fragrant snow) in the library of Beijing University. The work is a wood-block edition from the Qianlong reign (1736–96), and as such it cannot be photocopied, as the flash of light is harmful to the fragile paper. However, I found three pieces in this work written to or for Shi Zhenlin, and for a little over a dollar per page, I was able to have them microfilmed. The pieces include Cao's preface to Shi's *Random Notes* (which I already had in my copy of *Random Notes*), a personal letter to Shi, and the preface to a work that has not survived and that I had never before seen listed anywhere, *The Collected Prose and Poetry of Shi Wugang* (the *Wugang* being the style name of Zhenlin, meaning "Enlightenment Ridge"). In none of these pieces is there any reference to Xiaoshan, Shuangqing, or anything even remotely connected with her.

At one point in his *Random Notes,* Shi Zhenlin, in a typical non sequitur after quoting some sad poetry he had written with his friends, remarks, "That was when I began to regret that Cao Zhenting had never gotten to see Shuangqing" (*RN,* 4.44). Then, near the end of the memoir, Shi quotes Cao Zhenting himself, reporting the doubts of his friends concerning Shuangqing: "On the way here I have met many friends who are recluses, so many I should be quite proud. But many of them say they do not believe there can be such a person as Shuangqing in all of Heaven and earth." Shi Zhenlin then continues by quoting a long poem (4.65–66) that Cao Zhenting has supposedly written, which matches Shuangqing's "Autumn Lament" ("Qiu yin"), and which in effect affirms all that Shi Zhenlin has said about Shuangqing's life.

The poem contains a whole series of images associated with Shuangqing: washing clothes in the autumn stream, the ailing chrysanthemum, the crying mermaid, a single pearl in the ocean, Boluo the female immortal, sending meals to the fields, her shadow on the horizon, the gentleman immortal who beautifully records her story, the flying wild goose, the beautiful maiden with a heroic heart, the one who writes in powder on fallen leaves so that the poems disappear but remain fragrant, her autumn lament, planting melons, sacrificing to the flowers, writing the Heart Sutra on a cassia leaf, her malaria, the moon goddess Chang E, her pounding grain, sending food to the poor literatus, et cetera. The last couplet of the poem reads: "Fortunately *Xiqing* with such a skillful pen / Captures this sweetest flower in the world" (*RN*, 4.66).

This is a cleverly ambiguous way around the issue of Shuangqing's existence. Taken naively, it could be seen as Cao Zhenting's declaration of faith in the reality of Shuangqing. But it could just as well be seen to mean that Shuangqing exists precisely in the very poetic images associated with her, and nowhere else. The final couplet provides an almost postmodern twist; the pen (literally, brush) in the text captures this sweetest flower in the world. Without the text, we might well conclude, there would be no Shuangqing. Whatever the interpretation of Cao Zhenting's poem and the doubts he passes on concerning Shuangqing, it is important to remember that the only witness we have testifying to Cao Zhenting's attitude toward Shuangqing is Shi Zhenlin. In Cao's writings to or about Shi Zhenlin outside of the quotes in *Random Notes,* we find no mention of the peasant woman poet.

### *Yuan Mei's Silence*

A final interesting silence in the historical record concerns the great poet Yuan Mei. Yuan Mei was probably the most famous poet in the eighteenth century, in part because of his notoriety in promoting the education of women and the publication of women's poetry. Yuan was from Hangzhou, in neighboring Zhejiang Province, south and east of

Jintan. He personally taught a number of women disciples and published collections of their poetry. He also had a number of concubines and fancied himself as a shrewd judge of female beauty and character. He attracted the ire of conservative intellectuals, who attacked him for shamelessly fraternizing with women and corrupting them with poetry and publicity for their writings.

No one in the eighteenth century was more openly identified with the recruitment and the publicizing of female talent than Yuan Mei. Yuan and Shi were contemporaries, and Yuan won his metropolitan examination degree in 1739, two years after Shi Zhenlin. I have found no reference to Yuan Mei in Shi Zhenlin's writings, but Yuan Mei commented briefly on Shi Zhenlin in several places in his *Poetry Talks from Suiyuan* (Suiyuan being the name of Yuan Mei's famous beautiful garden). In one typical example, he describes Shi Zhenlin as a devotee of Chan Buddhism and a very original poet. He quotes one of Shi's poems, compares him to a small stream that yet carries great force, and praises Shi's poetic lines on flowers, on liberating a toad, and on butterflies breaking through a sunset all as "well worth chanting" (Yuan Mei 1974, supplement to *Suiyuan Poetry Talks,* 2.22a).

Since Yuan Mei knew Shi Zhenlin and refers to poems in *Random Notes,* he must have known of Shi's memoir. Yet he never mentions Shuangqing. His silence on Shuangqing may not mean very much, but given his familiarity with Shi Zhenlin, his strong commitment to praising and publishing women's poetry, his reputation as a connoisseur of female beauty and female talent, and Shi Zhenlin's declared central purpose in *Random Notes,* to "make Shuangqing's name known to the world," Yuan's silence is at least worth noting.

The doubts and silences discussed in this chapter do not prove anything, but they illuminate some ambiguities in the written record, reduce some probabilities, and increase others. At the very least, it is clear that Shi Zhenlin did not intend his *Random Notes* to be taken as a literal history. In several places, he deliberately left the question of Shuangqing's existence up in the air.

### *Possible Mixtures of Truth and Fantasy*

Grace Fong has noted some of the possible mixtures of truth and fantasy in Shi's memoir. Possibilities range from complete fabrication of the woman and her poems, to false attribution of another woman's poems to a beautiful and oppressed peasant, to the simple and straightforward collecting, editing, and recording of actual poems by an actual

Shuangqing (1994, 131–32). We may never know the precise mixture of truth and fantasy in Shi Zhenlin's portrayal on Shuangqing, but at the very least his narrative of Shuangqing, with its many improbabilities, evasions, and silences, suggests some fictionalization and some measure of male fantasy.

Despite the doubts and the silences in Shi's memoir, most Chinese literary critics and historians have treated Shuangqing as a real peasant woman poet. In recent years, several scholars (including my travel companion Du Laoshi) have discussed the question of Shuangqing's existence in greater detail than ever before. And these debates reverberated through our last two days of conversations in Jintan.

*eleven*

# *Conversations in Jintan*

JINTAN, SUNDAY, NOVEMBER 2, 1997

### *Mr. Yu Zhao on Shuangqing and the Xiaoshan Academy*

Thankful for a sound night of sleep back in the comfort of the Jintan Municipal Government Guest House (after our two-day adventure in Xuebu Township), we are up early, and ready for our eight o'clock breakfast appointment with Yu Zhao. Mr. Yu has already provided us with much excitement on this trip with his report of a Xiaoshan Academy that none of us had ever heard of before, but we are anxious to hear more of his earlier investigations, and to report to him our own findings of the past three days. Our host is Mr. Zhu, the head of security for the city of Jintan. Xiaowan joins us in our private dining room, and after introductions, we immediately begin discussing Shuangqing. Mr. Yu is a graduate of Nanjing University, where he majored in Chinese literature, although he is now the head of the Economic Commission of Jintan. He explains that he was born in Danyang and now lives in Jintan, just like Shuangqing (!), and thus he has long had a "strong interest in her poetry."

Mr. Yu immediately surprises us with another piece of information we have never heard before: "Shuangqing was actually born in Jianshan (a township in Danyang); that's an entirely different place from Jiangshu (where most sources claim she was born)."

"What source have you seen that makes this claim about Jianshan?" Du Laoshi asks.

"I heard this from an author who now works for the *Zhenjiang Daily News*. He says that Jianshan has a mountain called Xiaoshan, and that Xiaoshan and Jianshan are one and the same place, now located in Jianshan Township."

"If Jianshan is really Xiaoshan, then the actual location of Xiaoshan is getting very complicated," Du Laoshi notes with understatement. "Perhaps," she speculates, "Shi Zhenlin described Jianshan in Danyang but changed the location to Jintan. That's a possibility." I am pleased to be understanding this conversation, however confusing I find the information. To locate Xiaoshan in Danyang appears to contradict Shi Zhenlin's *Random Notes* as well as the earlier information Yu Zhao himself had given us about reports of a Xiaoshan Academy near Fang Shan in Jintan.

I try to clarify why we are puzzled by Mr. Yu's claim: "According to Shi Zhenlin's description of the location of Xiaoshan, it would have to be in Jintan near Fang Shan."

Sensing the possibility that we might get locked in a fruitless debate over the location of Xiaoshan, Du Laoshi comes to the rescue by changing the subject. "Well, in his *Random Notes* Shi Zhenlin mixed fiction and fact together. We've brought some materials to show you." She hands him a copy of her book, and I also pass him some of the materials I brought along and explain the growing interest in Shuangqing in Europe and North America.

When Hongsheng notes that Mr. Yu was one of the pioneers in the People's Republic in paying attention to Shuangqing and her poetry, he responds modestly, "There was also a lot of interest in Shuangqing in China before Liberation [the shorthand term in China for the 1949 Communist victory in the civil war with the Nationalist Party that then fled to Taiwan]."

Du Laoshi agrees, "Yes, Lin Yutang once said he planned to write a novel on Shuangqing."

Zhang adds, "And now Xiaowan is talking about writing, not only a novel, but also a play about Shuangqing."

Du remarks, "I say that if we can't find the Qing-dynasty Shuangqing, at least [in Xiaowan] we've found the contemporary Shuangqing!" This brings laughter all around, and for the first time, we begin to pass the food. The discussion is fast-paced enough to be hard for me to follow. Consequently, I tend to eat more than anyone else and just sit back and observe the scene. This is our most elegant breakfast, with *baozi,* rice gruel, pickled vegetables, eggs, toast, and steamed breads served in porcelain dishes on a white linen table cloth. We have our own private room and our own waitress who spends most of the time standing nearby and watching to see if anyone needs more tea or anything else. As my mind wanders briefly from the discussion, I can't help noticing this young woman. She is tall, perhaps five-eight, with square shoulders, and is wearing long brown pants and a matching jacket that almost has a military look. With her long hair pulled tight in a bun at the back of her head, her face is perfectly round and perfectly symmetrical, unmarred by makeup or jewelry. Feeling almost guilty for noticing this woman, who is attentive to our breakfast but not at all interested in our conversation, I am careful not to stare. (Maybe I'm just a voyeuristic "male gazer" after all, I silently fret to myself.)

Watching her out of the corner of my eye, I think to myself that hers is the kind of beauty most befitting a peasant woman like Shuangqing. I have noticed this hairstyle frequently in Jintan: hair in a simple bun, showing off a perfectly formed face with almond eyes and a gracefully curved nose that reminds me of the most handsome Buddha statues I have ever seen. My mother, who grew up in a Mennonite family in Missouri, has a nose like mine, hopelessly Germanic and triangular, but she once wore her hair in precisely this style, with a severely simple tightly wrapped bun. Adornments like jewelry and makeup, seen as breeding vanity, were forbidden. Aside from the ideological warnings against pride, wouldn't the simple bun-style hair be the most utilitarian both for Mennonite farm women and for Chinese peasants? Admittedly, this was not Shi Zhenlin's image of beauty. He preferred the aristocratic image of a woman's face with plucked, arched eyebrows, dangling earrings, and hair piled high in loops and adorned with jade pins. I would find his description more convincing if it were simpler and more utilitarian. Maybe my attraction to this elegant simplicity is part of my "peasant bias," or my Mennonite genes? My reverie lasts maybe five minutes, after which I try harder to follow the rapid-fire conversation.

To a question about available sources on Shi Zhenlin, Yu says he has read Shi's *Random Notes* and *Scattered Drafts from Huayang*, but has never seen *Scribbled Poetry of a Wandering Immortal* (a work mentioned in some sources, but one we have never seen). Sensing our keen interest in learning all we can on this trip, he laments that he once knew several people who were especially familiar with Shi Zhenlin and his writings, but some of them have died, and he has lost contact with the others. It sadly dawns on me that parts of the Shuangqing saga, from the eighteenth century to the present, have been irretrievably lost, as some of the most passionate local aficionados on Shuangqing had to suppress their passions in the Maoist years and have now passed from the scene. Even though Shuangqing had the right class background, her classical poetry was a long way from orthodoxy in the Cultural Revolution years. I could imagine some fervent Red Guards in the 1960s denouncing her as a class traitor for exchanging poetry with her exploiter enemies, the literati. That some of her poems had flirtatious overtones would have made her sins even more reactionary.

In our discussion of the location of the Xiaoshan Academy, Yu Zhao says he has never seen an artifact from such a place but was told that it once existed. He tends to believe the story because two of his three informants were illiterate and could not have read or been influenced by Shi Zhenlin's mention of a village called Xiaoshan. Du Laoshi seizes on this fact as particularly important evidence that Shuangqing must have existed independently of Shi Zhenlin's memoir. But to my mind, if a Xiaoshan Academy did exist in Jintan, it could just as easily have been founded by intellectuals who chose the name *in honor of* Shi Zhenlin's portrayal of a Xiaoshan village near Siping Shan. In any case, if the Taiping cataclysm destroyed everyone and everything in Jintan in the mid–nineteenth century, there is no way the descendants of late-nineteenth-century arrivals in Jintan could have remembered an academy from the early eighteenth century. So to me, the possible existence of a Xiaoshan Academy within living memory in Jintan is interesting evidence that Shi Zhenlin's memoir continued to be known and read long after his death, but it has little relevance to the question of Shuangqing's existence.

At another point, Yu Zhao startles me with the assertion that he believes the Xiaoshan Academy is simply another name for Ougeng Hall (Plowing-in-Pairs Hall), where Shi Zhenlin said he studied with Shuangqing's landlord Zhang Mengzhan. Mr. Yu gives no evidence for this view except the surmise that since Zhang Mengzhan's Ougeng Hall was the place where Shi and his friends studied at Xiaoshan, it must have been the same place as the Xiaoshan Academy. Du Laoshi sees this claim as quite logical and fitting the pattern of connection between Shi's memoir and the residue of Jintan popular lore.

Since the written sources on Shuangqing are so few, Yu Zhao believes we should pay more attention to whatever popular stories about Shuangqing we can find among the local population. This is a view Du Laoshi is very pleased to hear.

Xiaowan asks Mr. Yu directly, "Do you believe Shuangqing really lived? Or is she just a legendary figure?"

"Oh! I believe there really was such a person," he is quick to reply.

"In that case," Du Laoshi follows up, "if Shuangqing worked at this Xiaoshan Academy, what was the attitude of her husband and mother-in-law toward her having these kinds of relationships and writing poetry with these gentlemen scholars?"

"The popular story goes this way," Mr. Yu explains. "In the daytime she did her work for her husband's family, and at night she read books and wrote poetry. Her mother-in-law was definitely concerned about this. One time, it is said, Shuangqing was at the Xiaoshan Academy writing poetry with the scholars when her husband arrived. He was already quite ill, but he grabbed Shuangqing by her hair and dragged her all the way home."

He reports that Shuangqing did odd jobs for the scholars at the academy, and in turn, they taught her to write poems, assigned her topics to write on, and assisted her in revising and polishing her compositions. I am again impressed that this popular legend is in many ways more plausible than Shi Zhenlin's written account of Shuangqing. At least here we have a more believable explanation of the contact between a peasant woman and admiring scholars, and a more believable account of how a poor peasant woman could manage to produce such compelling poems. We also have a scene dramatizing the conflict between Shuangqing and her husband over her association with the literati, a conflict that seems strangely absent from *Random Notes.* It is as if the popular story helps people to make sense of the poems Shi Zhenlin has put in his memoir.

Du Laoshi finds the report of a Xiaoshan Academy and the story about Shuangqing working there as independent confirmation of Shi Zhenlin's narrative in *Random Notes.* Because the story comes from illiterates, she reasons, here is independent evidence that a peasant woman named Shuangqing must have existed and written the beautiful poetry attributed to her. By contrast, I see these reports as later interpolations, embellishments, and retellings of a Shuangqing story designed to make sense of the poetry in Shi Zhenlin's memoir and in the many anthologies that quote it. In my view, Shi's memoir remains the bedrock bottom layer in our archeological exploration.

### *Shuangqing: Real or Imagined?*

We ask Mr. Yu more questions about his earlier investigations. How many people had heard of Shuangqing? Not many, only a few very old people. In Mr. Yu's view, these older informants, including some illiterates, would have been unlikely to invent stories about Shuangqing. Thus, he puts a good deal of stock into popular stories. "There are two kinds of theories on Shuangqing," he summarizes. "One is that she didn't exist, but was entirely invented by Shi Zhenlin."

"Yes," interjects Hongsheng, "that was precisely the view of Hu Shi," a famous twentieth-century Chinese scholar whose ideas I discuss in chapter 14.

"And one theory," Yu Zhao continues, "is that these male scholars could not have made up the poetry and song lyrics attributed to Shuangqing."

"This is precisely my own view," Du Laoshi chimes in.

"Shi Zhenlin was the 'heroic' type," Yu continues, in reference to the heroic or masculine style of song lyrics. "He couldn't have written that kind of thing [i.e., the feminine style for which Shuangqing is famous]. That's my view: Shi Zhenlin was very direct and straightforward, not at all the feminine type." Once again, Du Laoshi is delighted to hear her own views articulated so clearly by Mr. Yu.

We then ask Mr. Yu to elaborate further on his view of the supposed Danyang origins of Shuangqing. He believes she came from Danyang because she is listed in the *Danyang County History*. When I ask how he thinks Shuangqing later acquired the surname He, his only response is to suggest that we might try to find a family genealogy for the He clan of Danyang.

This has been an interesting discussion, though we have raised more questions than we have answered. Although Mr. Yu's memory of his 1984 investigation is fuzzy, it is very interesting to have the tidbits of information he has provided us, especially the story about a Xiaoshan Academy where the peasant woman poet worked for the group of scholars studying there. It appears from our discussions with Yu Zhao that we are about a decade too late in looking for people with firsthand knowledge of stories about Shuangqing. Even so, we have discovered more connections between Shi Zhenlin's world and contemporary Jintan than I ever expected to find on this trip. The gulf between China's eighteenth century and its present is not quite as unbridgeable as I had imagined.

### *Televising the Search for Shuangqing*

The afternoon is fairly uneventful, except that we are joined not only by a TV crew, but also by the novelist Chu Fujin and the cultural official Meng Jiyuan, who are both curious to hear more about our research. We get a late start, and the overcast afternoon makes filming difficult, but I manage to take more pictures of the Shi Family Mountainside, the nearby prison, and the stone quarry. The television cameraman follows us on a walk around the Shi Family Mountainside, while Zhang Hongsheng and Du Laoshi point out our main conclusions from the previous day (see figure 22). The reporter interviews several of us about the significance of Shuangqing's poetry and our investigations. After our outing, we return to Xuebu Zhen for yet another lavish feast, where I am honored to sit between Security Chief Zhu and the novelist Chu Fujin.

We have been together now for three consecutive days, and everyone knows that our mission is fulfilled and we are about to leave. The mood is one of relaxed celebration of an event we will all remember. I sense that our Xuebu friends will probably welcome a return to normal life, but I think they have also enjoyed our visit, at least in some respects. From my perspective, they have been unbelievably accommodating to we three scholars on our quixotic quest in search of the vanished world of Shuangqing and Shi Zhenlin. At the end of the meal, I manage a short speech to thank our hosts.

> I'm very grateful for the wonderful hospitality you have shown us this weekend. I think I have discovered at least one profound difference between our two countries. If three scholars showed up at a local government office in America on a Friday afternoon, in search of some piece of eighteenth-century history, no matter how important their mission, they would be dismissed at 5:00 P.M., on Friday and told, if they still had business to conduct, to return on Monday morning. So I'm most grateful to all of you for your kindness, and I hope someday I can reciprocate by hosting some of you in the United States.

When someone remarks on the fact that my trip to Jintan has coincided exactly with Communist Party Chairman Jiang Zemin's trip to Washington, I reply, "Yes. I suppose in the larger scheme of things, his trip is much more important than mine, but I'm quite confident that I've had more fun than he has!"

As we rise to leave, our Xuebu host, Mr. Zhang, presents Du Laoshi, Hongsheng, and me each with a large bag of Jintan's most famous green tea, called Sparrow Tongue Tea (because the dried tea leaves are so small, they are said to resemble the tiny tongues of sparrows). I am surprised by this gift because the previous day, Du Laoshi and I had each purchased a half a kilo of just this tea. A half kilo amounts to a dozen or more small canisters, so I was already overloaded with tea. How will I add fifteen canisters of Sparrow Tongue Green Tea to my already bulging suitcase? When I later asked Hongsheng why they would give us the exact same thing we had already bought, he explained, "By buying a large amount of tea, you and Du Laoshi proved your interest in this local product. So they want to give you an equal amount to show their appreciation for your interest."

I am sad to wave goodbye to Mr. Zhang and his wife and granddaughter, Xiaomei, and to leave Xuebu Zhen for the last time. However, I feel confident that this will not be my last trip to Jintan. On our ride back to Jintan, Du Laoshi and Hongsheng kindly compliment me on the quick improvement in my spoken Chinese in just a few days' time. "The trouble is," I respond candidly, "my Chinese progresses for the few weeks I spend in China, and then regresses for years on end back in the States!"

### *Conversations in Jintan*

Back in Jintan, we invite Chu Fujin and Mr. Zhu to our room, along with Xiaowan and her lawyer friend Xu Donggong, the self-taught calligrapher. Mr. Xu presents Du Laoshi and Hongsheng and me with samples of his own calligraphy on Shuangqing-related themes, much to my delight. Sitting on the chairs and beds in our crowded room, Mr. Chu launches us on a wide-ranging and fast-paced discussion of everything under the sun. I am struck by his insatiable curiosity and cosmopolitan interests. Our topics include religion and its relation to economic development, a comparison of Chinese and Indian civilizations, the state of Chinese contemporary literature (which Mr. Chu sees as plagued with conformity and faddishness), and Samuel Huntington's writings on the clash of civilizations. Whatever improvement there has been in my Chinese in the past week, the intense discussion now leaves me reeling, and occasionally I check out of the conversation to keep my brain from a complete meltdown. At these times, I try to hide my weariness and continue to look interested in what is being said. At least three times, Mr. Chu finishes a short monologue, turns to me, and says, "And Professor Ropp, what do you think about this?"

Having just tried to look as though I understood and agreed with everything he had just said, I invariably turn to my reliable crutch, Hongsheng, and say, "I didn't quite catch the last couple of sentences. Could you summarize briefly? [meaning, whatever are we talking about?]" As Hongsheng explains slowly in his impeccably clear Mandarin, I try desperately to focus on what he says in order to be able to say something both relevant and intelligible. Mr. Chu is a truly delightful conversationalist, but his high energy level and high-octane vocabulary both leave me in the dust tonight. Our party finally breaks up around 11:00 P.M., and I retreat into the English language and try to summarize the evening's conversation in my journal before drifting off to sleep.

JINTAN, MONDAY, NOVEMBER 3, 1997

Today we plan to spend the morning at the Jintan County Archives, looking at the genealogical records of the Zhang family, in search of a listing for Zhang Mengzhan, Shi Zhenlin's friend and Shuangqing's landlord. After lunch with the mayor of Jintan, we will be taken to the neighboring county of Danyang, where Shuangqing was supposedly born. Hongsheng is anxious to get to Danyang so that he can introduce Du Laoshi and me to a former classmate of his who now works in the county government. Once he has us properly introduced there, he will return to Nanjing for his Tuesday class. After breakfast, I carefully pack my new treasures, calligraphy, roof tiles, and tea. Opening up the expandable pocket of my suitcase, I am delighted that I can squeeze in all thirty of my canisters of Jintan Sparrow Tongue Tea!

### *Change of Plans: One More Day in Jintan*

Just as I am feeling triumphant in my success, Xiaowan calls us with bad news: the mayor is tied up this noon, and has rescheduled us for dinner this evening. In addition, the Jintan TV crew wants to come to our hotel tomorrow (Tuesday) morning to interview each of us again, because time was too short on Sunday, and they have been studying more about our research, and so will be able to ask more detailed questions tomorrow. This news is a real blow to Hongsheng. His first inclination is to return to Nanjing anyway and miss dinner with the mayor. But Xiaowan is adamant. He can't miss dinner with the mayor! This is the culmination of all the work she has done for us and of all the connections she has made. And because we are so indebted to Xiaowan for all her work on our behalf, there is really no way Hongsheng can leave without having dinner with the Mayor.

### *The Downside of Connections* **(Guanxi)**

He is visibly distressed at having to call his department to cancel his Tuesday class, and he remarks at one point about how difficult it is to manage things in China. What he means is that one simply cannot avoid becoming enmeshed and entangled in an elaborate network of *guanxi,* human connections. On the one hand, as I noted already in chapter 1, we would not have made this trip at all, much less so successfully, without these many personal connections. My own connections with Du Laoshi and Hongsheng were crucial to begin with. And only Hongsheng's connections (through Nanjing University) with Xiaowan, and in turn, Xiaowan's connections with the mayor's office, have made possible all of our contacts in Jintan. But in the Chinese system of personal connections, each favor one accepts carries with it an obligation that must be repaid whether it is convenient or not, so we have little choice but to live, and die, by the system. And because the rules are so clear and universally known, Hongsheng does not have to agonize over his course of action. He knows he is trapped, so he makes his calls, readjusts his expectations, and we head off to the Jintan Public Records Office.

### *Searching for Shuangqing's Landlord Zhang Mengzhan*

After Xiaowan takes us to the public records office, only a few blocks from our hotel, Hongsheng explains to the young woman archivist our interest in the Zhang family genealogy. This young woman, in her thirties, is interested to hear our story of Shuangqing the Jintan peasant woman poet. She says she too likes to write poetry and hopes to resume writing poetry, not for publication but for her own enjoyment, once her child is grown up and she has more time. (Du Laoshi jokes that all the women in Jintan must be budding poets.) She brings us more than fifty volumes, each about one-inch thick, of the Zhang family genealogy, and we each take a dozen or so volumes and begin to page through them in search of a Zhang Mengzhan, Zhang Renchi, and Zhang Ling (Mengzhan's brothers) and Zhang Xiuyuan (their father). We have our own room and sit around a long conference table. The room is plain, with a concrete floor, but it is more than adequate for our needs. We are dressed warmly on this chilly autumn day, and further warmed by the hot glasses of green tea that our hosts periodically refill with boiling water. After the intensity of the last four days, it is a bit dull, but also relaxing, to sit quietly and thumb through piles of genealogies.

The work is straightforward and simple, almost mechanical. The genealogy traces all the branches of the Zhang family in Jintan for about a thousand years. We are only interested in the eighteenth century, so we can fly through those portions dealing with earlier periods. I skim the Chinese only half as fast as Du Laoshi and Hongsheng, but still manage to feel useful. Each person is listed in a family tree, with their names, wives' surnames, and birth and death dates. If a man won a civil service degree or served in office, that too is recorded. We are pleased to discover several Zhangs in the eighteenth century who have Meng as the first character of their given name: Zhang Mengzhe (b. 1700); Zhang Mengxiang (b. 1714); two brothers Zhang Menglin (b. 1710), and Zhang Mengyuan (b. 1725); and four brothers, Zhang Mengzhou, Zhang Menglong, Zhang Menghu, and Zhang Meng'an, all born between 1761 and 1785. But we find none of the Zhangs in Shi Zhenlin's *Random Notes:* Xiuyuan, Mengzhan, Renchi, or Ling.

Xiaowan has plans to visit her aunt in Zhenjiang today, so she leaves us once the introductions are finished and we have our stacks of genealogies to go through. We break for lunch and return for our fourth meal at Mr. Chen's Rainbow Elegance Restaurant. This time, without Xiaowan to order more food than we can eat, we insist on a simple meal of wonton soup. Mr. Chen obliges us as cheerfully as ever but still refuses to accept our money, as if we are on important government business with "all expenses paid." We are grateful for his warm hospitality, and as this is clearly our last meal here, we take pictures of Mr. Chen and his staff before heading back to the public records office (see figure 24). I get a little drowsy in the middle of the afternoon, but we diligently keep at it until we finish all fifty volumes by around five o'clock. "I like this collaboration with Chinese scholars!" I think to myself when I realize it would have taken me a fairly tedious week to get through the material we've surveyed in one day.

From our day's work, I see little of significance to illuminate the study of Shi Zhenlin's *Random Notes,* but Du Laoshi sees things differently. In her recent article on our investigative trip, she argues that all the given names of *Meng* in this genealogy suggest a connection between the main line of the Zhang family that lived in Xilitang in Liyang (a nearby county) and Shi Zhenlin's friend Zhang Mengzhan in Xiaoshan. She sees many significant parallels: both families combined farming and collecting rents from tenants with studying for the civil service examinations; both believed in communication with spirits through divination and planchette spirit writing; both families praised their most virtuous members, male and female alike, in their writings. These parallels suggest to Du Laoshi that Shi's *Random Notes* is a factual record of things seen and heard in the 1730s (Du 1998, 124–27).

Du Laoshi does note one contrast between the two Zhang families, with a humorous touch. Whereas Zhang Mengzhan once tried to convince Shuangqing to write him poems in exchange for grain, the Zhang genealogy contains a story about one Zhang son who was startled on one of his rent-collecting trips when a peasant woman came to his bedroom offering him wine and boiled eggs. Insulted by this affront to his virtue (or perhaps to his sense of class superiority?), he angrily chased her off and immediately boarded his boat for home. His boat was uncovered, and he traveled for dozens of *li* in a hard rain, arriving home at last with a splitting headache. Thereafter, he refused ever again to eat boiled eggs! (Du Fangqin 1988, 127). This story from the Zhang family genealogy beautifully illustrates the orthodox approach to peasant-tenant relations in the eighteenth century. Of course Shuangqing was never so bold as to approach her landlord in such a direct way, but from this kind of story, we can imagine that if the Liyang Zhangs ever read Shi Zhenlin's account of Zhang Mengzhan's dealings with Shuangqing, they would not have been inclined to include him in their illustrious genealogy.

### *Formal Dinner with the Mayor of Jintan*

At 6:00 P.M. we have our most formal meal of the trip, a banquet hosted by the mayor of Jintan City. He and several other city officials are dressed in dark suits with white shirts and ties. By contrast, we field-tripping scholars, including Meng Jiyuan and novelist Chu Fujin, are dressed informally. We have the potent *baijiu* in shot glasses, beer in tall glasses, and a sparkling red wine in wine glasses. In keeping with the higher rank of our hosts, the meal is more formal than our meals in Xuebu Zhen. I sit between the mayor and vice mayor, and ask myself, "Do these men host guests and eat like this every day?"

The food is even more lavish than we've had before, and the highlight comes when we are each served a large red boiled crab about eight inches in diameter. When I mockingly ask how one eats a crab with chopsticks, the vice mayor comes to my rescue with an expert demonstration. You pull off a leg or a claw, crack it between your teeth, dip it in a delicious soy-sugar-vinegar-garlic sauce, separate the tender rich meat from the pieces of shell with your tongue, swallow the meat and spit out the pieces of shell. I manage to do this with some difficulty. But the legs and claws are just a preliminary to the main attraction: the body of the crab. The vice mayor carefully instructs me to pull open the belly of the crab, dip the front part of the belly into the sauce and take a bite of the white part. Then you break the body in half, dip it in the sauce, and pull out the soft red and pink parts to eat, and discard the white parts around the edges. To me this is counterintuitive, as the white parts are all that I would identify as edible. I comfort myself in the knowledge that the Chinese experience in eating crabs is millions of times greater than mine. The soft red and pink parts—which I have no desire to identify—will never become my favorite part of the crab, but dipped in soy-sugar-vinegar-garlic sauce, they are quite tasty, and I suffer no adverse effects from this crab's "inner crab."

### *More Conversations on Shuangqing with Novelist Chu Fujin*

With our banquet finished by 8:00 P.M., we gather again in Hongsheng's and my room and begin discussing our hopes for future work on Shuangqing. Mr. Chu Fujin soon joins us, and he launches us into an intense discussion with a direct question to me: "So, Professor Ropp, what do you think about Shuangqing? Was there a real peasant woman poet named Shuangqing? Or did Shi Zhenlin simply create a fictional character?" Leave it to the ever-cheerful novelist, Mr. Chu, to put me on the spot. I surprise myself with the passion of my response. For the past few days I have mostly been a silent observer of these investigations, even when uncomfortable with the way we present our research, as if Shuangqing's existence is beyond doubt and we are simply trying to locate where, not whether, she once lived. Now my doubts come pouring out: her writing in powder on leaves, her early declaration about meeting scholars in or through *Random Notes,* her poverty, the abuse she cheerfully suffers, her brilliant poetry despite malaria, weakness, and daily farm drudgery, her wifely loyalty contradicted by her flirtations with the literati, the apparent obliviousness of Shi and his friends to the dangers they place her in with the fawning attention they lavish on her.

Having poured out all these doubts, I wait for a response. Hongsheng, who has heard me say these things before, shares some of my doubts, though he probably thinks I go too far at times. Du Laoshi also knows my views, though I have never stated them so directly or summarized them so completely in a single conversation before. She just smiles and even appears sympathetic, as if I'm having a dizzy spell that will soon pass. She agrees that Shi Zhenlin is sometimes contradictory, and that we may see him as a connoisseur of beautiful and talented women.

Yet she sees no reason to question Shi's account of Shuangqing. In her own published account of our trip, she would later write that "since Shi Zhenlin recorded all his encounters with his friends and stories of his friends in the form of a chronicle, why should we keep on doubting the existence of [Shuangqing as] a real woman? Shi Zhenlin was a rigorous and serious 'gentleman scholar' and an upright man of letters; why should we say that what he wrote was 'all lies'?" (Du 1998, 125).

In Du Laoshi's view, all the important findings thus far on our trip are indicative of the literal truth of Shi Zhenlin's account of

Shuangqing. The report of a Xiaoshan Academy is evidence that Shi Zhenlin's Xiaoshan was a real place. The Fang Shan area in general and the Shi Family Mountainside in particular match Shi Zhenlin's descriptions of Xiaoshan to a tee: the rocky mountain to the east, the bamboo grove, fields to the south, a body of water to the west, peasants making their own straw sandals and climbing Fang Shan to cut kindling. All these things suggest to Du Laoshi that Shi Zhenlin was simply describing a real place whose name got changed somewhere along the line to the Shi Family Mountainside. She also sees Jintan's and Xuebu Zhen's "high cultural level" as proof that a peasant woman like Shuangqing could have been educated sufficiently to produce the brilliant poetry attributed to her. As for the temple names at Fang Shan, she has no trouble with the assumption that the Grandma's Cave of recent times was Rouge Cave in Shi Zhenlin's day. And she is also inclined to accept Mr. Yu Zhao's view that the Xiaoshan Academy was simply another name for the Ougeng Hall where Shi Zhenlin says he studied with Zhang Mengzhan.

To me, all these correlations are not very central to the question of Shuangqing's existence. Because I read Shi Zhenlin's memoir as an imaginative reconstruction of his travels, "a book of Heavenly immortals," as his friend Wu Zhensheng characterized it, all the correspondences and parallels between this place and Shi's memoir simply help, in my view, to locate *Shi himself* in Xuebu Township and Jintan County in the 1730s. I am as delighted as Du Laoshi to think that we might have actually discovered the "real" setting of Shi's memoir, but the historical reality of the setting does little or nothing to prove the historical reality of Shuangqing. The existence of real covered bridges in Madison County, Iowa, provides the setting for the popular love story named after them, but it doesn't follow at all from the presence of such bridges that a real Iowa farmwife who looked like Meryl Streep ever had a love affair with a real traveling photographer the spitting image of Clint Eastwood.

Mr. Chu brings his novelist perspective to bear on these issues, and says, "Of course, in writing novels, one always combines observation with embellishment. If I met a talented peasant woman with an unappreciative husband, I would be inclined to beautify or idealize the woman and uglify her husband, simply for the sake of creating tension and drama in the story."

This helps me to visualize more clearly than I had before the many possible levels of truth and falsity in a single narrative. Just because parts of Shi Zhenlin's story seem to me unlikely does not in itself mean that the entire story is a complete fiction. Mr. Chu caps off the evening with my favorite line from the whole trip, in response to my question to him: "What do *you* think of the Shuangqing story and her poetry?"

With a wide grin, he replies, "If Shuangqing was a real peasant woman poet who suffered all the things Shi reports and still wrote such brilliant poetry, that's a very interesting story. But if she was the complete fabrication of Shi Zhenlin and still became famous as China's great peasant woman poet, that's an even more interesting story!" This last sentence pours out simultaneously with a deep belly laugh that makes me want to give him a bear hug.

"Exactly!" I blurt out with a laugh. "You have summed up precisely the point of view I want to convey in my book on Shuangqing."

Chu Fujin has helped me to formulate the challenge now before me: to tell Shi Zhenlin's story of Shuangqing, the story of Shuangqing in Chinese culture, and my own story of investigating these two stories. Before bidding farewell, he cheerfully gives me a last piece of excellent advice: "Just remember, the point of this story, of any story, is to keep the interest of the audience!"

JINTAN, TUESDAY, NOVEMBER 4, 1997

### *Terror of a Television Interview*

By five in the morning I find myself awake and worried about what I will say on camera in a few hours when the Jintan TV reporter asks me something about Shuangqing. Once I start thinking about this, it is hopeless to try to go back to sleep. We have agreed ahead of time that I am to provide the international perspective on research on Shuangqing. Du Laoshi will discuss Shuangqing's position in Chinese women's history, and Hongsheng will discuss her significance in Chinese poetry. Although I've already done one television interview on Saturday, I am terrified by the idea. I need to understand whatever question is asked the first time it's asked, and I won't have Hongsheng at my elbow to ask for clarification or to give me a ready Chinese equivalent for an English term. On the borderline between sleep and waking, the anxieties take over, and I can imagine being drummed out of the China field when my inarticulate television interview is broadcast to the world. By the end of my morning shower, I have recovered a semblance of sanity, and no longer fear a disgraceful end of my career. The worst that can happen is that Jintan TV finds my segment unusable. I still want to do well, and think, "How do I work postmodernism into this interview? That should impress them with the exotic foreign perspective!"

When it happens, the actual interview is mercifully short. The richness of Shi Zhenlin's memoir, I suggest, invites investigation from many angles: the poetry, the position of women in Chinese society, the growing literacy of women in the Qing period, and the uniqueness of a peasant woman poet. I note there is growing interest in Shuangqing and her poetry in the United States, Canada, Holland, Hong Kong, and Taiwan. Just as I feel my Chinese sentences are starting to flow, the interview is over. Thank you very much! My two minutes on camera pass by in a flash. Now we have finished everything we set out to do in Jintan. On to Danyang, the reputed birthplace of Shuangqing!

### *Farewell to Jintan and Xiaowan*

We settle our bill, which amounts to almost nothing, less than ten dollars per day by my calculation. Apart from breakfasts (which cost us about thirty cents per person), we have paid for no food on this whole trip, and Xiaowan and/or the local government have provided all our transportation.

After suggesting we might not leave until after lunch, Xiaowan makes more calls on her magical cellular phone and announces that the mayor's personal driver will take us to Danyang in the mayor's black limousine. We bid Xiaowan farewell, put our baggage in the trunk, and climb in. The two-lane highway is busy, and at one point our driver turns on a siren to warn oncoming traffic to make way for our car as we pass a series of slow-moving trucks. It is common on these two-lane highways for cars to straddle the center line to pass, even against a steady stream of oncoming traffic. As everyone understands this practice in China, my colleagues are not as alarmed as I am when we pull out and straddle the line. Common practice or no, our driver is clearly concerned enough about the tight squeeze ahead of us to turn on his siren, thereby letting oncoming traffic know that this is a car worth making room for. Fortunately, the cars do pull over enough to let us pass, and my confidence grows that we will indeed make it to Danyang.

*twelve* ·

# *Contemporary Scholarship*

### *1992: Harvard Conference*

In 1992 I presented a paper at an international conference called "Engendering China," organized at Harvard University and Wellesley College. Just back from my sabbatical year of work with Liu Laoshi, I naturally chose to do a paper on Shuangqing. In this paper, without formally declaring Shuangqing to be a fictional character, I quoted Shi's *Random Notes* at length and let the doubts accumulate of their own accord. Since Shuangqing's poetry is much better known than Shi Zhenlin's narrative of her life, I focused on Shi's portrayal of Shuangqing and the attitudes of Shi and his friends toward female talent and toward relations between men and women.

I noted the many implausibilities and ambiguities in Shi's memoir and suggested that Shuangqing is too idealized and Shi's story of her life too contradictory to be taken at face value, but I also acknowledged that the "most compelling" evidence for the existence of a real peasant woman poet lay in the haunting and original poems attributed to her. Despite these ambiguities, I emphasized her plausibility to most Chinese readers since Shi Zhenlin's time. The widespread acceptance of Shuangqing as a distinguished Qing-dynasty poet reflects an openness toward female literary talent that was important in late imperial China. Here is an important exception to the popular stereotype that Chinese in the eighteenth century saw literary talent as incompatible with female virtue. Shuangqing, I concluded, has a real place in Chinese culture, and a more prominent place than Shi himself (Ropp 1992).

Perhaps the best thing I did at the conference was to read Shuangqing's song lyric to the fading lamp in the original Chinese, with all those repeated characters. I tried to imitate Liu Laoshi's reading as best I could and was surprised by the polite applause that followed. Only years later would I hear Du Fangqin's kindly claim that my reading of this song lyric to the fading lamp first inspired her to take up Shuangqing's poetry in her own research.

### *1993: Yale Conference*

In June 1993 I participated in another international conference, at Yale University, on women and writing in late imperial China. This was the conference where I first met Kang Zhengguo, the brilliant and learned Chinese literature specialist from Xi'an Jiaotong University. I was delighted to room with him because this gave us ample opportunity to get acquainted. Since he spoke little English, our conversations helped me revive my spoken Chinese, which was already becoming rusty after my sabbatical in Taiwan the previous year. At our first meeting, I gave Kang a copy of my Harvard paper on Shuangqing and told him I had enjoyed his 1988 book on women and Chinese poetry. I looked forward to his own paper at this conference, as his topic was so similar to my Harvard conference paper from the year before: Shi Zhenlin and his narrative of Shuangqing.

### *Elsie Choy's* **Life and Poetry of He Shuangqing**

Meeting scholars from all over the world, rooming with Kang Zhengguo, and discussing Shuangqing and her poetry with him and others was an exhilarating experience. In addition to Kang Zhengguo, two other scholars discussed Shuangqing in their papers. Moreover, on the first day of the conference, Lin Shuen-fu, a colleague from my alma mater, the University of Michigan, showed me a newly published book, *Leaves of Prayer: The Life and Poetry of He Shuangqing, a Farmwife in Eighteenth-Century China*. Elsie Choy, a retired woman in Ann Arbor, had gotten interested in Shuangqing, had found Shi Zhenlin's *Random Notes* in the University of Michigan Library, and had written this book, a translation of all the portions of Shi Zhenlin's memoir pertaining to Shuangqing. She also had a reputable publisher, the University of Hong Kong Press, which had produced an attractive volume complete with Shuangqing's poems in English and in the elegant Chinese calligraphy of a well-known Hong Kong scholar and calligrapher, T. C. Lai.

Initially, my response was one of alarm. She had translated almost exactly the same portions of Shi's *Random Notes* that I had spent months of precious time deciphering with Liu Laoshi. All those hours, the best hours of a rare sabbatical, and here was the very same material in English and in print! Choy also included an introduction with much useful information on Shi Zhenlin and his eighteenth-century world. There may be hundreds of translations of the Bible and the *Daodejing*, but who would want to publish my version of something as obscure as *Random Notes* now that this book was out?

### *Discussions with Kang Zhengguo*

Fortunately, the excitement of the Yale conference easily overshadowed these anxieties. Every evening, when we should have been reading the next day's conference papers, Kang Zhengguo and I had long discussions on Shuangqing and her poetry. I was greatly encouraged to discover that many of our views uncannily coincided. We had both begun reading Shuangqing's poetry with the assumption that she was a historical figure. He first wrote on Shuangqing in his 1988 study of Chinese women's poetry, which I had read while on sabbatical in Taiwan. There he notes that the paucity of sources on her, and the amazing talent revealed in her poems despite her poor background, have caused some to raise doubts about her historical existence. However, he goes on to explain that her lack of formal education may have served her in positive ways.

> The poetry and song lyrics of He Shuangqing have not a trace of the affected sentimentality of women's poetry, and with her poetic pen she demolished the traps of classicism and elaborate ornamentation, and wrote in plain and simple language about the many difficulties she endured amidst poverty, farm life, and family affairs. (Kang 1988, 337)

Talking with him at Yale and reading his paper in Chinese, I discovered that he and I had recently developed many of the same doubts about the literal accuracy of Shi Zhenlin's narrative. In this regard, I was fascinated to see that Elsie Choy expressed views very different from ours. I raced through her introduction to see how she would present the issue of Shuangqing as a historical figure. Fortunately, she made it easy for me by summarizing her argument.

### *Elsie Choy: "No Doubt That Shuangqing Existed"*

> It has been suggested by some that He Shuangqing could have been a figment of Shi Zhenlin's imagination and than [sic] he

could have written the poetry attributed to her, as has been true with some scholars who have written lyric songs for their favorite courtesans and signed the women's names to them. From this we can see that the records of He Shuangqing are indeed so exceptional that she invites conjectures even today, just as she did in her own days, according to Shi Zhenlin.

In my mind there can be no doubt that she existed. In the first place, she is recorded in the county records of Danyang and Jintan, no matter how briefly. In the second place, her poetry is extremely feminine; its tenor, its contents, its colors are straight from the heart of a young woman in the sort of disgraceful life situation in which our poet found herself after her marriage. In the third place, the sensitivity in her work could not be faked by even the most sympathetic male. Fourth, if Shi Zhenlin had wanted to write an imaginary story, he could have written and acknowledged a fictional one. The fact is that his writings show him to be open, sincere, honest and sensitive to the feelings of others, with a certain amount of the detachment essential for a good objective biographer, though not a fiction writer. From his two notebooks we can see that he was interested in people and made it his life-long vocation to write sketches and portraits of them. He Shuangqing happened to be the largest canvas that he did, since she provided him with insightful material from both her life and work until she died. In a sense, her portrait was unfinished in his writings, but therein lies the real meaning or triumph of her life. Furthermore, Shi Zhenlin had no reason to fabricate He Shuangqing when many of his friends involved themselves in her life; and he certainly would not have portrayed his special friends, Anshu and Yuhan, in their infatuation for his own amusement. Finally, as recorded in his *Huayang sangao*, there are letters he wrote to some of these friends that refer to He Shuangqing's passing as something they all mourned. (Choy 1993, 31–32)

### *Su Zhecong: He Shuangqing, a Female Farmworker*

One of the Yale papers on Shuangqing was very similar to that of Elsie Choy in its approach. This was a Chinese paper by Su Zhecong, a senior professor of Chinese poetry at Wuhan University. Professor Su's 1987 anthology of Chinese women's poetry had provided me early on in my research with my first exposure to several of Shuangqing's most famous poems and song lyrics. I was naturally excited by the opportunity to meet her now, and to hear her discuss Shuangqing in greater detail. Professor Su's paper was entitled "The Poetry of He Shuangqing and Female Farm Workers." If anything, her interpretation of Shuangqing seems more unequivocal than Elsie Choy's. She does not even admit the possibility of doubt concerning the historical reality of a peasant woman poet named He Shuangqing. She simply assumes Shuangqing's existence.

Professor Su takes what I would call a Marxist-feminist-positivist approach. I say Marxist because she puts a great deal of emphasis on class relations and Shuangqing's position as a peasant. She is feminist in that she sees Shuangqing representing the voice of oppressed women in the Qing period, and demonstrating the genius of a woman who develops her talent against all odds. Perhaps most important of all the influences in her work is a positivist approach to the interpretation of sources, because she sees no problem in taking Shi Zhenlin literally at every turn. She takes in stride the idea of Shuangqing writing poems in powder on leaves. She sees proof of Shuangqing's existence in the realistic description of suffering in her poetry, in the distinctive quality of the poetry attributed to her, and in the close correspondence between Shuangqing's unhappiness as evident in her poetry and the oppressed position of women, especially peasant woman, in eighteenth-century China. Like Elsie Choy, Professor Su downplays the romantic elements in Shi Zhenlin's tale, and she sees Shuangqing as the modest, chaste, and loyal wife, not the flirtatious woman that Liu Laoshi and I had seen in some of the writings attributed to her.

### *Grace Fong: Shuangqing as a Feminine Ideal*

A very different approach was taken at the Yale conference by Grace Fong from McGill University. A specialist on Chinese poetry, Fong had earlier discussed Shuangqing in a 1990 conference paper on the development of a "woman's voice" in the song-lyric genre. In that paper (published in 1994), she acknowledges ambiguities in the question of Shuangqing's existence, but focuses primarily on the cultural significance of her poetry with its distinctive feminine voice. She gives an astute analysis of several of Shuangqing's song lyrics and praises them for having

> a highly individual and intense voice. The uncanny subjectivity and the overwhelming psychological dimension of these songs sometimes make them appear like the disturbed visions of an

> alienated woman. At the same time, her lyrics are crafted pieces with the naturalness and flow that conceal the artifice, in ways reminiscent of Li Qingzhao's art. Certain poetic devices, such as effective use of reduplication and cumulative repetition of words, are obvious emulations of Li Qingzhao's famous style. (1994, 130)

At the Yale conference, I eagerly anticipated Fong's paper. Applying contemporary literary theory in a perceptive analysis of Shi Zhenlin's narrative, she argued that Shi strove to create a feminine ideal of beauty, talent, sensibility, and virtue, all in the person and poetry of Shuangqing. In Fong's view, Shi Zhenlin's narrative is, at least in places, so "inscribed with male desire" that it "robs or dispossesses woman of her own voice." By the conclusion of *Random Notes,* Shuangqing "has been the object of his gaze, idealized, exploited, fetishized, and then forgotten." Yet, despite the male ideology permeating this memoir, Fong sees in the power of Shuangqing's poetry signs that "betray the 'otherness' of their origin" (1997, 274, 278). She elaborates in a footnote:

> I believe there was a real rural woman with poetic talent behind the representation in *Random Records.* But her image and story are aestheticized and subjugated to the overall design and tone of the work. We may call this process fictionalization. It is probable that Shi Zhenlin "edited" her poems in the process. (1997, 466 n. 18)

### *Kang Zhengguo: Marginalized Literati and Talented Women*

Kang Zhengguo delivered his Yale conference paper in Chinese and published it a year later in a Chinese journal. His topic is similar to that of Grace Fong, though he is a bit less theoretical in his approach, and a bit more concerned to relate Shi Zhenlin's writings to Chinese literary traditions and ideals. Slightly more agnostic than Fong on the question of Shuangqing's existence, he argues that it is impossible to know whether she existed or not, and not very productive to worry about it. The important thing is that Shuangqing represented an ideal of feminine beauty and talent that marginalized intellectuals like Shi Zhenlin and his friends identified with very deeply.

Taking up a theme from the prefaces to *Random Notes* written by Shi Zhenlin's friend, Wu Zhensheng, Kang Zhengguo notes the obsession of Shi and his friends with women of unmatched beauty, talent, feeling, and virtue. Every talented male scholar should be matched with a woman with these four qualities, which inspire the man to love the woman's beauty, to cherish (or pity) her talent, to sympathize with her feelings, and to respect her virtue. "Whether consciously or unconsciously, Shi was manifesting [through these qualities] his own self and the selves of his poor scholar friends" (Kang 1994, 95).

Kang points out Shi Zhenlin's fascination with the ambiguous relationship between dream and reality and praises Shi's narrative for its beauty and poetic power, whether it is a literal record of events or not. He also notes the popularity in the eighteenth century of numerous stories about talented and beautiful women who die young after unhappy lives of suffering and illness. Finally, he briefly sketches the evolution of commentaries on Shuangqing from the eighteenth century to the present, showing that most critics have taken her existence for granted. By contrast with most earlier Chinese critics, Kang is concerned, not to prove or disprove Shuangqing's historical reality, but to highlight her importance as a cultural ideal that has survived to the present day. He concludes his long erudite discussion with the observation that in the final analysis, only Shi Zhenlin knows who this "Cinderella" was. "As to the Shuangqing we have been discussing, she evidently exists in the 'fusing of horizons' [between fiction and fact, illusion and reality] as shown in this article" (1994, 104).

Both Kang Zhengguo and Grace Fong effectively apply contemporary literary theory in analyzing Shi Zhenlin's narrative representation of Shuangqing as a cultural ideal within the context of eighteenth-century China. I came away from the Yale conference pleased to have seen Shuangqing at the center of so much debate and encouraged in my own views by their congruence with those of Grace Fong and Kang Zhengguo. To be honest, I also felt uncertain as to the future of my own work on Shuangqing. Had I been "scooped" by Elsie Choy's book and the three Yale papers before I ever got into print? Was there anything I could add to the already rich discussion?

As soon as I got home from the Yale conference I ordered two copies of Elsie Choy's book on Shuangqing, one for me and one for Kang Zhengguo. When my copy came in the mail I spent two full days reading it very carefully. I discovered that Choy has uncovered some valuable information about the various ways Shuangqing's poetry had been anthologized and analyzed in the past. Her translations are generally accurate, and she includes informative notes on allusions in Shuangqing's poetry.

I was curiously relieved to discover how different Choy's interpretation is from my own. She simply is not troubled by the things that trouble me. She is not troubled by Shuangqing's given name, lack of a surname, writing on leaves with powder, or any of those things that caused me to doubt Shi Zhenlin's narrative as a literal or factual account. Whereas Liu Laoshi and I had detected flirtatious overtones with Shuangqing's use of the intimate term *lang* ("my dear"), Choy consistently interprets *lang* as a reference to Shuangqing's husband, thereby removing any connotation of flirtatiousness. Concentrating her narrative on Shuangqing, she pays little attention to Shi Zhenlin's and Wu Zhensheng's fascination with young beauties, their spirit-writing séances with female immortals, or the alternating spells of ecstasy and agony that Shuangqing casts on her most ardent admirers.

### *Du Fangqin:* Collected Materials on He Shuangqing

Less than a year after the Yale conference, I was surprised to find in my mailbox a copy of Du Fangqin's Chinese book, *Collected Materials on He Shuangqing*. Kang Zhengguo had sent me the book from China. I had not met Du Fangqin at the Harvard conference, and I didn't know that she was working on Shi Zhenlin and Shuangqing. I was particularly surprised to see her quote my Harvard paper in her book on the issue of Shuangqing's existence. Hers was by far the most detailed scholarly discussion of Shuangqing I had ever seen, and I was intrigued to read her argument. I slowly made my way through the book in whatever spare time I could find, working at the snail's pace of a few pages a week. (Little did I dream at this point that one day I would accompany her to Jintan and Danyang in search of modern traces of the Shuangqing story.)

In *Collected Materials on He Shuangqing*, Du includes most of Shi Zhenlin's narrative about Shuangqing's life, and all of the poetry and prose attributed to Shuangqing, with detailed annotations and explanatory notes. How I could have used this book when I first began reading *Random Notes* with Liu Laoshi! In a long section on "Research on He Shuangqing," Du presents arguments similar to those of Elsie Choy and Su Zhecong. In my view, she is more careful than they are to take into account the fanciful nature of much of Shi Zhenlin's *Random Notes*. She readily acknowledges, for example, that Shi was fascinated with dreams, imagination, popular religion, and female immortals. And she says his search for idealized women in the form of heavenly immortals was a kind of escapism from the pressures of examination life and the economic competition of eighteenth-century society.

## *Du Fangqin:* Random Notes *as Documentary History*

However, Du Fangqin sees a crucial distinction between Shi Zhenlin's infatuation with female immortals and the supernatural, and his portrayal of a mundane earthbound peasant woman poet. She points out that once Shuangqing appears in *Random Notes,* she replaces the female immortals as the focus of attention for Shi and his friends. Once Shuangqing comes on the scene, Shi and his friends hold only one more séance to communicate with the heavenly immortals.

Independently of each other, Kang Zhengguo and I had both seen similarities between Shi Zhenlin's aesthetic philosophy and that of the great eighteenth-century Chinese novelist Cao Xueqin. We were both encouraged in these views by a Chinese scholar, Hong Jingyuan, who wrote an article in 1984 comparing Shi's memoir and Cao's novel. Both men argued that fact and fiction, truth and illusion, dream and waking reality are inextricably bound up together and are ultimately indistinguishable from each other. Du Fangqin has a very different view. She contrasts *Random Notes* with Cao Xueqin's famous novel, *Dream of the Red Chamber.* Both works may feature many beautiful women, but from page 1, Cao Xueqin presents his work as a carefully crafted work of fiction, and the many women's poems in the novel are clearly the work of Cao himself. By contrast, Du argues, *Random Notes* is just what its title implies, random observations kept in the style of a journal. It records real places, and even Xiaoshan, the village where Shi found Shuangqing, is recorded in the county records of Danyang. *Random Notes,* in Du Fangqin's view, is a kind of rough-draft documentary record of Shi Zhenlin's observations.

## *Du Fangqin: Other Doubts Answered*

Du Fangqin goes beyond Elsie Choy in dealing with some of the doubts I and others have raised. Why is it that Shi's two most prominent friends, Wu Zhensheng and Cao Zhenting, who wrote prefaces for his work, never personally met Shuangqing? According to Du, this was just a coincidence because the two of them were not Jintan natives and never visited there during Shuangqing's short lifetime. Concerning the likelihood that a peasant woman could have received enough education to write poetry as well as Shuangqing did, Du points out that the number of female writers in the Qing period was ten times greater than the total number of women authors in all previous periods combined. Although born into a peasant family, her poetic talent was cultivated and nurtured by members of her family, especially her maternal uncle, the village tutor. After getting to know Shi Zhenlin, she was further inspired by the excitement of having found a truly understanding and appreciative counterpart. This makes her, in Du's view, the first female peasant poet ever recorded in history (Du 1993, 111–41).

### *Wang Ping: Pain as Inspiration*

In her recent book on footbinding, *Aching for Beauty,* Wang Ping writes insightfully about the ways that Shuangqing's story and her poetry parallel certain aspects of footbinding in late imperial China. Although Shi Zhenlin never mentions footbinding in his portrayal of Shuangqing, Wang Ping points out, his narrative highlights the unbearable pain that she endures with grace and dignity. She has the pain of exhausting farmwork, poverty, malaria with its chills and fevers, and the even more intense psychological pain of alienation and isolation made worse by her keen intelligence and sensitive poetic soul. Shuangqing's pain is essential to her greatness. As with the foot-bound maidens of the elite or the courtesan class, Shuangqing's "pain cleanses, procures, 'cooks' her earthly body into something utterly beautiful, spiritual, and immortal, transforming the flesh into writing—poetry. . . . Without her suffering or her stoic endurance, her beauty or talent wouldn't be worth a thing" (Wang Ping 2000, 129; see also 154–61). Wang Ping's book powerfully illustrates the close connections that many assumed between pain, feminine beauty, and literary talent in late imperial Chinese culture. In Shi Zhenlin's tale, what is so moving to the literati is precisely the transformation of Shuangqing's pain into poetry. This interpretation does not really depend on the historical existence of the peasant woman poet Shuangqing, but Wang Ping tells me that she was extremely moved by the first poems of Shuangqing's that she ever read, and her immediate assumption was that no man could have written such beautiful song lyrics in the feminine style.

### *Shuangqing's Distinctive Poetic Voice*

For Du Fangqin as for Elsie Choy (and to a lesser extent, for Grace Fong and Wang Ping), the most important argument for the historical reality of Shuangqing is the clear and distinctive poetic voice of the poems and song lyrics attributed to her. Shuangqing's poems are simply better than those of Shi or any of his male friends. She argues that it would have been impossible for Shi or any man to write so realistically about the life experiences and sentiments of a peasant woman.

### *Wilt Idema: Shuangqing as Fictional*

The most unequivocal dissent from this argument is by Professor Wilt Idema, a renowned authority on Chinese fiction and drama, formerly at the University of Leiden in the Netherlands, and now at Harvard. Professor Idema recently edited and translated into Dutch a large anthology of writings by Chinese women, and in the past several years we have discussed Shuangqing several times. In this anthology, he quotes parts of Shi Zhenlin's memoir in a section dealing with male fascination with such suffering women as Xiaoqing and Shuangqing. In introducing Shi's treatment of Shuangqing, he writes:

> It is not inconceivable that Shi Zhenlin in his description of Shuangqing was inspired by a real woman—many later male and female readers, including contemporary scholars, consider Shuangqing a historical character. However, at the same time it is obvious that Shi Zhenlin wanted to portray an ideal image of an exceptionally talented, patiently suffering woman—a symbol of the talented but unrecognized literatus. His Shuangqing is both more talented and more unfortunate than Xiaoqing. In subsequent passages of *Xiqing sanji* one may observe how Shi Zhenlin, time and again, redraws Shuangqing's portrait in order to underline her qualities, even if this results in logical inconsistencies. (1999, 404–05, translated from the Dutch by Professor Idema)

In Idema's view Shuangqing is an important figure in Chinese culture, even though Shi Zhenlin's "descriptions have little to do with historical facts and are, as far as I can see, purely fictional."

### *Zhou Wanyao: A Call for More Research*

In early 1997, I received in the mail from Professor Zhou Wanyao in Taiwan a very interesting Chinese article she had written entitled "The Story of Xiaoshan: A Review Article of Recent Works on He Shuangqing." Although Dr. Zhou is in the Institute of Taiwan History of Academia Sinica, she became interested in Shuangqing and Shi Zhenlin and has written the most comprehensive summary of current research on the subject. Her article arrived at a perfect time for me, just before I met Du Fangqin and Zhang Hongsheng. She summarizes most of the arguments I have discussed in this chapter, and she astutely refutes several of them.

For example, Zhou does not believe that the inclusion of Shuangqing in the county records of Danyang in 1885 can be taken as proof of anything. County histories are not infallible, and this particular record came out 150 years after Shi Zhenlin wrote his memoir. In Shi's memoir, Shuangqing's place of origin is not mentioned, but the implication is that her own family was not far from her husband's family in Xiaoshan. If Shuangqing were mentioned in the *Jintan County History* in, say, the mid–eighteenth century, that might be taken as good evidence of her historical existence. But mention of her over a century and a half later carries little weight.

Concerning the argument that Shuangqing's poetry is better than Shi Zhenlin's, Zhou agrees that her poetry *is* more interesting than that of the males quoted in *Random Notes*. However, she notes that some critics over the years have also praised Shi Zhenlin's poetry, and she suggests that a careful stylistic analysis of Shuangqing's poetry in comparison with that of Shi Zhenlin has not yet been done. Concerning the theoretical possibility of a man creating Shuangqing's life and poetry out of whole cloth, Zhou points out that many great authors in many cultures have created very believable characters of opposite genders and very different backgrounds from themselves.

Despite Zhou's criticisms of Du Fangqin, she praises Du for being the only scholar to take up the issue of Shuangqing's historical existence in detail. By contrast, Zhou criticizes Western and Western-influenced scholars, including Grace Fong, Kang Zhengguo, and me, for taking the position that the question of Shuangqing's original existence matters less than the fact that she has come to occupy a real place in Chinese culture, where she functions as a real iconic figure. She sees this position as based on contemporary Western-style literary criticism, and as insufficiently grounded in the original Chinese sources that are available. Zhou argues that more light can still be shed on the concrete question of Shuangqing's historical existence through a closer analysis of Shi Zhenlin's two major works, *Random Notes from Xiqing* and *Scattered Drafts from Huayang.*

### *Professor Zhou's Surmise and Compromise*

In the meantime, and pending that further detailed textual research, Zhou spells out her own compromise position between doubters and believers in Shuangqing. She suggests the likelihood that Shi Zhenlin did indeed come upon a beautiful peasant woman living in the

Xiaoshan area and possessing considerable poetic talent however unrefined or untrained. Shi Zhenlin probably used his imagination to idealize and perfect this woman and her writings. Thus the Shuangqing who so dominates Shi's memoir may well be idealized, but Zhou believes she has a firm basis in history (1996, 159–97).

### *How to Determine What Is Real?*

Was there a real peasant woman behind the poetry of Shuangqing? Perhaps more important than the different views on Shuangqing's existence are the different assumptions that guide our approaches to the question. The most important divide in these discussions is between those who assume the question of Shuangqing's historical existence can be answered empirically and those who do not. At one end of the spectrum is Su Zhecong, followed by Elsie Choy and Du Fangqin, who believe that empirical evidence is already sufficient (particularly in the form of her distinctive poetic voice) to prove Shuangqing's existence. Zhou Wanyao, Wang Ping, and Grace Fong straddle the fence on the issue, arguing for the likelihood that a real peasant woman poet served as a basis and inspiration for Shi Zhenlin's aestheticized and fictionalized Shuangqing. In arguing for more empirical research, more careful reading of Shi Zhenlin's extant writings, Dr. Zhou implies that the question of Shuangqing's existence should indeed be resolvable by empirical means. Without precluding the possibility that Shi was inspired by a real woman, Wilt Idema believes the empirical evidence of Shi's own memoir suggests quite clearly that Shuangqing was a fictional character. Kang Zhengguo, I, and to a lesser extent, Grace Fong, are doubtful that any empirical research will ever provide a definitive answer to this question. In our view, more important than the question of Shuangqing's historical existence are the indisputable facts that she was conceivable in eighteenth-century China, and she became a culturally important figure thereafter. She *is* real in Chinese culture, whether or not she ever existed in the ways that Shi Zhenlin claimed.

Although I doubt that there will ever be a complete consensus on the question of Shuangqing's existence, I agree with Zhou Wanyao that there is one aspect of Shi's *Random Notes* yet to be explored. In addition to the doubts, ambiguities, and silences in the memoir, there are also still some clues that I believe can help us better understand Shi's outlook on life, his aesthetic philosophy, his poetic abilities, and his motivation in writing such a work.

*thirteen* ·

# *Clues*

*The plums are just turning yellow, the baby swallow is born;*
*Deep in the woods everywhere one hears the yellow oriole's call.*
*Rains soften the fields, seedlings hunger for more moisture;*
*Clouds thick, in a thousand villages wheat welcomes clearing sky.*
*Mulberry leaves weight the branches down, making berries easy to pick;*
*Streams and fields full of water, making soft mud easy to plow.*
*Leisurely old men, having eaten their fill, without a thing to do,*
*Sit in the shade of the locust tree and chat about ages of peace.*

*That was a poem by* [Shi Zhenlin's friend, Yin] *Xiacun.*

*This year there was no rain from the third month on. By the beginning of the fifth, there was still little rain. Only wild vegetables and pulse grew in the fields, and it got so bad that even those hardy plants died. Once the second crop of wheat was cut, the fields could not even be plowed. So while chanting, "Streams and fields full of water, making soft mud easy to plow," one can only sigh in vain. Rummaging through my box of books I came also upon the following five- character ancient-style poem in three verses by Zhao Anshu* [on the disaster of a summer without rain—poems not included in this translation]. . . .

*Although it does not rain, one's hopes still intensify. When we do not see a sword-bearing immortal with our eyes, we need a "Hongxianzhuan"* [a well-known Tang classical tale of love] *in our hearts; when we do not see a living beauty with our eyes, we need a "Luoshen fu"* [famous prose poem *(fu)* by Cao Zhi (192–232) on the Goddess of Luo River] *in our hearts. Abroad there is a country where they regard what is seen in the daytime as false, and what is dreamed at night as real. Now, what we hope for intensely we may obtain in our dreams; what we see in our dreams may also become real. The reality may be short, but the dream long; the dream may be short, but the hope stirred by it long. But if the hope is only slight,*

> *there is no way of redeeming it. So between our hopes, our dreams, and our eyes, is there really any difference? On the seventh day it rained!* (*RN*, 2.36–37)

### *The Interplay of Illusion and Reality*

This bit of reflection on a rural drought and on the power of imagination is one of the clearer statements of the philosophy behind Shi's art and his portrayal of Shuangqing. Coming as it does between two sections on Shuangqing, it seems not only relevant, but central to Shi Zhenlin's aesthetic philosophy. As such, it is an important clue to our understanding of some of the puzzles his memoir presents. The idea of the interchangeableness or mutual interdependence of dreams and reality is a very old one in Chinese history. The most famous statement of this philosophy is the playful anecdote in the Daoist classic *Zhuangzi:*

> Once upon a time, Zhuang Zhou (Zhuangzi) dreamt that he was a butterfly, a butterfly fluttering about, enjoying himself. It did not know that it was really Zhuang Zhou. Suddenly he awoke with a start and he was Zhuang Zhou again. But he did not know whether he was Zhuang Zhou who had dreamed that he was a butterfly, or whether he was a butterfly dreaming that he was Zhuang Zhou. Between Zhuang Zhou and the butterfly there must be some distinction. This is what is called the transformation of things. (de Bary, Chan, and Watson 1960, 75)

This Daoist philosophy in China was reinforced by the introduction and growing popularity of Buddhism, which argued that all of material life is illusory, an illusion kept alive by the limitations and cravings of the individual human ego. As noted above, Shi Zhenlin was strongly attracted to Buddhism and assumed such Buddhist ideas as reincarnation and the workings of the Buddhist law of karma in which the deeds of one life are repaid with rewards and/or punishments in the next. Material existence is an illusion created by the self's craving for permanence. The Buddhist strives to see through the illusions of material existence, to attain enlightenment, and to free the ego from its cravings for fame, fortune, rank, and glory.

### *Buddhist-Daoist Romantic Aestheticism: "Life for Art's Sake"*

Although it may seem a contradiction in terms, Shi Zhenlin was a kind of Buddhist-Daoist romantic aesthete. Rather than enter a monastery and seek the complete extinction of the ego, he posited an alternative world where enlightenment is found in art and imagination. As a Buddhist, Shi saw the material world as impermanent and illusory, and he sought to extinguish those human cravings in himself for conventional rank, fame, wealth, and power. However, as an artist, he was not entirely free of ambition. He saw in art and the writer's imagination a way to create something more beautiful, more ennobling, and more permanent than material life and the temptations of wealth, rank, and power. He argued for the interchangeability of truth and illusion, fact and fiction, dreams and waking reality. He championed Buddhist values of compassion and criticized his own age for betraying those values more often than not. Yet, in the final analysis, he sought salvation not in Buddhist practice so much as in art and imagination, in aesthetic achievement and enjoyment. Ultimately, he believed in "life for art's sake."

In Shi Zhenlin's parable on the drought, he implies that one's hopes and wishes can come true if the hopes and wishes are sincerely and powerfully felt. One hopes for rain, longs for rain, dreams of rain, writes poems on rain . . . and the rain comes. When we do not see a real beauty with our eyes, we need to create one in our imaginations. Although Zhuangzi concludes that "between our dreams and reality, there must be some distinction," he leaves in doubt just what the distinction is, and his famous butterfly dream has long been interpreted to imply that between our dreams, hopes, and waking reality, ultimately there can be no distinction. This seems to be Shi Zhenlin's position, whatever Zhuangzi may have thought. Shortly before his parable on droughts and dreams, Shi quotes a poem by Zhang Mengzhan, Shuangqing's landlord. His last lines, "When the day's tea is all boiled / it's time for the dream to return," also hint that Shuangqing may be a product of these men's dreams.

### *"Composed in a Dream"*

As noted in chapter 4, "Biographer," Shi Zhenlin ends his own preface with the words, "Composed in a dream," which could be interpreted to suggest that the entire memoir is based on his dreams and ideals. As we see in that same chapter, the late Ming play *The Peony Pavilion*, which Shi Zhenlin undoubtedly knew, portrays dreams of love so powerful as to sicken a young woman unto death, and then to raise her back to life.

Judith Zeitlin writes, "A long intellectual tradition in China explores the difficulty of adjudicating between dreaming and waking states and accords an objective reality to dream experiences" (1993, 151). The greatest Chinese novel of all time, *Dream of the Red Chamber*, written in the late eighteenth century, is built around the importance of dreams and the permeable boundary between dream experience and waking experience, and between illusion and reality. Hong Jingyuan has noted the strong parallels between Shi Zhenlin and Cao Xueqin, the author of *Dream of the Red Chamber:* an interest in Buddhism, Daoism, karma, and the interchangeability of dreams and waking experience, of illusion and reality. Hong suggests the possibility that Cao Xueqin may have read and been influenced by Shi Zhenlin's *Random Notes* (Hong 1984). Of course, issues like the relationship between illusion and reality, and between appearance and reality, are central to the storytelling impulse and fictional traditions in all cultures.

### *Shi Zhenlin: "I Could Burn* **Random Notes"**

> *I intended to return to the Melon Bank of Yaohu early on the tenth* [of the twelfth lunar month of 1733], *but it rained so much that I could not go. On the evening of the eleventh, I discussed my* Random Notes *with* [Duan] *Yuhan. I closed the book and said, "In Heaven and on earth there are so many things that move us. Those people who love the writing in this book still doubt the things described in it; those who adhere to traditional doctrines find fault with its language. When I wrote it I did not consciously set out* [to write a book]. *Even if it were destroyed by fire, what cause would I have for regret?" Yuhan clapped his hands and shouted, "Bravo! Shuangqing is so elegant and refined; past or present her like has never been seen before. But perhaps you ought to be a little more circumspect in what you say about her." I replied, "When in Yangzhou I burned some ten* juan *of my old drafts. I burned them while staying at Shufengguan, and I could burn* Random Notes from Xiqing *as well. Human life is like a bolt of lightening; the spirit cannot be long maintained but soon vanishes, so why should our words last any longer?"* (*RN*, 3.52–53)

What is going on here? This seems another place where, in Robert Darnton's words, "the document is opaque," where things don't quite add up. If we can understand these kinds of places in *Random Notes,* perhaps we can use them as clues through which to interpret the work. In a casual conversation with his friend, Flower Lover Duan Yuhan, Shi mulls over the significance of the very memoir he is still writing and we are now reading. Ever aware of the work's reception, he notes two main responses from his readers: some love the writing but doubt its reality, and others who are traditionalists fault the book as immoral. Is he so discouraged by this as to be indifferent to its very survival? Is he preaching Buddhist detachment in recognition of the transience of all things? Or is he just asking a rhetorical question to get the response he knows will come? Given Duan Yuhan's important role in the book as one of the chief admirers of Shuangqing, we should not be surprised by his answer. He declares that Shuangqing is too refined and elegant to let disappear from the written record. However, he cautions Zhenlin to be more circumspect in what he writes about her. Duan Yuhan says, in effect, "Tone it down a bit." If you put in less controversial material, people will still love the writing, but they won't have so many grounds for criticism. He is concerned here about the reputation of Shi Zhenlin and Shuangqing. Apparently unmoved by this, Shi Zhenlin presses his point and says he may just burn the work anyway, "since life is so short."

### *Shuangqing's Response*

Given Shi Zhenlin's fascination with his memoir's reception, it is difficult to take this threat seriously. This seems no more than a rhetorical ploy to provoke a desired response from his supporters. And indeed, the very next line reads,

> *Shuangqing heard of this and wrote me a letter.*

The letter is quite learned in its discussion of the classics. She reports that when she was fifteen, her uncle once criticized Confucius and his disciples for leaving sensuous poems in the *Book of Songs,* a work that came to be one of the Five Classics and a basic part of every school curriculum. She says she responded by telling her uncle that he was no better than Confucius's worst students! And when her uncle criticized Mencius (second only to Confucius in the Confucian tradition) for being too outspoken, she told him he could not even learn to crawl from Chen Zhongzi, one of Mencius's disciples.

Her letter continues . . .

> *The Great Way has no one direction, the Great Teaching calls for no restraints. Those village pedants who preach the Doctrine of the Mean, spraying the entire table with their saliva and slobbering all over their whiskers, suppose themselves as accomplished as Zisi, or esteemed by Zhu Xi himself; yet their students all sleep at their desks. I spit on these people; they are fools deluding the deaf and misleading the blind. Mr. Moon-Admirer, for you to be so unsure, to write so well but behave so foolishly, to preach so brilliantly but vacillate like a pulley, this I cannot condone. You can burn this book,*

> *but then you had better keep silent thereafter. The butterfly can keep silent but still love the flower; the maggot can keep quiet but still crave the nightsoil. But people who keep silent do so to mislead others. Fragrance still attracts butterflies as stench draws maggots. I see this* [your threatening to burn your *Random Notes*] *and my malaria gets worse."* (*RN,* 3.53)

So much for peasant deference to the literati! It is an extraordinary image, the meek, malarial, shy, and docile peasant wife spitting on the village pedants for preaching their confining doctrines of Confucian ritual propriety. Shuangqing begins with a quote from the Daoist classic the *Daodejing:* "The Great Way has no one direction; the Great Teaching calls for no restraints." She then attacks the village schoolmasters who teach the Confucian classics to young aspiring examination candidates. They are idiots in her view, yet they put themselves on a par with Zisi, the grandson of Confucius who was traditionally credited as the author of the Confucian classic *The Doctrine of the Mean,* or of Zhu Xi himself, the great Song-dynasty synthesizer of the Neo-Confucian doctrines that came to define orthodoxy for seven centuries.

Shuangqing then lashes into Shi Zhenlin for even thinking about burning his book. We can almost see him bask with masochistic pleasure under the shower of her anger. She is, after all, paying him the ultimate compliment: you are such a brilliant writer, how dare you think of destroying your own work! Just as butterflies are attracted to flowers, so is Shi Zhenlin attracted to Shuangqing. And just as maggots are attracted to nightsoil!

"As Maggots Are Drawn to Nightsoil . . ." This metaphor threw me. I looked up from the text to Liu Laoshi and asked, "Is she really comparing herself to nightsoil and Shi Zhenlin to a maggot?"

"Well, yes, but the point is the attraction of one thing for another."

"But isn't this a rather strange way of describing an attraction, whether literary or sexual, between a man and a woman?"

"It seems rather crude, yes, but the attraction is the same as the butterfly (man) being drawn to the flower (woman). Maybe it's not so crude for a peasant woman! After all, they didn't have indoor plumbing in Xiaoshan!" Liu Laoshi giggled as she said this.

"Well," I couldn't resist bragging here, "I grew up on a farm, and I've seen maggots crawling all over stinking dead animals. They always looked pretty disgusting to me!"

"Okay, I concede the point!" she laughed. "This is another prose passage from Shuangqing that sounds more like Shi Zhenlin himself showing off by saying something mildly outrageous. In any case, it is difficult to see how this could have been written by the same person whose song lyrics are so elegant and refined."

For one of the few times in my year with Liu Laoshi, I felt almost like an equal in this discussion. I might have even influenced *her* view on the issue of maggots and nightsoil. We then returned to our reading and discovered that the letter's conclusion raised more doubts than it dispelled.

### *Shuangqing: "My Life Seems But a Dream"*

You are drawn to me, Shuangqing tells Shi Zhenlin, and even if you destroy *Random Notes,* you will still be drawn to me. Yet in destroying the record of your attraction, you will in effect be lying and deceiving people. "I see this, and my malaria gets worse." Shuangqing has as much stake in *Random Notes* as Shi Zhenlin, and in fact, it is difficult to tell the difference between them. Then comes one of the more intriguing statements in the entire book.

> *After all, my life seems but a dream anyway. What we meet in our dreams may not be the same as reality, but once we awake and think over what happened in our dreams, we have no regrets* [over what happened]. *Those who understand me and those who condemn me, won't they do so because of this book?* (*RN,* 3.53)

Once again we have that favorite theme of Shi Zhenlin, the relationship between dreams and reality. Her life "seems but a dream," yet dreams have their own reality too. Dreams create memories that are just as real as any other memories. We may make love in dreams, escape society's constraints in dreams, and have no regrets upon waking up. Shuangqing can be read to say, "I may well be the creation of your dreams, but don't slight your dreams, and by all means don't destroy this dream!" She ends with a paraphrase of Confucius who once said, "Those who understand me and those who condemn me will do so because of the *Spring and Autumn Annals,*" a chronicle of state affairs that praises the good deeds and condemns the evil deeds of statesmen. Shuangqing's use of such a quote suggests a literary ambition more consistent with Shi Zhenlin than with a woman who writes in powder on leaves because she does not want her work to survive.

### *Whose Words? Whose Ambition?*

At the very least, this letter raises many questions. Shuangqing has been the shy and reticent one all through the memoir. Her admirers try to draw her out at every opportunity. She stays in the shadows, writes in ephemeral powder on decaying leaves, and avoids the spotlight. Now Shi Zhenlin cavalierly suggests he might burn his memoir, and he has no concern to see it outlive him in any case (a bald-faced lie if ever there was one!). Suddenly Shuangqing goes on the offensive, writes in almost crude terms to condemn the critics of *Random Notes,* to chastise the memoirist for his lack of courage, to reflect on the possibility of her own fictionality, and to say in conclusion, "I want to be famous, the critics be damned, don't be such a weakling."

Liu Laoshi agreed, "This sounds more like Shi Zhenlin than Shuangqing."

"Is there really any difference between them?" I asked, referring to the whole portrait of Shuangqing in *Random Notes.*

"Well, Shuangqing's song lyrics seem real enough to me. 'The Autumn Chrysanthemum,' 'The Lone Goose,' 'The Fading Lamp,' these are all just too good and too distinctive. I don't see how he could have written them himself."

### *"Look at Tiny, Tiny Shuangqing!"*

Since leaving Taiwan in August 1991, I have continued, off and on, to revise my translations of Shuangqing's poems and song lyrics. While drafting chapter 7 on Shuangqing's song lyrics, I was struck by another oddity, the number of times she puts her own name, Shuangqing, in her lyrics.

1. In her third song lyric in *Random Notes,* to the tune of "Shiluoyi": "Looking at myself in the mirror, / I shock myself: so thin, erect, and alone. / It is not the face of spring; / It is not the face of autumn; / Is it really Shuangqing?"
2. To the chrysanthemum: "Is it just my own Shuangqing heartlessness / to abandon you in the quiet dusk out back?"
3. To the fading lamp: "Keep Shuangqing company for a little bit longer."
4. To her friend Hanxi: "I ask Heaven, no reply; / Look at tiny tiny Shuangqing, / Wavering, weary, and bored."

5. To the plum blossom: "Spring passions fill the sky, blossoms falling everywhere, / Enough to tire Shuangqing; / In my dream I pick them up in vain.
6. And to spring: "Spring has wronged Shuangqing."

I have not read a great number of song lyrics, but in the ones I have read, I have never seen poets or lyricists put their own given names in their poems or lyrics. I follow up my hunch by asking Steve Owen of Harvard about this. It is rare, he says, for a poet to refer to him- or herself in this way. I pose the same question by email to my friend Zhang Hongsheng at Nanjing University, prompting his interesting reply.

> You raise a very good question. I've thought this over for several days, and I can only think of a few cases in Chinese poetry where a famous poet mentions his *hao* or poetic name. Du Fu [712–770, often seen as China's greatest poet] referred to himself this way only once that I know of, in this line, "Fu is the old guest of the noblemen." Su Shi [1036–1101, one of the greatest literary figures in Chinese culture] occasionally mentioned his poetic name, "Dongpo" ["eastern hill," where he had built a studio] in his poetry, but never his given name, Shi. This was a way of referring to himself as the "other," apart from the author of the poem.
>
> I have read many song lyrics (of course not all of them!), and I have never found such an expression in a song lyric. I think it was not seen as in good taste to refer to oneself in such a direct way. It would have been seen as a bit vulgar. Now that you point out Shuangqing's lyrics, I realize this is the first time I have ever seen such a direct self-reference. In light of all this, if she was an actual historical figure, she was certainly unique. Yesterday, I discussed this question with my advisor, a famous classical scholar who just turned eighty-five. He agrees with me. (Email, January 6, 1998)

### *Whose Gaze Is It Anyway?*

If Shi Zhenlin wrote these lyrics in the voice of Shuangqing, the mentioning of the name Shuangqing makes much more sense. He is standing outside her, speaking as a ventriloquist, but occasionally his own voice comes through. This too would help explain how concerned she seems to be with describing her own appearance. Shi Zhenlin is obsessed with Shuangqing's appearance, and this same obsession is everywhere evident in the poems he attributes to her. If he wrote her poems, no wonder she is so often described as both object and subject.

### Random Notes: *"Destinies of Another World"*

Although Shi Zhenlin never mentioned Shuangqing in his later writings, in 1745 he commented briefly on *Random Notes* in a short poem for his friend Kong Ci'ou:

> One volume, *Xiqing*, on destinies of another world;
> Where can I bring up this passion *(qing)* again?
> The phoenix perches only on the *langgan* tree,
> But in the human world it still must listen to the cuckoo.
>
> (1935, 32)

With this brief poem on his *Random Notes of Xiqing*, Shi Zhenlin suggests that it is about "the destinies of another world," the world of immortals beyond the human realm. In asking "where" he can "bring up this passion again," he alludes to the story of Shuangqing and the passions she and her poetry generated. The fabulous mythological phoenix (Shuangqing) comes from the world of imagination; its beauty and its music (her beauty and her poetry) surpass anything in the human realm. The langgan tree has two meanings: 1) a fabulous mythological tree in the Kunlun Mountains; and 2) an alternative name for a kind of bamboo. Both these meanings can apply here because the phoenix is said to eat the seeds of the bamboo, yet as a mythological bird, it also could appropriately be confined to the mythological tree. But for all its splendor, when brought into the human realm (as in *Random Notes*) the phoenix is doomed to hear the mournful cry of the cuckoo. The phoenix (Shuangqing), in other words, is too good for the real world. In the "real" world of imperfect human beings, such a beautiful creature as the phoenix is doomed to suffer. Reality can never match or fully accommodate the world of beauty accessible to the imagination.

### *Signs of Fiction*

In *Fictional Truth* Michael Riffaterre notes common signs of fictionality in narrative texts. His long list includes

> narrators' intrusions . . . emblematic names for characters and places; incompatibilities between narrative voice and viewpoint

> and characters' voices and viewpoints; incompatibilities between viewpoint and verisimilitude, especially omniscient narrative; signs modifying the narrative's pace and altering the sequence of events . . . mimetic excesses, such as unlikely recording of unimportant speech or thought (unimportant but suggestive of actual happenings, of a live presence, creating atmosphere or characterizing persons); and finally, diegetic overkill, such as the representation of ostensibly insignificant details, the very insignificance of which is significant in a story as a feature of realism. Narratology seems to have neglected the constant coincidence between textual features declaring the fictionality of a story and a reassertion of the truth of that story. (1990, 29–30)

Although Riffaterre is discussing the genres of novels and short stories, all of the items in this list of signs of fictionality apply to Shi Zhenlin's memoir. As we have seen, there are inconsistencies and outright contradictions in Shuangqing's viewpoint; she has an emblematic given name with no surname; Shi is nearly omniscient in reporting her private conversations and inner thoughts; his extremely fragmentary narrative is full of flashbacks and "flash forwards" that destroy any sense of an orderly temporal sequence; and the literati behavior he describes is quite contradictory and implausible in treating Shuangqing as an object of worship while risking her reputation and her physical safety by rushing to have contact with her. Shi Zhenlin's periodic reassertion of the truth of his narrative and his occasional playful sparring with attacks on his veracity fit very nicely with Riffaterre's conventions of fictionality.

### *A Lyric by Shi Zhenlin*

As we have seen in earlier chapters, the most convincing argument for the historical reality of Shuangqing is that her song lyrics were too good and too distinctive to have been written by Shi Zhenlin. In this connection, I conclude this chapter with one more clue, a song lyric from Shi's *Random Notes.*

> *Wait for spring to come but spring is quickly gone;*
> *No place without flowers; none without wind and rain.*
> *How longsuffering is the Maiden of Huanshaxi* [Xi Shi]*;*
> *On seeing a wedding procession, she turns around and stares.*
> *All the way she grieves for spring, a grief that will not end;*
> *Alone she wronged the flower, so in tears she begs its pardon.*

*She still recalls deeply deeply, words deep into the night,*
*From living life to dying death, a thousand thousand declarations.*
(*RN*, 2.33)

This song lyric is about a poor beauty who is sad in the springtime. She waits for spring and laments its quick passing. There are flowers everywhere, but they are buffeted, troubled, or made inaccessible, by wind and rain. Huanshaxi is a river in Zhejiang Province where a beautiful country girl, Xi Shi, washed cotton cloth in the fifth century B.C. Discovered there by the enemies of the state of Wu, she was trained in music and dance, and sent to seduce and distract the prince of the kingdom of Wu, thereby "toppling his kingdom." This is not a historical commentary on Xi Shi, but a shorthand way of describing a contemporary beauty who is Xi Shi's equal. She sees a wedding procession pass her by, and she can only stare at it, longingly. She then returns home and grieves for spring, spring's disappointments or spring's passing. We are not told how she "wronged the flower" and why she now "begs its pardon." But she recalls "words deep into the night, / From living life to dying death, a thousand thousand declarations."

More important than the subject of this lyric is its style and its placement in *Random Notes.* It is a lyric by Shi Zhenlin, and it immediately precedes his introduction of Shuangqing in *Random Notes.* The lyric itself expresses the very feelings and uses some of the very techniques that Shuangqing would become famous for. There is a sense of love felt and love lost, of longing and disappointment, all expressed through natural imagery of springtime and flowers. That alone is not unusual because countless poets through the ages used such imagery to express such feelings. What is most striking is the poet's use of doublets, the repetition of characters in a natural way to build intensity as the lyric proceeds.

### *Doublets in a Feminine Style*

In the first line, we have two uses of "spring" *(chun),* a term Shuangqing would use twenty-one times in her bitter lyric on springtime disappointment. The second line has the negative character, *wu,* repeated four times: "Wu chu wu hua, wu chu wu yu" Literally, "no place no flowers no place no rain." To have this read clearly in English, we need three different words—"No place without flowers, none without wind and rain," but the meaning is equally clear in classical Chinese with four repeated *wu*'s. The next repetition is with the character *chou,* once as a verb, "grieve," and once as a noun, "grief." And finally, the lyric ends with an explosion of double characters, and one triple, in the last two lines. "She still recalls deeply deeply, words deep into the night, / From living life to dying death, a thousand thousand declarations." The repetitions are much more natural in the Chinese than any English version can capture, and their impact is much more forceful. What is striking about this lyric is how closely it resembles Shuangqing's, especially as seen in her lyric on the fading lamp, filled with repeated characters or doublets, and discussed in chapter 7, "Lyrics." At the very least, this demonstrates that Shi Zhenlin had the ability, and the inclination, to write in this "feminine style" first made famous by the great woman poet Li Qingzhao in the Song dynasty.

### *Summation*

So Shi Zhenlin was fascinated with dreams, with the interchangeableness of illusion and reality, and with the many perfections of Shuangqing. So he could write a song lyric in the feminine style in imitation of Li Qingzhao. "So what?" you might say. There will never be an airtight case, with absolute proof, concerning Shi's memoir and the reality or fictionality of Shuangqing. But the above excerpts from *Random Notes* all strike me as clues toward an interpretation of Shi Zhenlin and of Shuangqing. Shi signaled in various ways his motives for creating a fictional peasant woman poet and her poems. He believed in the power of poetry and song lyrics to move people in deep and mysterious ways. He believed that the world of dreams is as real or as illusory as the world of waking reality. What better way to demonstrate all these beliefs than by creating a heroine who gets taken for real and becomes a cultural icon?

Shi Zhenlin wanted his readers to have some doubts about his story. He raised doubts about Shuangqing himself and hinted in various ways that she was imaginary. Her own poetry is so focused on describing her visual appearance, and so self-referential with her frequent use of the name Shuangqing, that it suggests another author outside of Shuangqing observing her and naming her as an object. Finally, and this is my most controversial point, I believe he also had the ability to create the poetry of Shuangqing. He was a superbly talented prose stylist, a very talented poet, and he was obsessed with feminine beauty and feminine psychology.

It may just be that in Shuangqing, Shi Zhenlin found his own most original and authentic poetic voice. He had the motive, the opportunity, and the ability to create Shuangqing and her poetry out of his own imagination. He could have done it. That alone is not proof that he did it. The evidence will always remain circumstantial. This may seem an unsatisfying conclusion to a mystery, but we are not quite finished with the story yet. Whether a peasant woman poet named Shuangqing ever existed or not, the story of how she moved from Shi Zhenlin's rambling and contradictory memoir to her now-established place in Chinese culture is also something of a mystery.

*fourteen*

# *Reincarnations*

> He Shuangqing, style name Qiubi, came from Danyang (in the southwestern part of today's Jiangsu Province) in the Qing dynasty. Born into a peasant family, she lived in the vicinity of Siping Shan. Very beautiful, multitalented, and a lover of literary works, she was married in 1732 into a poor family of woodcutters surnamed Zhou. Her mother-in-law was wicked, her husband had a violent temper, and she herself suffered from chronic malaria. The family was very poor, and she had no money to buy writing materials, so she used powder instead of ink, and leaves in place of paper in order to write her poems and song lyrics. She showed great creativity in utilizing and combining materials from her daily life in a peasant village with her own innermost personal feelings, so that her poetry is extremely moving, deeply imbued with the flavor of country life and also with profound human feelings. Her poetry was cited in such Qing-dynasty works as *Poetry and Paintings of Famous Beauties* and *A Record of Poetry by Famous Qing-dynasty Beauties,* and she is recognized as a woman of genius.
>
> —Zheng Guangyi, *Critical Explanatory Guide to Poetry Published by Talented Women* (1991)

Since Shi Zhenlin's *Random Notes* was first published in 1737, Shuangqing has undergone many reincarnations through the works of critics and anthologists who have cited her poetry and recounted her biography, sometimes referring to Shi Zhenlin and sometimes ignoring him. A few of Shi's descriptions of Shuangqing are often quoted verbatim in these works, but most of his story has been left out. The above biography comes from a very large compilation of notable works by famous Chinese women poets. It is typical in the following ways: Shuangqing here has a surname, He, a style name, Qiubi, and a birthplace, Danyang. We learn of Shuangqing's beauty, her poetic talent, her illness, her persecution by her mother-in-law and husband, her high reputation as a poet, and her appearance in two anthologies from the Qing period. It is equally interesting to note what we are not told in this brief biography. We hear nothing of Shi Zhenlin's memoir, the literati worship of Shuangqing, or her occasional indulgence in flirtations with her admirers. Her story has been quite sanitized. How did Shuangqing get this way, cleansed of her dalliances with the literati, and gentrified with a surname, style name, and a birthplace removed from her husband's family? The answer entails a long, circuitous, and somewhat confused journey.

When I returned to the United States in 1991 after my sabbatical year in Taiwan, I was ready to write an article on Shuangqing but had no thought of doing a book. With the demands of teaching and chairing a department, I had no time for further research, and I didn't even think about the mysteries of how and when Shuangqing acquired a surname, a birthplace, and a style name. Even in my Harvard paper of 1992, I addressed none of these questions and only concentrated on Shi's *Random Notes.* A few years after that, on a whim one day, I checked the Harvard library and was astonished to find there the 1935 editions of Shi's *Random Notes of Xiqing* and *Scattered Drafts of Huayang.* I was thrilled to find these editions, which had been there all along, but also chagrined to realize that I had spent years walking past them in the Harvard stacks without even realizing they were sitting under my nose. Most importantly, at the back of *Random Notes* was an article by Zhang Gongliang that outlined the publishing history of the book and the history of commentaries on Shi Zhenlin and Shuangqing. Even with this gold mine of information, I was slow to turn my attention to it. When I finally did, after my trip to Jintan in 1997, I found in the same library most of the books cited by Zhang Gongliang. This chapter is the result.

### *1753: "Zhang Qingqing"*

The earliest known reference to Shuangqing after Shi Zhenlin's *Random Notes* came in a collection of miscellaneous writings by a man named Dong Chao in 1753. Dong Chao quoted two song lyrics by Shuangqing, on the lone goose and on the fading lamp, but nearly all his biographical information on the poet is at odds with Shi Zhenlin:

> Qingqing, surnamed Zhang, was from Runzhou in Jintan. A farmwife, she excelled in writing regulated verse and song lyrics, without ever having a teacher. She showed no dislike at all toward

> her illiterate commoner of a husband. A salt merchant tried to woo her in many different ways, but failed. She scolded and refused to answer all those who wrote to her to express their admiration for her. (Dong 1753, 3.6a)

If the poems were not Shuangqing's, we would not even suspect Dong Chao's poet to have any connection with Shi's Shuangqing. She has a surname, Zhang, and a new birthplace, Runzhou, in Jintan County. Her given name, Qingqing (慶青), consists of two different characters pronounced "qing," neither of which is the *qing* (卿) term of endearment, used in Shuangqing. She is wooed by a salt merchant, an incident not reported by Shi Zhenlin, and she refuses contact with all literati, which is not the case in *Random Records*. The quoted song lyrics have two minor mistakes each, but they are quite accurate renditions compared to Dong Chao's biography. How could this happen? To me, this interesting twist suggests that Shuangqing's poetry was copied or passed around orally, along with stories about the poetry's author. Oral transmission could explain how Shuangqing (Double qing) got transformed into Qingqing with entirely different characters. As for the surname and the stories about the poet, they also suggest oral transmission and transformation, which we all understand from the childhood game of gossip. In any case, this was not a terribly promising beginning for an accurate transmission of Shi Zhenlin's Shuangqing story, but it was promising beginning for the transmission of an image of great virtue in a poet of great talent.

### *Late Eighteenth Century: Shi Zhenlin's Writings and Wang Qishu's* Fragrant Flowers

In 1773, a wealthy Hangzhou salt merchant named Wang Qishu (1728–1799?) edited an eighty volume collection of writings by women entitled *Collection of Gathering Fragrant Flowers (Xiefang ji)*. Kang Zhengguo has determined from a third source that Wang Qishu's anthology included several of Shuangqing's poems and song lyrics taken from Shi's *Random Notes* (Kang 1994, 102–3). Although neither Kang Zhengguo nor I have seen this anthology, it appears that Wang Qishu cited Shi Zhenlin as his source and followed Shi in giving the peasant woman's name as Shuangqing, without any surname.

Shi Zhenlin died in 1779, the same year he completed a revised version of his *Random Notes* in eight chapters. In his postscript to this version, he reports that he has cut 20 percent out of his 1737 edition.

Thus, by the late eighteenth century, Shuangqing had attracted relatively little critical attention. Shi Zhenlin's *Random Notes* had been reprinted in a slightly condensed version, and a few of Shuangqing's poems had appeared in two anthologies, once under a completely different name, and once as the Shuangqing discovered by Shi Zhenlin.

### *Early Nineteenth Century: New Attention to "Shuangqing's Sad Story"*

Wu Dexuan (1767–1840) was a holder of a lower-level degree, a scholar, and a poet from Yixing, southeast of Jintan near Lake Tai, in Jiangsu Province. In his miscellaneous notes, *Continuing Record of Things Heard and Seen in the New Moon Pavilion (Chuyuelou xuwenjian lu),* dating from the early nineteenth century, Wu expressed deep admiration for Shi Zhenlin's writing. He described Zhang Qiongniang, the talented wife of Flower Lover Duan Yuhan, and reported that Duan's friend was Shi Zhenlin, whose *Random Notes from Xiqing* contained the "especially sad story" of the woman poet Shuangqing. He quoted briefly Shi's early description of Shuangqing and noted specifically that "her surname is not known." He recounted most of the details from Shin Zhenlin's introduction of Shuangqing but did not go beyond the painting of her portrait by the literati, and their recovery of her first three song lyrics (Wu Dexuan 1976, 2:1.4a–b). It appears that Wu Dexuan had seen only the second chapter of Shi's four-chapter *Random Notes;* thus he reported only a tiny fraction of Shi Zhenlin's Shuangqing story. Interestingly, Wu put much more emphasis on Shuangqing's virtue than on her talent, but he quoted directly from *Random Notes,* so he was far more accurate than Dong Chao in describing Shuangqing.

### *1831: Yun Zhu on "He Shuangqing from Danyang"*

In 1831, one of the great pioneer women scholars of the Qing dynasty, Yun Zhu (1771–1833), published a large anthology of women's writings, *Correct Beginnings: Women's Poetry from Our August Dynasty (Guochao guixiu zhengshi ji).* As the Chinese wife of a high-ranking Manchu military officer, Yun Zhu saw her anthology as setting the standard for women's writings. Fully aware of scholars' debates over the propriety or impropriety of women's writing and publishing poetry, Yun Zhu was determined to demonstrate that talent and virtue were not incompatible characteristics of women writers. The term *guixiu* in her title means "respectable women," or women from elite families. She noted in her preface that she excluded from her anthology the love poetry of courtesans and poetry by "female adepts and Buddhist nuns." Given her self-conscious emphasis on elite women writers, it is interesting that Yun Zhu quoted two poems by Shuangqing, despite her peasant background. And most curiously, for the first time that we find in the historical record, Yun Zhu gave Shuangqing the surname and birthplace that would be passed down to the twentieth century:

> *He Shuangqing.* From Danyang in Jiangsu Province, Shuangqing married into the Zhou family of woodcutters who for generations lived below Siping Mountain in Xiaoshan Li in Jinsha [another name for Jintan]. Brilliant from birth, she would chant pure and fresh poems. The *jinshi* degree holder Shi Zhenlin wrote about her in his *Random Notes from Xiqing.* (1831, 17.2a)

Yun Zhu followed this short biography with excerpts of two of Shuangqing's regulated verses but made no mention of Shuangqing's mastery of the (less orthodox) song-lyric form. She also ignored Shuangqing's relationship with her literati admirers. More intriguing than her selection of Shuangqing's poetry is Yun Zhu's report that Shuangqing was surnamed He and born in Danyang. This is the earliest mention of any He family in Danyang, and it comes nearly a century after Shi wrote his *Random Notes.* Given Yun Zhu's high rank and visibility, her work was extremely influential. In nearly every source thereafter, Shuangqing is listed as He Shuangqing from Danyang. We will never know how Yun Zhu came upon the surname He and the birthplace Danyang. Perhaps she heard about Shi Zhenlin and Shuangqing from some third source; perhaps Shuangqing's poems and stray anecdotes from Shi's *Random Notes* were simply being copied by hand and passed around in fragments. Yan Dichang in his *History of Qing-Dynasty Song Lyrics* (1990, 548), notes that the He family of Danyang produced a number of well-known women poets and song-lyric writers in the Qing period. Danyang is the next county to the north of Jintan, and perhaps the area closest to Jintan known for a family of women writers. Perhaps Yun Zhu or her informant simply assumed that such a talented female song-lyric poet in this area must have come from the He family of Danyang.

Of course, there is one alternative explanation for this chain of events, and that is that Shuangqing was indeed born into the He family in Danyang, and married into the Zhou family in Jintan. For Du Laoshi, this is at least one possibility, another being that Shuangqing was born in a Danyang village in Jintan, which was confused by her later biographers with Danyang County to the north. Others like Elsie Choy and Su Zhecong tend to take for granted that Shuangqing always came from the He family of Danyang, but they make no attempt to explain how or why it took nearly a century after Shi Zhenlin's memoir for anyone to "discover" Shuangqing's "true" surname and birthplace.

### *1839 and 1845: Wang Duan and Shen Shanbao on Shuangqing*

In 1993, Ellen Widmer kindly tipped me off that Wang Duan (1783–1839), one of the great pioneer women writers of the nineteenth century, also mentioned Shuangqing in her writings. A voracious reader, an independent, original, and insightful critic, novelist, and historian, Wang Duan was one of the most influential women writers of the Qing dynasty. In several places in her collected writings, *Collected Writings from the Natural Love of Learning Studio (Ziran haoxue zhai ji),* she mentions the suffering of Shuangqing, notes that she was married into a peasant family, that she expressed her suffering in her poetry, and that her story is recorded in *Random Notes from Xiqing.* Wang Duan quotes no poetry from Shuangqing and gives her no surname or location other than to refer the reader to Shi's *Random Notes.* Her references suggest, however, that Shi's *Random Notes* was in general circulation in the early nineteenth century.

Only recently I learned from Grace Fong that six years after Wang Duan's death, in 1845, another famous woman poet, Shen Shanbao (1808–1862), from Qiantang in Zhejiang Province, also mentioned Shuangqing in her *Notes on the Poetry of Famous Women (Mingyuan shihua),* on the lives and poetry of over five hundred women from the Ming and Qing dynasties. Following Yun Zhu, Shen refers to Shuangqing as having the surname He, though she identifies her only with the village of Xiaoshan, saying it is in Jurong (the next county west of Jintan). Shen reports that Shuangqing suffered from poverty and mistreatment at the hands of her husband and mother-in-law and says that she wrote in powder on leaves and flower petals because she did not want her writing to survive. She praises Shuangqing's poetic style and quotes two song lyrics, one poem and part of another. Without mentioning Shi Zhenlin, Shen cites *Random Notes from Xiqing* as reporting Shuangqing's virtue, beauty, suffering, and obscurity (Shen Shanbao 1987, 3.15b–16a).

### *1873: Huang Xieqing Gives Shuangqing a Book of Her Own*

In 1873, a famous connoisseur and anthologist of song lyrics named Huang Xieqing published a large compilation, *Collected Song Lyrics from Our August Dynasty, Continuation (Guochao cizong xubian),* a continuation of an earlier collection of Qing-dynasty song lyrics published in 1803. Huang includes in his collection the following biography of Shuangqing, as a preface to ten of her song lyrics. To the information in Shi Zhenlin's memoir Huang adds a surname and birthplace and two new elements: Shuangqing's style name and book of poems.

> He Shuangqing. Style name, Qiubi, from Danyang. She married into a peasant family named Zhou, in Jinsha, Xiaoshan, and wrote *Collected Poems and Song Lyrics from the Snow-Crushed Studio (Xueya xuan shici ji).* Huang Yunfu [Xieqing's style name] says: Shuangqing's song lyrics are like the loquacious ramblings and complaints of a young girl. She comments on the sights she daily sees, the sounds she hears, the thoughts she thinks, the musings she muses. Her music unfolds so naturally and orderly that the author does not seem to be writing song lyrics, and the reader easily forgets that these are lyrics. But the feelings are genuine and the language is simple and honest, in nearly three hundred pieces. Is this not heavenly music? Is this woman not a prodigy? However, she suffered from poverty as no talented woman ever suffered before! No one can read through her poems without a flood of tears. (Huang 1873, 22.2a–b)

Huang makes no mention of Shi Zhenlin, though in a note appended to Shuangqing's plum blossom lyric, he remarks that *Random Notes from Xiqing* has a different lyric on this same tune. Huang's anthology is one key, I think, to the way the Shuangqing story has come down to the twentieth century. It is the first time that so many of her lyrics appear in an anthology. There are almost no details from Shi Zhenlin's narrative, and only the barest reference to *Random Notes,* a reference that leaves the impression that Shi's memoir is simply one alternative source on the peasant woman poet, not the only source from which everything else originates.

Huang's anthology is also important for what it adds to the Shuangqing legend. Here, for the first time, she has another mark of the elite, a style name, Qiubi. Her birth in Danyang, first claimed in Yun Zhu's anthology, is reaffirmed here. Not coincidentally, Huang includes in his work several other song-lyric writers surnamed He from Danyang. In addition, and most intriguingly, he cites an independent work published under He Shuangqing's own name, *Collected Poems and Song Lyrics from the Snow-Crushed Studio.* As far as I am aware, no edition of this title survives, but the title listed in Huang's anthology inspired the Beijing Cultural Society to publish Shuangqing's poems and lyrics in 1927, under the title, *Collection from the Snow-Crushed Studio (Xueya xuanji).* Huang Xieqing's commentary evaluating Shuangqing's song lyrics is full of repeated characters, doublets, in the style of her own most famous lyrics. He finds her a unique voice, almost beyond description. These comments would often be repeated in the late nineteenth and early twentieth centuries.

### *1870s and 1880s: Shi Zhenlin Reprinted*

Perhaps in response to Huang Xieqing's high praise of Shuangqing's lyrics and his inclusion of ten of her works in his anthology, Shi Zhenlin's surviving works were reprinted several times in the 1870s and early 1880s, for the first time in nearly a century. Eight-chapter versions of *Random Notes* were published in 1874 and again in 1878. The 1878 edition, which Zhang Hongsheng and I found in the Nanjing Public Library, includes a supplementary chapter entitled "Appended Prose Sketches from Xiqing" ("Fu Xiqing wenlueh"). This appears to be virtually the same text as Shi's *Scattered Notes from Huayang,* which was also published independently in 1883. There are three other editions of *Random Notes* in the Nanjing Public Library without precise dates. All appear to come from the late Qing period. One is a wood-block edition dated simply "Qing period"; one is a wood-block edition with no dates; and one is dated "late Qing," published by the Old and New Book Company (Gujin shuju) in Shanghai.

### *1885:* Danyang County History *First Claims Shuangqing*

Shuangqing's Danyang birthplace, her style name Qiubi, and her own book of poetry were "officially" recognized in 1885 when the *County History of Danyang* included the following brief biography in the section on writers: "He Shuangqing, author of *Collected Poetry from the Snow-Crushed Studio,* had the style name Qiubi. From Jiangshu in Danyang County, she married a man surnamed Zhou who lived in Xiaoshan, Jintan." This biography added yet one more new detail to the changing life story of the peasant woman poet. Now she had a specific birthplace, Jiangshu, a small market town in the southeastern corner of Danyang, just across the border from Jintan County. Du Fangqin has pointed out that in *Random Notes* Shi Zhenlin mentioned briefly a man named He Dingfu, from this very same Jiangshu in Danyang (1993, 7). Given the surname He and the Danyang affiliation, Jiangshu was the logical place to locate Shuangqing at birth since it is the home of the He family that produced so many women poets.

### *Late-Nineteenth-Century Song-Lyric Anthologists Make Shuangqing Famous: Miao Quansun, Chen Tingzhuo, and Xu Naichang*

Miao Quansun (1844–1919), a prominent scholar and bibliophile, published *Collected Song Lyrics from Changzhou during Our August Dynasty (Guochao Changzhou cilu)* in 1889. In section 5, he described and quoted three poets from *Random Notes from Xiqing,* Duan Yuhan (Flower Lover), Jing Zhenxiang, and Zhang Tianshen, and he noted that they were all admirers of the beautiful and tragic heroine Shuangqing. He says that *Random Notes* is by a man named Shi Zhenyuan, mistakenly substituting *yuan* for *lin* in *Shi Zhenlin.* In Miao Quansun's collected prose writings, *Yifeng tang wenji,* he includes a "Preface to Shuangqing's Song Lyrics" ("Shuangqing ci xu"; 1973, section 5) for a collection compiled by Xu Naichang (described below) where he praises her lyrics in lavish terms as unique among more than eighty women song-lyric writers from the Qing dynasty. "Her poems are the most delicate and the deepest in feeling. Just like an olive or a betel nut, the more you chew it, the better the taste you will enjoy." Not only are there few women poets who can match her, Miao continues, but her lyrics surpass all the others in *Random Notes,* thanks to their dazzling originality. He went on to point out that Dong Chao had mistakenly given Shuangqing the name Zhang Qingqing. Although Miao wrote his preface for Xu Naichang, who used the surname He, Miao himself referred to her only as Shuangqing, and he made clear that Shi's *Random Notes* was the only source on her life and poetry (even though he mistakenly called the author Shi Zhenyuan) (Miao Quansun 1896, 5.18a–b). Miao was from Wujin, the next county east of Jintan, and to some extent he was exhibiting regional pride in the appearance of a poet as talented as Shuangqing in his area.

Regional pride was also important to another champion of Shuangqing's poetry in the late nineteenth century, Chen Tingzhuo (1853–1892), one of the most well known critics and editors of song lyrics in his day. From Dantu (today Zhenjiang), just to the north of Danyang, he championed the Changzhou school of poetry, named for the district where the school originated, just to the south of Danyang. In his main work of criticism, *Song-Lyric Talks from the White Rain Studio (Baiyuzhai cihua),* published in 1892, the year of his death, he wrote that Shi Zhenlin's *Random Notes* contained twelve song lyrics by this poor peasant woman named Shuangqing. He quoted several lyrics by Shuangqing and praised her skill in two other anthologies he compiled, *Principles of the Song Lyric (Ci ce)* and *Collection of Other Tunes (Bie diao ji).*

Chen called her lyric on the autumn chrysanthemum his favorite. "This lyric is very indirect in expressing desolation, so it is very moving. Not a single word is commonplace. It makes me so sad to read that I can hardly bear to read it to the end. The lyric is very profound, rooted in [Shuangqing's] disposition and personality." On this and her other lyrics he commented that although she wrote in the feminine style, her lyrics were too distinctive to be able to say that she followed closely any of the great masters of the past. "Is she an immortal, or a ghost? I can't really name her realm!" And of her lyric on her illness, he wrote, "Trifling matters of everyday life, picked up seemingly at random, made her lyrics shine in splendor. To have Shuangqing's lyrics in my *Collection of Other Tunes* will surely add luster to the collection" (Chen Tingzhuo 1983, 549–53).

Interestingly, in Chen Tingzhuo's original texts, he follows Shi Zhenlin closely in leaving Shuangqing without a surname, birthplace, style name, or book of her own. However, in a telling example of the ways that modern scholars, with the best of intentions, sometimes help to construct and perpetuate cultural myths, the 1983 edition of Chen's *Song-Lyric Talks from the White Rain Studio* includes careful annotations referring to He Shuangqing, with style name Qiubi, from Danyang. The modern reader will innocently assume that today's editors are clarifying information that Chen Tingzhuo left out, or perhaps assumed his readers would know. In fact, such annotations mislead by repeating claims for which no firm basis has ever been established. In the construction of historical memory through the publication of written texts, repetition often counts for more than concrete evidence or its absence.

In any case, even though Miao Quansun and Chen Tingzhuo followed Shi Zhenlin closely in their quoting and describing Shuangqing, they were soon followed by an even more famous bibliophile and a devotee of women's song lyrics, Xu Naichang, who resumed the practice of passing on Shuangqing's surname, birthplace, and style name. In 1896, Xu began publishing a large anthology of song lyrics by Qing-dynasty women, entitled *The Xiaotanluan Studio Collection of Women's Song Lyrics (Xiaotanluan shi huike guixiu ci)* in ten large volumes. He followed Huang Xieqing's 1873 description of He Shuangqing, including her surname, her Danyang origins, her style name of Qiubi, and the citation of a book of her own, *Collected Poetry from the Snow-Crushed Studio.*

By the late nineteenth century, Shi Zhenlin was sometimes identified with Shuangqing and sometimes not. Largely because of regional critics who praised and anthologized her as a distinctive poet from their own area, the peasant woman poet named He Shuangqing was increasingly recognized in the late nineteenth century as one of the most distinctive voices in the entire Qing-dynasty history of the song lyric. Not coincidentally, around this time of her growing fame, Shuangqing achieved the posthumous distinction of having a book of her own.

### *1895 and 1901: Baiyuan Publishes* Collection of Unpaid Remorse *(Excerpts from* Random Notes*)*

Baiyuan was a concubine of a man named Shen Zongchou. In 1895, she compiled all the references to Shuangqing in Shi's *Random Notes* and published them under the title *Collection of Unpaid Remorse (Qianchou ji).* Reprinted again in 1901, this work is the earliest *surviving* collection on Shuangqing independent of *Random Notes.* In a postscript, Shen Zongchou wrote that he had long had an original edition of *Random Notes,* and Baiyuan loved to copy the portions of Shi's memoir dealing with Shuangqing, including the poetry and song lyrics. When she had completed this, she asked Shen to publish the work, which he was happy to do. The title comes from a line in one of her lyrics: "The old remorse is still unpaid."

On November 7, 1997, near the end of my stay in Nanjing, Zhang Hongsheng and I visited the Nanjing Public Library, where we were delighted to find, among several treasures, this little collection, which I had never seen before. It was the middle of a Friday afternoon, two hours before closing time. The copy machine was broken, and we could not check out such a rare work, a tattered old wood-block edition from 1901. After a moment of panic mixed with despair, I proposed leaving the librarians however much money they needed to copy the work and mail it to me by airmail. We quickly had a deal, and I left three hundred yuan ($37.50). In less than a month, I had the copy in my hands. It includes almost everything in *Random Notes* dealing with Shuangqing: all her poems, lyrics and prose, as well as many literati comments on her and poems addressed to her.

The Shuangqing here was in many ways a reclamation of the original Shuangqing, with her living and breathing contradictions: her avowed disinterest in the literati followed by flirtatious poems. The romantic overtones of Shi Zhenlin's narrative, which were glossed over and downplayed in the anthologies that included only her poems, were here restored to their central place in the narrative. And the various accretions of elite markers that Shuangqing acquired in the course of the nineteenth century, here dropped away. We are back to a peasant women, simply Shuangqing, without a surname, a place of origin, or a literati-type style name. There is no embellishment of Shi's original narrative, no information on her death. As in the original, the story simply stops.

Baiyuan omitted from her collection everything not directly relevant to Shuangqing, including Shi Zhenlin's philosophical musings—on dreams and the power of imagination, for example—and his friend Cao Zhenting's comment that many people doubt the existence of Shuangqing. Nearly everything else was included in the collection. Without any references to Shi Zhenlin's "spirit writing," his Buddhist-inspired metaphysics, or his elliptical and evasive discussion of Shuangqing's existence, Baiyuan's version did not raise as many doubts as Shi's uncut original, but it gave by far the most complete account of Shi Zhenlin's narrative outside of his own work. By taking Shuangqing out of the original context of Shi Zhenlin's *Random Notes,* even though Baiyuan made the debt to Shi clear throughout, she helped to establish Shuangqing in the public eye independently of her biographer. As Shuangqing gained a certain independence from *Random Notes,* her surname, style name, and Danyang origins were seldom questioned in the many anthologies that included her work. It seems that few thought to ask why or how these discrepancies might have arisen. Readers of the original source on Shuangqing, on the other hand, were more likely to see her as a fictional creation. And in the last decade of the nineteenth century and the first decade of the twentieth, there would be more readers of Shi Zhenlin.

### *Qiu Weixuan (1897): "Ah Shuangqing! . . . between Being and Nonbeing"*

In 1897, Qiu Weixuan published a series of notes on fictional works and included in his collection a brief paragraph on Shi Zhenlin's *Random Notes.* He reports that Shi's memoir has become especially popular since it was reprinted in the 1870s. Noting that this memoir is not strictly a piece of fiction, Qiu singles out Shi's portrayal of the peasant woman poet Shuangqing as highly fictionalized. "Ah Shuangqing! Was she real or not? She seems entirely from the imaginary realm between being and nonbeing. In the descriptions of *Random Notes,* she is as ethereal as an immortal" (1960, 394). Clearly not everyone assumed that Shi Zhenlin's portrayal of Shuangqing was to be taken literally. In the next decade after Qiu Weixuan wrote, Chinese readers could make their own minds up about Shi's memoir, as a complete four-chapter edition of *Random Notes* was published in Shanghai in 1907. (This is the version that was reprinted in Beijing in 1987 and became the basis for all my translations.)

### *1910s and 1920s: The Virtuous and Talented He Shuangqing*

In the late teens and 1920s, as China was swept by a New Culture Movement that both criticized tradition and looked for modern precedents in China's past, there was another flurry of writing on Shi Zhenlin and on Shuangqing, who was now universally referred to as He Shuangqing. In 1916, Xu Ke included in the "Heroic Virtue" section of his enormous collection *Classified Collection of Qing-Dynasty Notes (Qingbai leichao)* a note on "He Shuangqing, Who Did Not Wish to Meet Scholars Face to Face." Most of Xu's account (except for giving her surname as He and her birthplace as Danyang) is quoted directly from the early part of Shi Zhenlin's narrative of Shuangqing's life, and though he notes that she did exchange poems and letters with her literati admirers, Xu concludes that Shuangqing lived a life of suffering yet did not react in anger (Xu Ke 1966, vol. 23, Zhenlie section, 4–5).

As if following Xu Ke's lead, the 1921 edition of the *Jintan County History* includes Shuangqing's biography in the section on women under the category "Virtuous and Understanding" (*xianshu,* 10.4a). Apart from listing her surname and style name, the brief biography follows closely Shi Zhenlin's early description of Shuangqing in *Random Notes,* including her listening in on her uncle the village teacher, her skillful calligraphy and love of poetry, her writing the Heart Sutra on a cassia leaf, and her loyal service to her husband and mother-in-law despite their mistreatment of her. There is no mention of a village called Xiaoshan, perhaps since such a place was not known in Jintan. In this same county history, Shi Zhenlin is listed under notable local authors (11.5b and 7a), and interestingly enough, his *Random Notes from Xiqing* is classified as a work of fiction. Perhaps the authors concurred with Qiu Weixuan's 1897 assessment of the fictional qualities of Shi's memoir.

In the 1920s, two more influential collections on women's writings in the Qing dynasty were published, both praising He Shuangqing of Danyang. Shi Shuyi, a Jiangsu native and female head of a school for girls, published *Brief Biographies of Refined Lady Poets from the Qing Dynasty (Qingdai guige shiren zhenglüe)* in 1922, listing 1,260 women poets from the period. She includes a short biography of "He Shuangqing, from Danyang" and quotes (with citations) several passages on Shuangqing from *Random Notes* and from Wu Dexuan's *Record of Things Seen and Heard in the New Moon Pavilion* (Shi Shuyi 1987, 192–95). In 1925, Liang Yizhen published a history of women's literature from the Qing period. This is the work, reprinted in 1958, that I first read on Shuangqing in the 1980s (discussed in the preface). Also listing her as He Shuangqing from Danyang, Liang calls Shuangqing one of his favorite poets in over two hundred years of literature by Qing-dynasty women. He quotes two of her regulated-verse poems and her three most famous lyrics, on the autumn chrysanthemum, on the tune of the lonesome phoenix, and on the lone wild goose. In introducing these poems he seems to quote from Shi Zhenlin but makes no mention of Shi Zhenlin or his *Random Notes* (Liang 1958, 42–46).

A new edition of the *Danyang County History* was published in 1926, largely following the 1885 edition that first listed He Shuangqing as a Danyang native. The section on anecdotes (section 24, *zhiyi*) quotes Shi Zhenlin on several details of Shuangqing's life and poetry. Most of these accounts in the early and middle 1920s assume the literal truth of Shi Zhenlin's narrative, though they cite only the first few pages. It seems that Shi's opening section on Shuangqing came to be accepted as a literal history of the peasant woman poet.

### *Late 1920s: Two Abridgements of* **Random Notes** *Feature Shuangqing*

In 1926, a man named Xue Qu edited and published a new abbreviated version of Shi Zhenlin's *Random Notes* under the title *Heaven and Earth (Tianshang renjian)*. This title is taken from Shi Zhenlin's own statement about contemplating burning his work: "In Heaven and on earth there are so many things that move us. Those people who love the writing in this book still doubt the things described in it; others who adhere to traditional doctrines find fault with its language. When I wrote it I did not consciously set out [to write a book]. Even if it were destroyed by fire, what cause would I have for regret?" (*RN*, 3.52). Xue includes about a tenth of the original, what he calls "the best parts," to make the work more widely available to the reading public. Although he does not mention Shuangqing in his preface, the Shuangqing narrative occupies about one-half of *Heaven and Earth* (as opposed to only one-fifth of *Random Notes*).

In his preface, Xue Qu heaps lavish praise on Shi Zhenlin's writing, and in his first paragraph he announces that the best part of *Random Notes* is Shi's "record of heavenly immortals and earthly beauties of great talent and emotion who suffer great calamities." He has traveled widely for ten years, he reports, always keeping *Random Notes* by his side for solace and inspiration. "It creates a world of profoundness and subtlety, a world of depth and clarity. It expresses tender emotions, pervasive and heart-rending. Alas, this is really a work of intoxicating power—a work that cleanses one's soul! How can I not love the talented poet!" What Xue Qu understands best about Shi's *Random Notes* is its aestheticism.

> These notes describe dubious stories on earth and absurdities in Heaven. Those novices unfamiliar with the correct way of reading should not concentrate only on such stories and absurdities. I have learned that the most beautiful is often beyond reality. If one knows how to enjoy the beauty of Greek sculptures, European fairy tales, poetry, and drama, then he will be able to enjoy them to his heart's content. On the other hand, if one attempts to slight those works because of their dubious details and absurdities, then he should not be regarded as someone who understands what beauty means. (Xue 1926, 3–4)

This is perhaps the most sophisticated commentary on *Random Notes* from an early admirer of Shi Zhenlin. If you worry about the literal truth or untruth of the book, Xue Qu argues, you will miss the point, fail to see and to appreciate its beauty. Just read it for its beautiful language, its profound sentiments. Read it and weep!

*Heaven and Earth* put before the reading public most of Shi Zhenlin's Shuangqing narrative, including her poems and lyrics, cutting mainly some of the third-party praise of her that fills the later pages of Shi Zhenlin's account. As with Baiyuan's edition of *Collection of Unpaid Remorse,* Xue Qu gives us the unvarnished, unretouched peasant woman named Shuangqing, without surname, Danyang origins, or style name. Even so, this was not the Shuangqing that was to be anthologized hereafter. The surname, given name, and Danyang origins had by this time appeared too often for anyone to question them now.

One year after the appearance of Xue Qu's abridgement of Shi Zhenlin's memoir, in 1927, Zhang Shoulin brought out an edition of Shuangqing's poetry under He Shuangqing's own name, *Collection from the Snow-Crushed Studio (Xueya xuan ji),* a title chosen because Huang Xieqing 1873 had referred to such a work by Shuangqing. Consisting of three chapters—song lyrics, regulated verse, and supplementary material on Shuangqing—this work was published by the Beijing Cultural Society (Beijing wenhua xueshe). Although I have not been able to locate a copy, Elsie Choy quotes extensively from it, showing that Zhang restored Shuangqing's surname and her Danyang birthplace. He seems to have downplayed Shuangqing's flirtatious relations with her literati admirers, and according to Choy, he also downplayed Shi Zhenlin's importance to the Shuangqing story (Choy 1993, 4–5, 8–11).

There was clearly a growing interest in Shuangqing and her poetry in the early twentieth century. By this time, she had undergone over a century of what I call gentrification: she acquired a surname, a style name, and a birthplace; her song lyrics were more frequently included in anthologies and praised by literary critics and historians; and her flirtatious exchanges with her literary admirers in poetry and prose tended to drop from view. Two exceptions to these trends were the publication of abridged versions of Shi's *Random Notes* in 1901 and 1927. Despite the implication of Xue Qu in 1927 that Shi's memoir was not to be taken literally, there were still few if any critics who openly questioned Shuangqing's existence as a historical persona. Not coincidentally, the two people who raised explicit doubts were two leaders of the New Culture Movement, Gu Jiegang and Hu Shi.

### *New Culture Movement: Doubts of Gu Jiegang and Hu Shi*

Part of the New Culture Movement was a critical reassessment of China's past, and Gu Jiegang was a champion of the application of critical and modern scientific methods in the exploration of China's past. In *Short Story Monthly* in 1924, he contributed a brief research note entitled "Shuangqing," where he reports his discovery that the Shuangqing of Shi Zhenlin's *Random Notes* is called Zhang Qingqing by Dong Chao (1753), and He Shuangqing by Huang Xieqing (1873). Gu Jiegang writes that he loved Shi's memoir from the time he was just over ten years old, and he especially appreciated the tragic story of Shuangqing. He concludes: "There are many readers of *Random Notes from Xiqing;* can any of them help me to solve these puzzling points?"

Gu Jiegang's note suggests that Shi's *Random Notes* was especially popular among young readers in the New Culture Movement. Gu's questions did not produce any immediate responses in the *Short Story Monthly,* but three years later, Hu Shi went far beyond Gu in raising questions about Shuangqing's existence.

One of the great educator-scholars in China in the early twentieth century, Hu Shi believed that the best way to promote a renaissance in Chinese culture was to reexamine China's myth-encrusted past in the cold light of scientific rationality. In 1929, Hu received a copy of Zhang Shoulin's *Collection from the Snow-Crushed Studio,* from the prominent romantic poet Xu Zhimo. After reading this collection of Shuangqing's poetry, Hu declares confidently that he finds her to be a fictional character. He notes the various contradictions between Shi Zhenlin's original account of Shuangqing and later accounts by Dong Chao in 1753 and Huang Xieqing in 1873. He finds inconsistencies in Shi's own account of Shuangqing's age, saying she was eighteen in 1732 and twenty-one in 1733. And most importantly, he sees *Random Notes* as lacking credibility on many counts, including Shuangqing's brilliant writing in tiny characters with powder on leaves despite her constant farmwork and suffering from malaria and the persecution of her husband and in-laws.

Despite his own suspicions, Hu Shi notes that many people believe that Shuangqing really lived, and some even proclaim her the greatest female song-lyric writer in the Qing period. Pressing his case, he cites Shi Zhenlin's own statement about dreams being as real as waking reality, and Wu Zhensheng's fanciful preface (which he quotes but mistakenly attributes to Cao Zhenting), in the style of an eight-legged essay crying over the sad fate of both heavenly and earthly beauties. In Hu Shi's view, Shi Zhenlin's *Random Notes* is nothing more than

> the bitter human philosophy of the failed examination candidate [*bagu xiucai,* that is the eight-legged *(bagu)* essay writer who only attains the lowest, *xiucai,* degree]; this is the bitter [failed] scholar's religion. The talented female poet Shuangqing is a female bodhisattva who takes on the sufferings of all the beauties in the world in this bitter scholars' religion. She comes out of the vain and anxious dreams of these embittered scholars, "the most beautiful, intelligent, profound, and virtuous woman in the world." (Hu Shi, 1971, 685)

After nearly two hundred years of commentary on Shuangqing, Hu Shi's essay was the first ever to cast such unequivocal doubt on her existence. I am struck now by his certainty, in 1929, that Shuangqing was a fictional character. Some of his arguments are a bit sloppy and unpersuasive. For example, the contradictions among later commentators concerning Shuangqing's names do not really bear on the veracity of Shi Zhenlin's narrative. The fact that Shi Zhenlin gave contradictory ages for Shuangqing could have meant simply that he was sloppy with dates, not that his entire narrative is fictional. Nevertheless, in the short space of three pages, Hu Shi delivered quite a devastating critique. He was the first and only Chinese critic to point out various improbabilities in Shi Zhenlin's narrative and to cite Shi's practice of communicating with female immortals through spirit writing, and Wu Zhensheng's ornate preface, as evidence that this is a fanciful work.

Whether he was right or wrong, the most striking thing about Hu Shi's clarion call of doubt is that it went largely unheard by his contemporaries and successors. It seemed to drop like a pebble in the ocean, without creating any ripples. I have never seen a response to Hu Shi's arguments by any of his contemporaries. So few references are made to his doubts in most twentieth-century commentaries that I discovered his article only recently, in the later stages of my own search, even though it has been sitting on my own bookshelf now for three decades, in Hu Shi's collected works.

While Hu Shi's arguments are powerful on one level, he seems oblivious to the aesthetic power of Shi Zhenlin's prose and Shuangqing's poetry. A brilliant analytical scholar, Hu Shi was in some ways emotionally and aesthetically tone deaf. Xue Qu had warned in his 1926 preface to *Heaven and Earth:* whoever worries only about the literal truth of Shi Zhenlin's memoir will surely miss the point of it. Judging from the lack of a Chinese response to Hu Shi's arguments, it seems fair to say that most Chinese also favored Xue Qu's approach. Most admirers of Shi Zhenlin's *Random Notes* do not believe it can so easily be dismissed as the lunatic ravings of a failed examination candidate. It may be a fanciful work, but it is also written with a power and beauty that many have found intoxicating.

### *1935: Shi Zhenlin's* **Random Notes** *and* **Huayang Drafts** *Reprinted*

The biggest publishing year ever for Shi Zhenlin came in 1935, when both *Random Notes* and *Scattered Drafts from Huayang* were published as part of a series of rare literary works, reprinted by the Shanghai Magazine Company. Three thousand copies of both works were printed, and *Random Notes* must have sold well, because an additional fifteen hundred copies were printed one year later.

### *Other Twentieth-Century Anthologies*

In addition to all of the above, Shuangqing is mentioned and quoted in many modern anthologies of women's literature. Elsie Choy has found her poetry in anthologies published in 1918, 1932, 1961, 1971, and 1978, and in one undated anthology published sometime between 1911 and 1932. Choy also quotes a 1973 history of Qing literature in which the author Han Shiqiu argues that Shuangqing was one of the three greatest women song-lyric writers of the Qing period. My own survey of modern anthologies and literary histories finds Shuangqing included in works by Su Zhide in 1975, Chen Xiang in 1977, Chen Xin, Zhou Weide, and Yu Huanping in 1985, Su Zhecong in 1987 and 1988, Kang Zhengguo in 1988, Bao Jialin in 1989, Yan Dichang in 1990, Zheng Guangyi in 1991 (quoted at the beginning of this chapter), Li Shaocheng et al. in 1992, and Gong Bao'an in 1992.

Two recent Chinese anthologies contradict the general trend of twentieth-century works by featuring Shi Zhenlin more than Shuangqing. The first of these is *Qing-Dynasty Song Lyrics: Contexts and Annotations,* (*Qing ci jishi huiping*) compiled by You Zhenzhong and You Yiding and published in 1995. The compilers include song lyrics by 354 poets from 1644 to 1911, including five by Shi Zhenlin, but none by Shuangqing. They explain the background of each lyric, and for some they cite what critics have said about the lyric and the author. The second work is *The Best Essays of Famous Writers from the Ming and Qing Dynasties,* (*Ming-Qing mingjia xiaopin jinghua*) an anthology of essays and vignettes, "small pieces" *(xiaopin)* of description and anecdote, compiled by Ou Mingjun and published in 1996. Shi Zhenlin's inclusion here is not so surprising because he clearly excelled in the *xiaopin* genre. All four selections are from *Random Notes,* and the longest one is Shi Zhenlin's introduction of Shuangqing (quoted in chapter 2, "First Encounters"), including her first three song lyrics. Thus, even where Shi Zhenlin gets recognition, his fame rests in large part on his description of Shuangqing and his quotations of her song lyrics.

### *English-Language Reincarnations: Lin Yutang (1960) and Rexroth and Chung (1973)*

In English, Shuangqing had comparatively few reincarnations before the 1990s. In 1960, Lin Yutang, the great interpreter of Chinese culture for American readers, discussed Shuangqing very briefly in *The Importance of Understanding: Translations from the Chinese.* He cited Shi Zhenlin as one of his favorite writers, along with Shen Fu, the author of *Six*

*Records of a Floating Life.* He praised their ability to capture beauty, moods, and feelings in their writings and noted that they shared with many Chinese the belief that "when genius produces something, the gods are jealous." He also mentioned Shuangqing as one of his favorite Chinese heroines and saw her too as fitting this pattern of doomed genius. He promised, some day, "to tell her story" (Lin 1960, 14–15, 86, 89). Unfortunately, he never got around to the task.

Obviously Lin Yutang was a kindred spirit with Shi Zhenlin. His own response to Shi's writings, so in line with Xue Qu and in contrast to the cold analytical approach of Hu Shi, helps explain why Hu remained a lonely voice expressing doubt concerning the story of Shuangqing and dismissing Shi Zhenlin's writings as the mutterings of a superstitious failed scholar. Lovers of literature were not likely to be moved by Hu Shi's coldly rational dismissal of *Random Notes* as "not reliable." Much more common were those who sang the praises of Shuangqing as one of the distinctive poetic voices of the Qing period, and of Shi Zhenlin as a great writer and poet himself.

As noted in my preface, Kenneth Rexroth and Ling Chung included two song lyrics by Shuangqing and short biography of her in their anthology of poetry by Chinese women entitled *Orchid Boat,* published in 1973. In chapter 12, I have already discussed the recent scholarly analyses of Shuangqing and her story that have appeared in the 1990s.

### *Lessons*

I see three main lessons in these many reincarnations of Shuangqing: First, her rise to fame was a gradual process. Seldom mentioned in the late eighteenth century, she came to be gentrified and noticed more prominently in the early nineteenth century. In 1831, for the first time, Yun Zhu reported her surname as He and her birthplace as Danyang. Soon after Yun Zhu, in the mid-nineteenth century, two other important women writers Wang Duan and Shen Shanbao, added Shuangqing to the canon of women writers they were then helping to create. Shuangqing's surname and Danyang birthplace gained wide acceptance, and in 1873 she was further gentrified when Huang Xieqing assigned her a style name (Qiubi) and a book of her own, *Collected Poems and Song Lyrics from the Snow-Crushed Studio.* Then in 1885, the *Danyang County History* listed a specific birthplace in Danyang, the town of Jiangshu. All these details were repeated in most later biographies of He Shuangqing. In the late nineteenth century, two prominent male literary critics, Miao Quansun and Chen Tingzhuo, praised Shuangqing's song lyrics as outstanding cultural products of their own region. Independently of Shi Zhenlin, Shuangqing was coming to be seen as one of the greatest female song-lyric writers in the Qing dynasty.

The second major lesson from Shuangqing's many reincarnations is that her independent appearance in many anthologies has never entirely obscured her ambiguous ties with Shi Zhenlin. *Random Notes* was reprinted several times in the 1870s and again in 1907, 1935, 1936, and 1987. Abridged versions featuring Shuangqing were published by Lady Baiyuan 1895 and 1901, by Xue Qu in 1926, and by the Beijing Cultural Society in 1927. The anthologies feature the beautiful song lyrics of Shuangqing, with only a few details of her unhappy life, and none of the doubts, ambiguities, and philosophical musings of *Random Notes.*

The third and most striking thing about Shuangqing's many reincarnations is how few have questioned her existence despite the doubts and ambiguities in Shi Zhenlin's memoir. Before the 1990s, the most direct claims for a fictional Shuangqing were made by Qiu Weixuan in 1897 and Hu Shi in 1929. Despite the inconsistencies Hu Shi found in Shi Zhenlin's and subsequent accounts, few have joined him in challenging the standard biography of He Shuangqing. As seen in chapter 12, scholars in recent days have begun to analyze Shuangqing's story and her song lyrics in greater detail than ever before. Although some, including myself, have raised doubts about the literal truth of Shi Zhenlin's story of Shuangqing, all agree that the poetry attributed to her belongs in any anthology of Chinese women's poetry. Now that Shuangqing's origins are being questioned as never before, her poems and song lyrics are probably better known today than at any time in the twentieth century. Her place as a Chinese cultural icon is secure.

By now the circle, from 1737 to the present, is nearly complete. The last stop on this journey is in Danyang, where Du Laoshi and I found one more local reincarnation of Shuangqing's story.

*fifteen* ·

# *Exploring Danyang*

DANYANG, TUESDAY, NOVEMBER 4, 1997

Shortly before noon, Du Laoshi, Hongsheng, and I arrive at the Danyang municipal government headquarters, unload our bags, and bid farewell to our driver, who immediately departs for the return trip to Jintan. Hongsheng calls his friend in the Danyang municipal government and arranges a 2:00 P.M. meeting for us at the Danyang County Local History Office. We wheel our bags to the nearby Danyang Guest House, which is larger and more lavish than the Jintan Guest House we have just left. On our way, we notice a slogan written in large characters on a wall, in the same style as the political slogans of the Maoist era. Only this one seems far removed from the days of Chairman Mao: "Help Danyang progress; manage well the Yellow Wine Festival" (see figure 26).

Danyang is famous for its yellow wine, and the woman clerk on duty at the Guest House tells us they have no rooms available because of the expected influx of guests, starting tomorrow, for the three-day Yellow Wine Festival. When we offer to check out by 8:00 A.M. tomorrow, she agrees to register us for the night. After introducing us to several Danyang officials this afternoon, Hongsheng will take a bus back to Nanjing. Du Laoshi and I will stay here tonight and return to Nanjing tomorrow afternoon. We have two major goals: to learn what we can from the compilers of Danyang's county history, and to visit Jiangshu, the small town in the southeastern corner of the county most often identified as the birthplace of Shuangqing.

### *Shuangqing in the History of Danyang County*

After a quick lunch at a local restaurant, we arrive at 2:00 P.M. at the Danyang County Local History Office. Mr. Rong Mingru, editor of the *Danyang County History,* greets us warmly and presents us each with the latest hardbound edition. This seems unduly generous, as all we have to offer in return is one copy of Du Laoshi's book and the loan of some of our other materials for photocopying. When we explain our interest in Shuangqing, Mr. Rong says that there are many opinions concerning whether Shuangqing ever existed or not. Since he and his colleagues were unable to verify her existence, they did not include much about her in this version of the local history. Because I have checked this same volume out of Harvard's library, I delight Du Laoshi by flipping immediately to the one place I know (p. 1010) where a song lyric by Shuangqing is included.

### *Mr. Shi Shenghua: A New View of Shuangqing*

Mr. Rong also gives us a short book entitled *Danyang*, published in 1991, which includes an article on Shuangqing by Mr. Shi Shenghua, a reporter for the *Danyang Daily*. Almost immediately, Mr. Shi himself arrives. Briefly, I check out of the conversation in order to look over this article. I am impressed with Shi Shenghua's way of embellishing on Shi Zhenlin's prose. (In romanized form, Mr. Shi's surname looks the same as Shi Zhenlin's, but it's a different character.)

> In a thatched hut with a shabby door, she grew up in a common peasant family, like an apricot blossom hanging over a courtyard wall.
>
> In the fifty-fourth year of the Kangxi reign (1715), He Shuangqing was born into a peasant family of Jiangshu in Danyang. The fertile lands and clear waters of the village nurtured her, surrounded by the lakes and rivers of Jiangnan (the southern lower Yangzi valley). "The cardamom flower opens in early February." As described in this poem (i.e., like the cardamom) Shuangqing grew up a pretty and charming maiden. Pale as a pear blossom, her body was like jade, her skin white as snow. She had no makeup, no jewels, and no jade hair ornaments; her black long hair was like a bolt of silk draping down to her shoulders. Her beauty was inborn and natural. Countless young men from wealthy and noble families were overwhelmed by her beauty.
>
> Her uncle on her mother's side was a well-known teacher at a local school, and he lived next door to Shuangqing. From her early childhood, she was deeply influenced by everything she saw and heard, and thus she developed a profound love for poetry and prose. She was clever, with dexterous hands. By ten years of age,

> she did exquisite needlework that she exchanged for books to read. When her uncle was teaching, she would lean quietly against the wall under the window and listen attentively, committing all she heard to memory. In her spare time in her own room, she would write and recite poems and practice calligraphy and painting in order to express the feelings and emotions of her budding maidenhood. (Shi Shenghua 1991, 141)

### *Shi Zhenlin and Shuangqing: An Early Love Affair?*

The story is so familiar that I skim these paragraphs quickly, until coming to a passage that fairly leaps off the page. It departs from Shi Zhenlin's *Random Notes* so radically that I wonder whether I am understanding it. Just at this point, Mr. Rong and Mr. Shi leave us to ourselves for a minute. They go out to check on arrangements for this evening. "Look at this," I whisper to Du Laoshi. She gives the paragraph a quick glance and shows it immediately to Hongsheng, saying, "This is an entirely new story!" I feel reassured that I am not just imagining things.

> Among her uncle's students was one called Shi Zhenlin, a native of Jintan, a well-mannered and easygoing young man. At first glance, he fell in love with Shuangqing, and she likewise fell in love with him. But her family was strictly bound by the rules of propriety, and she could only bury her feelings and hide her love deep in her heart. When she was eighteen, her father, He Migao, died, leaving her paternal uncle in charge. In exchange for a betrothal gift of 150 kilos of unhusked grain, this uncle married her to a man surnamed Zhou, a native of Xiaoshan in Jintan. Her husband was over ten years older than she was. (Shi Shenghua 1991, 141)

### *Questions for Shi Shenghua*

Here we have a name for Shuangqing's father, He Migao, and a youthful romance between Shuangqing and Shi Zhenlin. When Mr. Shi returns, we greet him with a series of rapid-fire questions about his sources for this article. We also explain that we've studied Shi Zhenlin's *Random Notes* for years and read countless biographies of He Shuangqing, and we have never come across this information about Shuangqing's father or her early acquaintance with Shi Zhenlin.

Mr. Shi seems curiously withdrawn, and he answers our questions with a frown on his face. For one thing, it seems he is not well. He has a nasty hacking cough that seems to convulse his entire thin frame. Although wincing in pain with each cough, he lights up a fresh cigarette every thirty minutes. I can understand that our arrival might not be an exciting development for him. We three scholars have shown up on the eve of a major city festival, full of probing questions about one short article he wrote six years ago. We show him our own supply of Shuangqing materials, including the books by Du Laoshi and Elsie Choy, my Harvard conference paper, and Zhou Wanyao's article from Taiwan. He is clearly surprised and a bit nonplused by all this. He scans our material with a resigned look and shows no interest in photocopying it. For him this is a minor story, one among hundreds he has written over the years, about a piece of local culture. Yet we are scholars who have spent years researching this topic, and now, in effect, we are questioning his use of sources for his article.

"Where did you get all this information?" Du Laoshi asks excitedly. "We have never before heard this story about Shuangqing and Shi Zhenlin falling in love in their youth before she was ever married."

"Years ago someone gave me some materials on He Shuangqing, including the poems I quote in the article. Unfortunately, there was no name identifying the source of the material, and I don't even remember who gave it to me. I don't have it anymore. It's all been lost."

"As far as we know, the only original source on He Shuangqing is the memoir, *Random Notes from Xiqing*, by Shi Zhenlin," Hongsheng explains. "Have you read it?"

"No, but I've heard of it."

"Shi Zhenlin never mentioned Danyang as the original home of Shuangqing, nor did he mention the surname He. He simply called her Shuangqing."

"Sources on Shuangqing are extremely limited," he readily acknowledges, "but she appears in earlier editions of the *Danyang County History*, and in a compilation of Danyang literary works that was compiled by the Danyang County Association on Taiwan [made up of former residents of Danyang who fled to Taiwan in 1949]."

"What evidence is there that Shuangqing really came from Danyang?" Hongsheng asks.

"Well, the *Danyang County History* says she was born in Jiangshu, and there are many people surnamed He in that district."

Having long had doubts about Danyang being the birthplace of Shuangqing, I had not been very excited about our visit here. However, Shi Shenghua's article alone has made the trip worthwhile. As the conversation continues, I turn back to the article to see what other surprises it might hold. The next several paragraphs appear to be based on the Shuangqing narrative in *Random Notes.*

### *Shi Shenghua's Story of Shuangqing, Continued*

Her life after marriage was extremely unhappy. No matter how completely she complied with the requirements of wifely loyalty and service, and no matter how hard she worked or how docile she remained, she was frequently scolded, beaten, and mistreated by her ignorant, stupid, domineering, and tyrannical husband and mother-in-law. Even when she was stricken with malaria and bedfast as a result, her husband forced her out of bed and into the fields to work.

Oppressed by the feudal ethical codes and a life of privation, she was tightly confined to this tiny narrow mountain village. The ardor and hopes of her youth she kept deep in her inner courtyard, and they gradually dissipated altogether. She was sorrowful, melancholy, and lonely, and she had no one with whom to share her sufferings. The only outlet she had was to express her thoughts and feelings in poetry and song lyrics.

At the foot of Mao Shan, the village of Xiaoshan was a beautiful place. Shuangqing lived on the west side of the village. In front of the door of her hut flowed a stream with its bubbling waves; along the stream there were willows with their pliable twigs swaying in the breeze. To the north of the village there was a huge stone sticking up like a screen, pine trees standing proudly, old vines interwoven and tangled, and green bamboo rocking and swaying. To the southwest were the Xiangxia pavilion and the Plowing-in-Pairs (Ougeng) Hall. Beyond the hall was a rocky precipice on which stood the Temple of the Flower Goddess. There was a beautiful statue of the Goddess of Flowers for people to worship. No one knew how many times Shuangqing had knelt before it and prayed, and no one knew how many tears she had shed when she was there by herself. The springtime flowers withered, the autumn leaves fell, the swallows flew away, and wild geese came. . . . Year in and year out, her plight was always the same, with no sign of change for the better.

The showers of early summer scattered over the valleys and fields. Newly harvested wheat sent forth its delicate and pleasant fragrance from the threshing floor. Herdboys with fresh flowers on their heads enjoyed their leisure on the backs of their water

> buffaloes. After she finished all her farmwork in the fields, Shuangqing had to rush home to cook for the family. She toiled so much that her whole body was racked with pain. Even so, all she heard were scoldings and reproaches. Bearing all this, to express her sad feelings, she wrote this song lyric to the tune of "Huanxisha": [here Mr. Shi quotes Shuangqing's first lyric in *Random Notes* (see chapter 2, "First Encounters")].
>
> There were no flowery phrases or expressions used in this lyric. The language she used was that of common everyday speech. She excelled at expressing her feelings within and through her natural setting, thus revealing the beauty of her tragic life. In this manner, she captured in her work moments of high aesthetic value. She was also comfortable using different and intricate meters and rhyme schemes to express her ever-changing moods and sentiments. Her lyric to the tune of "Fenghuang taishang yichuixiao" is a good example: [here he quotes Shuangqing's famous lyric to the fading lamp, filled with doublets or repeated characters (see chapter 7, "Lyrics")].
>
> The language used in this lyric is simple and common. Many repetitions are cleverly employed and thus is achieved an artistic effect of chanting circling back on itself. The poem is exceedingly sentimental and melodious, and it carries a lingering charm. It is a lament that expresses the sorrow and sadness of Shuangqing herself.
>
> Shuangqing wrote her poems only to express her own feelings and sentiments; she did not wish to see them handed down or passed on to others. She wrote her poems in the regular script in very small characters, very carefully and beautifully, on reed leaves, bamboo leaves, and cassia leaves—leaves that she dearly loved. Then, she would let the leaves wither and the poems fade away. However, some of her poems and lyrics were discovered, copied, and treasured by lovers of her poetry. (Shi Shenghua 1991, 142–43)

I skim this material quickly and listen to the conversation with one ear while Du Laoshi asks some general questions about Danyang. Hongsheng's friend who has helped us arrange this meeting arrives, and they chat briefly outside the office. Just as I am about to put the essay aside, my eyes fall on two more paragraphs that present an entirely new interpretation of Shi Zhenlin's Xiaoshan encounter with Shuangqing.

*Tearful Silent Reunion of Parted Lovers*

> One summer, the Jintan provincial-degree holder Shi Zhenlin, who had just failed in the metropolitan examination, came to Xiaoshan with his friend Duan Yuhan, to study at Duan's Plowing-in-Pairs Hall, and to escape the summer heat. One day, he chanced to meet a slender woman coming out carrying a trash basket. Shi Zhenlin felt very strange and wondered how such a beautiful woman could be living in such a poor and remote place as this. He fixed his gaze upon her, and to his astonishment, he recognized his beloved Shuangqing whom he had longed for and pined for day and night. To meet like this after their prolonged separation, Shuangqing was overcome with feelings of both joy and sadness. Staring at each other, speechless, there was only a flood of hot tears.
>
> During his days in Xiaoshan, Shi Zhenlin collected some of her poems and lyrics. He was profoundly shattered to read the sad and touching works of such a talented woman. That a woman of such great talent and great beauty should live a life of such great misery! "No one could surpass Shuangqing in both talent and beauty; no one could suffer more than Shuangqing in poverty and illness!" In his notes he grievingly recorded her tragic story. A few years later, he passed the metropolitan examination and came to Xiaoshan once again. But to his shock, Shuangqing had already died from her long illness brought on by her prolonged sadness and despair. She was buried at the foot of Mao Shan. From a woman who had been Shuangqing's neighbor, he received a poem Shuangqing had left for him. (Shi Shenghua 1991, 143)

I am amazed by this account of Shi Zhenlin's tearful silent reunion with Shuangqing, and I show it to Du Laoshi immediately. The poem that Shuangqing left for Shi Zhenlin is also one I have never seen before. There is no time to translate it now, but I have to admit to myself how wrong I was to think the trip to Danyang was not necessary. Shi Shenghua's account is as interesting and as original as Shi Zhenlin's!

After Hongsheng leaves to catch his bus at 3:15, we continue our conversation for an hour more. Mr. Rong says that the vice mayor, Chen Guohua, wants to treat Du Laoshi and me to dinner this evening. However, because of the Yellow Wine Festival, Mr. Chen cannot join us himself. (I take this to mean he will foot the bill!) Mr. Rong and Mr. Shi will join us, along with Miss Yin, a young woman from the local history office.

When we first arrived, Du Laoshi had mentioned our keen interest in visiting Jiangshu, the supposed birthplace of He Shuangqing. Mr. Shi made several phone calls, arranged for a car from his office to take us to Jiangshu tomorrow, and made an appointment for us at the Jiangshu local government. Du Laoshi has hopes that we might be able to meet some older people in Jiangshu, as we did in Xuebu Zhen. Mr. Shi says that he and Miss Yin will accompany us to Jiangshu. Whatever Mr. Shi might think of our probing questions and our quixotic quest for information about Shuangqing, he is certainly making every effort to accommodate our needs.

### *Dinner in Danyang*

At dinner this evening, I quickly realize how dependent I have been on Hongsheng. He speaks a crystal clear Mandarin, and he knows enough English that I can always turn to him for a Chinese equivalent of an English word. Du Laoshi is patient and helpful but doesn't speak much English, and I still don't understand her as easily as Hongsheng. Even so, I rightly anticipate another delightful feast with our gracious and generous hosts.

Our main host at dinner is a Mr. Pan, who fills in for the absent vice mayor. Our delicious and bountiful meal (including whole crabs for the second night in a row) is served along with the ever-potent *baijiu* liquor, and a special treat, Danyang yellow wine, the main excuse for tomorrow's festival. Mr. Rong is in a jovial mood, and Mr. Shi seems much more relaxed than earlier in the day. We discuss the general state of economic development in China, U.S.-Chinese relations, and just a bit about our research on He Shuangqing. I remark on the contrasts between China today and the China I first visited twenty-two years ago. This identifies me as an "old friend" of China's who visited already in the "bad old days." Mr. Rong and I discover we were both born in 1944, the Year of the Monkey, which requires a "bottoms up" toast of yellow wine. The wine looks more red than yellow to me; it's a sweet wine made from glutinous rice. Having had little wine for the past month, I relish it! We finish our meal by 8:00 P.M., and Du Laoshi and I are free for the evening, a welcome reprieve from the intensity of the past few days in Jintan.

### *A "Lost Shuangqing Lyric"*

For awhile after dinner, Du Laoshi helps me work on the beginnings of a translation of the Shuangqing song lyric we have not seen before. Months later, I would polish the translation of this "lost Shuangqing lyric" that she supposedly left for Shi Zhenlin just before she died:

*All day I think of you and shed my tears in vain;*
*Chang'an is more distant every day;*
*Each night I visit several times in dreams.*
*The plight of this lyric writer is laughable;*
*I study the village girls and boys,*
*Early and late, burn the incense and make the three kowtows.*
*I pray to Heaven to bless and protect you:*
*May the distant one win rank and fame,*
*And soon find himself a sweet companion.*
*You must forget the pining woman who is sick and thin;*
*In the next life, who knows* [if we'll be together];
*As for this life, it is finished.*
(Quoted in Shi Shenghua 1991, 144)

Although we are excited to see this new "Shuangqing lyric," it clearly does not match the quality of the other lyrics attributed to Shuangqing. It is a conventional lyric to an absent male lover who has gone to the distant capital to compete in the civil service examinations. It is simple enough, and the poet implies that these lovers are separated both by space and by social class. She therefore urges him to achieve rank and fame, and to find a proper marriage partner worthy of his high status. Although he may have sought rank and fame in the examination system, in *Random Notes* Shi Zhenlin studiously ignored that quest, and Shuangqing never expressed the slightest concern for the examination experiences of her literati admirers. The lyric also lacks most of the hallmarks of the Shuangqing style: the vivid imagery of Shuangqing, the intense identification of the poet with the object she describes, the obsession with her own appearance, the skillful repetition of characters in a natural and expressive way, the simple recounting of daily life. Of course, even if the lyric were more skillfully done, there would be no reason to attribute it to Shuangqing since it appears nowhere in Shi Zhenlin's *Random Notes,* nor in any other source within two centuries of the memoir.

DANYANG, WEDNESDAY, NOVEMBER 5, 1997

### *Trip to Jiangshu Township: Shuangqing's Birthplace?*

It is a bright sunny day, and Du Laoshi and I check out of our rooms early, as promised, after enjoying a lavish dim sum breakfast. Our driver soon arrives, with Mr. Shi and Miss Yin, and by nine o'clock we are having tea in a reception room of the Jiangshu township government headquarters. Mr. Shi seems much more comfortable and animated than he did yesterday. Perhaps he also enjoys this unusual trip chaperoning two scholars to Jiangshu, a town he tells us he has only rarely visited.

In Jiangshu, we are greeted by a young woman, Miss He (not the same He as He Shuangqing), who is not familiar with Shuangqing. She is nevertheless eager to hear about the purpose of our visit, and she quickly skims through Du Laoshi's book and looks over our copy of Shi Zhenlin's *Random Notes*.

### *Spirit Writing in Danyang*

An elderly man named Sun soon joins us as we begin to discuss some of the Daoist practices associated with Mao Shan and described in Shi Zhenlin's *Random Notes*. Though he has not read this memoir, Mr. Shi is quite familiar with the practice of spirit writing. "There are many superstitious practices that are quite popular in this area still today. And in the eighteenth century, the belief in immortals was particularly widespread in Danyang."

"To engage an immortal through spirit writing," I ask, "did one need to hire a shaman or specialist of some kind? Or could anyone engage in this on their own?"

"Anyone could do this!" he replies. "There were, and still are, many shamanistic practices in this region. Some specialists treated illness [by casting out and protecting against malevolent spirits]; others did fortune telling."

"Were these people often women?" Du Laoshi asks.

"The healers were mostly women, but some men also specialized in these practices."

### *Shuangqing as a Role Model for a Jiangshu Middle School Class*

The elderly Mr. Sun is the only one we meet in Jiangshu who has heard of Shuangqing. He says he remembers reading in the newspaper a short while back about a middle school teacher who used the example of Shuangqing's poetry as a way of encouraging the young women in her class to develop their literary talents.

### *Doubts on Shuangqing Not Welcome Here*

During a lull in our discussions, I show Miss He the passage in Shi Zhenlin's *Random Notes* where he says Shuangqing wrote the Heart Sutra on a cassia leaf and many of her lyrics in powder on leaves. Suggesting that some parts of Shi Zhenlin's story seem fictionalized, I am curious to test the reaction of someone who has not heard of Shuangqing before. Miss He will have no part of my attempt to sow seeds of doubt. "What's so strange about that?" she says with a hint of indignation in her voice. "It seems perfectly possible for me that she wrote on leaves using powder." Sorry I mentioned it! End of discussion.

### *Lunch in Jiangshu*

At noon, after a round of picture taking (see figure 27), Miss He takes us to lunch in a private dining room at a local restaurant. As has become our custom on this trip, we eat a lavish meal of a dozen delicious dishes.

Mr. Shi is curious to hear how I became interested in China, and I note truthfully that I literally fell into it. "Growing up on a farm in the Midwest, I knew absolutely nothing about China when I went to graduate school to study European history in 1966. But the 'Vietnam War to contain China' and American television coverage of Chairman Mao's Cultural Revolution both brought China to my attention, and I decided to do something about my ignorance and take a couple of classes on China. After my first ten days in graduate school, I liked my China courses so much that I decided to abandon European history and study China instead. As my advisor warned at the time, the decision prolonged my graduate school career by a few years in order to study Chinese and Japanese, but I never had any regrets. Such was the optimism of the 1960s that my wife and I started our family during those tumultuous years, and before I had my first job six years later, we had two sons and an adopted Chinese daughter. So, with a Chinese daughter who now has a half-Chinese son, I must be considered at least part Chinese."

Du Laoshi, hearing this story for the first time, deadpans a quick response. "You *must* have been Chinese in an earlier incarnation! Perhaps you really are the reincarnation of Shi Zhenlin!"

I have to admit, through my laughter, that reincarnation is somehow a more satisfying explanation than my "falling into" Chinese studies by accident.

After lunch, we visit a local store selling its own Jiangshu-produced freshwater pearls. We all buy some pearls, and I take pictures up and down the street while Du Laoshi takes the opportunity to buy many small strings of Jiangshu pearls as souvenirs for her friends and family. Then, finished by two o'clock, we head back to Danyang, and catch the same 3:30 bus that Hongsheng had taken the day before. Du Laoshi wants to take the overnight train back to her home in Tianjin, so once we get back to Nanjing University, we hurry off to the train station to see if she can still get a ticket. Sleepers are all sold out, but she gets a seat on the 7:30 train, and she and I find a nearby restaurant for a quick dinner.

NANJING, WEDNESDAY–SATURDAY, NOVEMBER 5–8, 1997

### *Nanjing Interlude*

We have agreed that I will stop in Tianjin on my way back to Beijing and spend a day seeing the city. Du Laoshi will reserve a room for me at the guest house at her university. Reflecting back on our week of travel together, I marvel at all we have discovered. Du Laoshi and I are equally excited by our findings, though not surprisingly, we have each found confirmation of our previously held views. Most importantly, Du Laoshi sees the popular stories about Shuangqing as independent confirmation of her historical existence; and she sees all the parallels between Shi's memoir and the setting of Fang Shan in Jintan as evidence for the view that *Random Notes* was a straightforward factual account of Shi Zhenlin's observations. By contrast, I see the popular stories about Shuangqing as later retellings, interpolations, misreadings, and mishearings of the Shuangqing story originated by Shi Zhenlin.

Our differing views, however, have never caused us the slightest problem on this trip, in part because we share the same enthusiasms. Through the course of the week, we have also discussed possibilities for more collaboration in the future. Seeing that even local officials in Jintan and Danyang do not have editions of Shi Zhenlin's *Random Notes,* Du Laoshi has decided that she would like to edit a new punctuated and annotated edition of the memoir. If she does this, Hongsheng and I have told her that we might try to cooperate on a complete translation of Shi's memoir into English. Thus far, I (and independently, Elsie Choy) have translated perhaps one-fourth of the memoir. We think a complete translation would help make Shi Zhenlin's literary skill better understood in the West; and it would help the Western scholarly world see the Shuangqing story in its original context, something not previously possible.

Curiously, back on my own in Nanjing after an exciting week with my colleagues exploring Jintan and Danyang, I feel as if the spell of the past has been broken, and I, a news junkie all my adult life, am suddenly hungry for news of the present. For tonight, however, my first night back in Nanjing, I put off looking for a newspaper until tomorrow and turn to Shi Shenghua's concluding paragraphs of his short biography of Shuangqing.

### *Shi Shenghua's Conclusion on Shuangqing*

When he finished reading [the last poem Shuangqing had left behind for him], Shi Zhenlin burst into tears, and two icy streams flowed down his cheeks. In his grief and anguish, he then wrote the story of the ill-fated but talented woman in his *Random Notes from Xiqing,* and he handed it down to later generations.

Most of the works of He Shuangqing have been preserved in the *Collection from the Snow-Crushed Studio,* which was compiled by someone later. What she wrote in her poetry and song lyrics was mostly about her own misfortune in life, and her lament for that misfortune. Her works are permeated with feelings of suppression, desolation, and sadness. Given the confines of her own life experiences, her work was necessarily narrow in scope. However, her personal tragedy reflects the dark shadows of her own time and her own society and helps us to see the mistreatment of women, especially in the lower social strata, and to understand how their talents were suppressed and destroyed. Moreover, with her ardent and authentic feelings being expressed with such a high level of artistic ability, she produced works of unquestionably high aesthetic value. People of later generations have called her the Li Qingzhao of the Qing dynasty [Li Qingzhao being China's most famous woman poet]. Huang Xieqing, a poet in the last years of the Qing dynasty, commented on Shuangqing's poems by saying they are "like the loquacious ramblings and complaints of a young girl." [Here Mr. Shi continues with the famous quote from Huang Xieqing in which he praises her poetry using her own style of repeated characters or doublets (see chapter 14, "Reincarnations.")]

Wang Zhefu wrote in the beginning chapter of his *History of the New Literature Movement in China:* "We read Shen Fu's *Six Records of a Floating Life* [a nineteenth-century memoir of a loving married couple] and He Shuangqing's *Collection from the Snow-Crushed Studio,* but can we stay untouched and unmoved after reading these stories full of sadness and sorrow?" Mr. Xu Zhimo [the great poet who introduced Hu Shi to Shuangqing's poetry] once strongly recommended *Collection from the Snow-Crushed Studio* to the reading public. Mr. Hu Shi [see "Reincarnations," year 1929] also wrote "Investigations on He Shuangqing." Her poetry and song lyrics had a definite influence on the development of the New Literature Movement in China [in the 1920s].

He Shuangqing, the talented peasant woman poet of Danyang, suffered immensely during her miserable and tragic life, but what she left to humanity is a very rich and precious literary heritage. She will always have an important place in the history of Chinese literature. (Shi Shenghua 1991, 144)

I appreciate Mr. Shi's conclusions on Shuangqing's place in Chinese literary history, and I am particularly pleased to see his reference to Xu Zhimo. A leader of a romantic literary movement in China in the 1920s, Xu was a colorful figure who once studied at my own Clark University in Worcester, Massachusetts, before transferring to Oxford. He was killed in an airplane crash in 1933. Thanks in part to a popular new soap opera on Xu's life, a "Xu Zhimo craze" has recently developed in Taiwan. It is a sweet coincidence that this most famous Chinese poet of the twentieth century once studied at my university and was an ardent fan of Shuangqing's poetry.

Before closing this little volume entitled simply *Danyang,* I read one more time Shi Shenghua's remarkable account of Shi Zhenlin's tearful reunion in Xiaoshan, having found her by accident after a long separation. This story seems designed to make sense of Shi Zhenlin's relationship with Shuangqing and his concern to make her poetry known to the world. If this were all true—if she was his childhood sweetheart; if she was forced by her parents to marry a poor peasant; and if he found her years later only by accident—it would help explain the air of tragedy that pervades Shi Zhenlin's account and the erotic overtones in their poetic exchanges. But of course this account has its own implausibilities. Why would a family marry their daughter to a poor peasant after she's been courted by a privileged and educated literatus? And if Shi Zhenlin gave no hint of any earlier contact with Shuangqing, how would a twentieth-century author be able to uncover such a long-hidden love affair? The point of this story is not its plausibility or implausibility, but rather its way of "making sense" of the magical poetry attributed to Shuangqing and the worshipful attitude of Shi Zhenlin toward his peasant heroine.

### *Shi Shenghua's Final Anecdote: "He Just Imagined It!"*

I had been so intent on reading and understanding Shi Shenghua's article while we sat in the local history office in Danyang that I missed one of the key admissions by Mr. Shi. Two days later, on the way to the Nanjing Public Library with Hongsheng, I mention Mr. Shi's "new information" to Hongsheng to see what he thinks of it. "In fact," Hongsheng says with a chuckle, "Mr. Shi based the early part of his article on the anonymous source that is now lost. The Shuangqing poem he quotes also came from that source. But the description of the tearful silent reunion of Shuangqing and Shi Zhenlin, Mr. Shi admitted that he 'just imagined' that!"

"Imagined it?" I ask, incredulously.

"Yes! He made it up!"

What an appropriate conclusion to our investigations in Jintan and Danyang, I think to myself. How often in the past have people "made up" things to try to make sense of the poetry attributed to the peasant woman poet Shuangqing? She acquired a surname, a style name, and a birthplace in Danyang to explain how she could be so literate and so skilled in poetry. Now, in the most recent version of her story, she has acquired a clandestine-yet-innocent early love affair and an accidental tearful reunion to make sense of her poetic exchanges with Shi Zhenlin.

### *A New Alternative Site for the Village of Xiaoshan*

"Oh, that's not all," Hongsheng continues. "Du Laoshi called me last night to say she had gotten a call from Secretary Sun at Xuebu Zhen. He says, since our visit to Jintan, our friends in Xuebu Zhen have been thinking more about the scenic descriptions in Shi Zhenlin's *Random Notes.* They now think there is another nearby site, the Ninth Brigade of Fang Shan (a term that harks back to the Cultural Revolution when villages were organized into "production brigades") that bears a striking resemblance to Shi's description of Xiaoshan!"

"So," I remark to Hongsheng with a laugh, "our investigations still aren't quite finished!" As this news sinks in, I think to myself, there must be a dozen places in Jintan with bamboo groves and a stream beside a rock-strewn mountain. When we first visited Fang Shan and the stone quarry at the Shi Family Mountainside, I had wondered how the authorities would ever manage to create a tourist site on the grounds of a prison beside a stone quarry? Now I think we have an answer: If they can find a more fitting place for Xiaoshan, they won't have to put it beside a prison!

In her 1998 article of our investigative trip to Jintan, Du Laoshi reports that she later received a number of letters and requests for her book from people in Jintan, in reaction to the newspaper and television reports on our visit there. There was something of a "Shuangqing fever" in Jintan and Danyang. One of her correspondents, Mr. Zhao Suolong, a native of Xuebu Township and now in the College of Population Management in Nanjing, wrote that he had earlier made a thorough study of Shi Zhenlin's *Random Notes*, and he had located the site of Xiaoshan at the Tenth Brigade of Fang Shan, near Wild Boar Pond (Du 1998, 122–23). So now we have two additional possibilities for the location of Xiaoshan, all near Fang Shan and the Shi Family Mountainside, but just not on the site of a provincial prison.

### *Du Laoshi's Conclusions*

Reflecting back on the trip just completed, Du Laoshi and I feel exhilarated by the connections we have made. Although we have been studying Shuangqing now for years, we had not known of these local stories of a Xiaoshan Academy and a childhood relationship between Shi Zhenlin and Shuangqing. And the local scholars who have come across and recorded these stories had not known of our work on Shuangqing, or the work of our colleagues abroad.

We have discovered some common ground in our views of Shuangqing, but the trip has done little to resolve our differences. Du Laoshi and I agree that Shi Shenghua's account of Shi Zhenlin's unsuccessful courtship of Shuangqing is most likely based on oral retellings, or corrupted reprintings, of the Shuangqing narrative in *Random Notes*. We also agree that ironclad proof one way or another will never be possible concerning the historical existence of a peasant woman poet named Shuangqing. Our most fundamental disagreement is over the significance of our possible discovery of the site of Xiaoshan village. For Du Laoshi, the existence of such a site in itself (wherever it might actually be) is important as evidence that Shi Zhenlin's memoir is an unembellished factual account of his experiences and observations. For me, the possible existence of a real Xiaoshan village does not fundamentally alter my reading of Shi's memoir. His description of the scenery and layout of Xiaoshan, while not terribly detailed, was never a problem in my mind. I simply find his account of Shuangqing and her interactions with him and his friends unpersuasive as a historical document.

For Du Laoshi, if Xiaoshan was based on a real place, it suggests that Shuangqing was based on a real person. If other characters in *Random Notes* can be shown to be real historical figures, why should we doubt that Shuangqing was a real historical figure? Jintan's high cultural level, its contemporary women poets, its talented schoolchildren, all provide evidence for the historical reality of a peasant woman poet. And the parallels between the Fang Shan area and Shi Zhenlin's Xiaoshan (from straw sandals to peasants cutting kindling on the mountainside to the popular belief in spirit writing) all fit into a jigsaw puzzle that Du Laoshi sees as an accurate and realistic account of Jintan in the eighteenth century. As for the inclusion of Shuangqing in the local histories of Jintan and Danyang counties, she believes there must be some factual basis for that beyond misreadings of *Random Notes.*

This is not to say that Du Laoshi uncritically accepts everything in the local histories. For example, she has been particularly troubled by conflicting accounts of Shuangqing's birthplace, and this was a major reason she wanted to visit Danyang. Based on our visit there, and on further library research afterward, she has proposed a new "solution" to the problem of Shuangqing's native place. It particularly troubled her that Shi Zhenlin describes Shuangqing as growing up in a mountainous area because the Jiangshu district is quite flat. After our visit to Danyang, she was excited to discover a reference to a "Danyang li" in the District of the Wandering Immortals in Jintan. Thus, in her view, this "Danyang li" in Jintan was probably later mistaken for the neighboring county of Danyang. This means that Shuangqing could have been born into a mountainous place named Danyang, and she could have married into a village not far from where she was born.

She concludes her trip report by noting that in establishing a proposed location for Xiaoshan village, and in our historical verification of numerous parts of Shi Zhenlin's *Random Notes,* we have moved far beyond Hu Shi's bold claim in the 1920s that Shuangqing was a complete fabrication (Du 1998, 133).

TIANJIN, SUNDAY, NOVEMBER 9, 1997

### *A Busy Day with Du Laoshi*

On the "soft-sleeper" to Tianjin, I share a compartment with two congenial Chinese gentlemen from Beijing, who keep me talking and listening half the night. On my arrival in Tianjin at 7:30 A.M., Du Laoshi greets me with her customary good cheer, and we are off on a whirlwind of activity. We visit a popular temple, a calligraphy exhibit, a museum of popular culture, and a delightful open-air antique market. I have to try the local food specialties, including *erduo yan* ("fried ears"), a deep-fried dough filled with sweet bean paste, followed later in the day by a large bowl of a thick sweet "tea soup" *(cha-tang).* Made with fine ground tea leaves, rice flour, sugar, nuts, raisins, and dates, all mixed with boiling water poured from a giant pot with a dragon face and a long spout, it has the consistency of a thick milkshake. The colorful and verbose "tea soup" peddler, on Ancient Culture Street, keeps up an incessant chatter to attract customers, and he claims to have the only surviving Ming-dynasty recipe for his delicious concoction.

We take a break from our Shuangqing discussions for the day, but I can't resist some Buddhist souvenirs in her honor: four miniature statues of Buddhist bodhisattvas (compassionate saints who work for the enlightenment of others), and a "ringing" brass bowl that resonates with a beautiful tone when tapped with a wooden mallet. Buddhists ring this kind of bowl to mark the beginning and ending of meditation sessions. For my wife, Marjorie, Du Laoshi insists on buying a very lifelike clay statue of a squatting bald grandpa (who looks like me except for his Chinese eyes) with a baby boy on his shoulders. We have a delicious dinner of pork and vegetable dumplings *(jiaozi)* expertly made by Du Laoshi's husband at their comfortable apartment. Already Du Laoshi has typed up a dozen single-spaced pages summarizing the conversations on our trip. I use her computer to send an email to Marjorie. After the formal banquets in Jintan and Danyang, the tasty *jiaozi* dinner in an informal and relaxed setting makes me feel like I am already home.

*sixteen* ·

# *Reflections*

A wise man once said that a good historian has a paradoxical task: to take a simple story and make it complicated, and to take a complex story and make it simple. Keeping that in mind, I have tried to tell the story of three journeys through Chinese culture: Shi Zhenlin's, Shuangqing's, and my own. The simplest lesson of these explorations is that understanding Shuangqing and her significance is not a simple matter. There are many layers of meaning to be peeled away, even within the memoir, *Random Notes from Xiqing*. Beyond Shuangqing's appearance in *Random Notes,* new, complicated, and sometimes contradictory layers of meaning were attached to her person and her poetry in Chinese culture, from 1737 to the present.

When I began studying the poetry of Shuangqing, all I knew about her came from a few anthologies. I was impressed by the song lyrics attributed to her, and I wanted to believe that a great peasant woman poet had indeed lived and written in early-eighteenth-century China; however, my impressions were based on the very top layer of a deep archaeological site. Thanks to Dorothy Ko, I suddenly found in my mailbox one day "the original source," Shi Zhenlin's *Random Notes,* as if magically extracted from the bottom layer of many strata. With my teacher Liu Laoshi, I began reading Shi's memoir in the conviction that I would discover there the truth about Shuangqing. The more I read in this meandering fragmentary tale, the more I came to realize that I would never understand the enigma of Shuangqing without first understanding the enigma of Shi Zhenlin.

By its very strangeness, Shi's memoir reminds us how far we are removed from his time and place. In Robert Darnton's terms, *Random Notes* contains many "opaque points" that seem to defy explanation. Yet, as Darnton rightly observes, it is precisely these puzzles that provide us the best opportunity "to pick at" the document in an attempt "to unravel an alien system of meaning." Once we become familiar with Shi's memoir, once our eyes adjust to the light that at first seems so dim, we gradually come to see his concerns, his assumptions, and his obsessions. He provides us a window on one corner of the literati culture of his time.

### *Artful Autobiography*

Wu Pei-yi has called the period 1565–1680 "the golden age of Chinese autobiography" because autobiographies written during those tumultuous years of Ming decline and Qing conquest are so rich in personal self-exploration in contrast to the conventional Chinese "annalistic autobiographies" that simply chart one's career and experiences with a minimum of introspection and self-revelation.

Quoting Paul Jay, Wu defines effective autobiographical writing as "private, meditative, nostalgic, and seemingly informal, preoccupied more often than not with the personal life, and imbued with sentiment and a kind of wistfulness" (Wu 1990, 236). In Wu Pei-yi's view, Shen Fu's *Six Records of a Floating Life,* written in the early nineteenth century (and discussed in chapter 4 above), is the only piece of Chinese autobiographical writing after 1680 that meets Jay's description. I think Shi Zhenlin's *Random Notes* is a striking exception and perhaps a bridge from the rich autobiographical writings of the sixteenth century to Shen Fu's celebrated *Six Records.* I do not know that Shen Fu ever read Shi's *Random Notes,* but the two works are strikingly similar in their obsession with private life, their seeming indifference to public careers and officialdom, and their wistful, sad, and nostalgic incorporation of the scholar-beauty romance tradition into their autobiographical musings.

What are the implications of these parallels for our interpretation of Shi Zhenlin's memoir? The most important point is that the memoir in Shi's hands is above all a work of art. That doesn't mean the book is entirely a fiction; in fact it is more self-revelatory than most memoirs of its time. However, as with Shen Fu's highly artful autobiography, it does mean that the work is carefully constructed even (perhaps especially) where it appears to be casual and "random" in its recollections. In some ways, Shi Zhenlin is more philosophical than Shen Fu, more insistent that "life is but a dream," and more explicit in arguing that the products of imagination and experience are equally valid and equally "real." Just as a jazz player improvises on a theme, Shi Zhenlin improvised on his observations, dreams, hopes, and experiences to create a beautiful piece of writing. What it reveals is not so much the concrete events and experiences of Shi Zhenlin in the 1730s as the inner consciousness and ideals of Shi and his circle of friends.

### *Buddhist-Daoist Romantic Aestheticism*

I have called Shi Zhenlin's philosophy of life a kind of Buddhist-Daoist romantic aestheticism. In the eighteenth century, people like Shi Zhenlin easily felt threatened by many forces. A growing money economy and rising social mobility undermined the traditional high status of intellectuals. Intense examination competition made a government career less and less likely for hundreds of thousands of highly educated young men. Even if they succeeded in climbing the examination ladder of success, strong and aggressive Manchu emperors concentrated power in their own hands and viewed their Chinese officials as servants, not as moral examples or voices of conscience.

In these circumstances, Buddhist-Daoist romantic aestheticism offered consolation to the sensitive and civilized poets and writers—including Shi Zhenlin, the novelist Cao Xueqin, and the memoirist Shen Fu—who found "the real world" of moneymaking, examinations, and an official's way of life too insipid, constraining, and distasteful to be attractive. One Japanese scholar has called this type of aesthetic escapism "the several thousand year-old misty tradition of the resignation of Chinese men of letters" (Iida 1953, 46). There is indeed a sense of resigned melancholy that pervades Shi's memoir, a sense that he and his friends are poor yet proud and sensitive souls in a cold cruel world.

Perhaps this sense of resignation reflects the fact that Shi and most of his friends had not passed the all-important provincial examination during the main period when he wrote *Random Notes*. In this regard, it is interesting that Shi Zhenlin's descriptions of Shuangqing date from the fourth lunar month of 1733 to the second lunar month of 1735. In the eighth month of 1735, he passed the all-important provincial examination that qualified him for government service and for the metropolitan examination at the capital. It may not be a coincidence that Shi seemed so obsessed with Shuangqing during the anxious years of preparation leading up to the provincial examination in 1735, but never mentioned her again once he had passed that examination.

Although Shi Zhenlin worked hard not to appear obsessed with examinations, or with the rank, wealth, and fame that accompanied success, he retained a strong sense of literary and artistic ambition. He may have been resigned to his private life outside of officialdom, but he also embraced the freedom of imagination, of wandering in the mountains, and of engagement with painting and poetry, with a joy that belies the term *resignation*. In the love of poetry, painting, nature, and beauty, he found more than solace. He found delight, humor, a sense of fulfillment, and a way to become known and respected in the world.

### *Sublimated Scholar-Beauty Romantic Tragedy*

What has all this to do with the peasant woman poet Shuangqing? It has everything to do with the attraction of Shi and his friends to the ideals Shuangqing represents. Shi's friends who wrote prefaces for his memoir commented on his obsession with the sad fate of women of talent and beauty. Shi described Shuangqing as the most talented and the most beautiful woman in the world. She was also the most tragic because her great talent and beauty were entirely unrecognized by her family. Instead of being appreciated, she was abused, persecuted, and taken for granted. Shuangqing was a mirror for the self-image of Shi Zhenlin and his nonconformist friends in the competitive status-crazed and money-grubbing society of their day. They saw themselves as talented, erudite, attractive, ambitious, passionate, sensitive, and virtuous, and yet, many in society looked down on them as losers, failures, and bohemians. Their great talents—and especially their artistic abilities—went unrecognized and unrewarded by society at large.

As noted in chapter 4, the romantic ideal of a talented, passionate, and attractive couple became especially popular in the sixteenth century. There was a reaction against such ideals after the Manchu conquest of China in 1644, but Shi Zhenlin's memoir suggests that these ideals continued to have a powerful appeal in some sectors of the Chinese elite. The story of Shuangqing is a sublimated and tragic version of the scholar-beauty romance. Romance is sublimated in the sense that sexuality is expressed only indirectly, in terms of intense longing, the stirrings of springtime, the love of butterflies for flowers, et cetera. And the story is tragic insofar as the intense longings inspired by poetry, flowers, and springtime are left unfulfilled. The beautiful woman is fated to live out her short life in misery, obscurity, and persecution.

Even in this sublimated and tragic version of the scholar-beauty romance we can still see the hold of romantic ideals on some Chinese intellectuals and their lament over the difficulty of realizing these ideals in Chinese society. In their prefaces to *Random Notes,* Shi's friends Cao Zhenting and Wu Zhensheng take for granted the scholar-beauty ideal that a talented scholar finds his greatest fulfillment in being united with a beautiful and talented woman. They also assume that talented women in Chinese society are likely to meet with disappointment.

### *Remnants of Late-Ming Romanticism and Individualism in a Confucian Age*

In several other ways Shi Zhenlin's memoir and Wu Zhensheng's preface represent an eighteenth-century echo (albeit in sublimated form) of romantic ideals that had flourished in the sixteenth century. Whereas late-Ming romanticism centered on the courtesan quarters and liaisons between prominent literati and talented courtesans, in these mid-eighteenth century writings, the love that is celebrated is either sublimated into a platonic literary exercise (as with Shi Zhenlin and the peasant poet Shuangqing), or celebrated within marriage (as with Wu Zhensheng's love for his own talented and deceased wife).

These men also echoed the theme of individualism that had flourished in the late sixteenth and early seventeenth centuries. Their obsession with private life contrasts sharply with traditional Confucian literati obligations toward the state and public service. Although they were perennial examination candidates, both Shi Zhenlin and Wu Zhensheng make no mention of politics or official careers. Implicit in these elegant and obscure writings is a self-consciously proclaimed love of nature, poetry, spontaneity, friends, and private life that we associate with philosophical Daoism. There is no mention here of filial or wifely obligations, no discussion of social etiquette, proper forms or ceremonies; no concern is expressed for the financial welfare of the family, and no reference is made to the responsibility of the Confucian elite for the preservation of the social and political order. Instead, personal meaning and fulfillment are defined in terms of aesthetic pleasure, communing with one's friends and with nature, and cultivating talent, not for public service but for its own sake. Romantic love, a central part of private life, is seen as a highly refined ethical and aesthetic response between equally elegant, talented, sensitive, and virtuous people.

Although Shi Zhenlin and Wu Zhensheng never became widely known, in the late imperial period, they parallel such important artists as the dramatist Tang Xianzu, the novelist Cao Xueqin, and the memoirist Shen Fu, in their proclaimed indifference to official life, their devotion to the power of imagination, their fascination with Daoism and Buddhism, their love of literary art, and their close identification with women. These artists and these themes may not qualify as a cultural revolution in eighteenth-century China, but nevertheless, I believe that Shi Zhenlin and Wu Zhensheng represent an undercurrent of cultural ferment beneath the calm surface of the "high Qing." For they made a significant attempt to proclaim the importance of private life against the counterclaims of official career, to reaffirm some of the individualistic ideals popular in the late Ming, and to reassert the legitimacy of romantic love or intimacy across gender lines against the counterclaims of Confucian propriety.

### *Shi Zhenlin: Connoisseur of Feminine Beauty and Talent*

As Craig Clunas has demonstrated in *Superfluous Things,* late imperial China was a great age of connoisseurship. In an era of increasing social mobility and heightened status anxieties, down-and-out literati could still claim their high status by demonstrating their "good taste." Their aesthetic judgment became the only solid basis left for their exalted self-image. In Shi Zhenlin's circle, being able to recognize artistic greatness was almost as important as embodying greatness oneself.

In his narrative of Shuangqing, Shi Zhenlin demonstrated his refined poetic taste, as well as his qualifications as a connoisseur of feminine beauty, another hallmark of the refined gentleman scholar. With his story of Shuangqing, he showed that his aesthetic sensibilities and romantic idealism were pure and strong. He was the discoverer, interpreter, and understanding companion *(zhiyin)* of the most talented, beautiful, sensitive, and suffering woman in the world. No flesh-and-blood wife or courtesan or concubine could match Shuangqing's story for its sheer poignancy and beauty.

### *"A Woman's Voice"*

Perhaps the most interesting question raised by Shi Zhenlin's narrative and Shuangqing's poetry is the issue of "a woman's voice." There was a long tradition of men writing from behind a woman's mask, "in a feminine voice." If we see masculinity and femininity as artificial and archetypal categories along a continuum, and we recognize that all people embody elements of both in their persons, it is quite possible to imagine that Shi Zhenlin found his own most powerful voice in the poetry of Shuangqing. Readers of Cao Xueqin's great novel *Dream of the Red Chamber* have long been captivated by the poetry of Cao's heroine Lin Daiyu, and they see her poetry as superior to that of the male characters in the novel (including Cao's autobiographical antihero Jia Baoyu). I cite the example to show how easily Chinese readers *can* take for granted the power of a male author to create believable female characters and "feminine style poetry."

Shi Zhenlin did not match the creative genius of Cao Xueqin, but he was a talented writer, a favorite of many, and he shared with Cao a commitment to Buddhist-Daoist romantic aestheticism. As a Buddhist, Shi Zhenlin was a skeptic about conventional distinctions between truth and illusion, dream and waking reality. In his view the world of the imagination was every bit as real as the so-called real world. He shared the skepticism of the ancient philosopher Zhuangzi about the difficulty of discriminating between truth and illusion. Throughout his memoir, he drops hints and signposts that suggest his work is both fiction and fact, dream and reality, hope and disappointment, illusion and truth, and all of these polarities are inextricably intertwined, interdependent, and inseparable. The truth is in the fiction and vice versa. He seems to say "Shuangqing is my invention, and she's very real!"

### *Shi Zhenlin's Place in Chinese Culture*

When I began the study of Shuangqing, I saw Shi Zhenlin as a forgotten figure in Chinese culture, but I discovered that I was wrong. As noted in chapter 14, "Reincarnations," Shi's *Random Notes* had become very popular in literary circles from the 1870s onward. It has been reprinted in full or abridged versions several times in the twentieth century, and a number of notable intellectuals have proclaimed their fondness for the book. In 1993, when I gave a conference paper on Wu Zhensheng's prefaces to *Random Notes,* the eminent historian Hsu Choyun (Xu Zhuoyun) told me how pleased he was to see me working on this topic because in his own youth Shi Zhenlin had been one of his favorite authors. Shi's inclusion in the recent anthology of "best essays from the Ming and Qing," edited by Ou Mingjun, and in the anthology of Qing-dynasty song lyrics, edited by You Zhenzhong and You Yiding, also testify to his solid reputation down to the present day.

I believe it quite possible that Shuangqing was primarily the literary creation of Shi Zhenlin, given Shi's artistic talents, his aesthetic philosophy, his deep identification with female psychology, his concern to set himself apart from the conventional crowd, and his faith in the coequal status of truth and illusion. He had the ability and the motivation to create such a heroine, to circulate her poetry, and to proclaim himself as her discoverer. Whether he created her from whole cloth or not, he wanted to leave that impression.

### *Multiple Readings of the Shuangqing Story*

One of the most interesting parts of the Shuangqing story is the evolution of her image following the publication of Shi's memoir in 1737. In studying Shuangqing's many reincarnations in the modern history of Chinese culture, we have seen that there is no one "Chinese response" to Shi Zhenlin, to his Shuangqing narrative, or to the poetry of Shuangqing. Instead there have been multiple responses from multiple constituencies at different times.

From the early nineteenth century onward, literary critics and historians have included Shuangqing in their anthologies and histories to illustrate the expanding literacy of women in the late imperial period, the rich local culture of Jintan and Danyang, the mistreatment of women in Chinese society, and a distinctive feminine voice representing a social strata, the peasantry, not normally included in the voluminous canon of Chinese poems and song lyrics. Shuangqing was gradually gentrified with a surname (He), a specific birthplace (Jiangshu in Danyang), a style name (Qiubi), and a book of her own *(Poems and Song Lyrics from the Snow-Crushed Studio),* as if the compilers of anthologies and local histories could not imagine a female poet without all these accoutrements.

Since Shuangqing's song lyrics were distinctive and original, it was easy to assume a real peasant woman had produced them. Interestingly, most Qing-dynasty literary critics seemed to believe that women might have as much literary talent as men. No one that I know of ever claimed that Shuangqing's poetry was "too good" to have been written by a woman. On the contrary, the argument usually went the other way: her poetry was too good to have been written by Shi Zhenlin. Regional pride was also a major factor in bringing Shuangqing's poetry to the attention of the world. Concerning this latter point, it is no coincidence that Wu Dexuan (early nineteenth century), Miao Quansun (1889), and Chen Tingzhuo (1892) all celebrated Shuangqing's poems as a unique product of their own region.

In China's May Fourth Movement of the 1920s, we see two contrasting responses to Shuangqing and Shi Zhenlin. With the demythologizing impulse of a Western-trained Chinese intellectual, Hu Shi saw Shuangqing as the fictional creation of a failed self-pitying literatus. But Hu Shi himself also wanted to find themes, issues, and accomplishments in China's past that would be relevant to China's present and future. In this vein, the romanticism and aestheticism of Shi Zhenlin struck a chord with many May Fourth readers. More popular than Hu Shi's skepticism concerning Shuangqing was the attitude of Xue Qu, who admonished readers to appreciate Shi Zhenlin for the beauty of his language and the power of his writing. Shi Zhenlin appeals to the aesthetic, literary, and sentimental side of Chinese culture. Hu Shi's coldly rational reading of Shi Zhenlin was not likely to convince the people most drawn to read *Random Notes.*

Another common response to Shi Zhenlin's tale has been that of my teacher, Liu Laoshi. Her reactions taught me as much about Shuangqing as my own reading of Shi's narrative. She had some of the same doubts I did about the literal truth of *Random Notes,* and she raised doubts I would not have thought to raise. She was especially sensitive, for example, to the flirtatious overtones in the poetry and prose exchanged by Shuangqing and her admirers. She did not believe a proper woman, peasant or otherwise, would have written to Shi and his friends the way Shuangqing sometimes did. Yet she was convinced by the powerful and distinctive song lyrics attributed to Shuangqing that such a woman must have lived and provided the inspiration for Shi Zhenlin's story.

Regarding the ambiguities and implausibilities in Shi's *Random Notes,* her solution was a kind of bifocal reading. She saw most of the song lyrics attributed to Shuangqing as authentic products of a peasant woman poet. Yet she suspected that much of Shi's narrative, some of the poems, and most of the prose he attributed to Shuangqing were his own fabrications. Years later I discovered that Du Fangqin had a similar view. As noted earlier, I am struck by how closely this response to Shi Zhenlin's story parallels the treatment of Shuangqing and her poetry through many of her reincarnations in poetry anthologies and literary histories. As a fragmentary tale, Shi Zhenlin's *Random Notes* invites a fragmentary reading. For many readers, the point is not to find a coherent story, since there is no coherent story, but to browse through the book in order to find and savor one's favorite parts.

In more recent times, a different dynamic is at work. In the People's Republic of China under Mao, historians were duty bound to celebrate the peasantry and other oppressed groups. Shuangqing was naturally hailed as a heroine illustrating the genius, virtue, courage, and perseverance of a peasant woman under the old feudal regime. The traditional anthology view of Shuangqing was particularly suited to Maoist or Marxist analysis because the romantic and erotic aspects of Shi's tale were omitted from the anthologies. This nonflirtatious Shuangqing seems made to order for a Marxist positivist feminist approach. She illustrates victimhood and agency, the irrepressible natural-born genius of the peasantry, and the perseverance of a Chinese woman under the most oppressive of circumstances. In this context, to deny the historical existence of Shuangqing would seem to be a betrayal of contemporary Chinese Marxism and feminism.

In my travels with Du Laoshi, it gradually dawned on me that the source of our differences on Shuangqing's historical existence comes from the different ways we read Shi's *Random Notes*. For Du Laoshi, the inconsistencies and improbabilities in the memoir are minor embellishments that do not really call into question the historical reality of a peasant woman named Shuangqing. Where I see Wu Zhensheng's preface to *Random Notes,* on the qualities of heavenly beauties, as a philosophical clue about the shared belief of Wu and Shi Zhenlin in the power of imagination to shape reality, Du Laoshi sees the preface as reflecting little more than Wu's own dreamy erudition and his desire to show off his parallel prose. She remains convinced that *Random Notes* is a factual chronological record of Shi Zhenlin's experiences.

In the post-Mao era, it is possible to celebrate Shuangqing primarily for her literary talent, and to celebrate Shi Zhenlin for his, without reading her story as a morality tale of class struggle. It is easier to recognize in Shuangqing's story romantic elements that cross the boundaries of class. It is also possible to question the literal truth of Shi's narrative without being attacked as a "bourgeois revisionist." Having read the arguments of Du Fangqin, Elsie Choy, and Su Zhecong (summarized in chapter 12, "Contemporary Scholarship") in favor of a literal interpretation of Shi Zhenlin, I had once assumed that few if any contemporary Chinese doubted the historical existence of a peasant woman poet named He Shuangqing. But as I discovered on my travels in 1997, there are skeptics about Shi Zhenlin's Shuangqing narrative even in Jintan and Danyang. We heard the same story from the compilers of the histories of those two counties: "The case of He Shuangqing is not clear; the facts are in dispute, so we did not include very much about her." They did not claim that Shuangqing was a fictional figure, but only that her case was not clear.

If Shuangqing seems "made to order" for contemporary Chinese feminists, in the West she seems "made to order" for an argument about the ways cultures are constructed. In the last generation, students of history and literature in the United States have become much more skeptical toward their sources. Today we are preoccupied more than ever before by questions like these: Whose interests are being served and expressed by this source? What is the hidden agenda of this author? How does the genre he or she writes in shape the message he or she sends? How did any particular document come to be written, preserved, circulated? How do words reflect, shape, bolster, or confront power relations in a society?

Shi Zhenlin's text, his Shuangqing narrative, and Shuangqing's many reincarnations since 1737 nicely illustrate the complex ways that a cultural icon gets constructed. Shi Zhenlin himself seems to share the skepticism of the postmodernist toward any simple interpretation of a text as a straightforward reflection of reality. He implies that fiction can be true and that history, even a history that is "literally true" can be "false" in the sense that it may be misleading or unimportant. In his view, if essays are original and well written, even though on fanciful or "trivial" topics, they are true in the sense that they are worth reading. On the other hand, even if essays are written on something as important as the classics, if they are derivative, dry, and dull, they are "false" and not worth reading. I think Shi Zhenlin would appreciate the view that other things are more important than the literal truth or falsity of his account: namely, the emotional power of his prose and poetry, the genuine appeal of his tale to Chinese readers past and present, and the meaningfulness of his narrative as a window on one small corner of eighteenth-century China.

Storytelling is a powerful way to make sense of life. The story of Shuangqing has been a meaningful one in the evolution of Chinese culture. Despite implausibilities in Shi Zhenlin's narrative of Shuangqing, parts of his story "ring true." Shuangqing's unhappiness is a natural result of her high intelligence, her keen sensitivity, her strong literary ambition, and her miserable circumstances. Literacy raises her expectations and exposes her to ideals that cannot be realized in the real society of her time. Whether or not Shuangqing ever existed in the way she was described in Shi's *Random Notes* or in subsequent reincarnations, she illustrates some profound truths about Chinese society and its evolution from the eighteenth century to the present.

The most intriguing aspects of Shi Zhenlin's story of Shuangqing are precisely the powerful ambiguities involved: ambiguities of male and female voice, of elite and peasant relations, of truth and illusion, fact and fiction, dream and waking reality. Although we will never "prove" the existence or nonexistence of an eighteenth-century peasant woman poet named Shuangqing, the ambiguities of her case will surely retain their appeal for future generations. As Chu Fujin so delightfully puts it, "If Shuangqing really lived, that's a very interesting story; if she was fabricated by Shi Zhenlin, that's even more interesting."

### *Shuangqing and Poetic Culture in China Today*

Shuangqing's image will no doubt continue to evolve with future reincarnations. It took me years to realize this simple fact. When I began reading about Shuangqing and her poetry, I only thought of uncovering a bit of China's eighteenth century. It never occurred to me to see connections between the eighteenth century and the present—or even the future—state of Chinese culture. I never contemplated the possibility of visiting the area where Shi Zhenlin once lived and worked. I assumed that China's break with its own past has been so radical and so complete that I would find no trace of the world Shi Zhenlin once occupied. I was wrong.

In Jintan and Danyang, I was delighted to meet scholars, writers, reporters, artists, and officials for whom China's past is important and relevant to contemporary life. To Du Fangqin, Shuangqing's life and poetry are important for contemporary Chinese feminism. To Zhang Hongsheng, China's entire literary heritage, including the story of Shuangqing, is a precious gift to the present. To writers and artists in Jintan and Danyang, including Wan Lijun, Yu Zhao, Meng Jiyuan, Chu Fujin, Shi Han, and Shi Shenghua, Shuangqing is a matter of pride in the rich regional culture of this rural part of Jiangsu Province. To the mayor of Jintan and to Zhang Jinsheng and his colleagues in the local government of Xuebu Zhen, the story of Shuangqing is a newly discovered reason for local pride that holds out the possible development of a tourist site of national importance.

Throughout this book I have emphasized the centrality of poetry in Chinese culture. I was particularly pleased to see in Jintan and Danyang a poetic culture that still survives and thrives. When Yu Zhao, head of the Economic Commission of Jintan, heard of Shuangqing and the report of a Xiaoshan Academy, his natural response was to write a poem. At our calligraphy party at the gallery of Shi Han in Jintan, the focus was on poetry. Wan Lijun (Xiaowan), our indefatigable guide in Jintan, published a book of poetry while she was still a college student. Her good friends include Xu Donggong, a lawyer with a passion for calligraphy, and Xu Shuping, a young woman who writes delightful song lyrics. On our travels to Jintan and Danyang, I wrote continually in my journal, to make sure to capture all we had seen and heard. My roommate, Hongsheng, wrote only poems. He later sent me a few of them as fond mementos of our trip.

In our travels through Jintan and Danyang, Du Laoshi, Hongsheng and I developed our own private joke and rallying cry: "Shuangqing still lives!" We saw her reflected in the dramatic sunset at Fang Shan and in the bright yellow chrysanthemums blooming under cool blue skies on a sunny autumn morning in Jintan. And most especially we saw her reflected in the poetry and passion of Wan Lijun, the bright precocity of seven-year-old Zhang Ting, and the keen interest of many local people in Jintan and Danyang in their cultural heritage and in Shuangqing's story and her poetry.

### *Kang Zhengguo: "The Fusion of Horizons"*

My friend Kang Zhengguo first planted in my mind the idea of traveling to rural Jintan and Danyang to look for the origins of Shuangqing's story. We share a fascination with Shuangqing in part because we share a respect for rural life. He once worked on a farm in China in the aftermath of the Cultural Revolution. When I told him of my farm background, he said he has always wanted to visit, and to work on, an American farm. In the summer of 1998, I finally delivered on a six-year-old promise to take him to the Ropp farm in central Illinois, where he could engage in "real farmwork." We drove from New Haven out to the corn belt on two brilliantly sunny days in early August. Our visit coincided with the McLean County 4-H Fair, where we spent a day looking at machinery displays and watching livestock shows. Because my cousin and my brother were busy with the fair, we were spared the experience of baling hay, but we helped feed some Chester White pigs and some Jersey calves. It was hot and humid, as it always is in Illinois in August, and we spent part of our time under a cool fan in my brother's farmhouse kitchen, discussing Shuangqing and recalling what it must have been like in August 1733, in Jintan's sultry humidity when Shi Zhenlin visited his rural friends at Fang Shan to try to escape the summer heat.

On our last evening in Illinois, we went for a walk around a small lake near my parents' home. On the lake were dozens of wild geese (now fat and semidomesticated by picnic-goers with surplus food). In the flatness of central Illinois, the sky seemed many times larger than the landscape. The sunset was a brilliant mix of scattered clouds extending over the entire western sky to the very edge of the low horizon. As we circled the lake, we joked at how many Shuangqing themes we had here before us: a rural setting in the August heat, a flock of wild geese on still water, a vivid sunset with dazzling multicolored clouds scattered over the horizon. Kang Zhengguo began to recite Shuangqing's most famous song lyric: "Tiny tiny flecks of cloud, / Fine fine threads of light," and I responded by finishing the sentence: "here and gone, bright and dim, hard to quench." We broke into laughter, unable to continue.

"Here is the 'fusion of horizons' you discuss in your article," I remarked, in reference to his conclusion that Shuangqing's story and poetry represent the fusion of horizons of "truth and illusion," "reality and fiction." "And speaking of horizons," I continued, "this brilliant sunset also conjures up the conclusion of Shuangqing's song lyric to her friend, the neighbor girl Hanxi: 'The sunset hurts the eyes; / Don't look to the horizon, / The horizon only shows a few cold clouds drifting apart.' "

"Yes," Zhengguo agreed, "Shuangqing *is* here in the sunset, just as Shi Zhenlin demonstrated. This is our Xiaoshan!"

However humble and uncertain her origins, Shuangqing has achieved the immortal status that Shi Zhenlin claimed for her. Whether or not she ever existed as a peasant woman poet, it is significant that she was thinkable in the eighteenth century and remembered thereafter. Shi Zhenlin's faith in the primacy of art and the power of imagination was not misplaced; cultures are in a profound sense mentally constructed and maintained. However frustratingly ambiguous the portrait Shi has left, his memoir had the kind of impact he hoped for. He remained a relatively obscure painter and writer, while Shuangqing became famous as one of the most captivating poetic voices in late imperial Chinese culture. In Shi's *Random Notes,* the boundary lines between literature and life, between dream and waking reality, between Shuangqing the beautiful peasant poet and Shi Zhenlin the marginalized literatus have been erased. Whatever the likelihood of Shi Zhenlin's veracity as historical witness, he was altogether convincing in proclaiming the transformative power of his and Shuangqing's art.

# *Guide to Sources and Further Reading*

Although I have not wanted to burden the general reader with detailed footnotes, I list here my most important sources, and suggestions for further reading. In some chapters my main sources are all acknowledged in the text, and it seems unnecessary to repeat them here.

## General

In the past decade, there has been an explosion of publishing on women and gender relations in late imperial China. Important recent books in English include those by Francesca Bray (1997), Charlotte Furth (1999), Dorothy Ko (1994), and Susan Mann (1997), and edited volumes by Ellen Widmer and Kang-i Sun Chang (1997) and by Harriet Zurndorfer (1999). My review article (1994) on English-language scholarship on this topic covers work from the late 1980s and early 1990s. Susan Mann's 1993 article examines the relevance of feminist theory for the study of Chinese history and includes numerous examples of English-language works on Chinese women. There are too many recent articles to cite here, but those most relevant to this study are included in the bibliography. A major anthology of Chinese women's poetry and poetry criticism is edited by Kang-i Sun Chang and Haun Saussy (1999). A new journal founded in 1999 and devoted to gender relations in China is *Nannü: Men, Women, and Gender in Early and Imperial China* (Leiden).

## Chapter 1: "Departure"

Kang Zhengguo's 1988 book *Fengsao yu yanqing* (A study of Chinese classical poetry by women and on women), which has just a few pages on

Shuangqing, seemed especially remarkable to me when I first read it in 1991. It showed a subtlety, sophistication, and independence from the Marxist "class struggle" view of literature that had been so prevalent in the years of Maoist rule in China. Here was a fresh approach that clearly signaled a post-Mao renaissance of classical Chinese scholarship.

Du Fangqin's 1993 book on Shuangqing was preceded by her pioneering 1988 book, in which she traced the development of gender ideology in China from very early times down to the twentieth century. Interestingly, both Kang Zhengguo's and Du Fangqin's books were published in the same series.

Zhang Hongsheng's first book (1995) was a revision of his 1989 doctoral dissertation, on a particular school of poetry in the late Song dynasty (early thirteenth century), a subject far removed from Shuangqing and Shi Zhenlin. His recent (1998) study of Qing-dynasty song lyrics is much more relevant to the themes of this book.

**Chapter 2: "First Encounters"**

All translations of Shi Zhenlin's *Random Notes* in this book are based on the 1987 edition that was published in Beijing by Zhongguo shudian. It is a reprint of a four-chapter edition that was published in 1907 by the Shanghai Guangzhi shuju. Another useful reprint is the 1935 edition, also in four chapters, published by Shanghai zazhi gongsi, with modern punctuation and subdivisions in the text. Both of these versions appear to be based on the original text that Shi Zhenlin published in 1737. Elsie Choy has translated all the passages from *Random Notes* that deal directly with Shuangqing in her 1993 book, *Leaves of Prayer: The Life and Poetry of He Shuangqing, a Farmwife in Eighteenth-Century China.* In addition to these main sources, Du Fangqin's book on Shuangqing is extremely useful because she supplies annotations for all the poems attributed to Shuangqing and gives a vernacular Chinese translation of each poem. She also quotes some of the nineteenth-century commentaries on Shuangqing and her poetry that I discuss in chapter 14. An important English-language source for me early on in my research on Shi's *Random Notes* was Grace Fong's essay "Engendering the Lyric: Her Image and Voice in Song," which she shared with me in manuscript form in 1990 and which was eventually published in 1994. She demonstrated the importance of Shuangqing's song lyrics, their distinctive qualities, the ambiguities of their authorship, and the possibility of rendering them accurately and elegantly in English.

## Chapter 3: "Portraits"

In addition to the main sources I cite in this chapter on the definition of feminine beauty for members of the Chinese elite in the Qing period, a particularly useful Chinese source is Shen Yizheng, *Lidai meiren hua xuan* (Selected paintings of beauties through the ages), published in 1984. This book provides representative paintings of beautiful women from the Song period (960–1279) up to 1911 and includes the two paintings I discuss in this chapter (see figures 3 and 4). Interestingly, as late as the Tang period (618–906) beautiful women in China were portrayed as relatively plump and robust, but there was a shift in the Song period toward a more frail and fragile waiflike image of feminine beauty. Patricia Ebrey includes interesting speculations on this change in her essay "Women, Marriage, and the Family in Chinese History" (1990). Wu Hung's "Beyond Stereotypes" (1997) provides an illuminating discussion of definitions of feminine beauty in early Qing court art and the eighteenth-century masterpiece of fiction, *Dream of the Red Chamber.*

## Chapter 4: "Biographer"

The most important source on Shi Zhenlin's life is a yearly chronicle of Shi's life by Yuan Hua (1988). Other brief but useful biographies of Shi are in the *Jintan County History (Jintan xianzhi)* (1885, 1921, 1993), in the encyclopedic *Morohashi Chinese-Japanese Dictionary,* in the standard *Chinese Biographical Dictionary (Zhongguo renming da zidian),* in Feng Jinbo's early-nineteenth-century collection of biographies of Qing-dynasty painters, and in Elsie Choy's *Leaves of Prayer* (1993). Kang Zhengguo (1994) also includes many useful details on Shi Zhenlin in his essay on the "talented woman plot" of the marginalized literatus.

On Chinese society in the Qing period, good introductions are Susan Naquin and Evelyn Rawski (1987), Richard Smith (1994), and Lloyd Eastman (1988). On the examination system, see Benjamin Elman (1991, 1999) and Miyazaki Ichisada (1976). On the fascination of Ming-Qing literati with ill-fated young beauties, see Ann Waltner on Tanyangzi (1987), Ellen Widmer (1992) on Xiaoqing, Dorothy Ko (1994) on Xiaoqing and the sisters Ye Xiaoluan and Ye Wanwan, and Judith Zeitlin (1998) on spirit writing. On the Chinese scholar's tradition of miscellaneous notes or jottings, *biji,* see Y. W. Ma's "*Pi-chi*" (1986). An excellent compilation of Chinese travel writings is Richard

E. Strassberg (1994). On companionate marriages in the late imperial period, see Dorothy Ko (1994) and Paul Ropp (1993a).

Cyril Birch's delightful translation of Tang Xianzu's sixteenth-century romantic comedy *The Peony Pavilion* (1980) beautifully illustrates the romanticism of that age, a romanticism that still inspired Shi Zhenlin two centuries later. The two works of Qing literature most relevant to Shi Zhenlin's preoccupations are Cao Xueqin's *Dream of the Red Chamber* (also known as *The Story of the Stone*), marvelously translated by David Hawkes and John Minford (1973–86), and Shen Fu's *Six Records of a Floating Life,* translated by Leonard Pratt and Chiang Su-hui (1983). Li Wai-yee's *Enchantment and Disenchantment* (1993) is an insightful study of China's romantic literary tradition and the dialectical interplay of love and desire as vehicles of illusion and disillusion, enchantment and disenchantment, delusion and enlightenment.

**Chapter 6: "Poems"**

On the techniques, traditions, and cultural importance of classical Chinese poetry, including regulated verse, see excellent introductions by Stephen Owen, *Traditional Chinese Poetry and Poetics* (1985), the essay, "Shih," on regulated verse, by Richard Bodman and Shirleen S. Wong in Nienhauser (1986), the essay "Chinese Poetry" by Kang-i Sun Chang (1993), and James J. Y. Liu (1962). Elsie Choy translates all of Shuangqing's regulated verse in her *Leaves of Prayer.* An inspiring book on the art of translating poetry is Douglas Hofstadter (1997).

**Chapter 7: "Lyrics"**

On the song-lyric tradition, see Marsha Wagner (1984), Pauline Yu (1994), Kang-i Sun Chang (1980, 1993), and her essay on the song lyric, "Tz'u," in Nienhauser (1986). Grace Fong expertly analyzes several of Shuangqing's lyrics in "Engendering the Lyric" (1994).

**Chapter 9: "Flirtations and Admirers"**

Keith McMahon's 1995 study of male-female relations in eighteenth-century Chinese fiction deals mostly with erotic literature, against which Shi Zhenlin's memoir appears very tame. Yet McMahon's chapter 5 on the "chaste scholar-beauty romance" is very important in clarifying some of the ideals that Shi and his friends strongly embraced.

On the cult of *qing,* which can be translated as "passion" or as "love," see Li Wai-yee (1993), Dorothy Ko (1994), and Hua-yuan Li Mowry (1983). Mowry's work is a translation of many short anecdotes from Feng Menglong's seventeenth-century compilation of *Qing shi* (A history of *qing*).

On debates over women's literacy, talent, and virtue in the Qing period, see works by Clara Wing-chung Ho (1995 and 1998), Susan Mann (1991, 1992, 1994, 1997), and Dorothy Ko (1992, 1994). On the rise of women's literacy in the Qing period, and the concomitant rise of networks of mutually supportive women, see especially Dorothy Ko (1994), Susan Mann (1997), and Ellen Widmer (1989). On the obsessive concern with female virtue in the late imperial period, see Katherine Carlitz (1991), Du Fangqin and Susan Mann (1998), Mark Elvin (1984), Charlotte Furth (1990), and T'ien Ju-k'ang (1988).

### Chapter 14: "Reincarnations"

The most important source for this chapter is the extremely useful essay on reference materials on *Random Notes from Xiqing,* written by Zhang Gongliang and appended to the 1935 edition of the memoir. Zhang quotes most of the references made to Shuangqing in surviving writings from the eighteenth, nineteenth, and early twentieth centuries. In most cases I have been able to locate the sources quoted by Zhang, and they are listed in the bibliography.

On Yun Zhu and her extremely influential 1831 anthology, *Correct Beginnings,* see Susan Mann's *Precious Records* (1997).

Among the extant editions of Shi Zhenlin's *Random Notes from Xiqing,* the Nanjing Public Library has by far the best collection, including three four-chapter editions listed in the bibliography, one dated the Qianlong reign (1736–1796), one dated Qing (1644–1911), and one "late Qing." The Qianlong-reign version could well be the first edition published in four chapters in 1737. Also at the Nanjing public Library are two eight-chapter editions of *Random Notes,* published in 1874 and 1878 respectively. These appear to be based on the 1779 version that Shi Zhenlin edited shortly before his death.

# *Bibliography*


Balazs, Etienne. 1965. *Political Theory and Administrative Reality in Traditional China*. London: School of Oriental and African Studies, University of London.

Bao Jialin. 1989. "Nongjia nüshiren He Shuangqing" (Peasant woman poet He Shuangqing). In *Funü wenti suixiang lu* (Notes on women's issues). Taipei: Daoxiang chubanshe.

Bodman, Richard, and Shirleen S. Wong. 1986. "Shih." In *The Indiana Companion to Traditional Chinese Literature*, ed. William H. Nienhauser Jr., 682–89. Bloomington: Indiana University Press.

Bray, Francesca. 1997. *Technology and Gender: Fabrics of Power in Late Imperial China*. Berkeley and Los Angeles: University of California Press.

Bruneau, Marie Florine. 1992. "Learned and Literary Women in Late Imperial China and Early Modern Europe." *Late Imperial China* 13.1 (June): 156–72.

Cao Xueqin and Gao E. 1973–86. *The Story of the Stone*. Trans. David Hawkes and John Minford. 5 vols. Harmondsworth: Penguin.

Cao Zhenting. 1751. *Xiangxue wenchao* (Prose writings from the fragrant snow). N.p.

Carlitz, Katherine. 1987. "Gender Ideals in Ming Epitaph Literature." Paper presented to the Annual Meeting of the Association for Asian Studies, Boston, April.

———. 1991. "The Social Uses of Female Virtue in Late Ming Editions of *Lienü zhuan*." *Late Imperial China* 12.2 (December): 117–48.

Chang, Kang-i Sun. 1980. *The Evolution of Chinese Tz'u Poetry: From Late T'ang to Norther Sung*. Princeton: Princeton University Press.

———. 1986. "Tz'u." In *The Indiana Companion to Traditional Chinese Literature*, ed. William H. Nienhauser Jr., 846–49. Bloomington: Indiana University Press.

———. 1988. "The Ideal of the Mask in Wu Wei-yeh (1609–1671)." *Harvard Journal of Asiatic Studies* 48.2: 289–320.

———. 1990. *The Late Ming Poet Ch'en Tzu-lung: Crises of Love and Loyalism*. New Haven: Yale University Press.

———. 1993. "Chinese Poetry." In *The New Princeton Encyclopedia of Poetry and Poetics*, eds. Alex Preminger and T.V.F. Brogan, 190–98. Princeton: Princeton University Press.

Chang, Kang-i Sun, and Haun Saussy, eds. 1999. *Women Writers in Traditional China: An Anthology of Poetry and Criticism.* Stanford: Stanford University Press.

Chen Dongyuan. 1967. *Zhongguo funü shenghuo shi* (A history of the lives of Chinese women). 1937; reprint, Taipei: Shangwu yinshuguan.

Chen Tingzhuo. 1983. *Baiyuzhai cihua* (Song-lyric talks from the White Rain Studio). 1892; reprint, Jinan: Qilu shushe.

———. 1984. *Ci ze* (Principles of the song lyric). 1890; reprint, 2 vols., Shanghai: Shanghai guji chubanshe.

Chen Xiang, ed. 1977. *Qingdai nüshiren xuanji* (Selected works of Qing-dynasty women poets). 2 vols. Taipei: Taiwan Shangwu yinshuguan.

Chen Xin, Zhou Weide, and Yu Huanping. 1985. *Lidai funü shici xuanzhu* (Selected and annotated poetry by women through the ages). Beijing: Zhongguo funü chubanshe.

Chou, Wan-yao (see Zhou Wanyao).

Choy, Elsie. 1993. *Leaves of Prayer: The Life and Poetry of He Shuangqing, a Farmwife in Eighteenth-Century China.* Hong Kong: Chinese University of Hong Kong Press.

Clunas, Craig. 1991. *Superfluous Things: Material Culture and Social Status in Early Modern China.* Urbana: University of Illinois Press.

Cooper, Arthur. *Li Po and Tu Fu.* Harmondsworth: Penguin.

Crawford, William Bruce. 1976. "'The Oil Vender and the Courtesan' in the Ts'ai-tzu Chia-ren Novels." In *Critical Essays on Chinese Literature,* ed. William H. Nienhauser Jr., 31–42. Hong Kong: Chinese University of Hong Kong Press.

*Danyang xianzhi* (Danyang County history). 1885. N.p.: Bancang mingfeng shuyuan.

*Danyang xianzhi* (Danyang County history). 1961. Comp. Su Yunzhang. Taipei: Huaxin yinshuguan.

*Danyang xianzhi* (Danyang County history). 1992. Comp. Danyang County History Editorial Committee. Nanjing: Jiangsu renmin chuban she.

Darnton, Robert. 1985. *The Great Cat Massacre.* New York: Vintage.

de Bary, William Theodore, Wing-tsit Chan, and Burton Watson, comps. 1960. *Sources of Chinese Tradition.* Vol. 1. New York: Columbia University Press.

Dong Chao. 1753. *Donggao zachao.* (Miscellaneous notes from the eastern shore). In *Yi hai zhu chen* (Yi hai zhu chen collectanea), ed. Wu Shenglan, vol. 46. N.p.: Tingyi tang, Jiaqing reign (1796–1819).

Du Fangqin. 1988. *Nüxing guannian de yanbian* (The evolution of concepts of women). Henan: Henan renmin chubanshe.

———. 1993. *He Shuangqing ji* (Collected materials on He Shuangqing). Zhengzhou, Henan: Zhongzhou guji chubanshe.

———. 1998. "Xiaoshan gushi jiudi xunfang he wenben zhongdu—guanyu He Shuangqing he Shi Zhenlin de tianye kaocha" (Rereading the texts and looking for the old sites and stories of Xiaoshan—field investigations concerning He Shuangqing and Shi Zhenlin). In *Zhongguo shehui xingbie de lishi wenhua xunzong* (Investigations on the history and culture of gender and society in China). Tianjin: Tianjin shehui kexue yuan chubanshe.

Du Fangqin and Susan Mann. 1998. "Competing Claims on Womanly Virtue in

Late Imperial China." In *Zhongguo shehui xingbie de lishi wenhua xunzong* (Investigations on the history and culture of gender and society in China), by Du Fangqin, 229–78. Tianjin: Tianjin shehui kexue yuan chubanshe.

Eastman, Lloyd E. 1988. *Family, Fields, and Ancestors: Constancy and Change in China's Social and Economic History, 1550–1949*. New York and Oxford: Oxford University Press.

Eberhard, Wolfram. 1971. "What Is Beautiful in a Chinese Woman?" In *Moral and Social Values of the Chinese: Collected Essays*. Taipei: Ch'eng-wen Publishing.

———. 1986. *A Dictionary of Chinese Symbols*. London: Routledge.

Ebrey, Patricia. 1990. "Women, Marriage, and the Family in Chinese History." In *Heritage of China: Contemporary Perspectives on Chinese Civilization*, ed. Paul S. Ropp, 197–223. Berkeley and Los Angeles: University of California Press.

Edwards, Louise P. 1994. *Men and Women in Qing China: Gender in "The Red Chamber Dream."* Leiden: E. J. Brill.

Elman, Benjamin A. 1991. "Political, Social, and Cultural Reproduction via Civil Service Examinations in Late Imperial China." *Journal of Asian Studies* 50.1 (February): 7–28.

———. 1999. *A Cultural History of Civil Examinations in Late Imperial China*. Berkeley and Los Angeles: University of California Press.

Elman, Benjamin A., and Alexander Woodside, eds. 1994. *Education and Society in Late Imperial China, 1600–1900*. Berkeley and Los Angeles: University of California Press.

Elvin, Mark. 1984. "Female Virtue and the State in China." *Past and Present* 104:111–52.

Epstein, Maram. 2001. *Competing Discourses: Orthodoxy, Authenticity, and Engendered Meanings in Late-Imperial Chinese Fiction*. Cambridge: Harvard University Press.

———. 1999. "Reflections of Desire: The Poetics of Gender in *Dream of the Red Chamber*." *Nan nü: Men, Women and Gender in Early and Imperial China* 1.1: 64–106.

Feng Jinbo. N.d. *Moxiangju huazhi* (Moxiangju's biographies of painters). N.p.: n.p., Jiaqing reign (1796–1820).

Fong, Grace S. 1990. "Persona and Mask in the Song Lyric *(Ci)*." *Harvard Journal of Asiatic Studies* 50.2 (December): 459–84.

———. 1994. "Engendering the Lyric: Her Image and Voice in Song." In *Voices of the Song Lyric in China*, ed. Pauline Yu 107–44. Berkeley and Los Angeles: University of California Press.

———. 1997. "De/Constructing a Feminine Ideal in the Eighteenth Century: *Random Records of West-Green* and the Story of Shuangqing." In *Writing Women in Late Imperial China*, ed. Ellen Widmer and Kang-i Sun Chang, 264–81. Stanford: Stanford University Press.

Furth, Charlotte. 1990. "The Patriarch's Legacy: Household Instructions and the Transmission of Orthodox Values." In *Orthodoxy in Late Imperial China*, ed. K. C. Liu, 187–211. Berkeley and Los Angeles: University of California Press.

———. 1992. "Poetry and Women's Culture in Late Imperial China: Editor's Introduction." *Late Imperial China* 13.1 (June): 1–8.

———. 1999. *A Flourishing Yin: Gender in China's Medical History, 960–1665*. Berkeley: University of California Press.

Gates, Hill. 1989. "The Commoditization of Chinese Women." *Signs* 14.4 (summer): 799–832.

Gertz, SunHee Kim, and Paul S. Ropp. 1998. "Literary Women, Fiction, and Marginalization: Nicolette and Shuangqing." *Comparative Literature Studies* 35.3: 219–54.

Giles, Herbert A. 1968. *A Chinese Biographical Dictionary*. 1898; reprint, Taipei: Ch'eng-wen Publishing.

Gong Bao'an, ed. 1992. *Qing ci sanbaishou jinyi* (Contemporary explanations of three hundred Qing-dynasty song lyrics). Xi'an: Shaanxi renmin chubanshe.

Goyama Kiwamu. 1994. "*Seisei sanki* no sekai" (The world of *Random Notes from Xiqing*). *Bungaku Ronshu* (Essays on literature) 39: 23–48.

Gu Jiegang. 1924. "Shuangqing." *Xiaoshuo yuebao* (Short story monthly) 15.11: 6.

Hales, Dell R. 1976. "Dreams and the Daemonic in Traditional Chinese Stories." In *Critical Essays on Chinese Literature,* ed. William H. Nienhauser Jr., 71–87. Hong Kong: Chinese University of Hong Kong Press.

He Shuangqing. 1927. *Xueya xuan ji* (Collection from the Snow-Crushed Studio), ed. Zhang Shoulin. Beijing: Beijing wenhua xueshe.

Hegel, Robert E., and Richard C. Hessney, eds. 1985. *Expressions of Self in Chinese Literature.* New York: Columbia University Press.

Hessney, Richard C. 1979. "Beautiful, Talented, and Brave: Seventeenth-Century Chinese Scholar-Beauty Romances." Ph.D. diss., University of California at Berkeley.

Ho, Clara Wing-chung [Liu Yongcong]. 1995. "The Cultivation of Female Talent: Views on Women's Education in China during the Early and High Qing Periods." *Journal of the Economic and Social History of the Orient* 38.2: 191–223.

———. 1998. *De, cai, se, quan: Lun Zhongguo gudai nüxing* (Virtue, talent, beauty and power: Women in ancient China). Taipei: Maitian chuban gufen youxian gongsi.

Hofstadter, Douglas R. 1997. *Le Ton beau de Marot: In Praise of the Music of Language.* New York: Basic Books.

Hong Jingyuan. 1984. "*Xiqing sanji* he *Hongloumeng*" *(Random Notes from Xiqing* and *Dream of the Red Chamber). Wenxian* 6:61–65.

Hu Shi. 1971. "He Shuangqing kao" (Investigations on He Shuangqing). In *Hu Shi wencun* (Collected essays of Hu Shi), vol. 3, 3d ed., 683–85. Taipei: Yuandong tushu gongsi.

Hu Wenkai. 1985. *Lidai funü zhuzuokao* (An examination of women's writings through the dynasties). Rev. ed. Shanghai: Guji chubanshe.

Huang Xieqing. 1873. *Guochao cizong xubian* (Collected song lyrics from our august dynasty, continuation). N.p.: n.p.

Hummel, Arthur W., ed. 1967. *Eminent Chinese of the Ch'ing Period.* 1943; reprint, Taipei: Ch'eng-wen Publishing.

Idema, Wilt. 1999. *De onthoofde feministe, Leven en werk von schrijvende vrouwen in het Chinese keizerrijk van de vroege tweede eeuw v. Chr. tot de eerste jaren van de twintigste eeuw* (The beheaded feminist, Lives and works of writing women in imperial China from the early second century B.C. to the earliest years of the twentieth century). Amsterdam: Atlas.

Iida Kichiro. 1953. "*Jurin gaishi* ni okeru fushi no kitei o naserumono" (On the background of the satire in *Rulin waishi*). *Kambun gakkai kaiho* (Bulletin of the Association of Chinese Literature, Tokyo University of Education) 14:42–46.

Jiang Minfan and Wang Ruifang, comps. 1984. *Zhongguo lidai cainü xiaozhuan* (Short biographies of talented women throughout Chinese history). Zhejiang: Zhejiang wenji chubanshe.

*Jintan xianzhi* (Jintan County history). 1885. Comp. Wang Guofeng et al. N.p.: n.p.

*Jintan xianzhi* (Jintan County history). 1921. Comp. Feng Xu et al. [Shanghai]: Shangwu yinshuguan.

*Jintan xianzhi* (Jintan County history). 1993. Comp. Jintan County History Editorial Committee. Nanjing: Jiangsu renmin chubanshe.

Kang Zhengguo. 1988. *Fengsao yu yanqing* (A study of Chinese classical poetry by women and on women). Zhengzhou: Henan renmin chubanshe.

———. 1994. "Bianyuan wenren cainu qingjie jiqi suo chuanda de shiyi—*Xiqing sanji* chutan" (The "talented woman plot" of the marginalized literatus and its poetic flavor: The case of *Xiqing sanji*). *Jiu zhou xuekan* (Chinese culture quarterly) 6.2 (summer): 87–104.

Ko, Dorothy. 1992. "Pursuing Talent and Virtue: Education and Women's Culture in Seventeenth- and Eighteenth-Century China." *Late Imperial China* 13.1 (June): 9–39.

———. 1994. *Teachers of the Inner Chambers: Women and Culture in China, 1573–1722*. Stanford: Stanford University Press.

Levy, Dore. 1999. *Ideal and Actual in "The Story of the Stone."* New York: Columbia University Press.

Li Ruzhen. 1966. *Flowers in the Mirror*. Trans. and ed. Lin Tai-yi. Berkeley and Los Angeles: University of California Press.

Li Shaocheng et al., eds. 1992. *Jiangsu lidai wenxuejia* (Jiangsu authors through the ages). Zhenjiang: Jiangsu guji chubanshe.

Li Wai-yee. 1993. *Enchantment and Disenchantment: Love and Illusion in Chinese Literature*. Princeton: Princeton University Press.

Liang Yizhen. 1958. *Qingdai funü wenxue shi* (A history of women's literature in the Qing dynasty). 1925; reprint, Taipei: Taiwan Zhonghua shuju.

Lin Yutang. 1963. *The Importance of Understanding: Translations from the Chinese*. Cleveland: World Publishing.

Liu, James J. Y. 1962. *The Art of Chinese Poetry*. Chicago: University of Chicago Press.

Ma, Y. W. 1986. *"Pi-chi."* In *The Indiana Companion to Traditional Chinese Literature*, ed. William H. Nienhauser Jr. 650–52. Bloomington: Indiana University Press.

Mann, Susan. 1991. "Grooming a Daughter for Marriage: Brides and Wives in the Mid-Ch'ing Period." In *Marriage and Inequality in Chinese Society*, ed. Rubie S. Watson and Patricia Buckley Ebrey, 204–30. Berkeley and Los Angeles: University of California Press.

———. 1992. "'Fuxue' (Women's Learning) by Zhang Xuecheng

(1738–1801): China's First History of Women's Culture." *Late Imperial China* 13.1 (June): 40–62.

———. 1993. "What Can Feminist Theory Do for the Study of Chinese History? A Brief Review of Scholarship in the U.S." *Jindai Zhongguo funüshi yanjiu* (Research on women in modern Chinese history) 1 (June): 241–60.

———. 1994. "The Education of Daughters in the Mid-Ch'ing Period." In *Society and Education in the Ch'ing Period,* ed. Benjamin Elman and Alexander Woodside. Berkeley and Los Angeles: University of California Press, 19–49.

———. 1997. *Precious Records: Women in China's Long Eighteenth Century.* Stanford: Stanford University Press.

McMahon, Keith. 1995. *Misers, Shrews, and Polygamists: Sexuality and Male-Female Relations in Eighteenth-Century Chinese Fiction.* Durham: Duke University Press.

Meng Jiyuan. 1992. "He Shuangqing." In *Jiangsu lidai wenxuejia* (Jiangsu authors through the ages), ed. Li Shaocheng et al., 427–31. Zhenjiang: Jiangsu guji chubanshe.

———. 1994. "'Xihua wulei kezhanyi'—Jieshao Qingdai nongmin nüciren He Shuangqing" ("You pity the flowers but have no tears left to soak your shirt"—introducing the Qing peasant woman poet He Shuangqing). In *Mao Shan sanji* (Essays on Mao Shan). Nanjing: Jiangsu renmin chubanshe.

Miao Quansun. 1896. *Guochao Changzhou cilu* (Collected song lyrics from Changzhou during our august dynasty). N.p.: Yunzizaikan.

———. 1973. *Yifeng tang wenji.* Reprint, Taipei: Wenhai chubanshe.

Miyazaki, Ichisada. 1963. *Kakyo* (The examination system). Tokyo: Chūō kōron sha.

———. 1976. *China's Examination Hell.* Trans. Conrad Schirokauer. New York: Weatherhill.

Mowry, Hua-yuan Li. 1983. *Chinese Love Stories from Ch'ing-shih.* Hamden, Conn.: Archon Books.

Naquin, Susan, and Evelyn Rawski. 1987. *Chinese Society in the Eighteenth Century.* New Haven: Yale University Press.

Overmyer, Daniel L. 1985. "Values in Chinese Sectarian Literature: Ming and Ch'ing *Pao-chuan.*" In *Popular Culture in Late Imperial China,* ed. David Johnson, Andrew J. Nathan, and Evelyn S. Rawski, 219–54. Berkeley and Los Angeles: University of California Press.

———. 1991. "Women in Chinese Religions: Submission, Struggle, Transcendence." In *From Benares to Beijing: Essays on Buddhism and Chinese Religion in Honour of Prof. Jan Yun-hua,* ed. Koichi Shinohara and Gregory Schopen, 91–120. New York: Mosaic Press.

Ou Mingjun, ed. 1966. *Ming-Qing mingjia xiaopin jinghua* (The best essays of famous writers from the Ming and Qing dynasties). Hefei: Anhui wenyi chubanshe.

Owen, Stephen. 1985. *Traditional Chinese Poetry and Poetics: Omen of the World.* Madison: University of Wisconsin Press.

———. 1986. *Remembrances: The Experience of the Past in Classical Chinese Literature.* Cambridge: Harvard University Press.

———. 1989. *Mi-Lou: Poetry and the Labyrinth of Desire.* Cambridge: Harvard University Press.

———. 1990. "Poetry in the Chinese Tradition." In *Heritage of China: Contempo-*

*rary Perspectives on Chinese Civilization,* ed. Paul S. Ropp, 294–308. Berkeley and Los Angeles: University of California Press.

Pao Chia-lin [Bao Jialin]. 1989. "Nongjia nüshiren: He Shuangqing" (Peasant woman poet: He Shuangqing). *Taiwan shibao* (Taiwan times), December 12, 1978; reprinted in Bao Jialin, *Funü wenti: Suixianglu* (Random thoughts on women's issues), 89–92. Taipei: Daoxiang chubanshe.

Peterson, Willard J. 1979. *Bitter Gourd: Fang I-chih and the Impetus for Intellectual Change.* New Haven: Yale University Press.

Qiu Weixuan. 1960. "Shuyuan aotan" (Idle talks under the bean arbor) (1897). Included in Qiu Weixuan, *Keyun lu xiaoshuo hua* (Fiction talks by the Keyun Cottage), in *Wan Qing wenxue congchao* (Collected works on late Qing literature), ed. A Ying, vol. 2, *Xiaoshuo xiqu yenjiu* (Studies on fiction and drama), 377–426. Reprint, Beijing: Zhonghua shuju.

Rawski, Evelyn Sakakida. 1979. *Education and Popular Literacy in Ch'ing China.* Ann Arbor: University of Michigan Press.

Rexroth, Kenneth, and Ling Chung. 1972. *The Orchid Boat: Women Poets of China.* New York: McGraw-Hill.

Riffaterre, Michael. 1990. *Fictional Truth.* Baltimore: Johns Hopkins University Press.

Robertson, Maureen. 1992. "Voicing the Feminine: Constructions of the Gendered Subject in Lyric Poetry by Women of Medieval and Late Imperial China." *Late Imperial China* 13.1 (June): 63–110.

Roddy, Stephen J. 1998. *Literati Identity and Its Fictional Representations in Late Imperial China.* Stanford: Stanford University Press.

Ropp, Paul S. 1981. *Dissent in Early Modern China: "Ju-lin wai-shih" and Ch'ing Social Criticism.* Ann Arbor: University of Michigan Press.

———. 1992a. "A Confucian View of Women in the Ch'ing Period: Literati Laments for Women in the *Ch'ing shih tuo.*" *Chinese Studies* 10.2 (December): 399–435.

———. 1992b. "Shi Zhenlin and the Poetess Shuangqing: Gender, Class, and Literary Talent in an Eighteenth-Century Memoir." Paper presented at the conference "Engendering China," Harvard University, February.

———. 1993a. "Love, Literacy, and Laments: Themes of Women Writers in Late Imperial China." *Women's History Review* 2.1: 107–41.

———. 1993b. "A Meditation on the Tragedies of Talented and Beautiful Women: Wu Zhensheng's Preface to Shi Zhenlin's *Xiqing sanji.*" Paper presented at a meeting of the American Association for Chinese Studies, Columbia, S.C., October.

———. 1994. "Women in Late Imperial China: A Review of Recent English-Language Scholarship." *Women's History Review* 3.3: 347–83.

Sangren, Steven P. 1983. "Female Gender in Chinese Religious Symbols: Kuan-yin, Ma-tsu, and the 'Eternal Mother.'" *Signs* 9.1: 4–25.

Shen Fu. 1981. *Fusheng liuji* (Six chapters from a floating life). Tainan: Xinshiji chubanshe.

———. 1983. *Six Records of a Floating Life.* Trans. Leonard Pratt and Chiang Su-hui. Harmondsworth: Penguin Books.

Shen Shanbao. 1987. *Mingyuan shihua* (Notes on the poetry of famous women).

1845; reprint, in *Qing shihua fangyi chubian*, ed. Du Songbo, vol. 9. Taipei: Xinwenfeng chubanshe.

Shen Yizheng. 1984. *Lidai meiren hua xuan* (Selected paintings of beauties through the ages). Taipei: Yishu tushu gongsi.

Shi Shenghua. 1991. "Nongjia cainü He Shuangqing" (The brilliant peasant woman He Shuangqing). In Zhou Songlin, ed., *Danyang* (Nanjing: Jiangsu renmin chubanshe), 141–44.

Shi Shuyi. 1987. *Qingdai guige shiren zhenglue* (Brief biographies of refined lady poets from the Qing dynasty). 1922; reprint, Shanghai: Shanghai shudian.

Shi Zhenlin. 1874. *Xiqing sanji* (Random notes from Xiqing). 8 chaps. N.p.: n.p. Lead type ed.

———. 1878. *Xiqing sanji* (Random notes from Xiqing). 8 chaps. *Fu Xiqing wenlue* (Appended Prose Sketches from Xiqing), 1 vol. N.p.: n.p.

———. 1883. *Huayang sangao* (Scattered drafts from Huayang). N.p.: n.p. Lead type ed.

———. 1895. *Qianchou ji* (Collection of unpaid remorse). Ed. Baiyuan. N.p.: Baiyuan lou. Wood-block ed.

———. 1901. *Qianchou ji* (Collection of unpaid remorse). Ed. Baiyuan. N.p.: Shen Zongchou. Wood-block ed.

———. 1926. *Tianshang renjian* (Heaven and earth). Ed. Xue Qu. Shanghai: Hezuo she.

———. 1935a. *Huayang sangao* (Scattered drafts from Huayang). Zhongguo wenxue zhenben congshu (Collections of rare manuscripts in Chinese literature), 1st collection, no. 9. Shanghai: Shanghai zazhi gongsi.

———. 1935b. *Xiqing sanji* (Random notes from Xiqing). 1737; reprint, Zhongguo wenxue zhenben congshu (Collections of rare manuscripts in Chinese literature), 1st collection, no. 5. Shanghai: Shanghai zazhi gongsi.

———. 1987. *Xiqing sanji* (Random notes from Xiqing). 4 chaps. 1907 (with preface dated 1737); reprint, Beijing: Zhongguo shudian.

———. N.d. *Xiqing sanji* (Random notes from Xiqing). 4 chaps. N.p.: Qianlong reign (1736–96). Wood-block ed.

———. N.d. *Xiqing sanji* (Random notes from Xiqing). 4 chaps. N.p.: Sanyu tang, Qing period. Wood-block ed.

———. N.d. *Xiqing sanji* (Random notes form Xiqing). 4 chaps. Shanghai: Gujin shuju, late Qing.

Smith, Richard J. 1994. *China's Cultural Heritage: The Qing Dynasty, 1644–1911*. 2d ed. Boulder: Westview Press.

Spence, Jonathan. 1978. *The Death of Woman Wang*. New York: Viking Press.

Strassberg, Richard E. 1994. *Inscribed Landscapes: Travel writing from Imperial China*. Berkeley: University of California Press.

Su Zhecong. 1987. *Lidai funü zuopinxuan* (Selections from women's writings through the ages). Shanghai: Shanghai guji chubanshe.

———. 1988. *Lidai nüzi cixuan* (Selected song lyrics from women poets through the ages). Chengdu: Bashu shushe.

———. 1993. "Cong He Shuangqing shici kan Qingdai nongfu de sixiang xingge" (The poetry of He Shuangqing and the Qing female farmworkers). Paper presented to the Conference "Women and Literature in Ming-Qing China," Yale University, June.

Tang Xianzu. 1980. *The Peony Pavilion.* Trans. Cyril Birch. Bloomington: Indiana University Press.

T'ien Ju-k'ang [Tian Rukang]. 1988. *Male Anxiety and Female Chastity: A Comparative Study of Chinese Ethical Values in Ming-Ch'ing Times.* Leiden: E. J. Brill.

Virgillo, Carmelo, and Naomi Lindstrom, eds. 1985. *Woman as Myth and Metaphor.* Columbia: University of Missouri Press.

Wagner, Marsha L. 1984. *The Lotus Boat: The Origins of Chinese Tz'u Poetry in T'ang Popular Culture.* New York: Columbia University Press.

Waltner, Ann. 1987. "T'an-yang-tzu and Wang Shih-chen: Visionary and Bureaucrat in the Late Ming." *Late Imperial China* 8.1 (June): 105–33.

Wan Lijun. 1996. *Meili de liulang* (Beautiful wandering). Jintan: Jiangsu wenyi chubanshe.

Wang Duan. 1839. *Ziran haoxue zhai ji* (Collected writings from the Natural Love of Learning Studio). Reprinted in *Rubuji zhai huichao* (Transcribed collected writings of Rubuji Studio), ed. Chen Kun. N.p.: 1872.

Wang Ping. 2000. *Aching for Beauty: Footbinding as Cultural Fetish and Discourse of Body and Language.* Minneapolis: University of Minnesota Press.

Watson, Rubie S. 1986. "The Named and the Nameless: Gender and Person in Chinese Society." *American Ethnologist* 13.4 (November): 619–31.

Watson, Rubie S., and Patricia Buckley Ebrey, eds. 1991. *Marriage and Inequality in Chinese Society.* Berkeley and Los Angeles: University of California Press.

Widmer, Ellen. 1989. "The Epistolary World of Female Talent in Seventeenth-Century China." *Late Imperial China* 10.2 (December): 1–43.

———. 1992. "Xiaoqing's Literary Legacy and the Place of the Woman Writer in Late Imperial China." *Late Imperial China* 13.1 (June): 111–55.

Widmer, Ellen, and Kang-i Sun Chang, eds. 1997. *Writing Women in Late Imperial China.* Stanford: Stanford University Press.

Wu Dexuan. 1976. *Chuyuelou wenjianlu* (A record of things seen and heard from the New Moon Pavilion). 2 vols. Reprint, Taipei: Taiwan Shangwu yinshuguan.

Wu Hung. 1997. "Beyond Stereotypes: The Twelve Beauties in Qing Court Art and the *Dream of the Red Chamber.*" In *Writing Women in Late Imperial China,* ed. Ellen Widmer and Kang-i Sun Chang, 306–65. Stanford: Stanford University Press.

Wu Pei-yi. 1990. *The Confucian's Progress: Autobiographical Writings in Traditional China.* Princeton: Princeton University Press.

Xu Ke, comp. 1966. *Qingbai leichao* (Classified collection of Qing-dynasty notes). 48 vols. Shanghai, 1916; reprint, Taipei: Taiwan Shangwu yinshuguan.

Xu Naichang, comp. 1896. *Xiaotanluan shi huike guixiu ci* (The Xiaotanluan Studio collection of women's song lyrics). N.p.: n.p.

Xue Qu, ed. 1926. *Tianshang renjian* (Heaven and earth), by Shi Zhenlin. Shanghai: Hezuo she.

Yan Dichang. 1990. *Qing ci shi* (A history of Qing-dynasty song lyrics). Jiangsu: Jiangsu guji chubanshe.

Ye Gongchuo. 1982. *Quan Qing cichao* (Song lyrics of the Qing dynasty). Reprint, Beijing: Zhonghua shuju.

You Zhenzhong and You Yiding, eds. 1995. *Qing ci jishi huiping* (Qing-dynasty song lyrics: Contexts and annotations). Hefei: Huangshan shushe.

Yu, Anthony C. 1997. *Rereading the Stone: Desire and the Making of Fiction in Dream of the Red Chamber.* Princeton: Princeton University Press.

Yu, Pauline, ed. 1994. *Voices of the Song Lyric in China.* Berkeley and Los Angeles: University of California Press.

Yuan Hua. 1988. "Shi Zhenlin nianbiao" (Chronological biography of Shi Zhenlin). *Wenjiao ziliao* (Reference materials on culture and education) 5:98–113.

Yuan Mei. 1974. *Jianzhu Suiyuan shihua* (Poetry-talks from Suiyan, with notes and commentary). Reprint, Taipei: Dingwen shuju.

Yun Zhu. 1831. *Guochao Guixiu zhengshi ji* (Correct beginnings: Women's poetry of our august dynasty). N.p.: Hongxiangguan.

Zeitlin, Judith T. 1993. *Historian of the Strange: Pu Songling and the Chinese Classical Tale.* Stanford: Stanford University Press.

———. 1998. "Spirit Writing and Performance in the Work of You Tong (1618–1704)." *T'oung Pao* 84:102–35.

Zhang Gongliang. 1935. "*Xiqing sanji* cankao ziliao" (Reference materials on *Random Notes from Xiqing*). Appended to Shi Zhenlin, *Xiqing sanji.* Shanghai: Shanghai zazhi gongsi.

Zhang Hongsheng. 1995. *Jianghu shipai yanjiu* (Studies on the Jianghu school of poetry). Beijing: Zhonghua shuju.

———. 1998. *Qingdai cixue de jian'gou* (The structure of Qing-dynasty song lyrics). Nanjing: Jiangsu guji chubanshe.

Zheng Guangyi, ed. 1991. *Zhongguo lidai cainü shige jianshang cidian* (A critical explanatory guide to poetry published by talented women through the dynasties). Beijing: Zhongguo gongren chubanshe.

Zhong Huiling. 1981. "Qingdai nü shiren yanjiu" (Studies on Qing women poets). Ph.D. diss., National Zhengzhi University.

Zhou Wanyao. 1996. "Xiaoshan chuanqi: He Shuangqing yanjiu zhi jiantao yu zhanwang" (The story of Xiaoshan: A review article of recent works on He Shuangqing). *Xinshixue* (New history) 7.4 (December): 159–97.

Zurndorfer, Harriet, ed. 1999. *Chinese Women in the Imperial Past: New Perspectives.* Leiden: Brill.

# Index